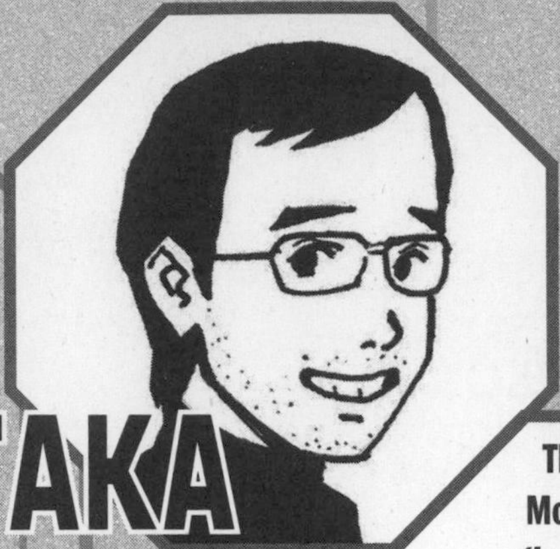

YUTAKA IZUBUCHI

The girls Takeaki Momose draws are *(just nasty enough)* GOOD!! *...no, really.*

Profile
Born 12/8/58 in Tokyo.
Mech-Designer, Illustrator, Comic Artist. Script, Direction of TV Animation, *RAHXEPHON*. Notable work: *MOBILE POLICE PATLABOR, MOBILE SUIT GUNDAM: CHAR'S COUNTERATTACK* (Mecha Designer).

TAKEAK MOMOS

The themes of this comic are "family" and "happiness." Pretty heavy themes, but I plan on writing it without any tension in my shoulders. What? Too relaxed? Heh-heh....you smart-mouth.

Profile
Born 11/8/76.
Debuts in *WEEKLY SHONEN SUNDAY*.
Notable work *MIAMI GUNS* (Kodansha).

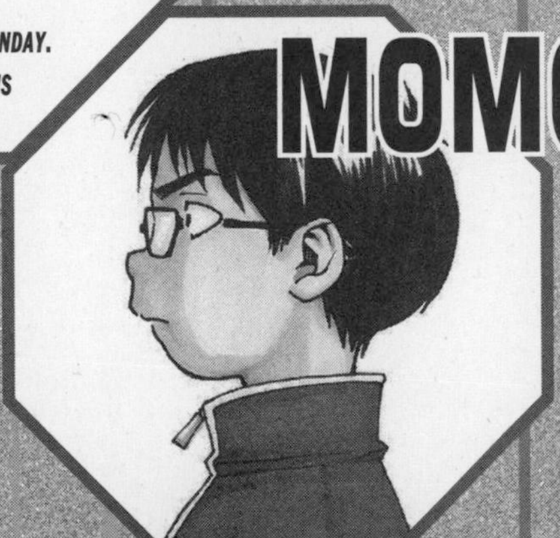

RahXephon
Vol. 1

Action Edition

CREATED BY
YUTAKA IZUBUCHI & BONES
ART BY
TAKEAKI MOMOSE

English Adaptation/Gerard Jones
Translation/Joe Yamazaki
Touch-up & Lettering/Kathryn Renta
Cover, Graphics & Design/Mark Schumann
Editor/Kit Fox

Managing Editor/Annette Roman
Editor in Chief/William Flanagan
Production Manager/Noboru Watanabe
Sr. Director of Licensing & Acquisitions/Rika Inouye
V.P. of Marketing/Liza Coppola
Sr. V.P. of Editorial/Hyoe Narita
Publisher/Seiji Horibuchi

Printed in Canada.

Published by VIZ, LLC
P.O. Box 77010
San Francisco, CA 94107

Action Edition
10 9 8 7 6 5 4 3 2 1
First printing, March 2004

www.viz.com   store.viz.com   www.animerica-mag.com

RahXephon

1

CREATED BY   **YUTAKA IZUBUCHI**

&   **BONES**

ART BY   **TAKEAKI MOMOSE**

1

CONTENTS

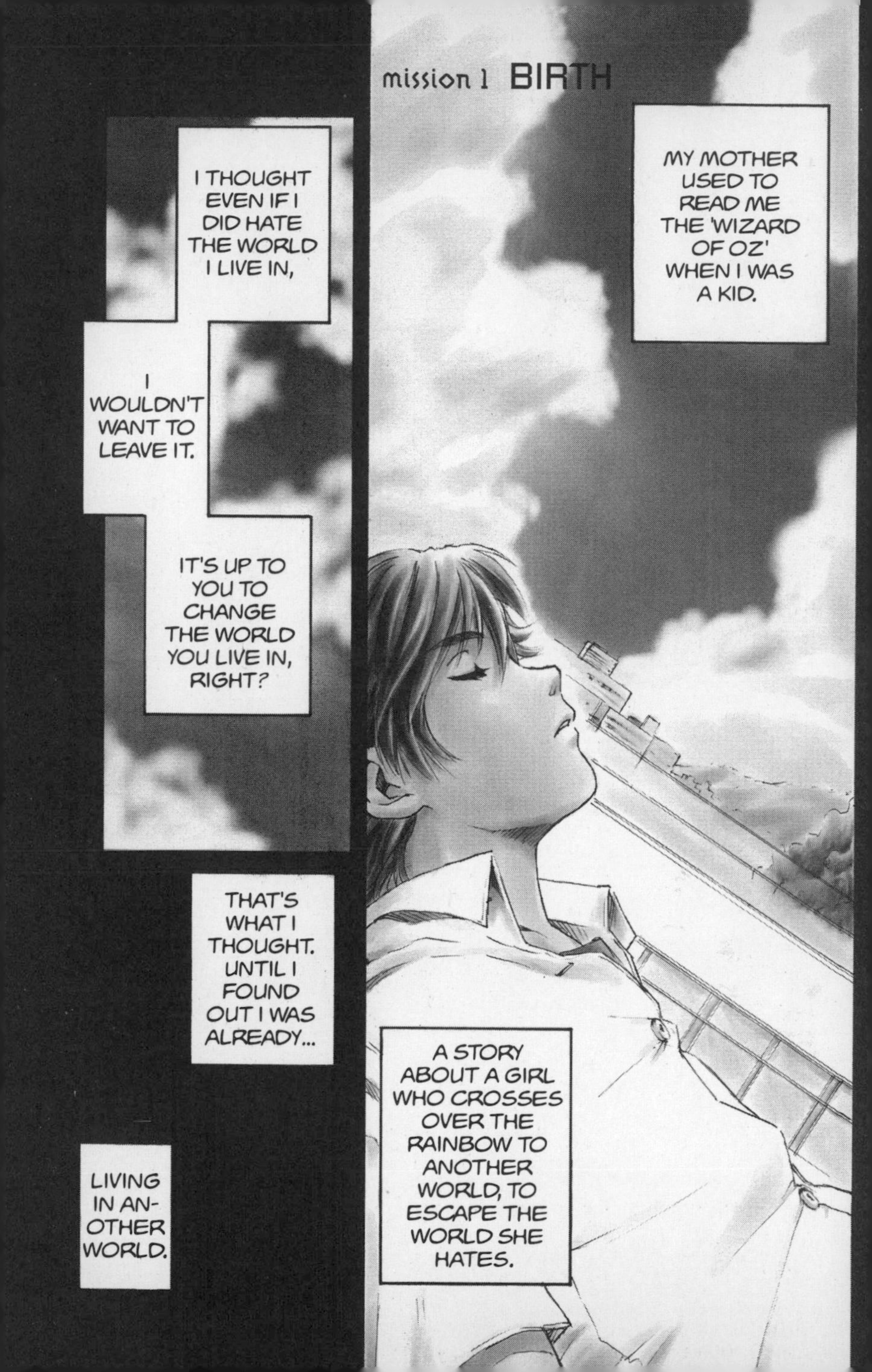
mission 1 BIRTH
MY MOTHER USED TO READ ME THE 'WIZARD OF OZ' WHEN I WAS A KID.
A STORY ABOUT A GIRL WHO CROSSES OVER THE RAINBOW TO ANOTHER WORLD, TO ESCAPE THE WORLD SHE HATES.
I THOUGHT EVEN IF I DID HATE THE WORLD I LIVE IN,
I WOULDN'T WANT TO LEAVE IT.
IT'S UP TO YOU TO CHANGE THE WORLD YOU LIVE IN, RIGHT?
THAT'S WHAT I THOUGHT. UNTIL I FOUND OUT I WAS ALREADY...
LIVING IN AN-OTHER WORLD.

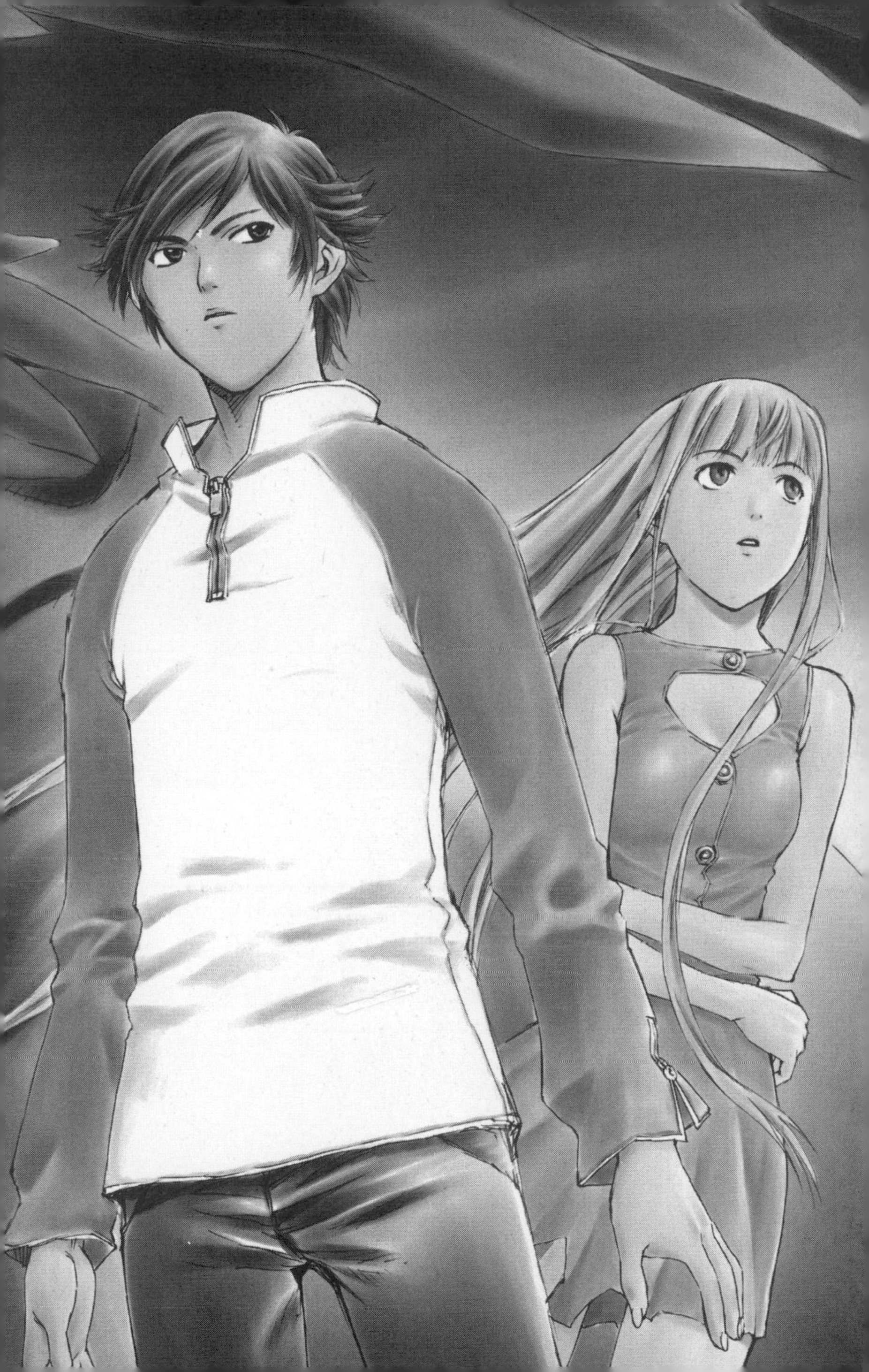

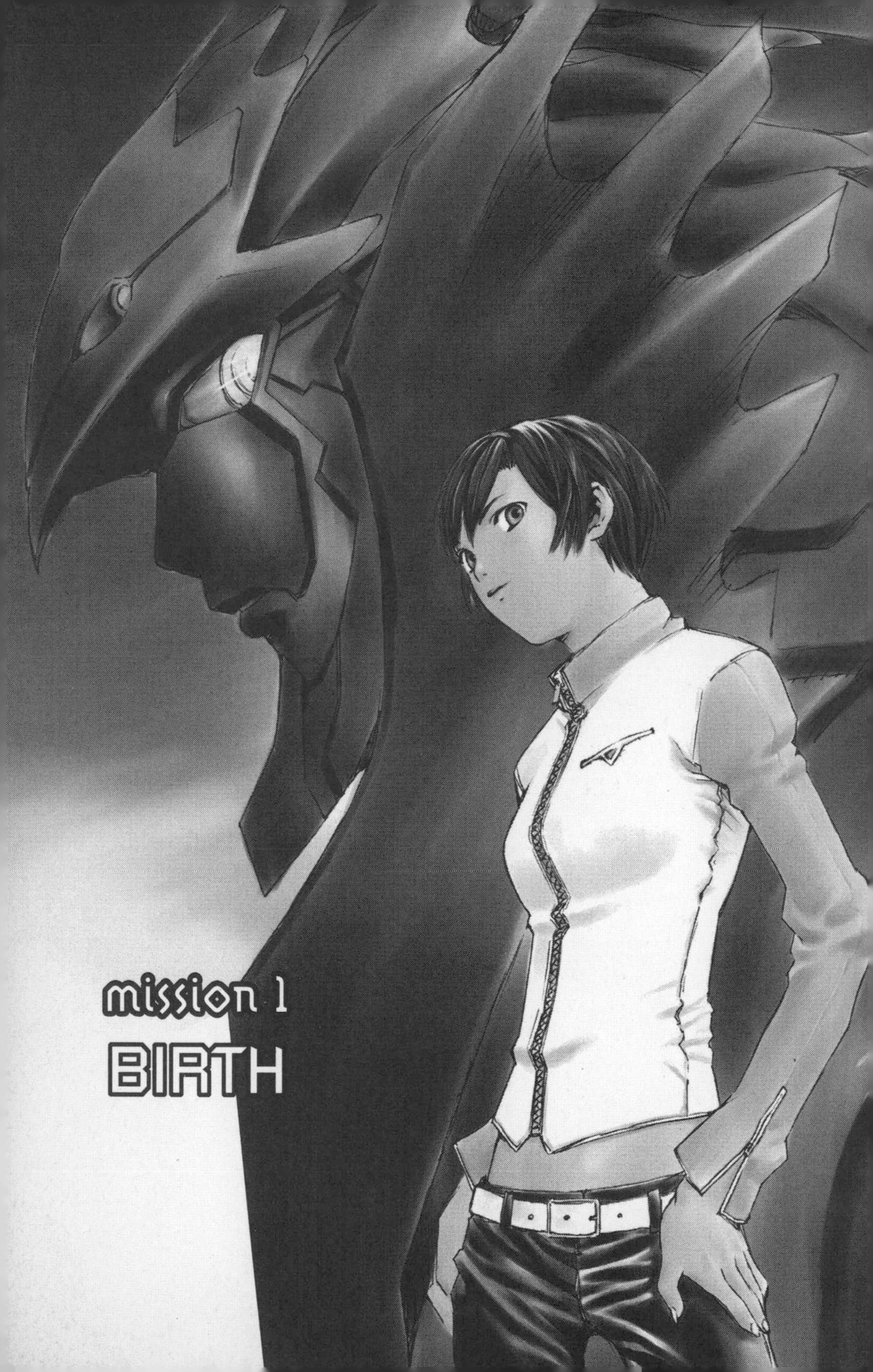
mission 1
BIRTH

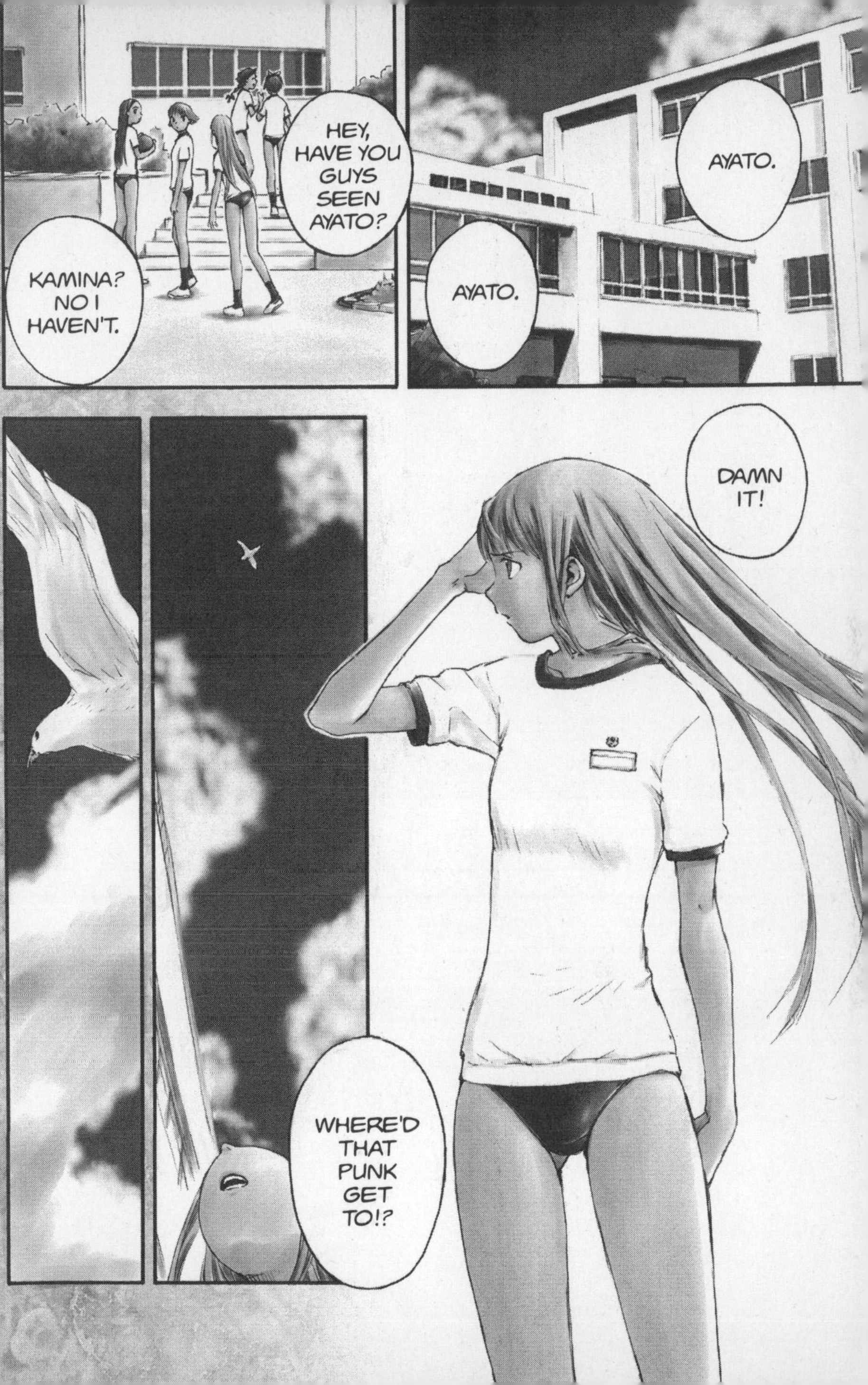
AYATO.
AYATO.
HEY, HAVE YOU GUYS SEEN AYATO?
KAMINA? NO I HAVEN'T.
DAMN IT!
WHERE'D THAT PUNK GET TO!?

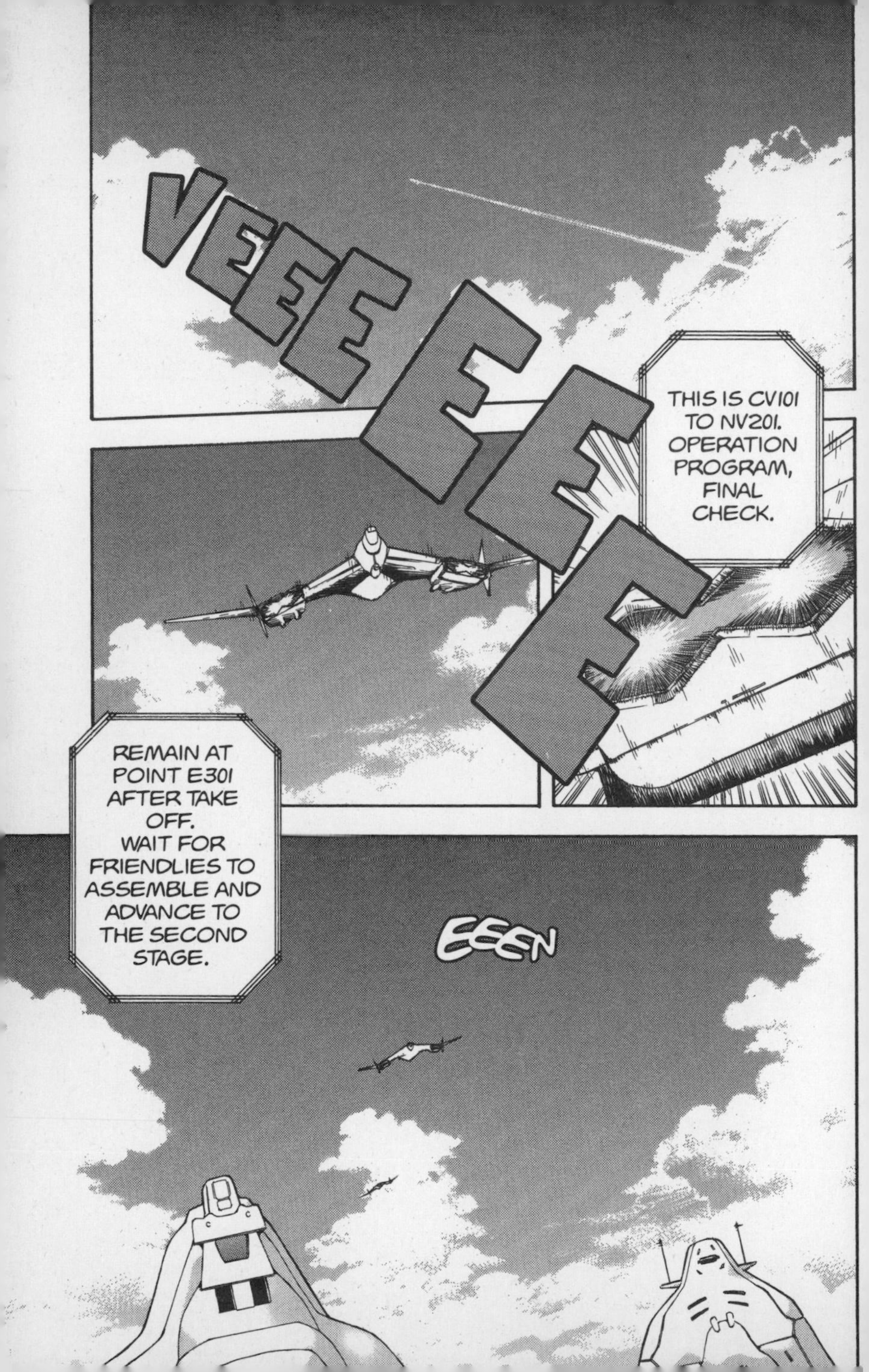
VEEEEEE
THIS IS CV101 TO NV201. OPERATION PROGRAM, FINAL CHECK.
REMAIN AT POINT E301 AFTER TAKE OFF. WAIT FOR FRIENDLIES TO ASSEMBLE AND ADVANCE TO THE SECOND STAGE.
EEEN

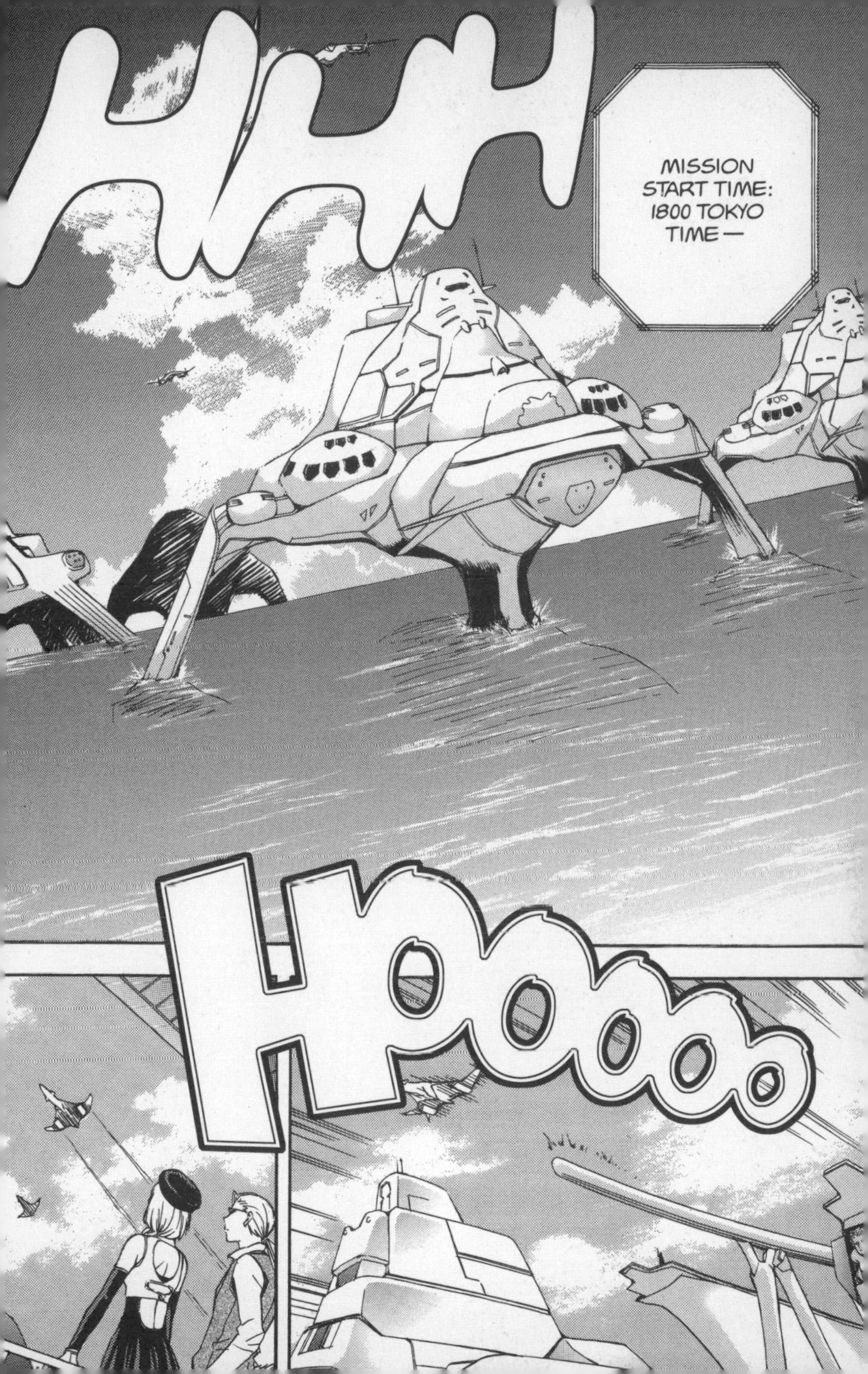
MISSION START TIME: 1800 TOKYO TIME—

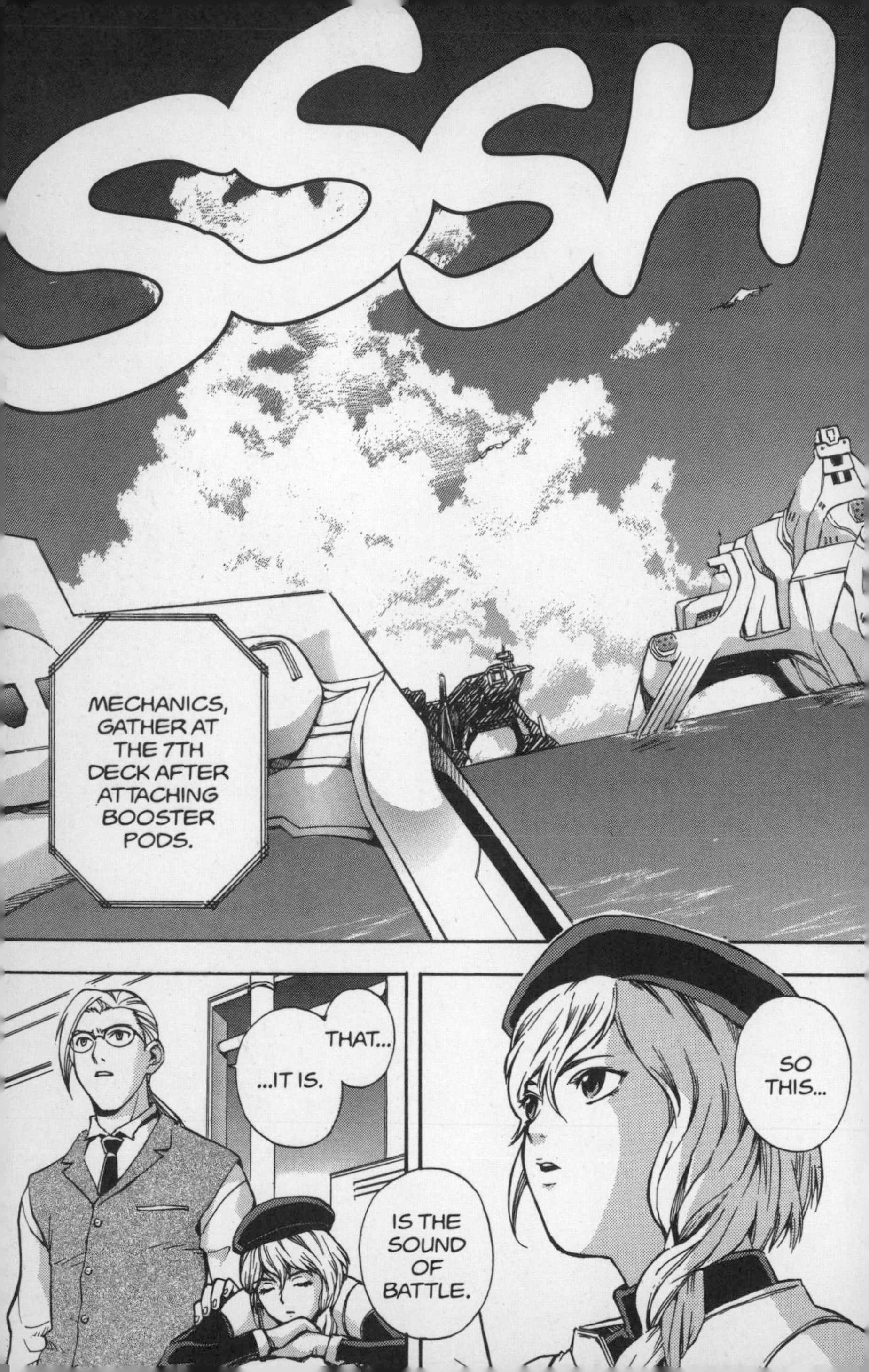
SSSH
MECHANICS, GATHER AT THE 7TH DECK AFTER ATTACHING BOOSTER PODS.
SO THIS...
IS THE SOUND OF BATTLE.
THAT...
...IT IS.

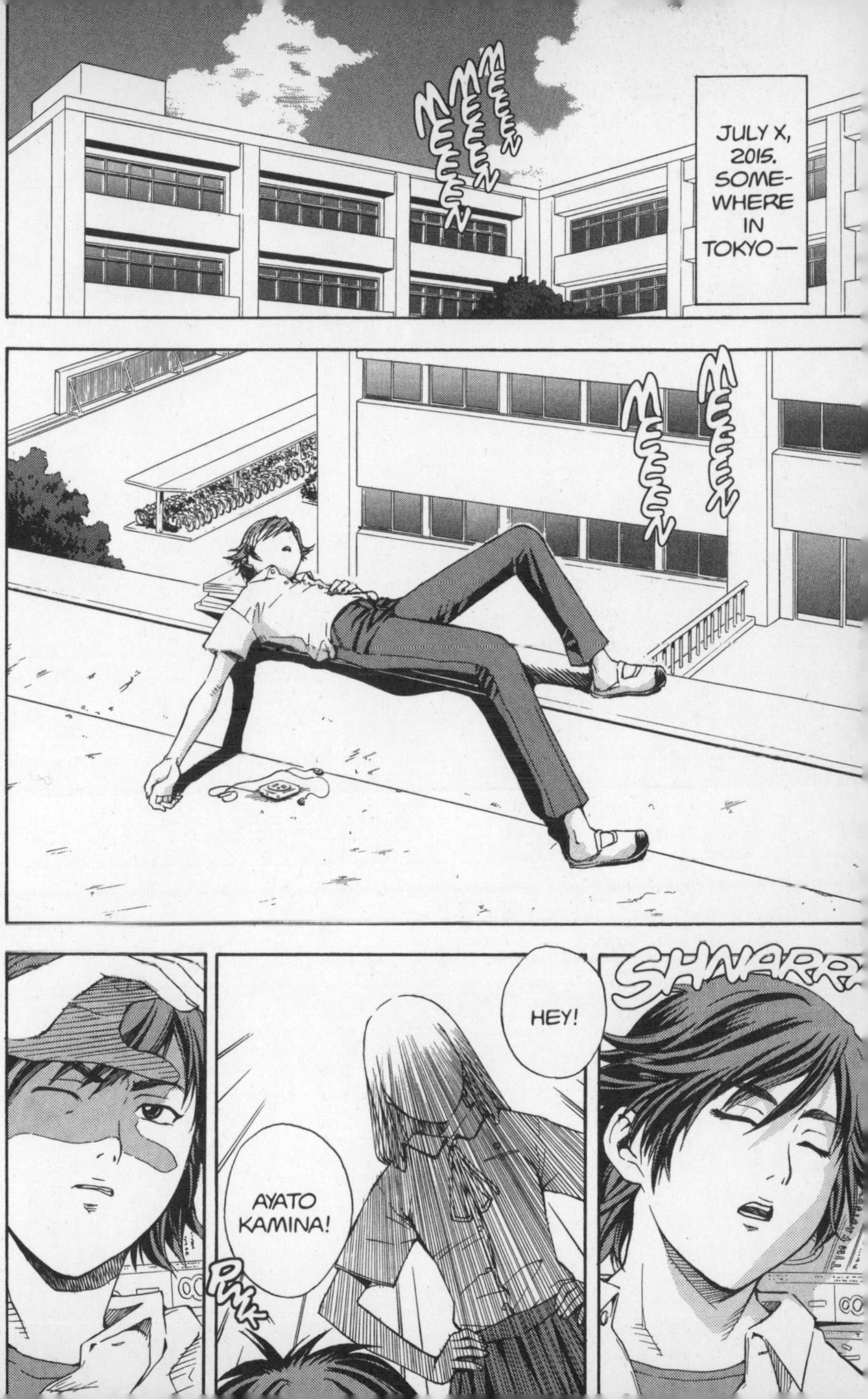
JULY X, 2015. SOMEWHERE IN TOKYO—
MEEEEN
MEEEEN
MEEEEN
MEEEEN
MEEEEN
SHWARR
HEY!
AYATO KAMINA!
PINK

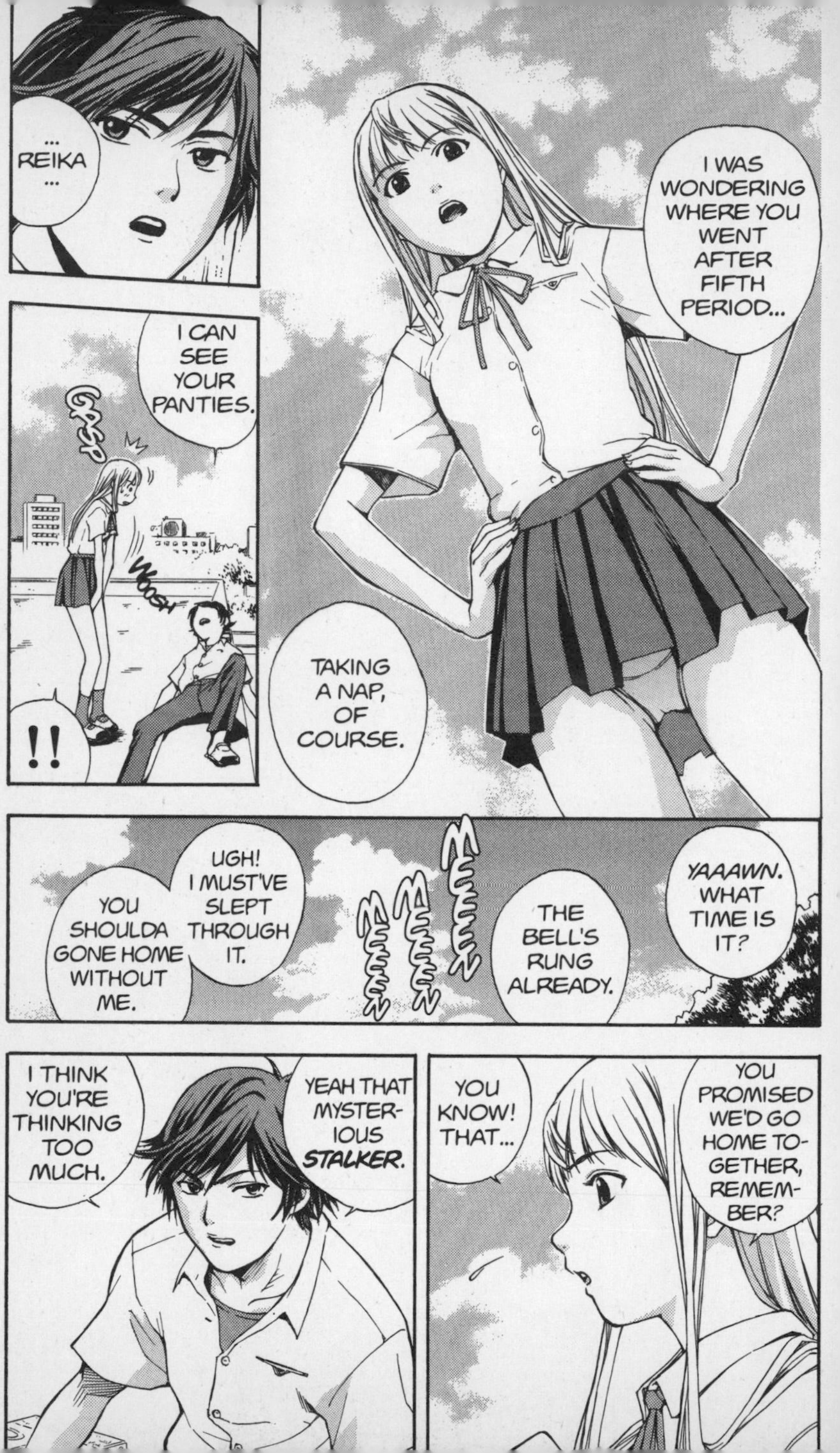
I WAS WONDERING WHERE YOU WENT AFTER FIFTH PERIOD...
TAKING A NAP, OF COURSE.
... REIKA ...
I CAN SEE YOUR PANTIES.
GASP
WOOSH
!!
YAAAWN. WHAT TIME IS IT?
THE BELL'S RUNG ALREADY.
MEEEN
MEEEN
MEEEN
UGH! I MUST'VE SLEPT THROUGH IT.
YOU SHOULDA GONE HOME WITHOUT ME.
YOU PROMISED WE'D GO HOME TO-GETHER, REMEM-BER?
YOU KNOW! THAT...
YEAH THAT MYSTER-IOUS *STALKER*.
I THINK YOU'RE THINKING TOO MUCH.

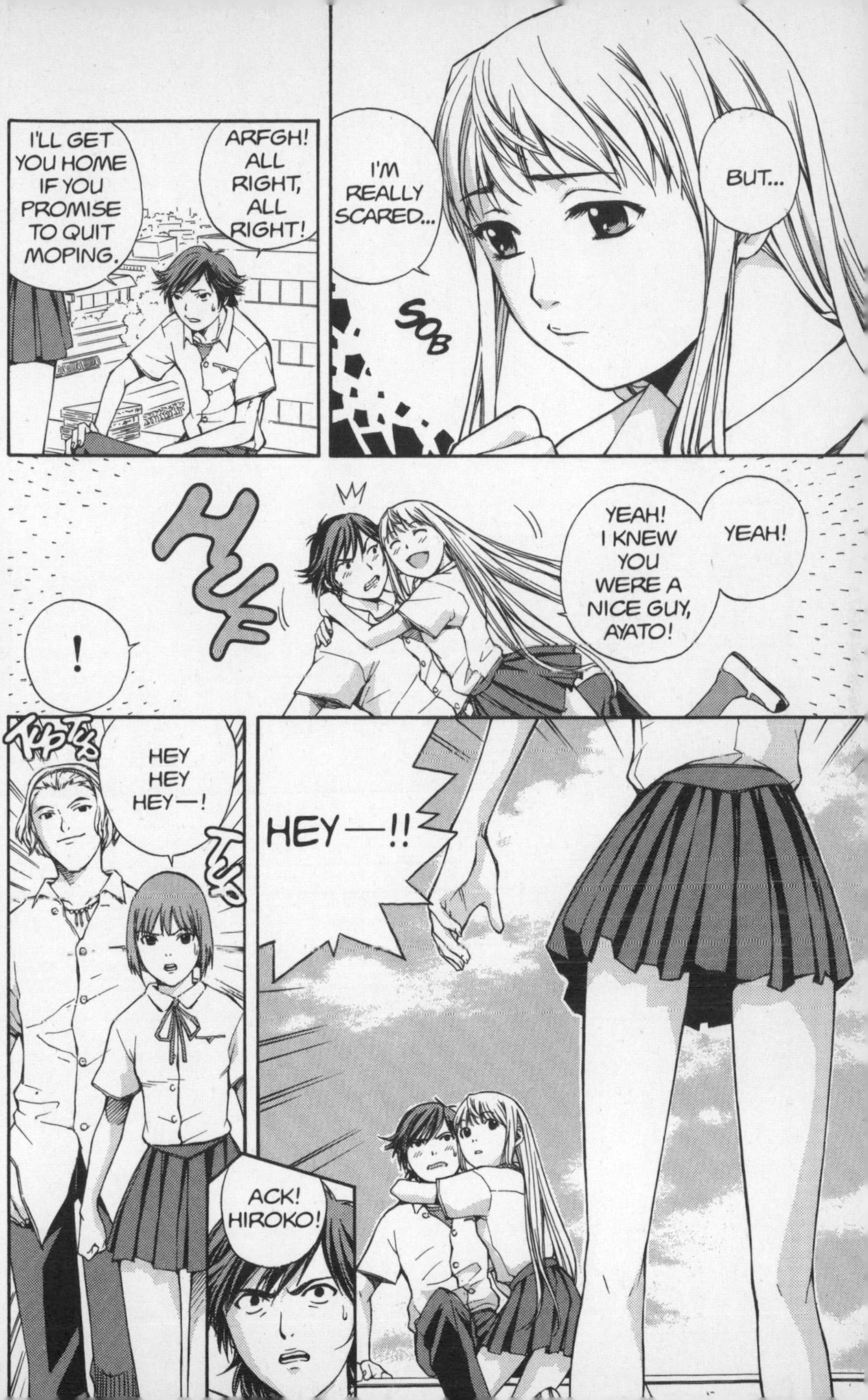
BUT...
I'M REALLY SCARED...
SOB
ARFGH! ALL RIGHT, ALL RIGHT!
I'LL GET YOU HOME IF YOU PROMISE TO QUIT MOPING.
YEAH!
YEAH! I KNEW YOU WERE A NICE GUY, AYATO!
!
HEY—!!
HEY HEY HEY—!
ACK! HIROKO!

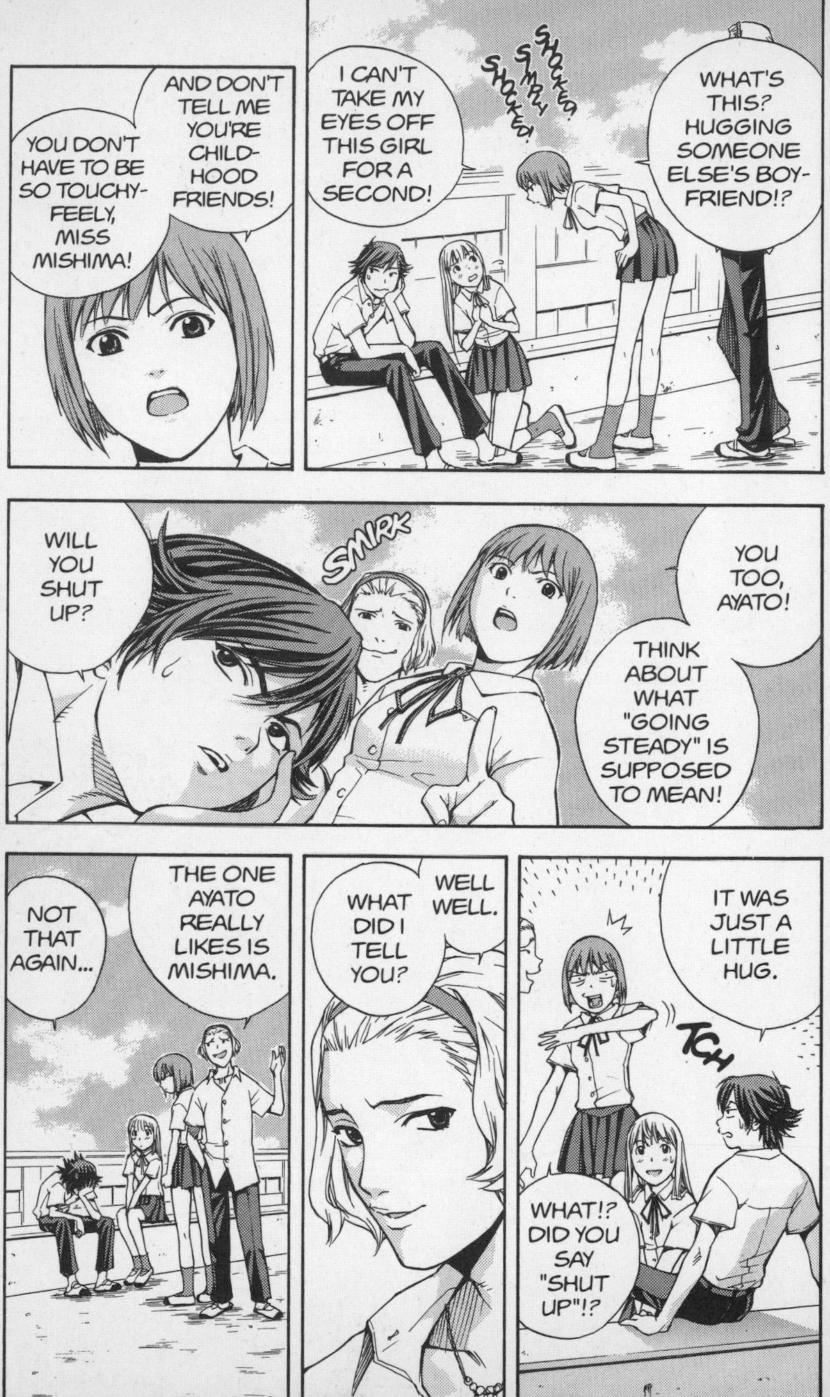
WHAT'S THIS? HUGGING SOMEONE ELSE'S BOY-FRIEND!?
SHOCKED!
SIMPLY
SHOCKED!
I CAN'T TAKE MY EYES OFF THIS GIRL FOR A SECOND!
AND DON'T TELL ME YOU'RE CHILD-HOOD FRIENDS!
YOU DON'T HAVE TO BE SO TOUCHY-FEELY, MISS MISHIMA!
YOU TOO, AYATO!
THINK ABOUT WHAT "GOING STEADY" IS SUPPOSED TO MEAN!
SMIRK
WILL YOU SHUT UP?
IT WAS JUST A LITTLE HUG.
TCH
WHAT!? DID YOU SAY "SHUT UP"!?
WELL WELL.
WHAT DID I TELL YOU?
THE ONE AYATO REALLY LIKES IS MISHIMA.
NOT THAT AGAIN...

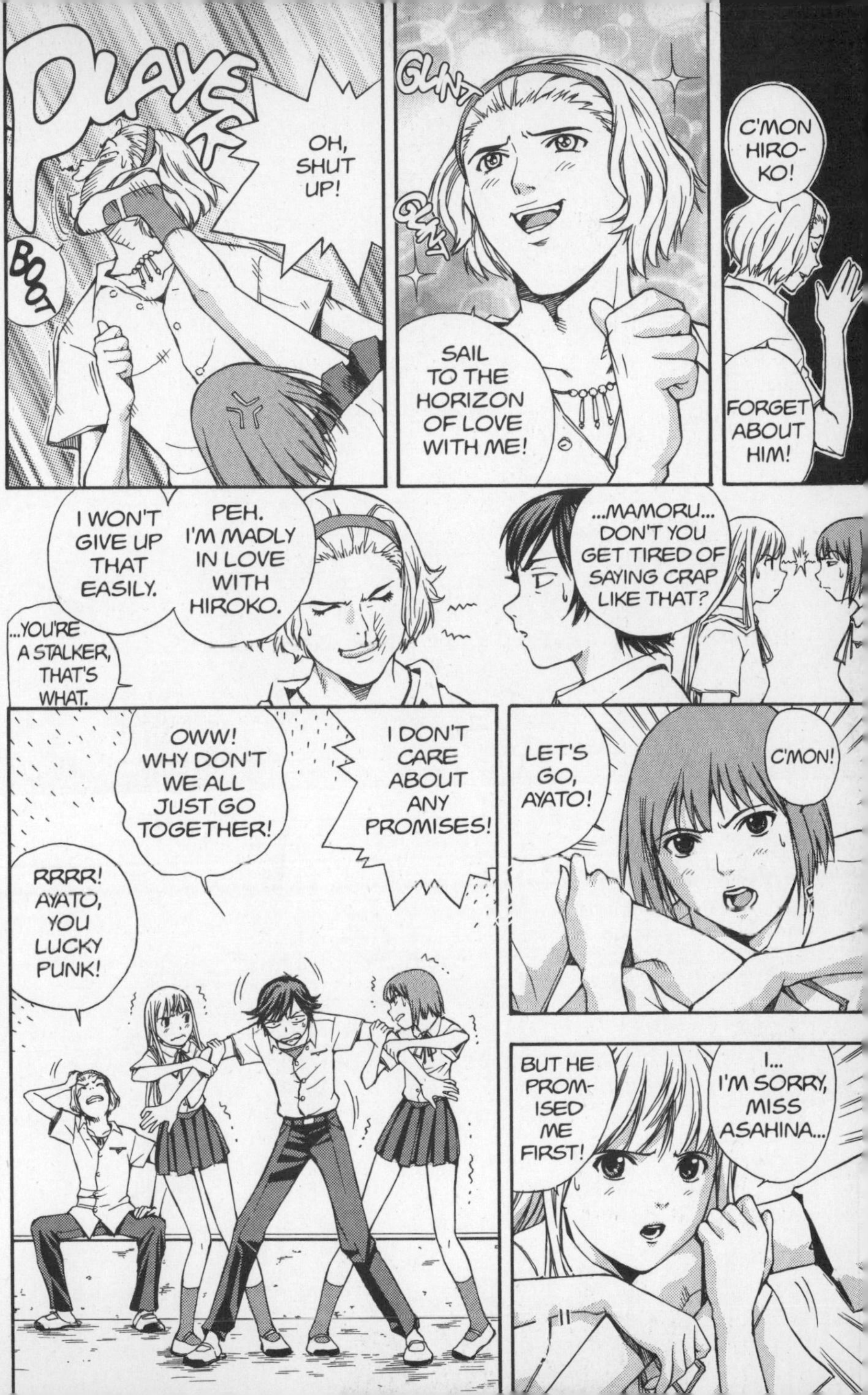
C'MON HIRO-KO!
FORGET ABOUT HIM!
GLINT
GLINT
SAIL TO THE HORIZON OF LOVE WITH ME!
OH, SHUT UP!
BOOT
...MAMORU... DON'T YOU GET TIRED OF SAYING CRAP LIKE THAT?
PEH. I'M MADLY IN LOVE WITH HIROKO.
I WON'T GIVE UP THAT EASILY.
...YOU'RE A STALKER, THAT'S WHAT.
C'MON!
LET'S GO, AYATO!
I... I'M SORRY, MISS ASAHINA...
BUT HE PROMISED ME FIRST!
I DON'T CARE ABOUT ANY PROMISES!
OWW! WHY DON'T WE ALL JUST GO TOGETHER!
RRRR! AYATO, YOU LUCKY PUNK!

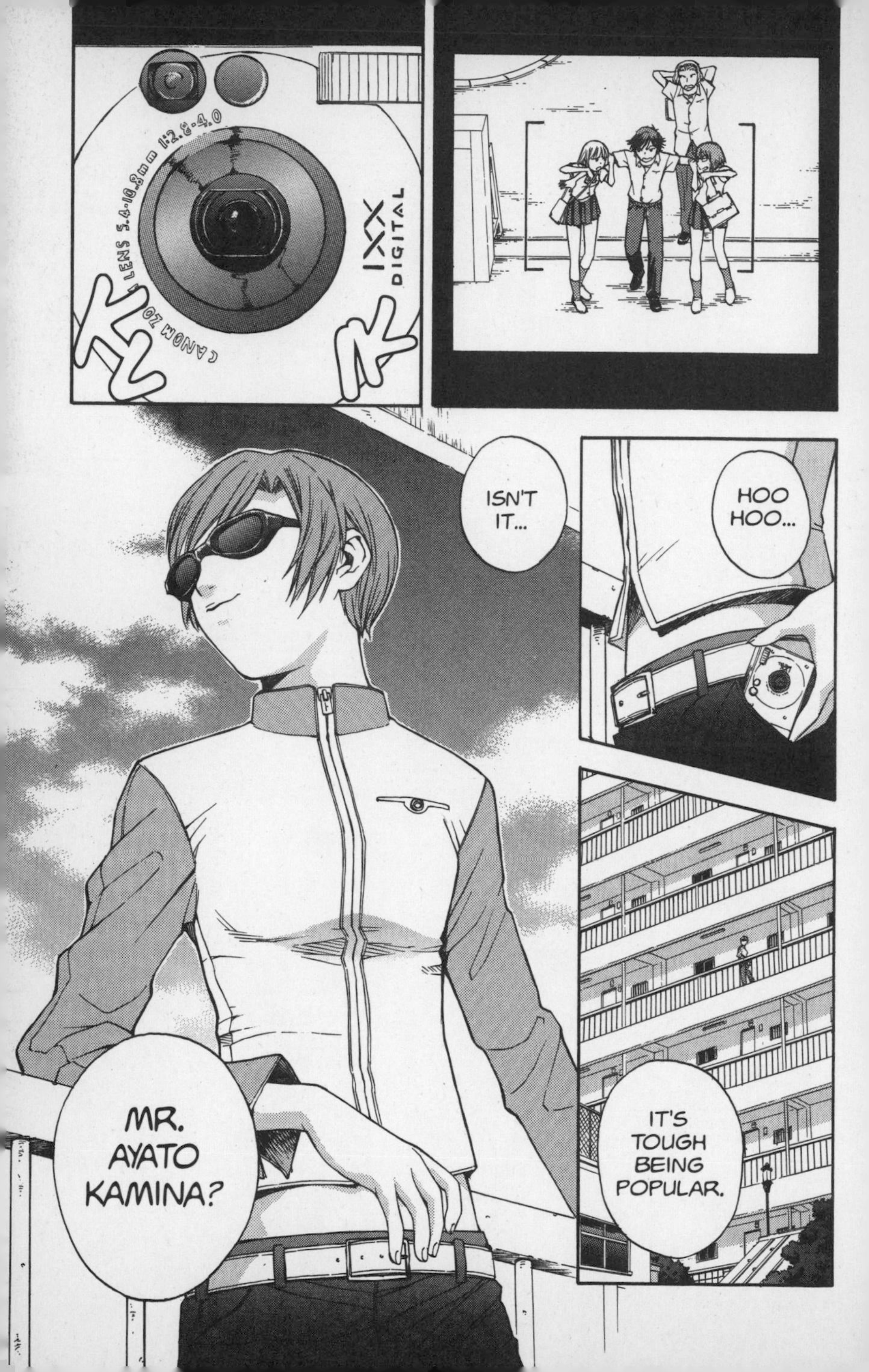
LENS 5.4-10.8mm 1:2.8-4.0
IXY DIGITAL
HOO HOO...
IT'S TOUGH BEING POPULAR.
ISN'T IT...
MR. AYATO KAMINA?

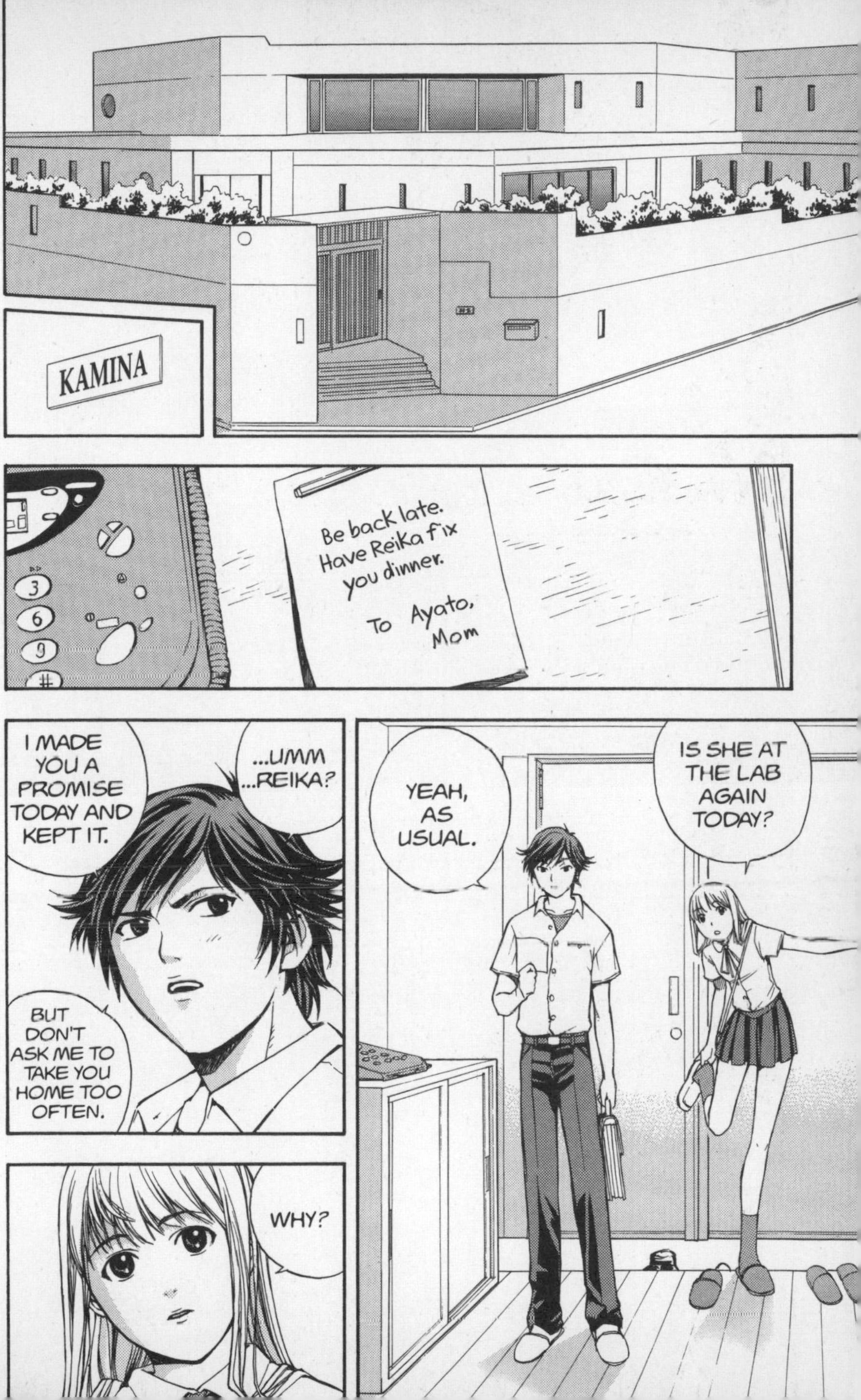
KAMINA
Be back late. Have Reika fix you dinner. To Ayato, Mom
IS SHE AT THE LAB AGAIN TODAY?
YEAH, AS USUAL.
...UMM ...REIKA?
I MADE YOU A PROMISE TODAY AND KEPT IT.
BUT DON'T ASK ME TO TAKE YOU HOME TOO OFTEN.
WHY?

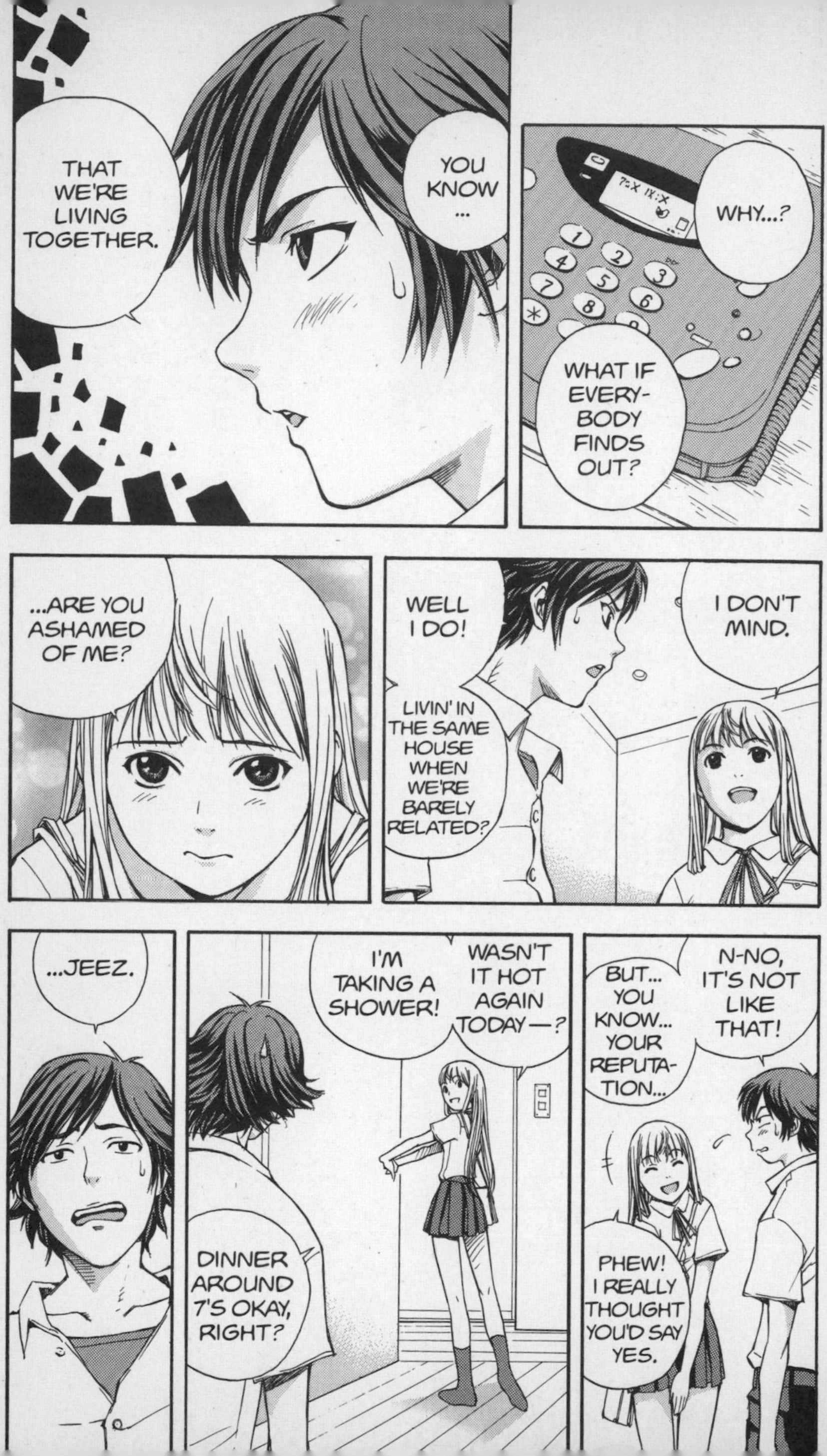
WHY...?
WHAT IF EVERY-BODY FINDS OUT?
YOU KNOW ...
THAT WE'RE LIVING TOGETHER.
I DON'T MIND.
WELL I DO!
LIVIN' IN THE SAME HOUSE WHEN WE'RE BARELY RELATED?
...ARE YOU ASHAMED OF ME?
N-NO, IT'S NOT LIKE THAT!
BUT... YOU KNOW... YOUR REPUTA-TION...
PHEW! I REALLY THOUGHT YOU'D SAY YES.
WASN'T IT HOT AGAIN TODAY—?
I'M TAKING A SHOWER!
DINNER AROUND 7'S OKAY, RIGHT?
...JEEZ.

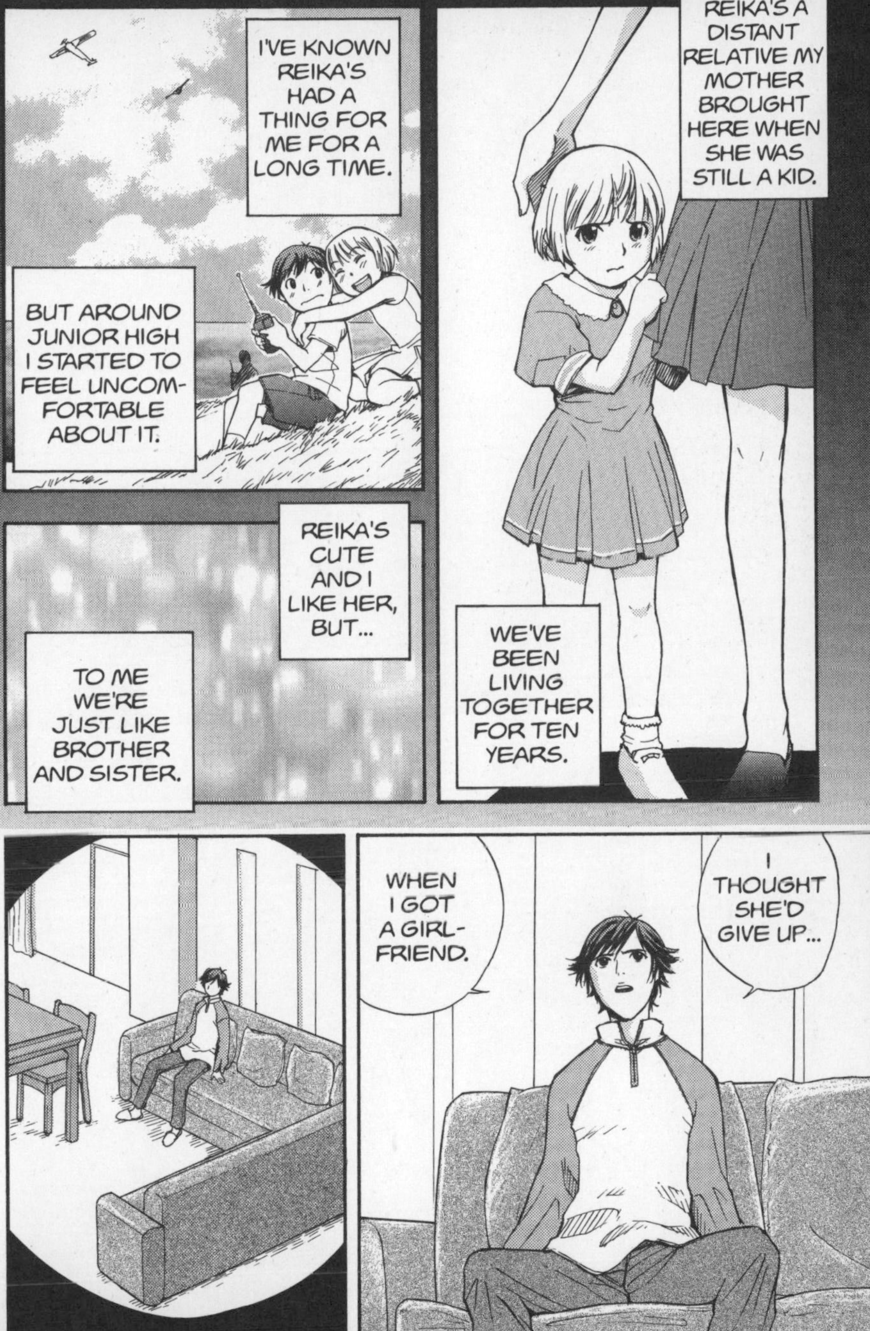
REIKA'S A DISTANT RELATIVE MY MOTHER BROUGHT HERE WHEN SHE WAS STILL A KID.
WE'VE BEEN LIVING TOGETHER FOR TEN YEARS.
I'VE KNOWN REIKA'S HAD A THING FOR ME FOR A LONG TIME.
BUT AROUND JUNIOR HIGH I STARTED TO FEEL UNCOM-FORTABLE ABOUT IT.
REIKA'S CUTE AND I LIKE HER, BUT...
TO ME WE'RE JUST LIKE BROTHER AND SISTER.
I THOUGHT SHE'D GIVE UP...
WHEN I GOT A GIRL-FRIEND.

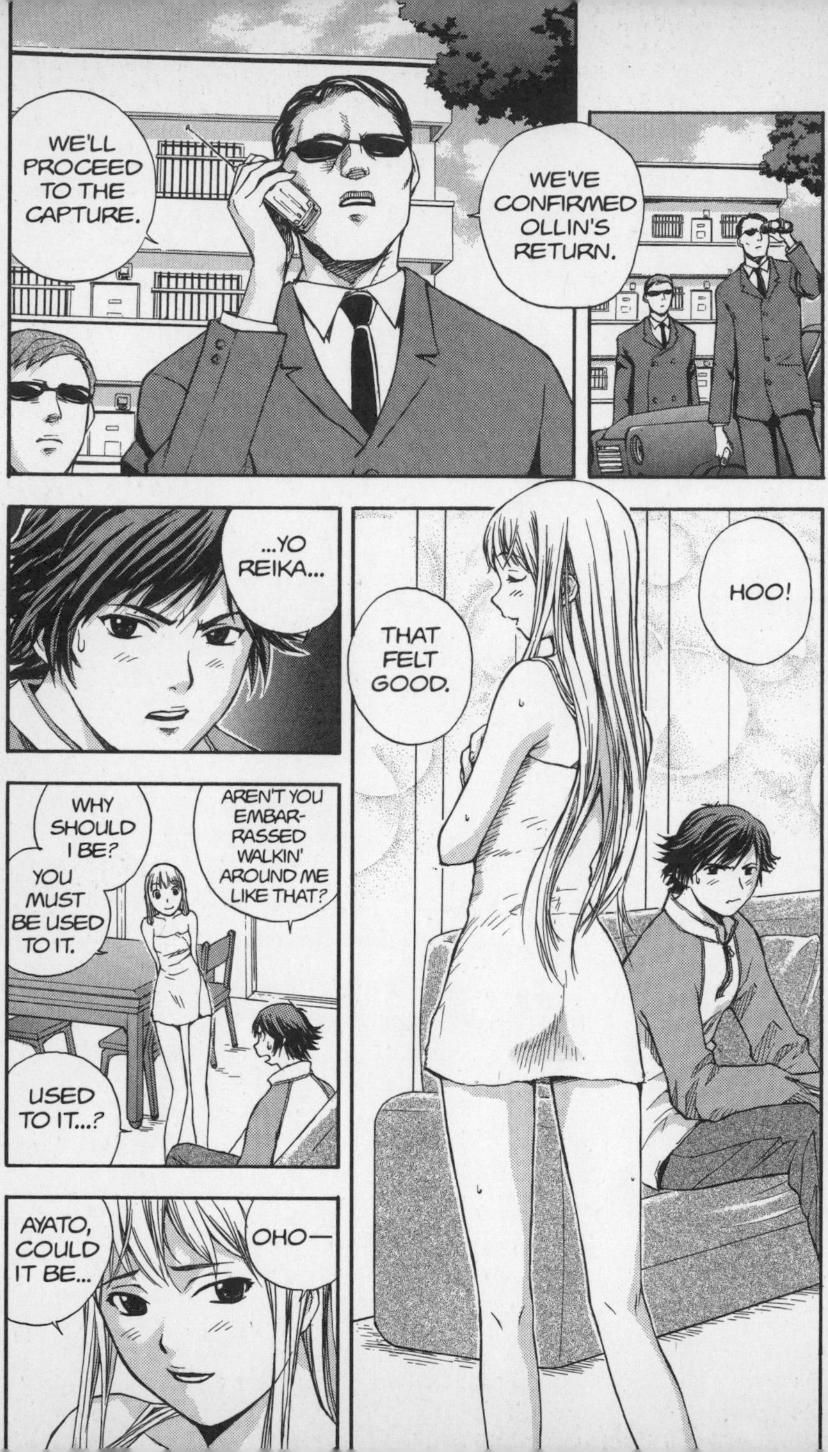
WE'VE CONFIRMED OLLIN'S RETURN.
WE'LL PROCEED TO THE CAPTURE.
HOO!
THAT FELT GOOD.
...YO REIKA...
AREN'T YOU EMBAR-RASSED WALKIN' AROUND ME LIKE THAT?
WHY SHOULD I BE?
YOU MUST BE USED TO IT.
USED TO IT...?
OHO—
AYATO, COULD IT BE...

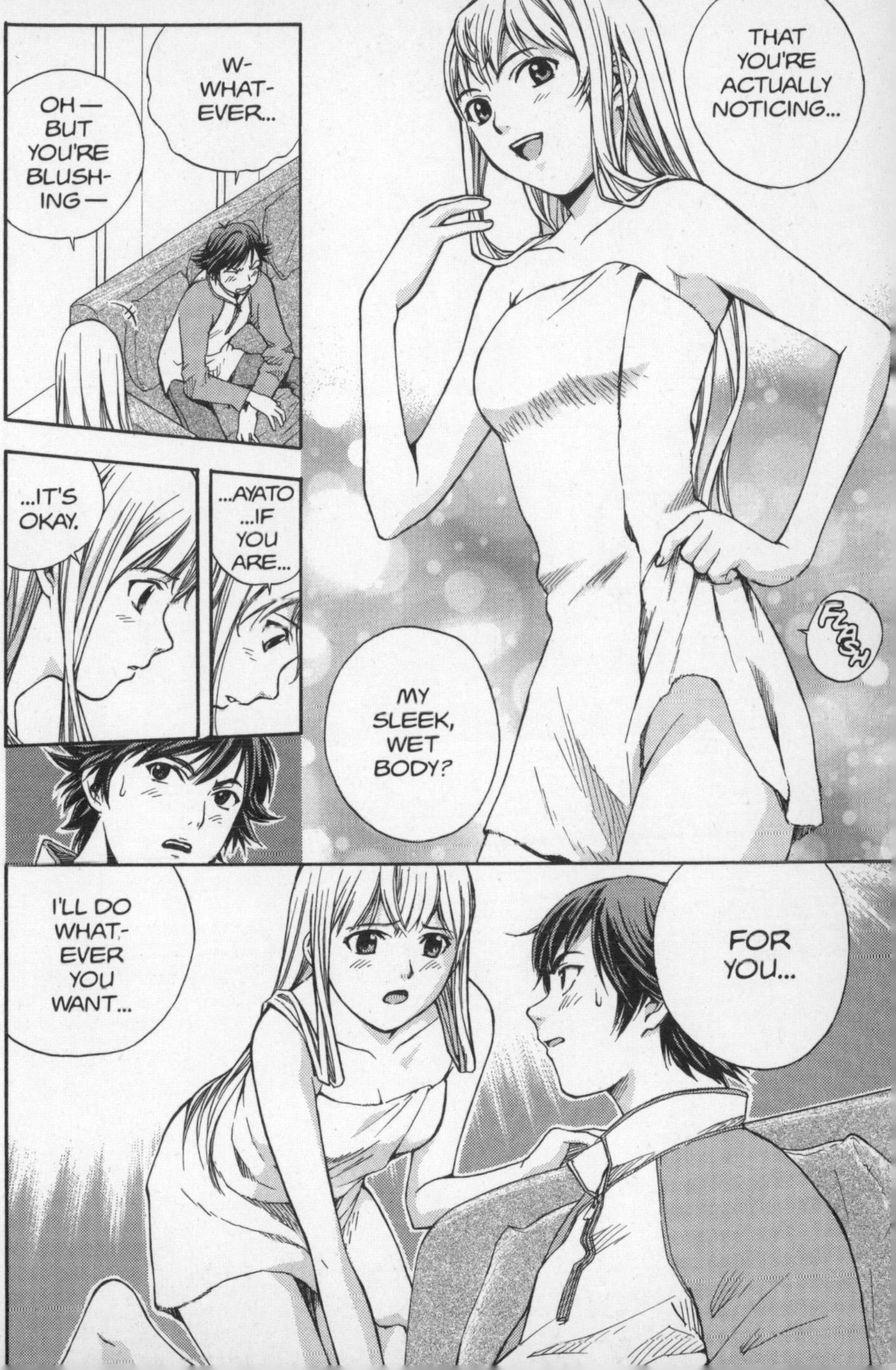
THAT YOU'RE ACTUALLY NOTICING...
MY SLEEK, WET BODY?
FLASH
OH— BUT YOU'RE BLUSH-ING—
W-WHAT-EVER...
...AYATO ...IF YOU ARE...
...IT'S OKAY.
FOR YOU...
I'LL DO WHAT-EVER YOU WANT...

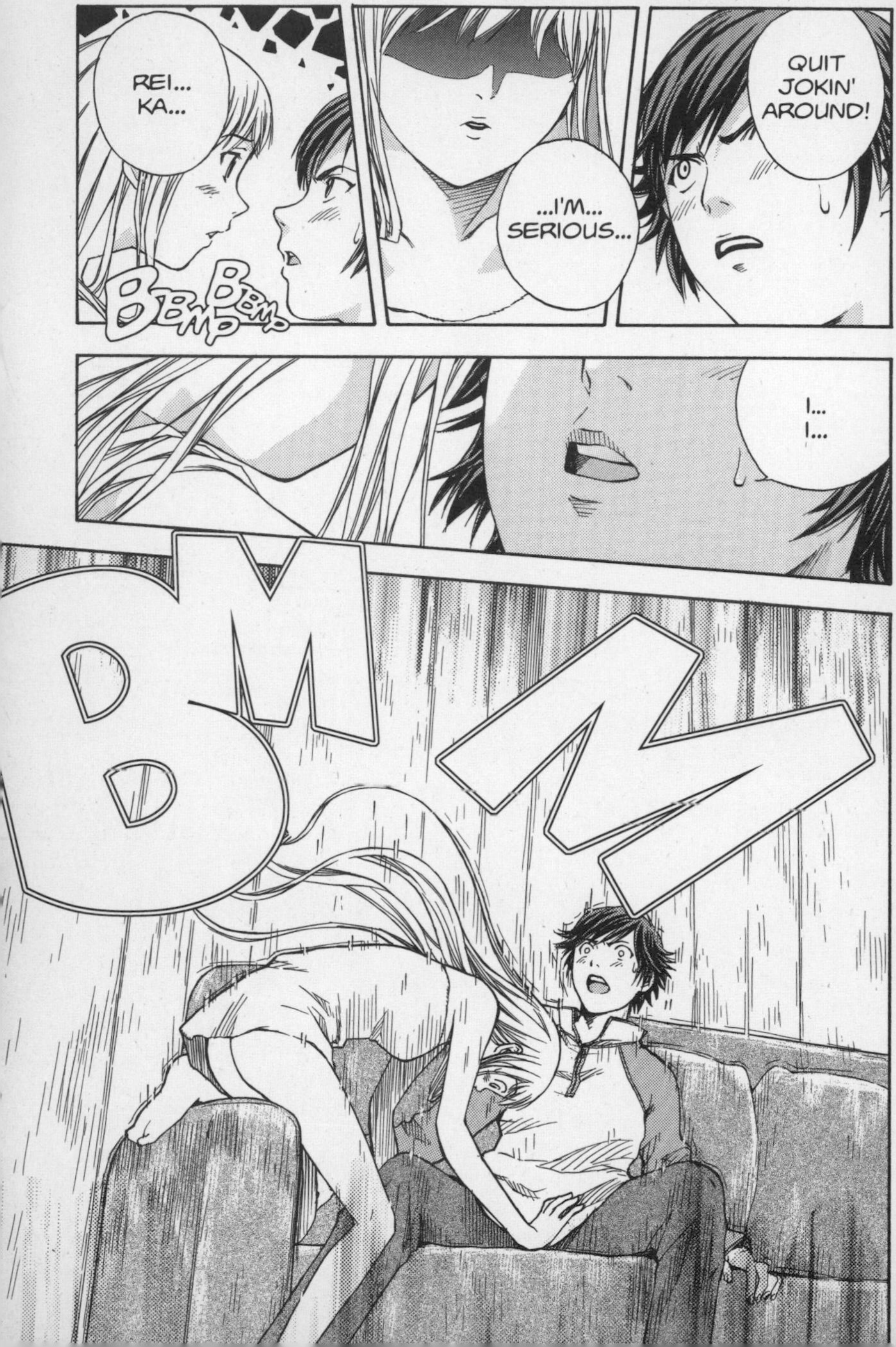
QUIT JOKIN' AROUND!
...I'M... SERIOUS...
REI... KA...
BBMP BBMP
I... I...

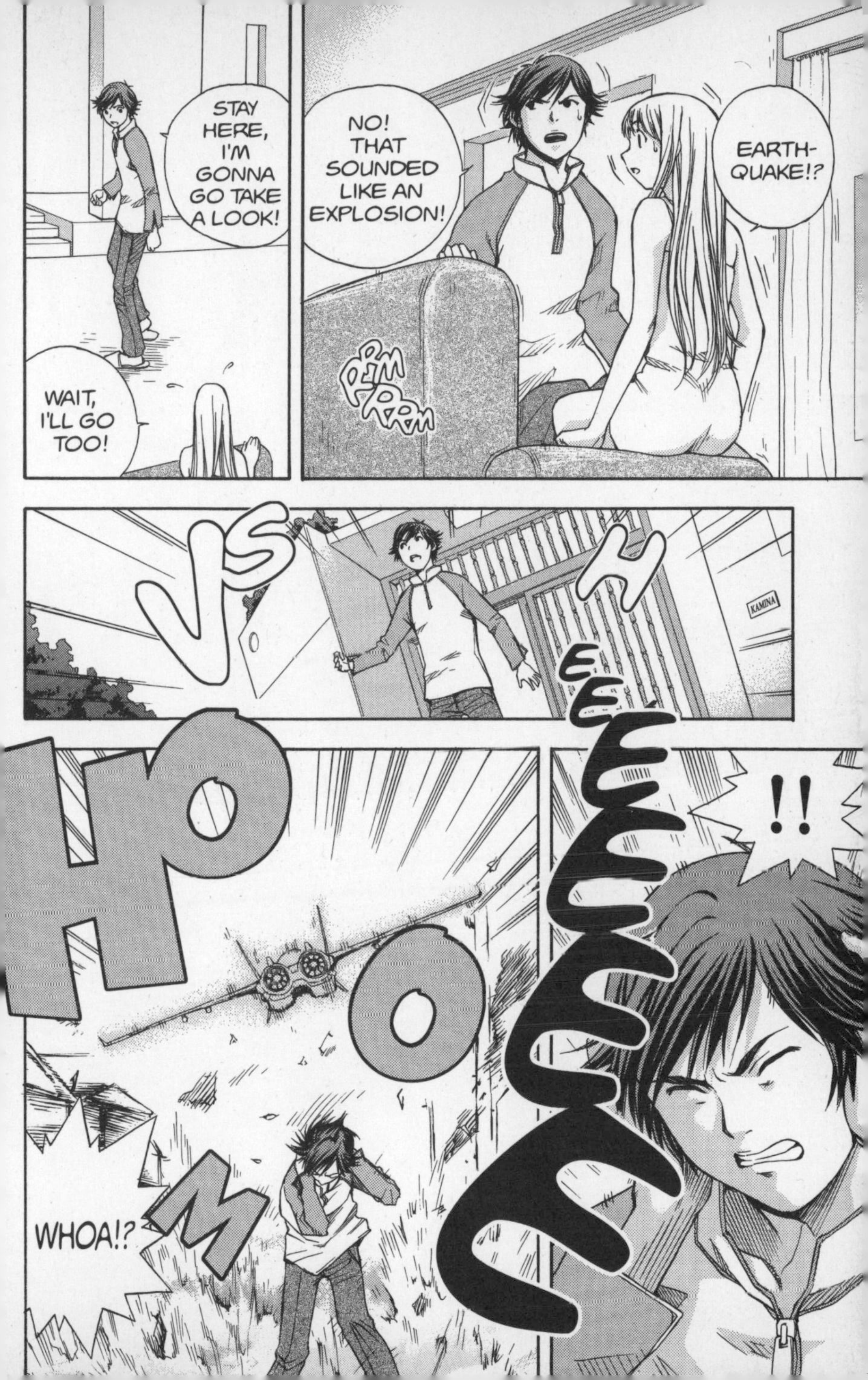
EARTH-QUAKE!?
NO! THAT SOUNDED LIKE AN EXPLOSION!
RRM RRM
STAY HERE, I'M GONNA GO TAKE A LOOK!
WAIT, I'LL GO TOO!
VS
H
KAMINA
EEEEEEEE
!!
HOOM
WHOA!?

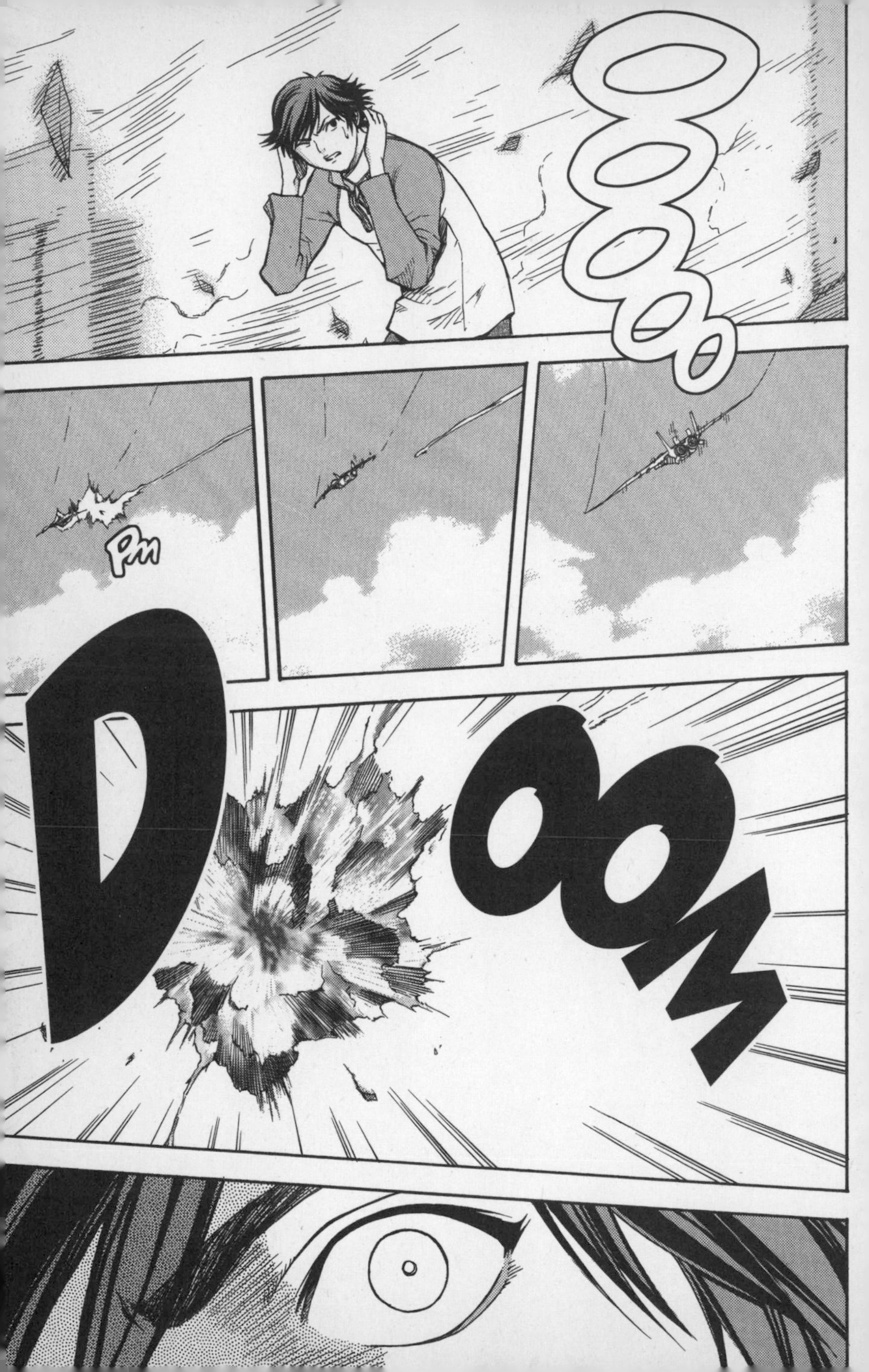
OOOOOO
Pm
DOOM

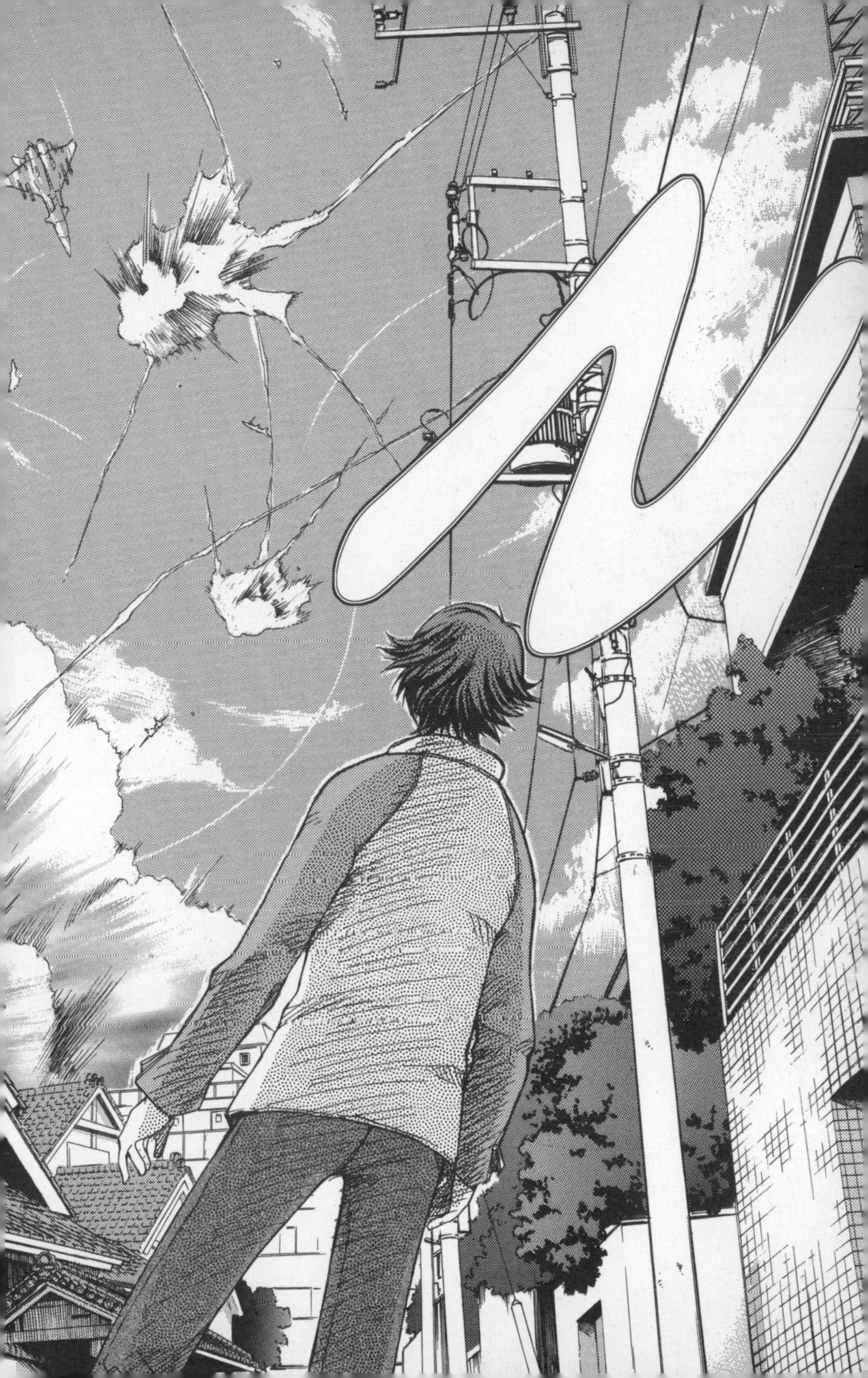

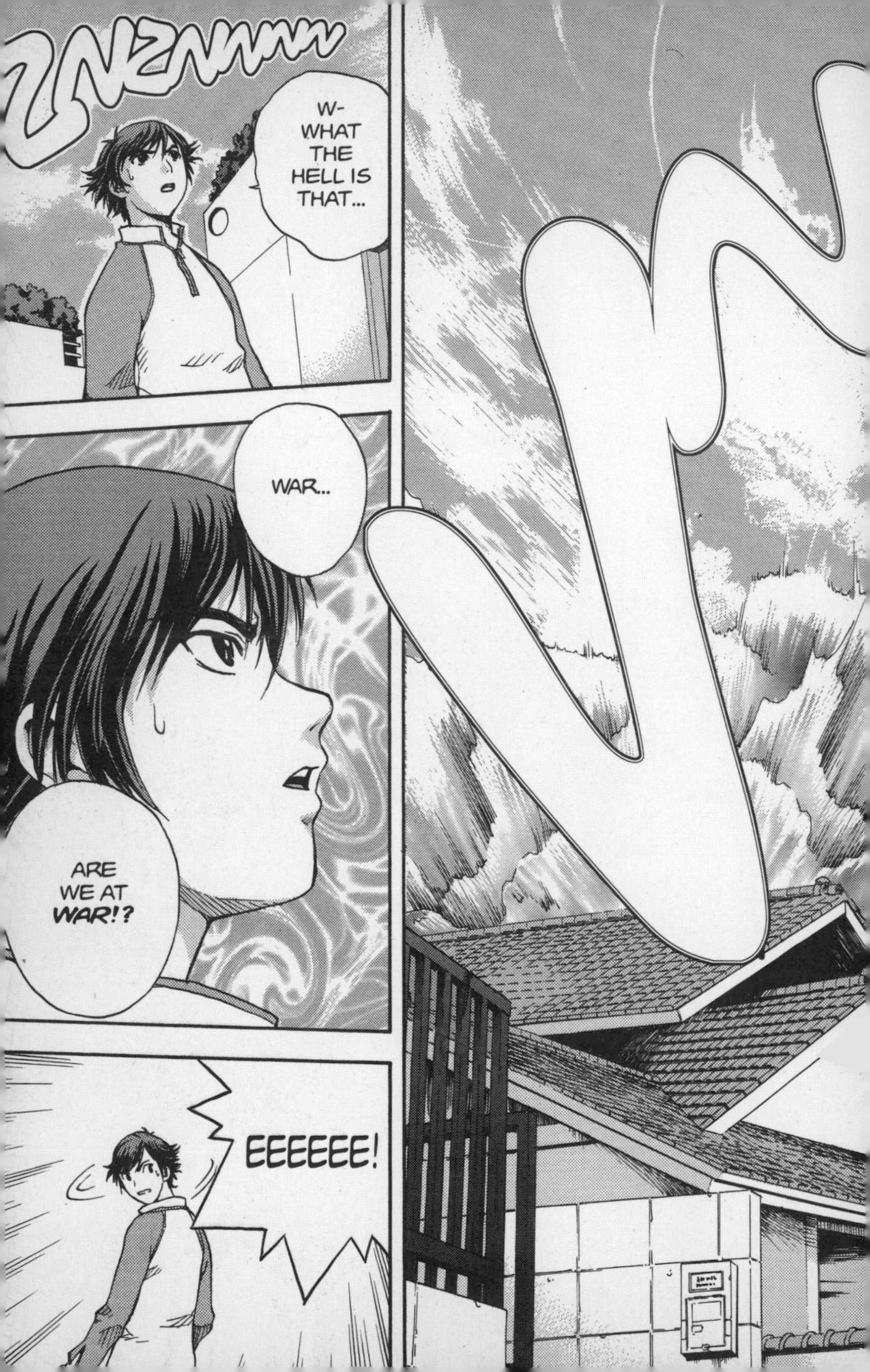
W- WHAT THE HELL IS THAT...
WAR...
ARE WE AT WAR!?
EEEEEEE!

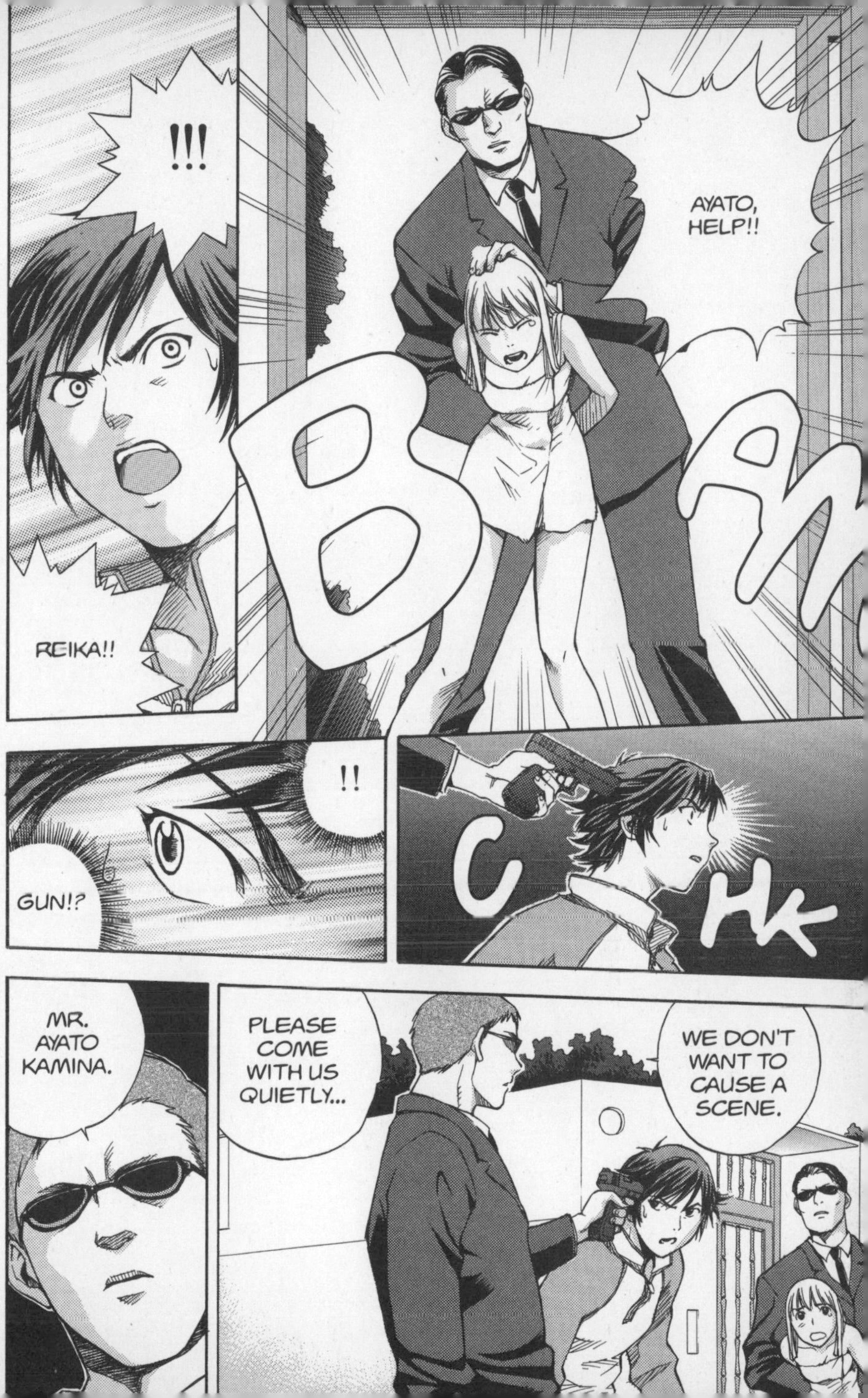
AYATO, HELP!!
BAN
!!!
REIKA!!
CHK
!!
GUN!?
WE DON'T WANT TO CAUSE A SCENE.
PLEASE COME WITH US QUIETLY...
MR. AYATO KAMINA.

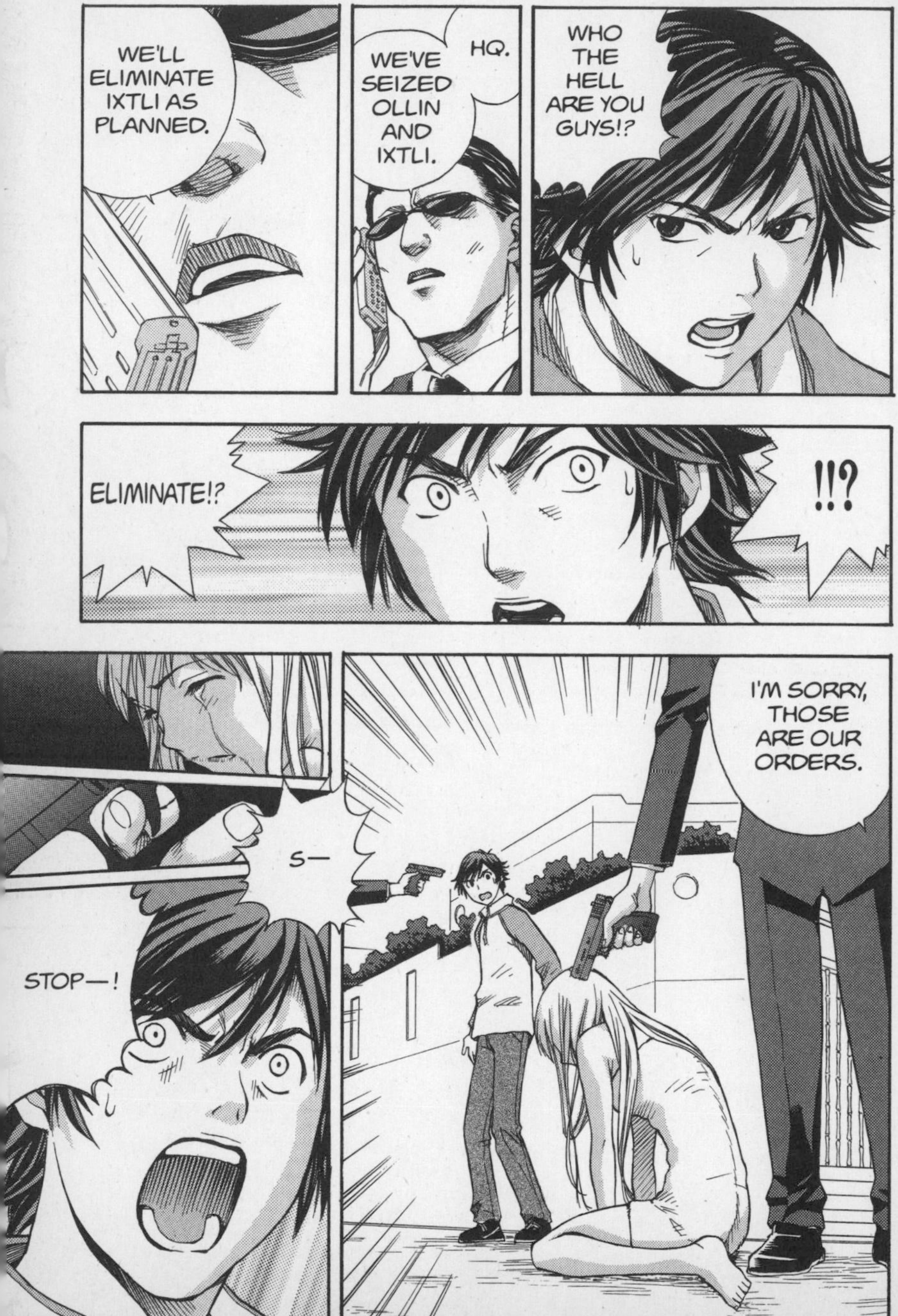
WHO THE HELL ARE YOU GUYS!?
HQ.
WE'VE SEIZED OLLIN AND IXTLI.
WE'LL ELIMINATE IXTLI AS PLANNED.
!!?
ELIMINATE!?
I'M SORRY, THOSE ARE OUR ORDERS.
S—
STOP—!

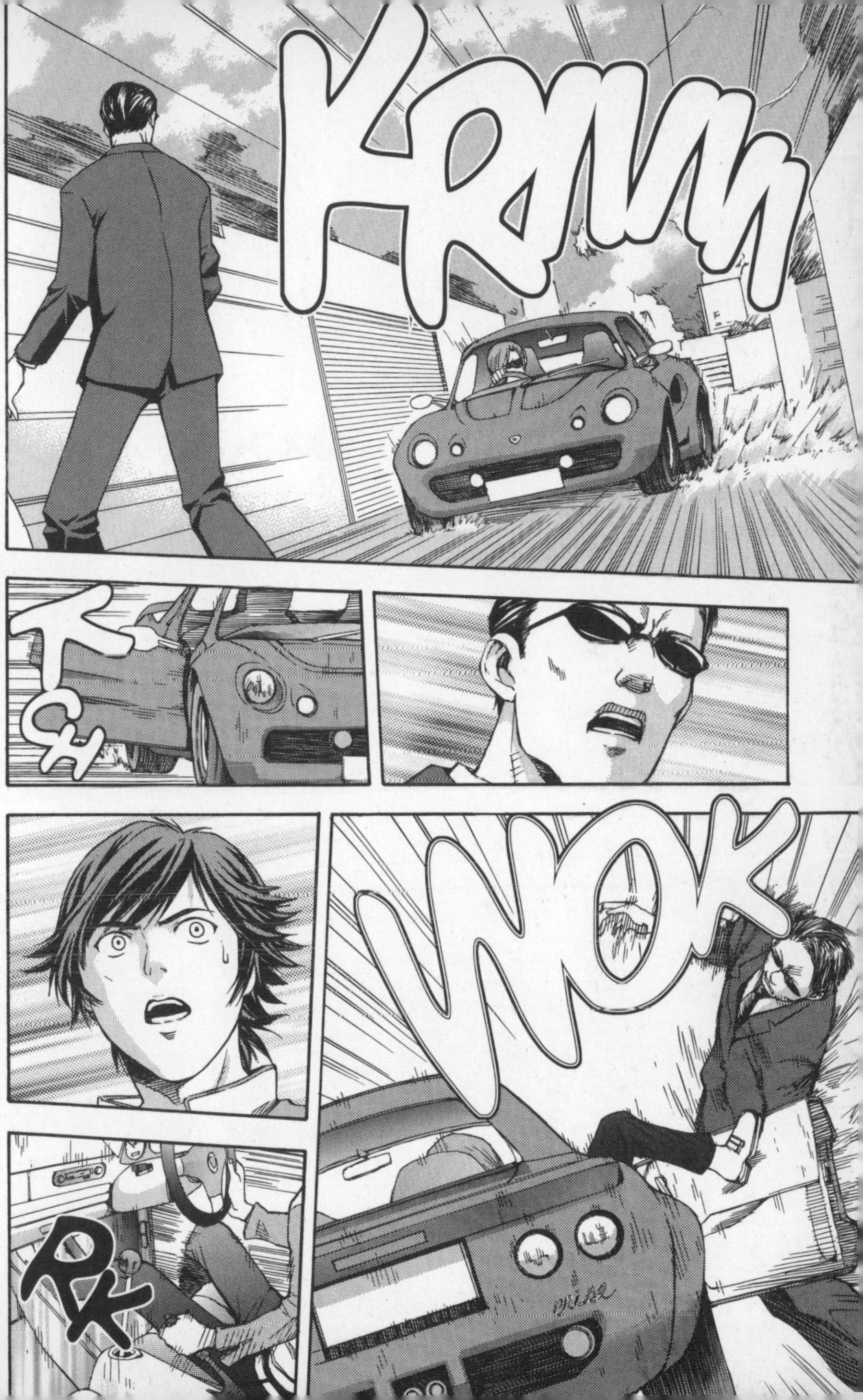
WOK

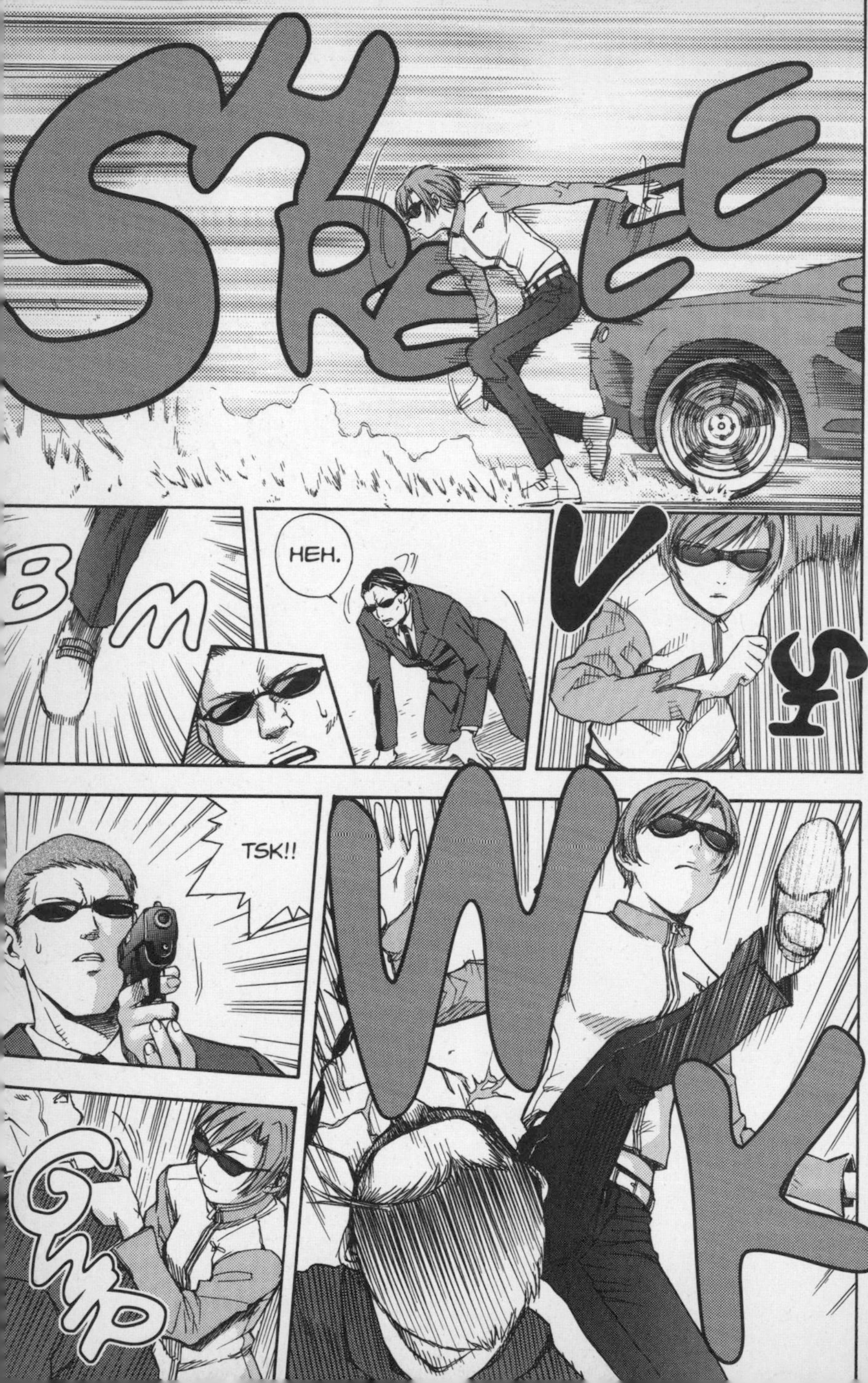
HEH.
TSK!!

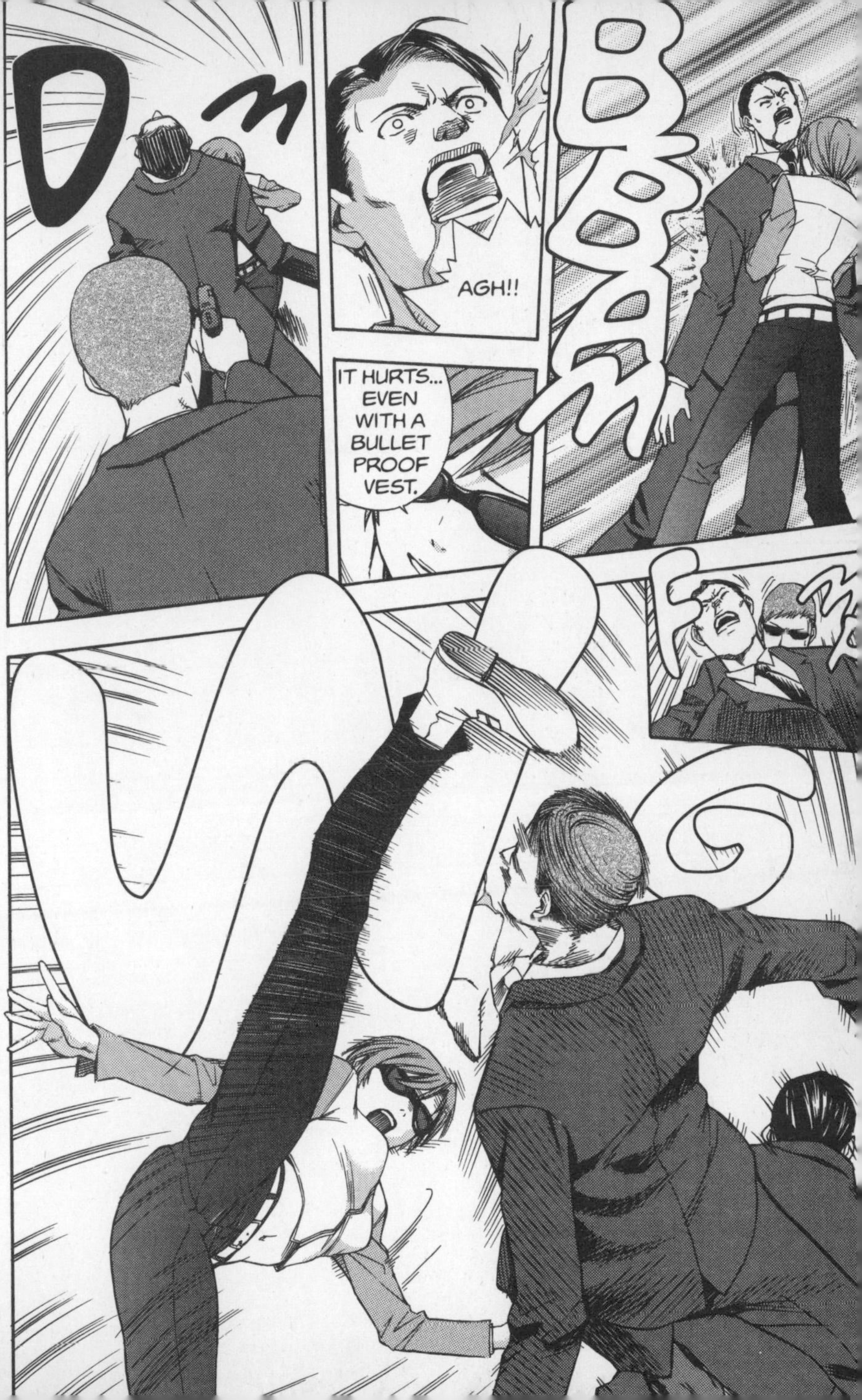
AGH!!
IT HURTS... EVEN WITH A BULLET PROOF VEST.

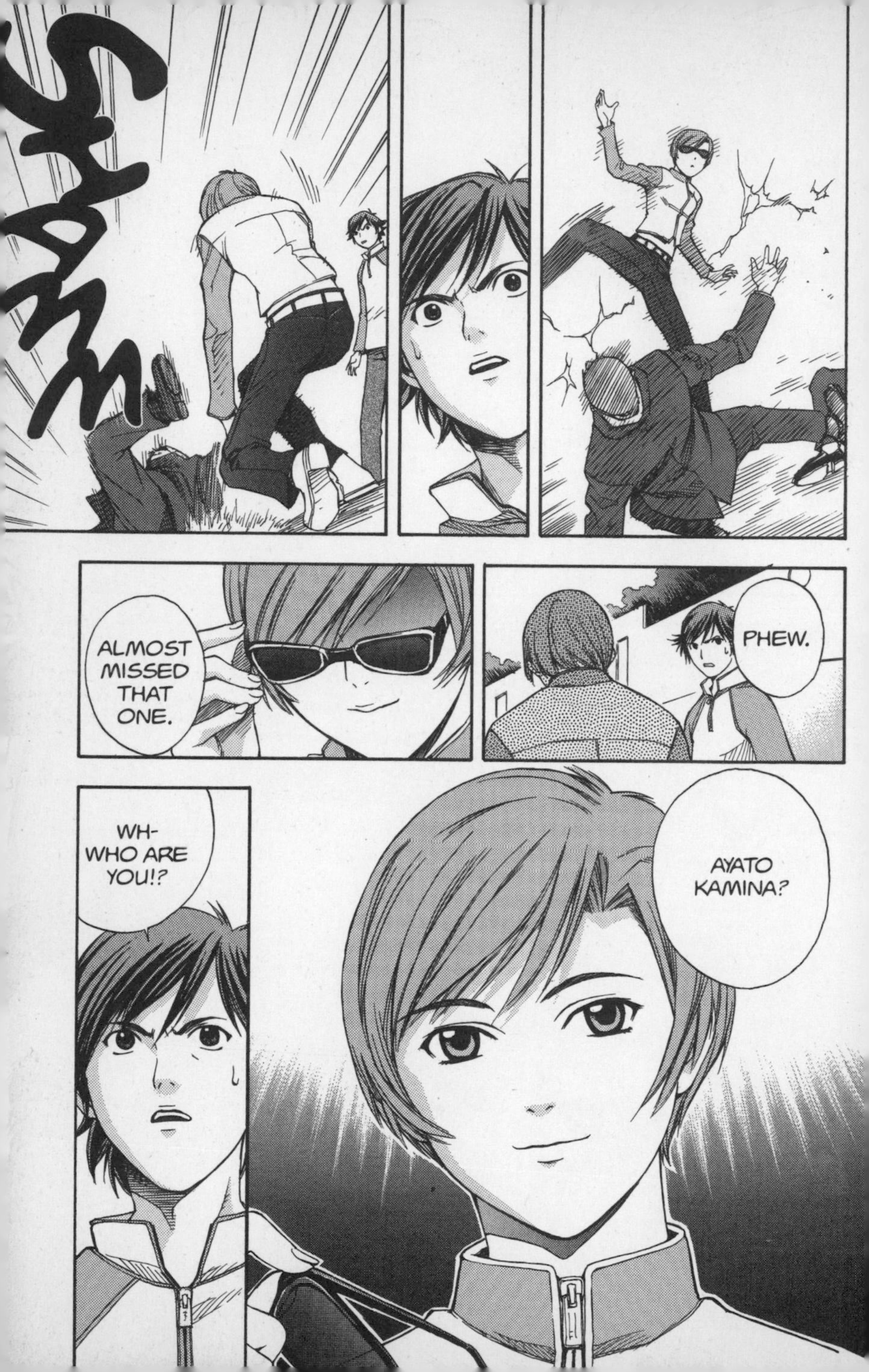
SLAM
PHEW.
ALMOST MISSED THAT ONE.
AYATO KAMINA?
WH- WHO ARE YOU!?

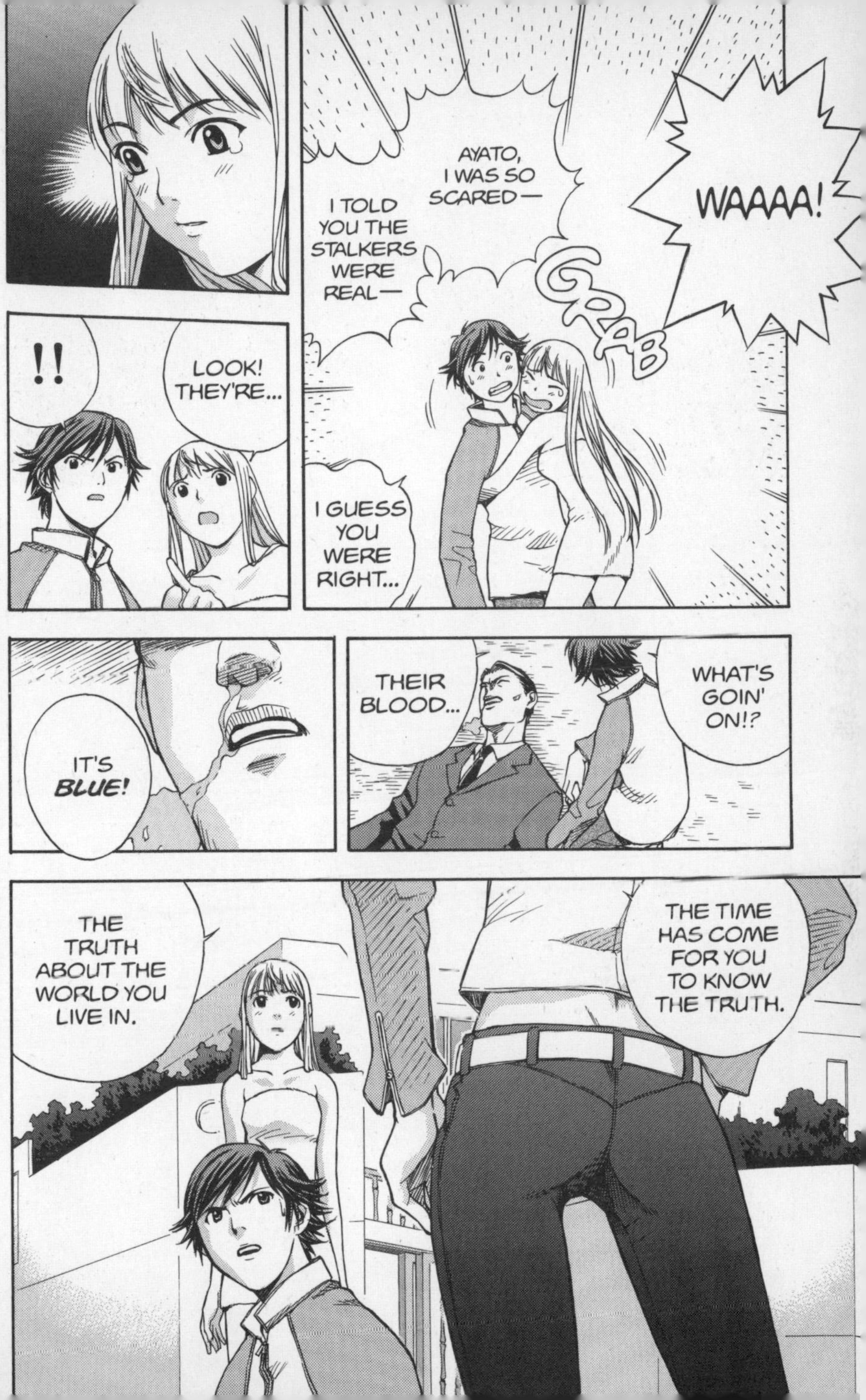
WAAAA!
GRAB
AYATO, I WAS SO SCARED—
I TOLD YOU THE STALKERS WERE REAL—
I GUESS YOU WERE RIGHT...
LOOK! THEY'RE...
!!
WHAT'S GOIN' ON!?
THEIR BLOOD...
IT'S *BLUE*!
THE TIME HAS COME FOR YOU TO KNOW THE TRUTH.
THE TRUTH ABOUT THE WORLD YOU LIVE IN.

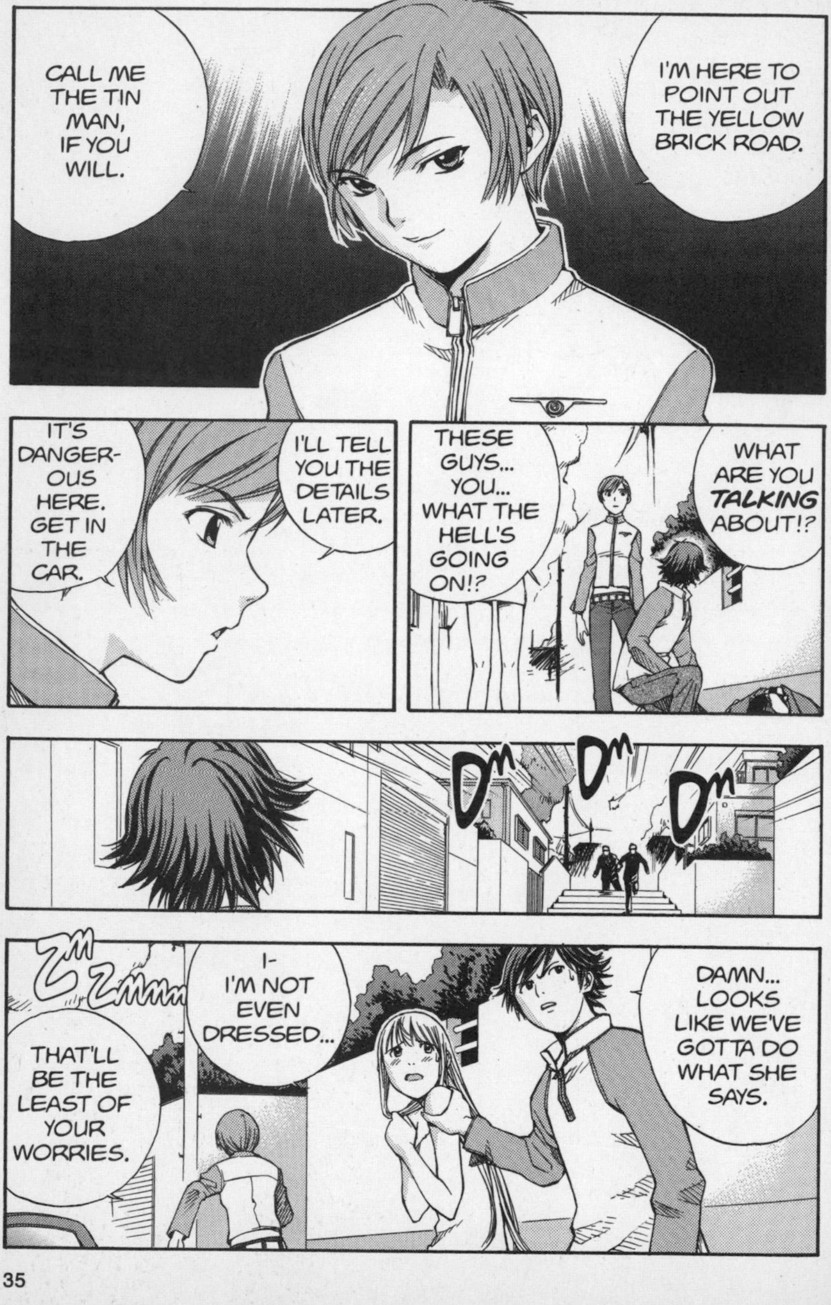
I'M HERE TO POINT OUT THE YELLOW BRICK ROAD.
CALL ME THE TIN MAN, IF YOU WILL.
WHAT ARE YOU *TALKING* ABOUT!?
THESE GUYS... YOU... WHAT THE HELL'S GOING ON!?
I'LL TELL YOU THE DETAILS LATER.
IT'S DANGER-OUS HERE. GET IN THE CAR.
Dm
Dm
Dm
DAMN... LOOKS LIKE WE'VE GOTTA DO WHAT SHE SAYS.
I- I'M NOT EVEN DRESSED...
Zm Zmmm
THAT'LL BE THE LEAST OF YOUR WORRIES.

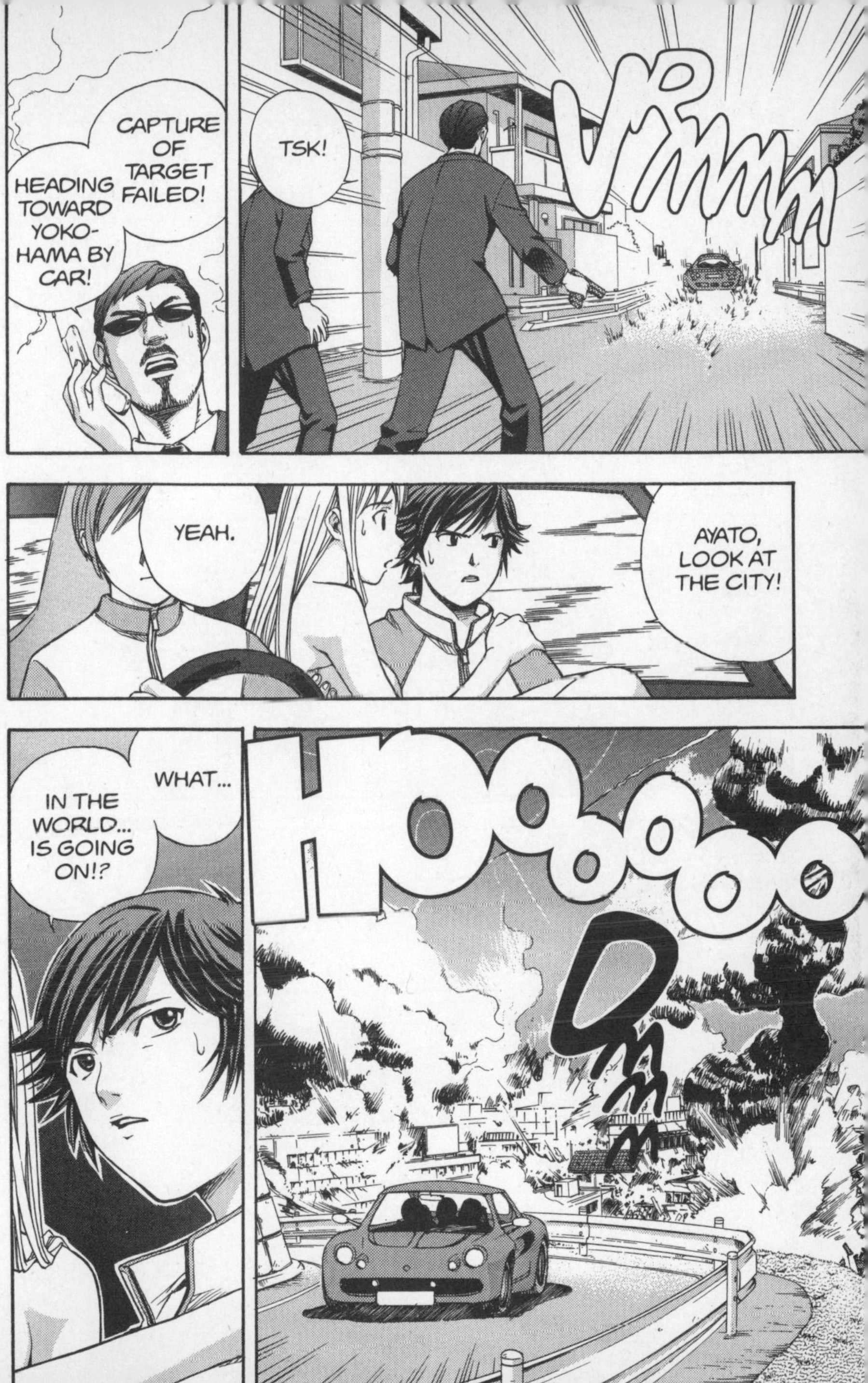
TSK!
CAPTURE OF TARGET FAILED!
HEADING TOWARD YOKO-HAMA BY CAR!
AYATO, LOOK AT THE CITY!
YEAH.
WHAT...
IN THE WORLD... IS GOING ON!?

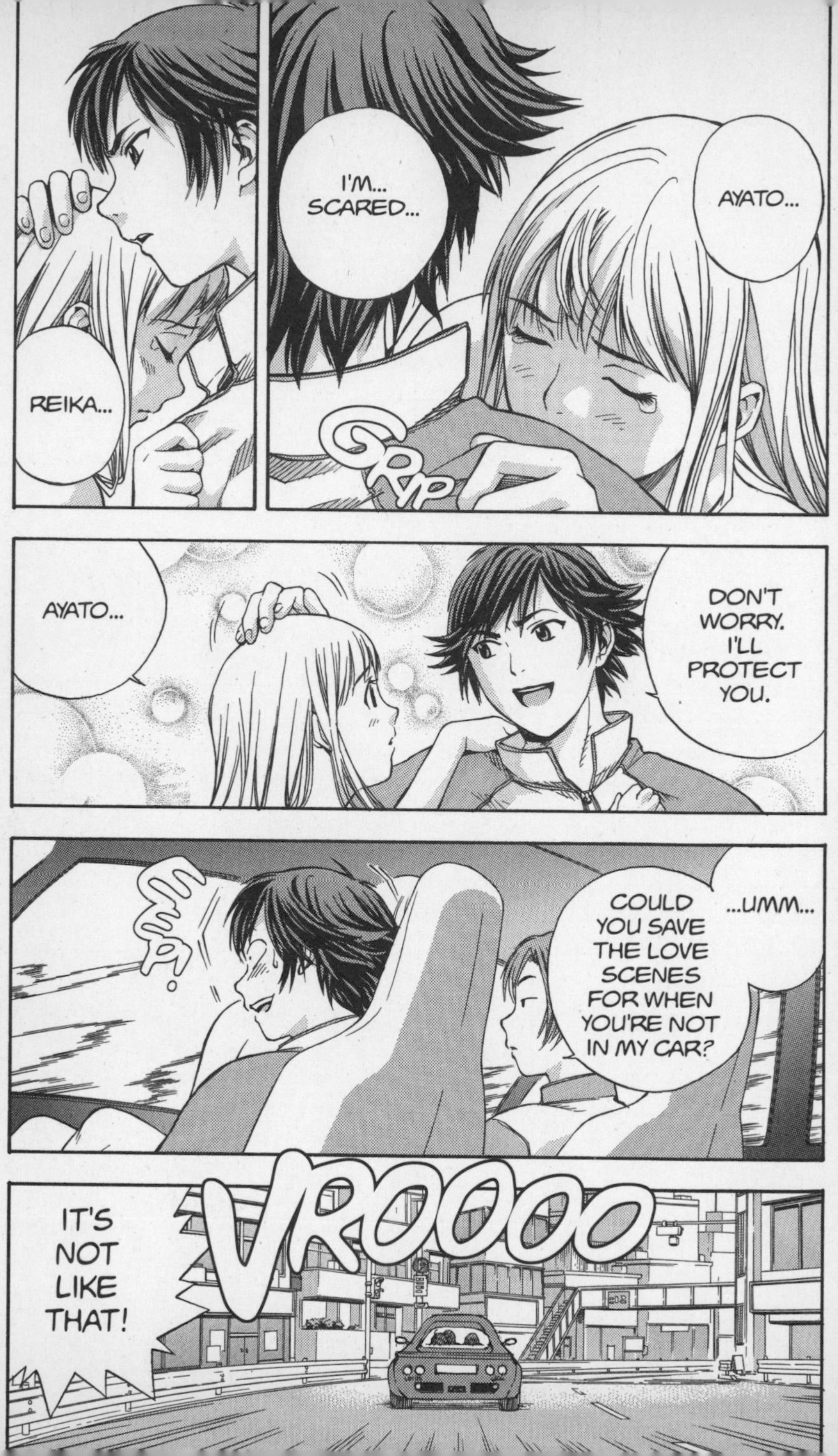
AYATO...
I'M... SCARED...
GRIP
REIKA...
DON'T WORRY. I'LL PROTECT YOU.
AYATO...
...UMM...
COULD YOU SAVE THE LOVE SCENES FOR WHEN YOU'RE NOT IN MY CAR?
EEP!
VROOOO
IT'S NOT LIKE THAT!

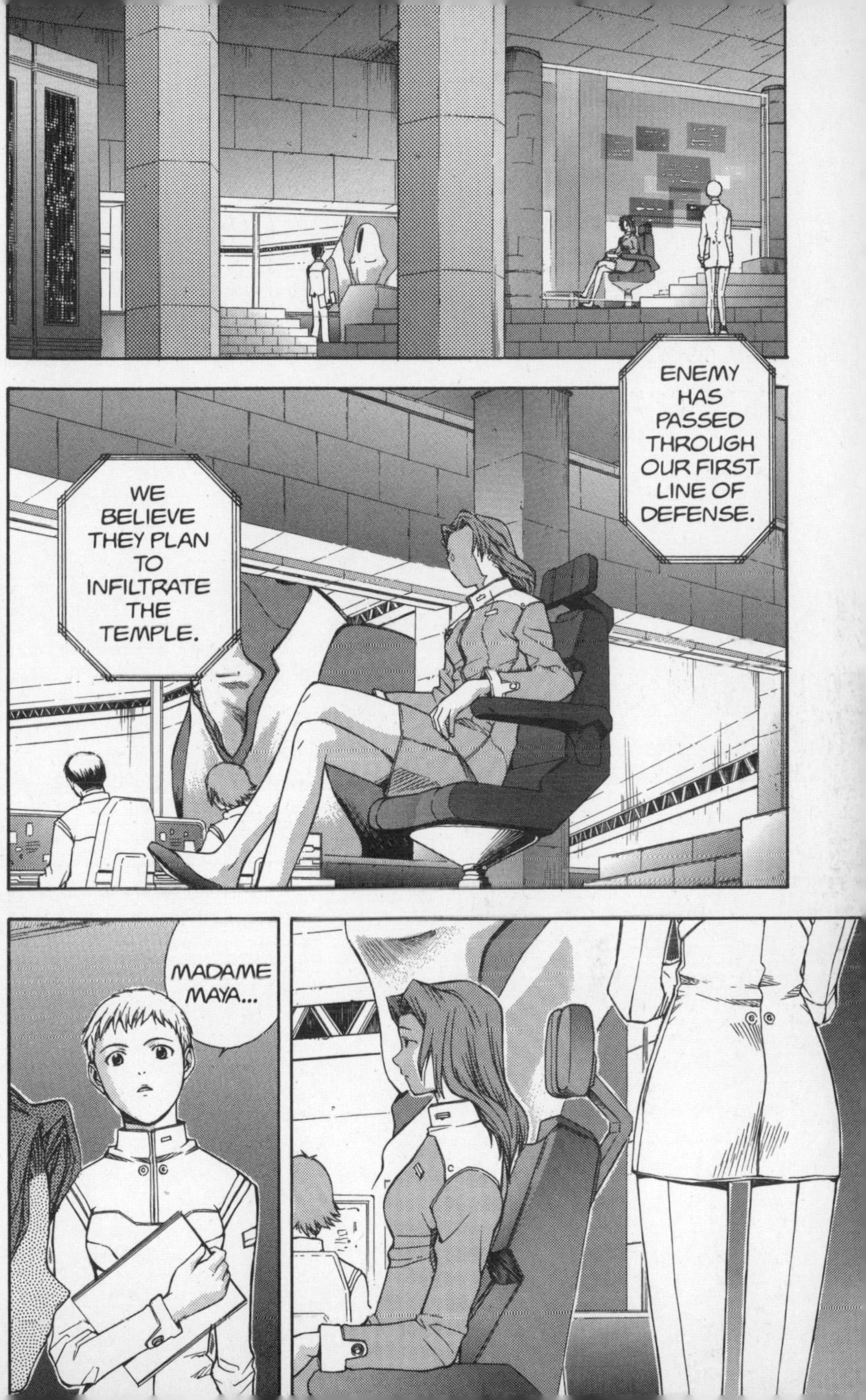
ENEMY HAS PASSED THROUGH OUR FIRST LINE OF DEFENSE.
WE BELIEVE THEY PLAN TO INFILTRATE THE TEMPLE.
MADAME MAYA...

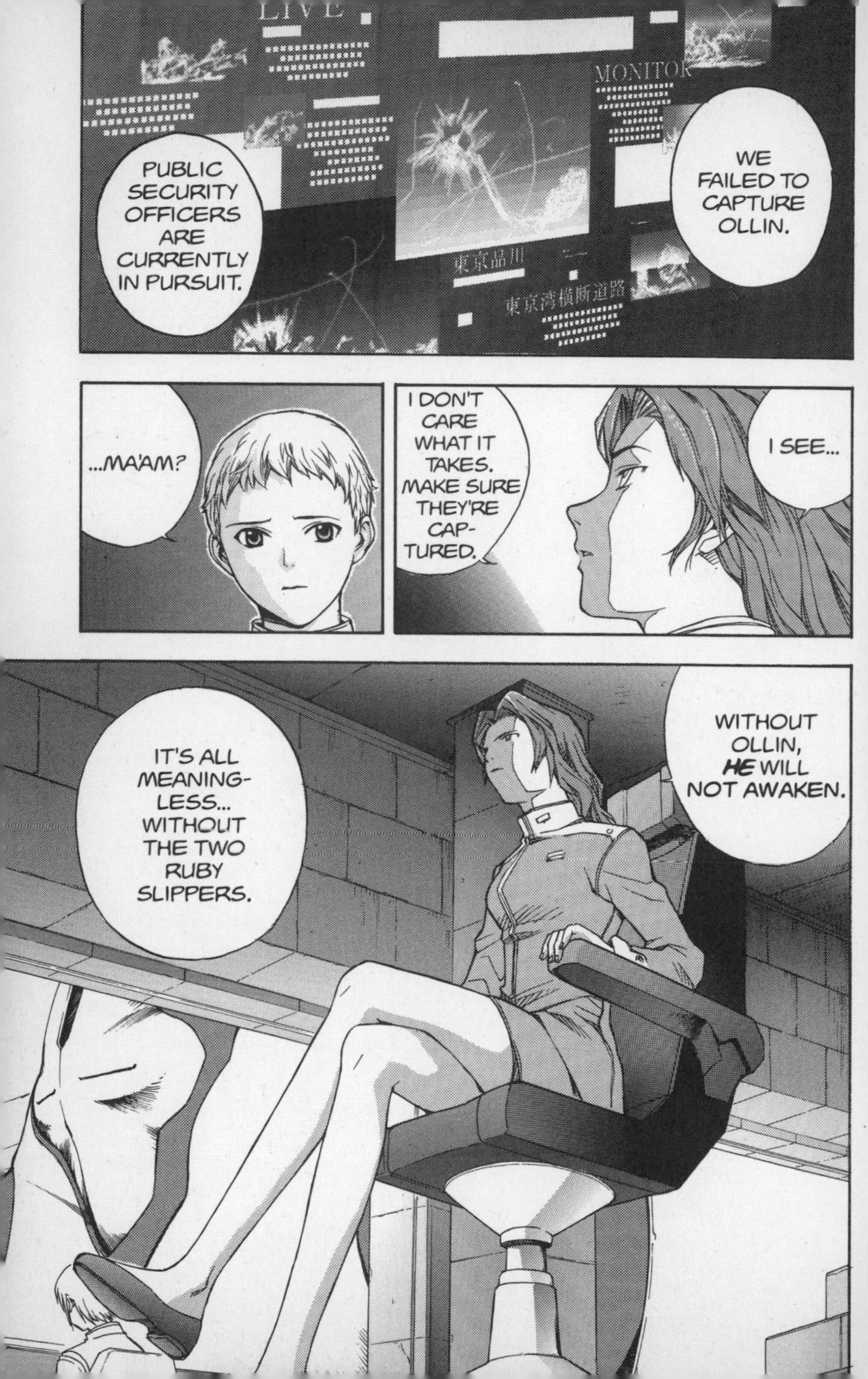
LIVE
MONITOR
東京品川
東京湾横断道路
WE FAILED TO CAPTURE OLLIN.
PUBLIC SECURITY OFFICERS ARE CURRENTLY IN PURSUIT.
I SEE...
I DON'T CARE WHAT IT TAKES. MAKE SURE THEY'RE CAP-TURED.
...MA'AM?
WITHOUT OLLIN, ***HE*** WILL NOT AWAKEN.
IT'S ALL MEANING-LESS... WITHOUT THE TWO RUBY SLIPPERS.

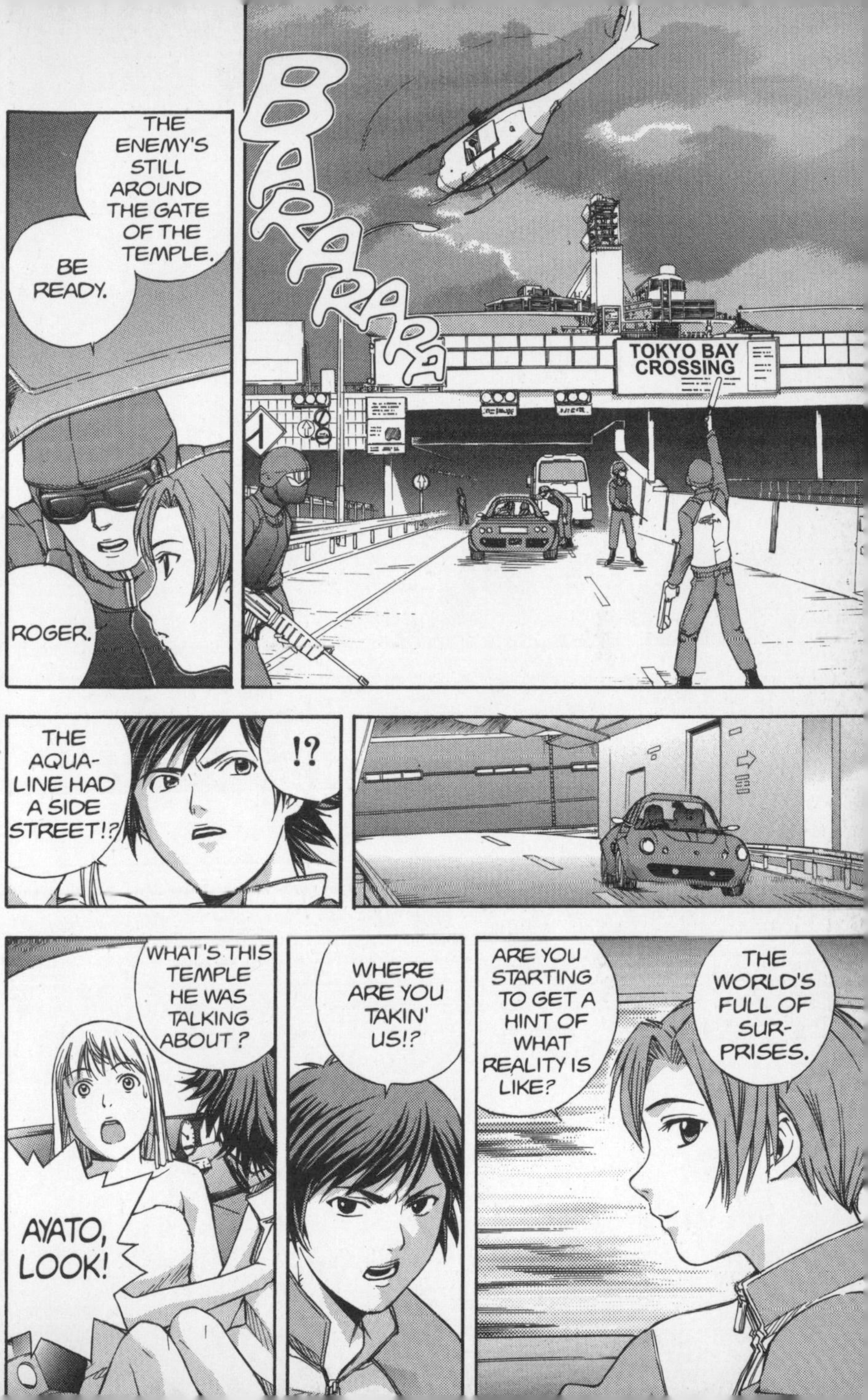
BARARARARA
TOKYO BAY CROSSING
THE ENEMY'S STILL AROUND THE GATE OF THE TEMPLE.
BE READY.
ROGER.
!?
THE AQUA-LINE HAD A SIDE STREET!?
THE WORLD'S FULL OF SUR-PRISES.
ARE YOU STARTING TO GET A HINT OF WHAT REALITY IS LIKE?
WHERE ARE YOU TAKIN' US!?
WHAT'S THIS TEMPLE HE WAS TALKING ABOUT?
AYATO, LOOK!

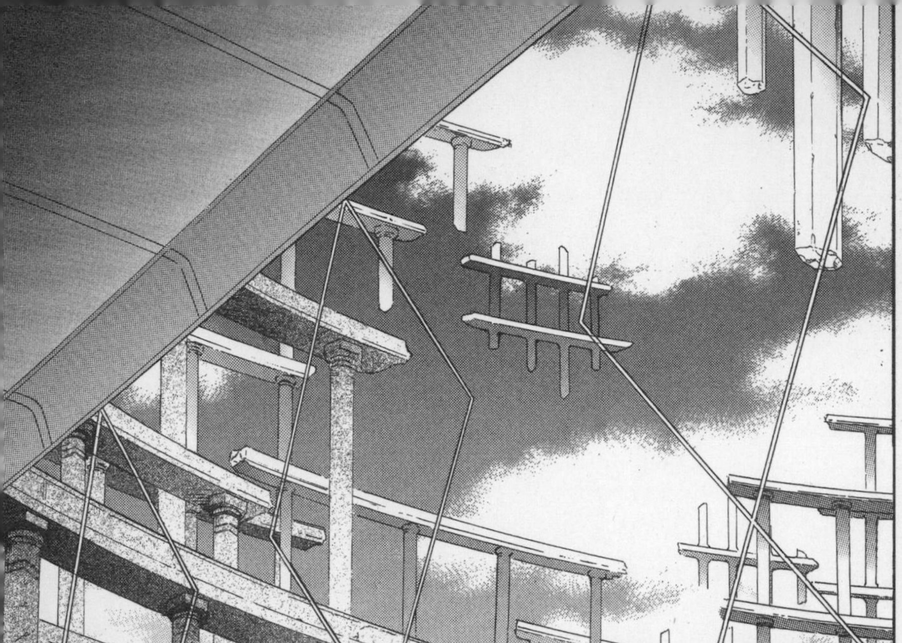

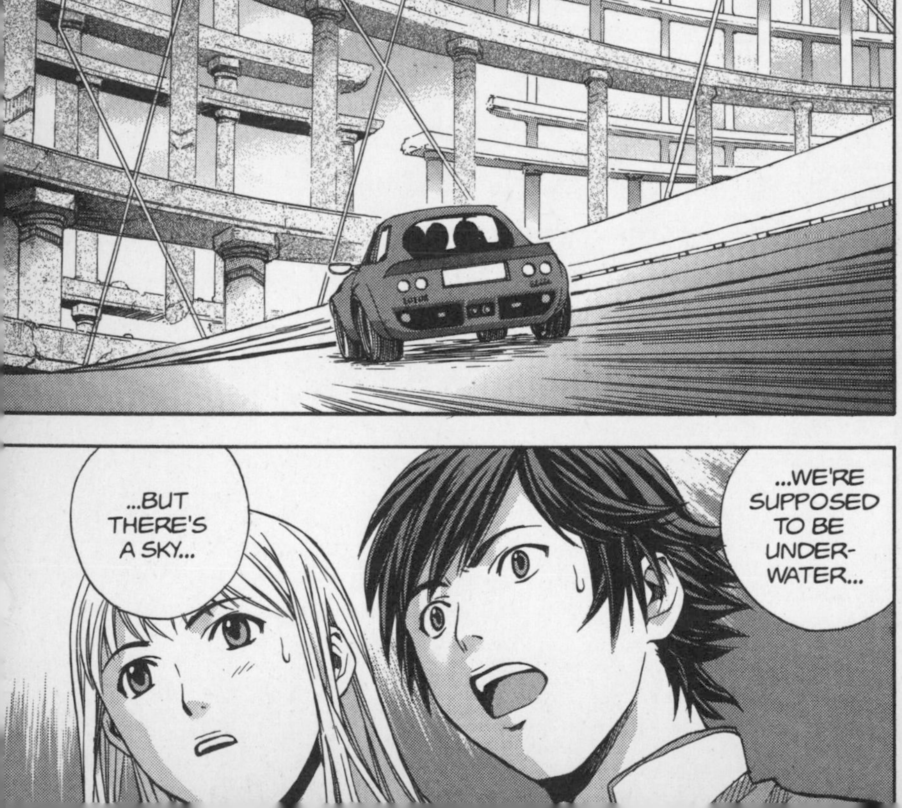
...WE'RE SUPPOSED TO BE UNDER-WATER...
...BUT THERE'S A SKY...

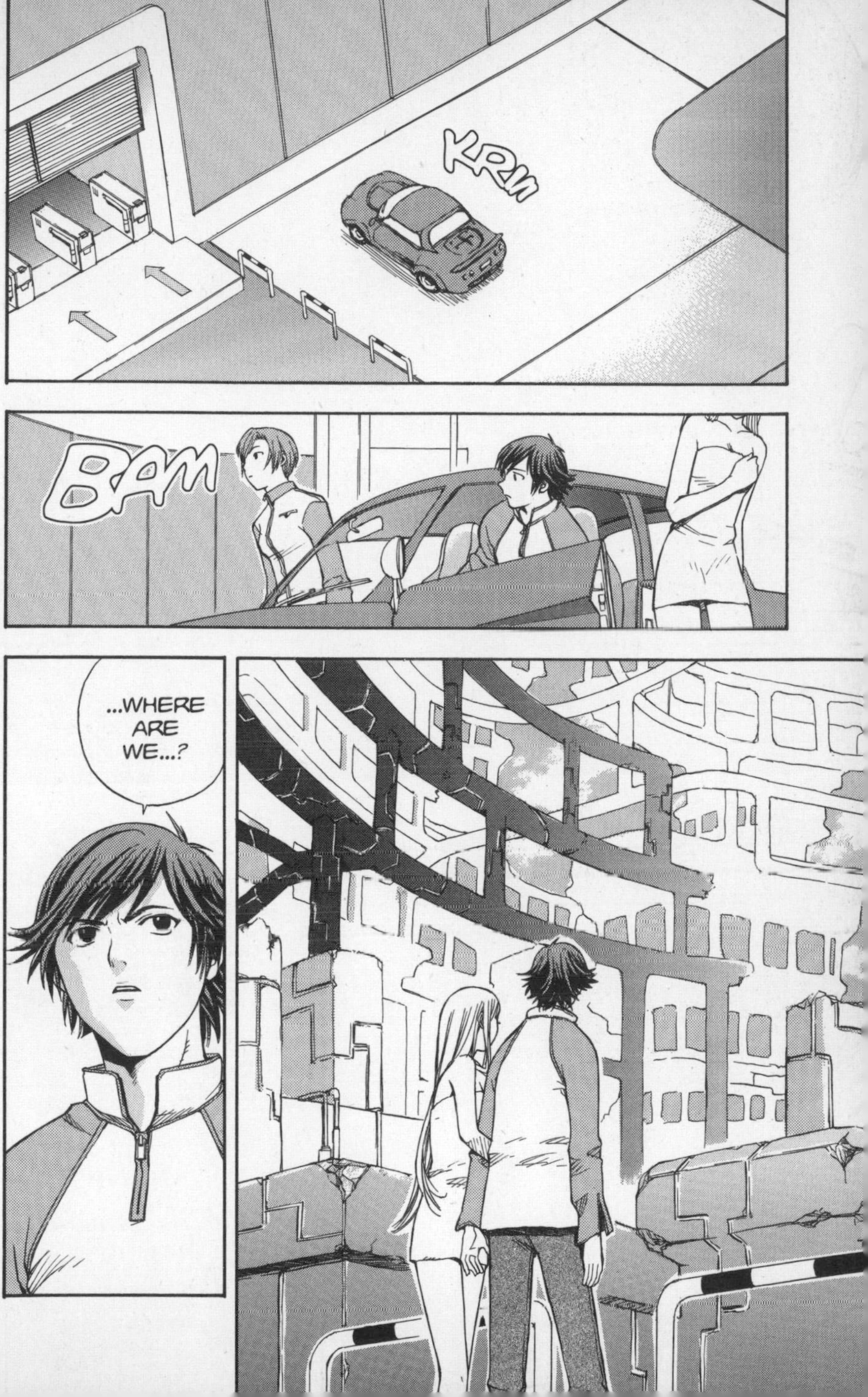
KRIII
BAM
...WHERE ARE WE...?

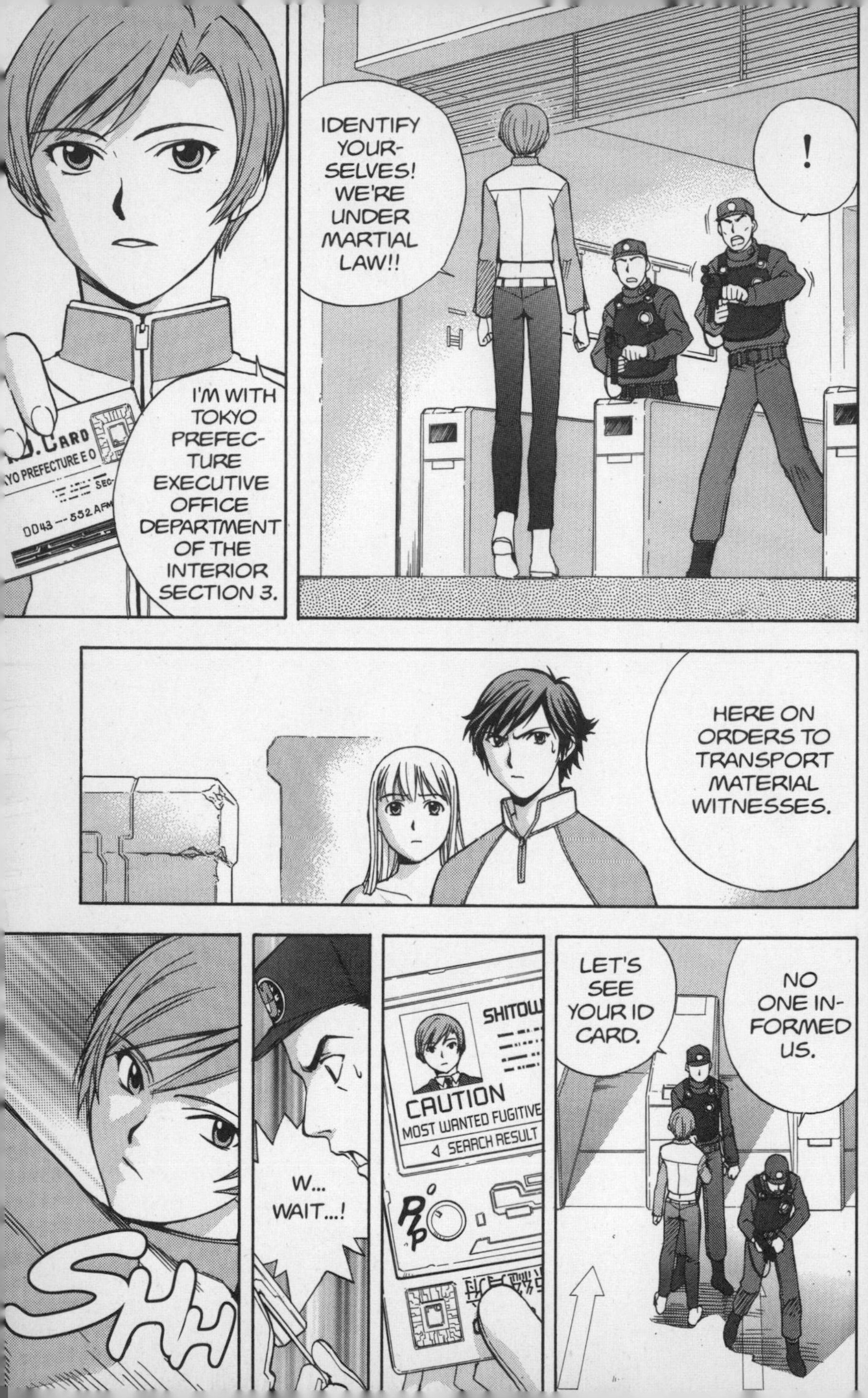
!
IDENTIFY YOUR-SELVES! WE'RE UNDER MARTIAL LAW!!
I'M WITH TOKYO PREFEC-TURE EXECUTIVE OFFICE DEPARTMENT OF THE INTERIOR SECTION 3.
HERE ON ORDERS TO TRANSPORT MATERIAL WITNESSES.
NO ONE IN-FORMED US.
LET'S SEE YOUR ID CARD.
SHITOW
CAUTION
MOST WANTED FUGITIVE
SEARCH RESULT
PiP
W... WAIT...!
SHH

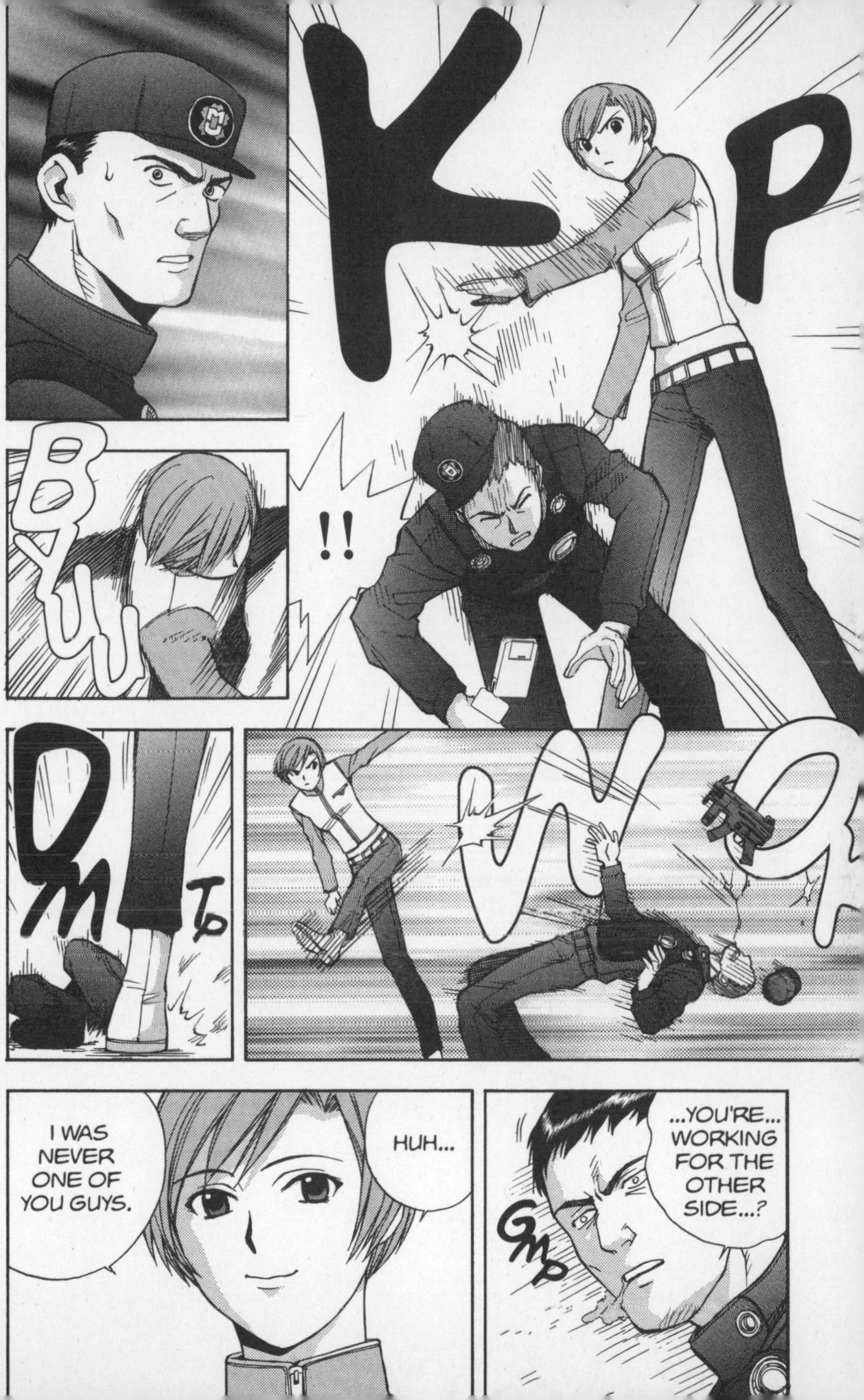
KYP
BYUU
!!
DMTO
WHO
...YOU'RE... WORKING FOR THE OTHER SIDE...?
GMP
HUH...
I WAS NEVER ONE OF YOU GUYS.

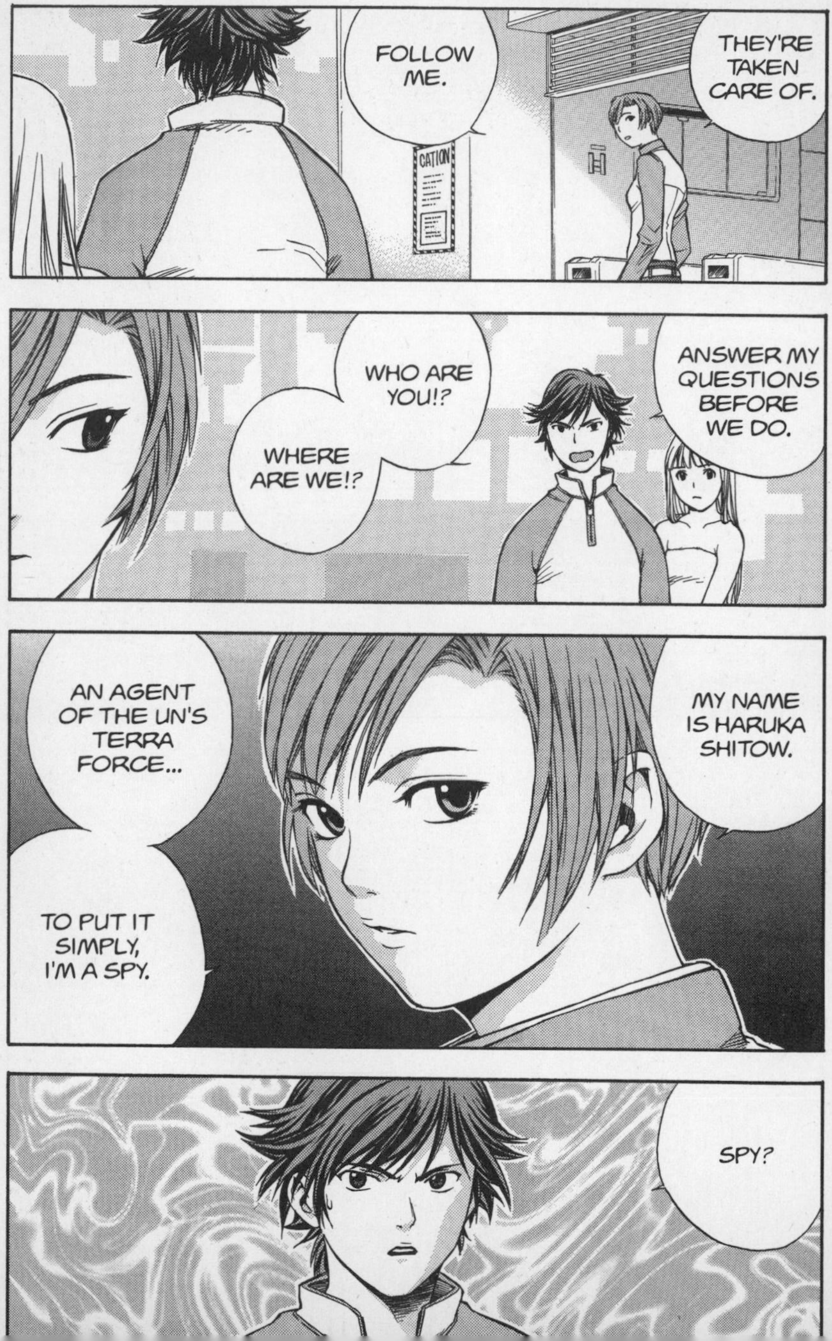
THEY'RE TAKEN CARE OF.
CATION
FOLLOW ME.
ANSWER MY QUESTIONS BEFORE WE DO.
WHO ARE YOU!?
WHERE ARE WE!?
MY NAME IS HARUKA SHITOW.
AN AGENT OF THE UN'S TERRA FORCE...
TO PUT IT SIMPLY, I'M A SPY.
SPY?

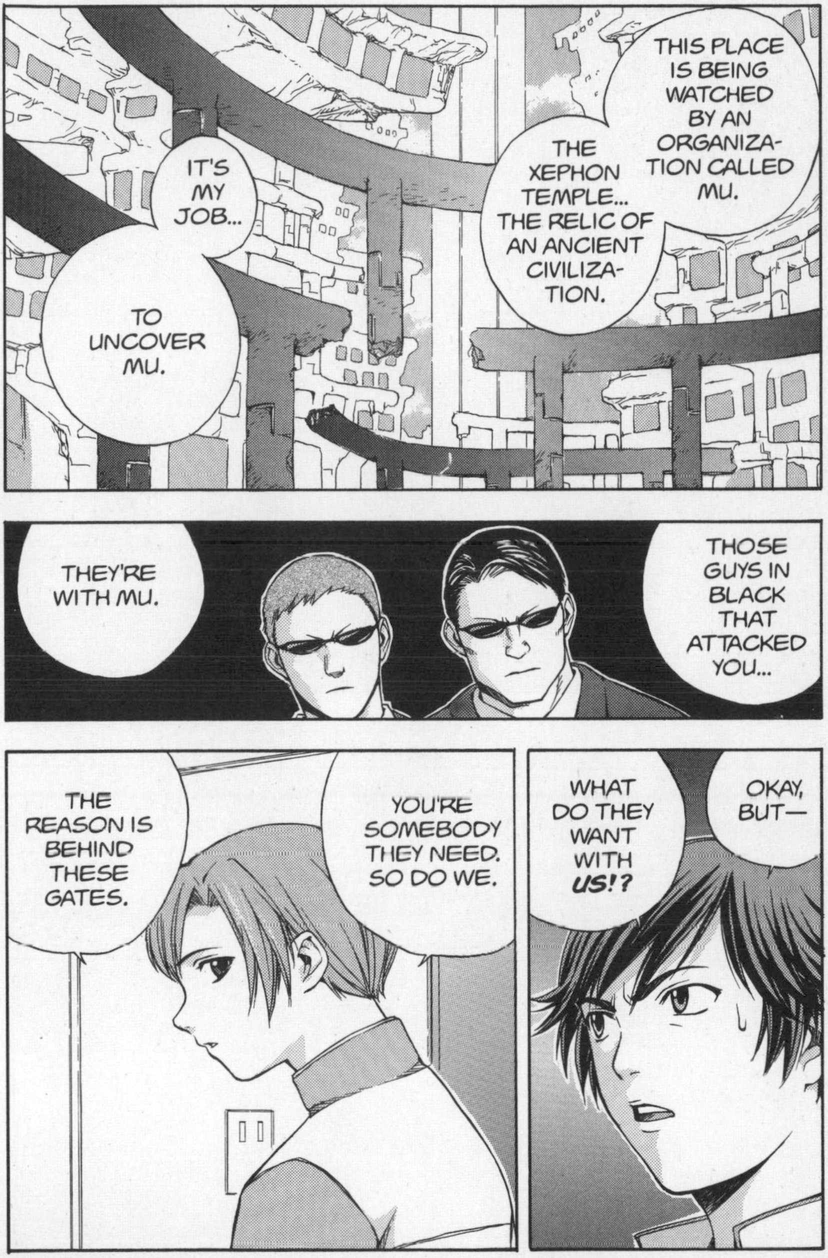
THIS PLACE IS BEING WATCHED BY AN ORGANIZATION CALLED MU.
THE XEPHON TEMPLE... THE RELIC OF AN ANCIENT CIVILIZATION.
IT'S MY JOB...
TO UNCOVER MU.
THOSE GUYS IN BLACK THAT ATTACKED YOU...
THEY'RE WITH MU.
OKAY, BUT—
WHAT DO THEY WANT WITH ***US!?***
YOU'RE SOMEBODY THEY NEED. SO DO WE.
THE REASON IS BEHIND THESE GATES.

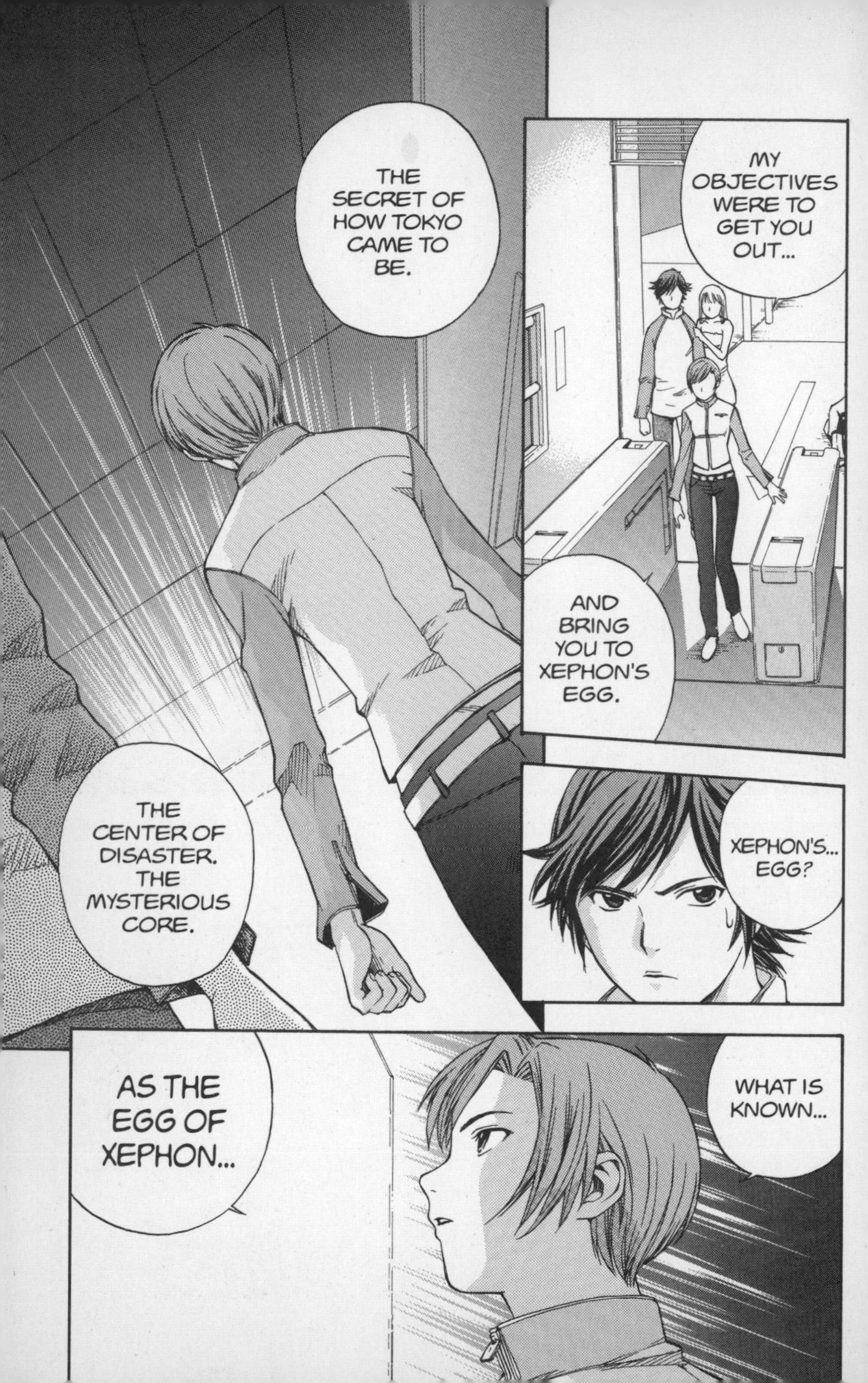
MY OBJECTIVES WERE TO GET YOU OUT...
AND BRING YOU TO XEPHON'S EGG.
XEPHON'S... EGG?
THE SECRET OF HOW TOKYO CAME TO BE.
THE CENTER OF DISASTER. THE MYSTERIOUS CORE.
WHAT IS KNOWN...
AS THE EGG OF XEPHON...

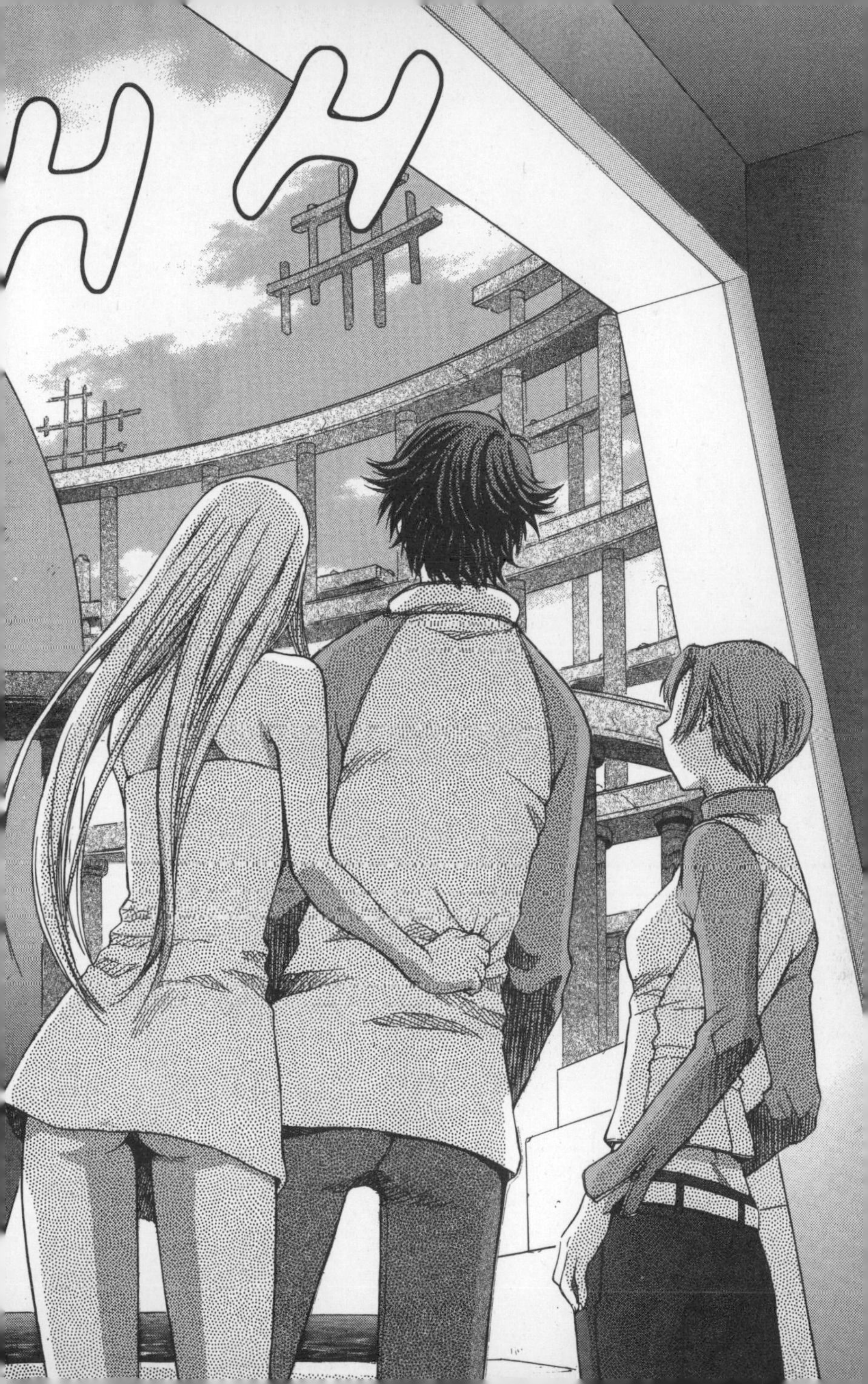
HH

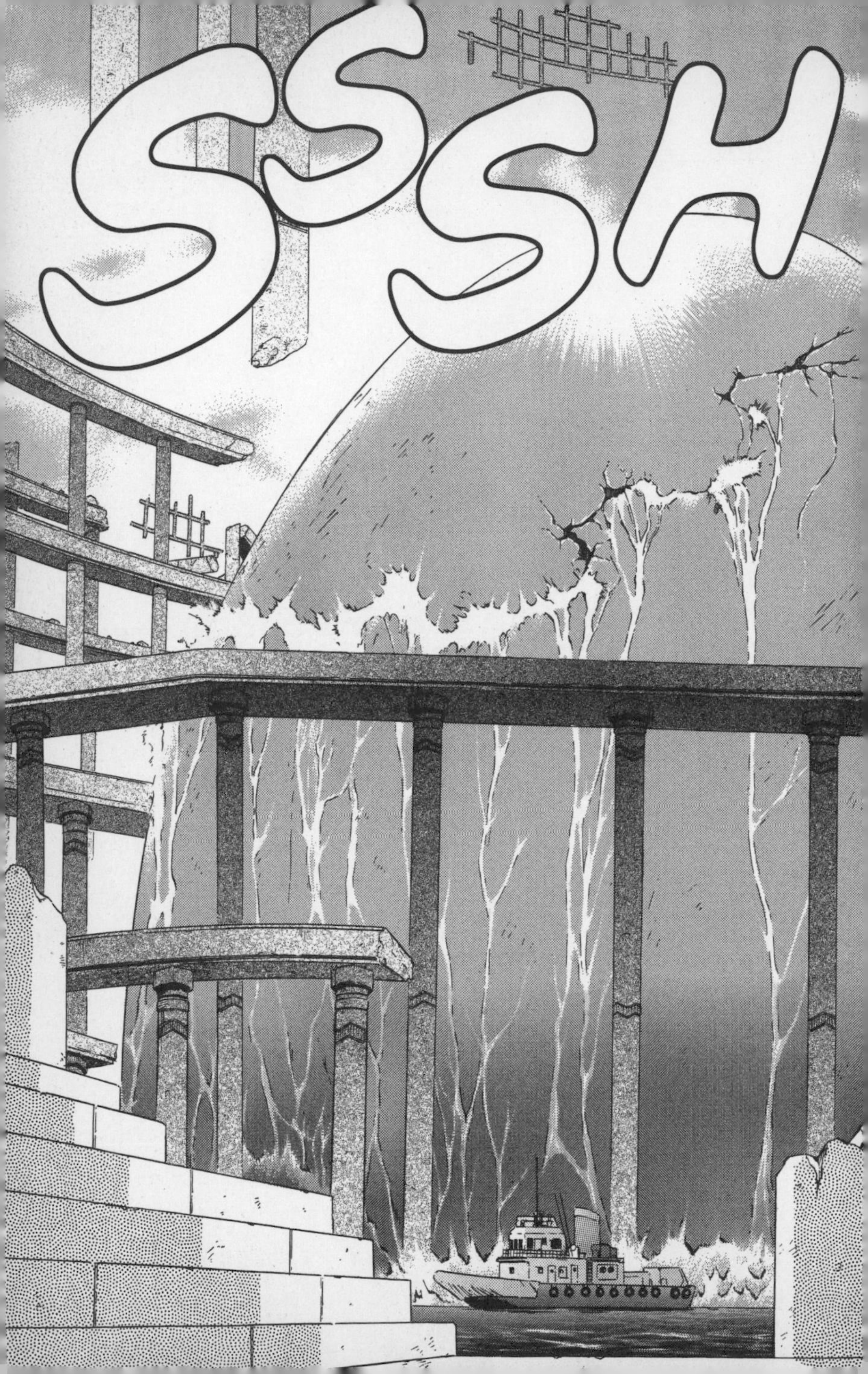
SSSH

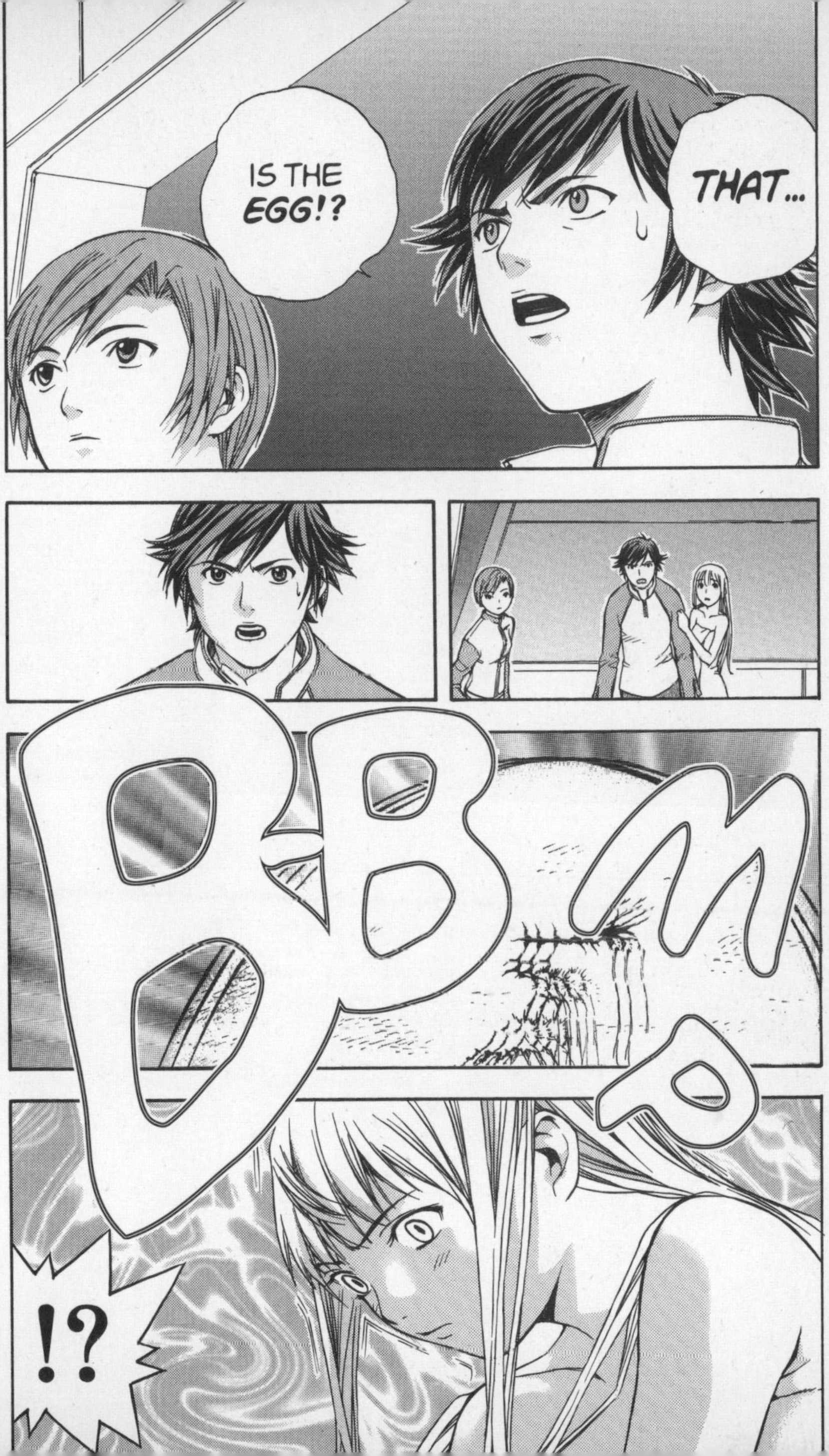
THAT...
IS THE EGG!?
!?

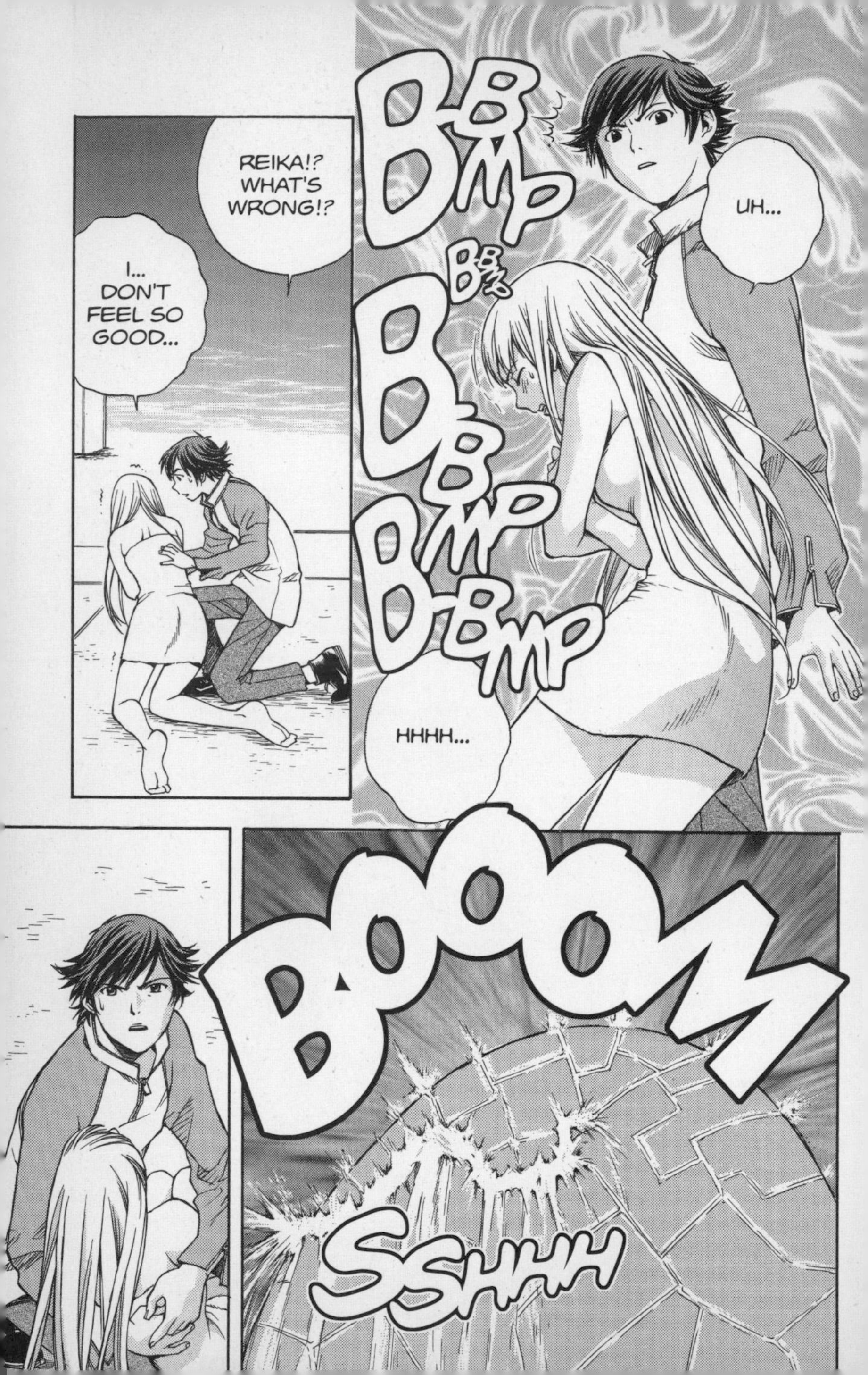
B-BMP
BBMP
BBMP
UH...
B-BMP
B-BMP
HHHH...
REIKA!? WHAT'S WRONG!?
I... DON'T FEEL SO GOOD...
BOOOM
SSHHH

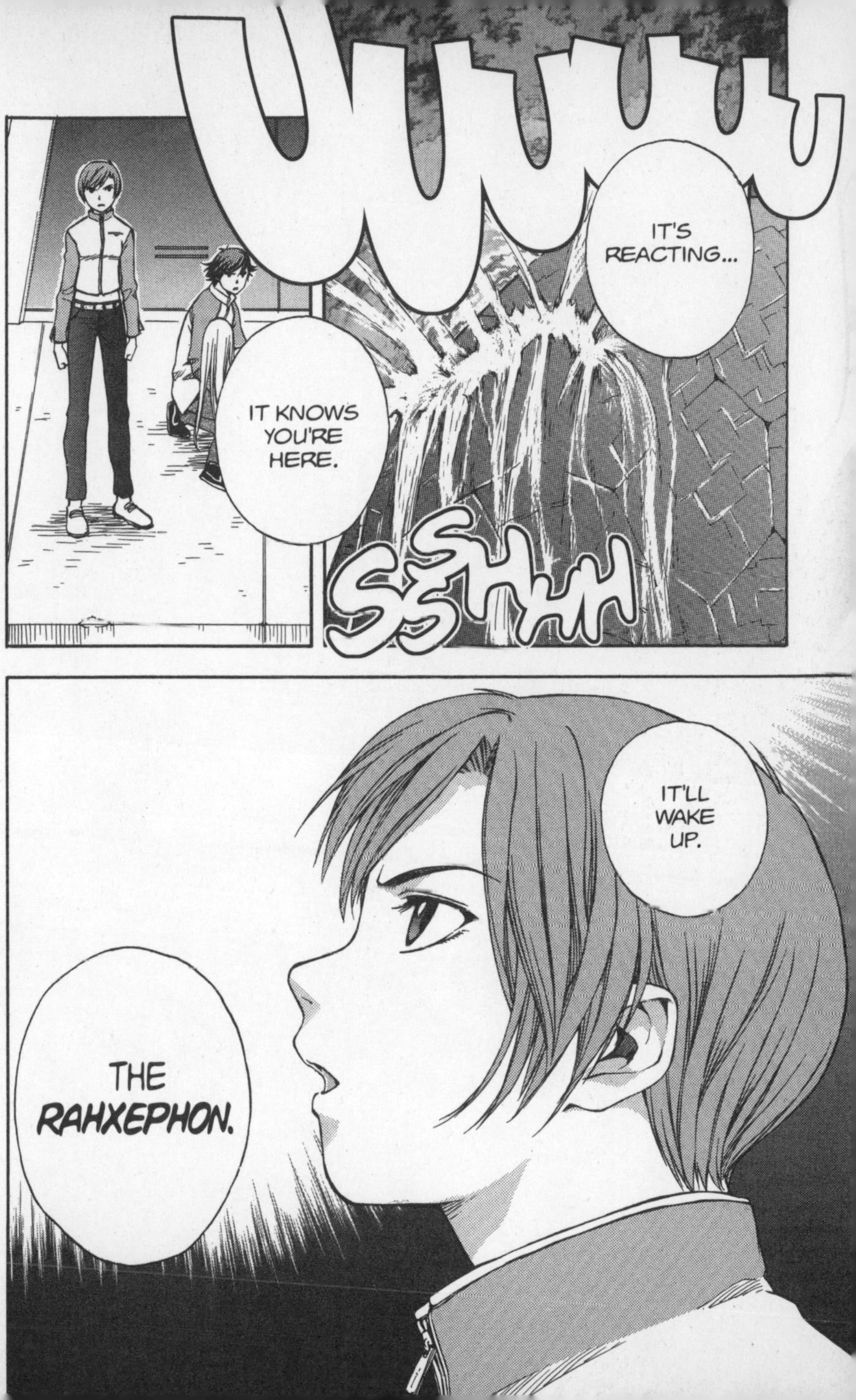
IT'S REACTING...
IT KNOWS YOU'RE HERE.
IT'LL WAKE UP.
THE RAHXEPHON.

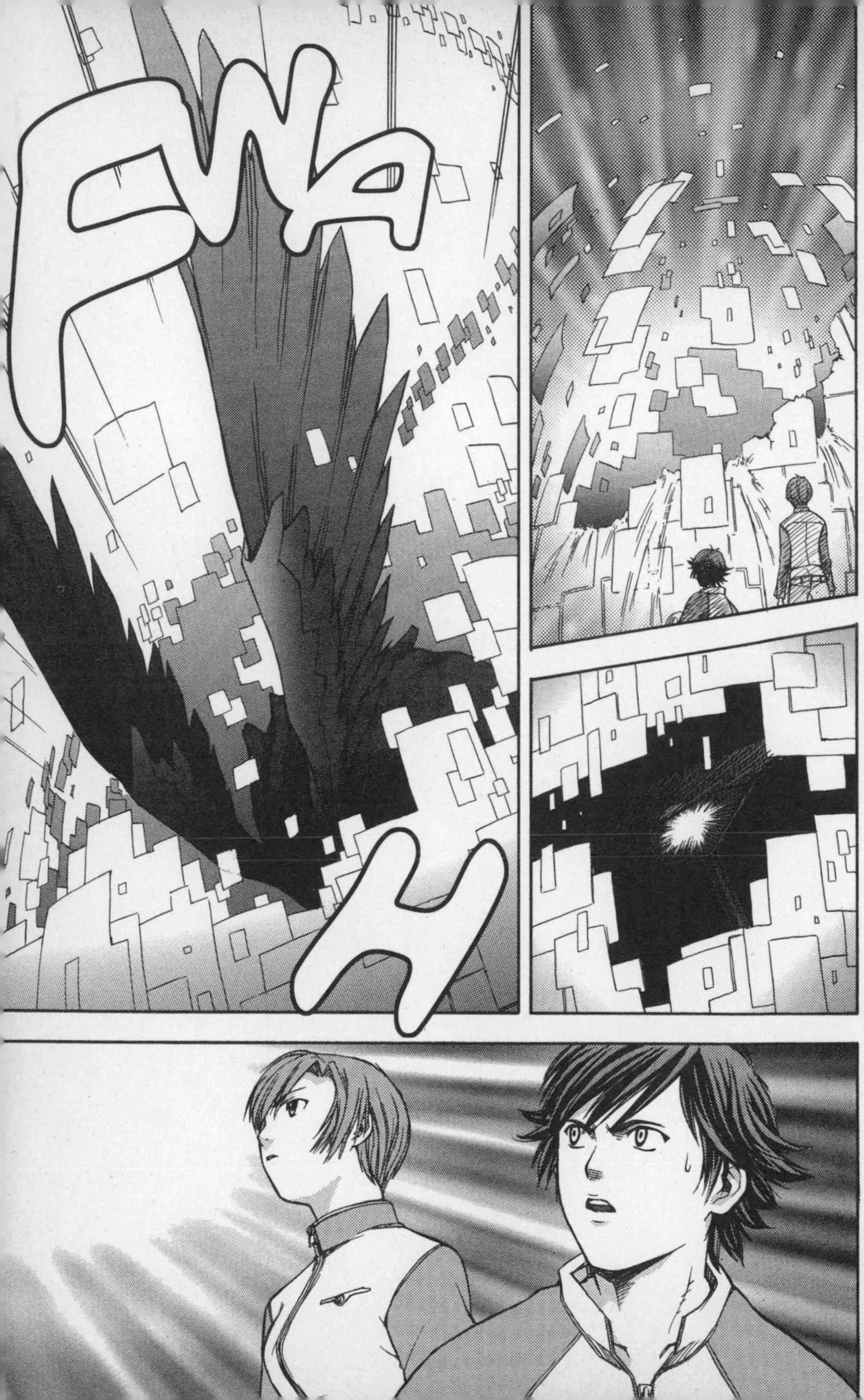
FWAH

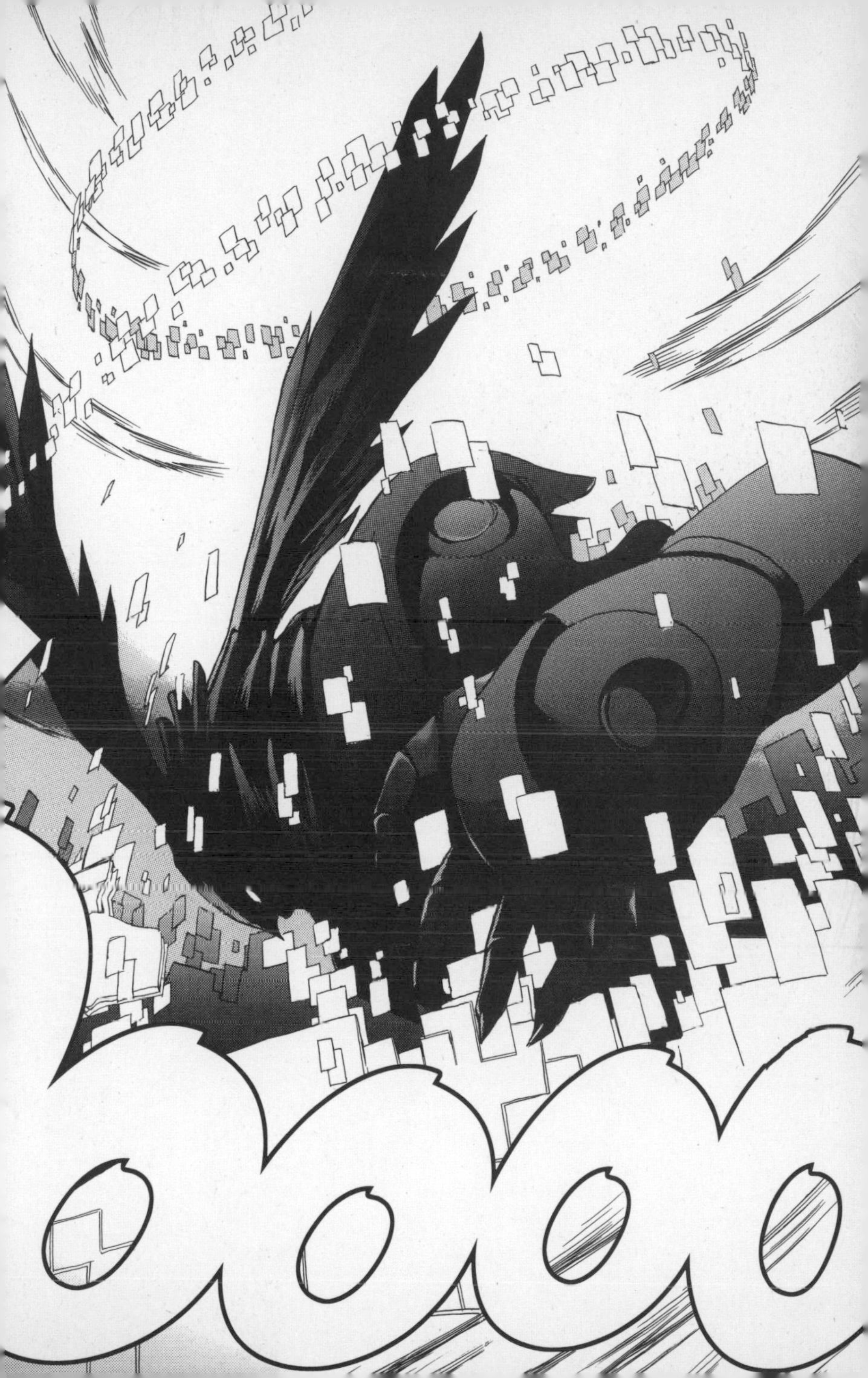
OOOO

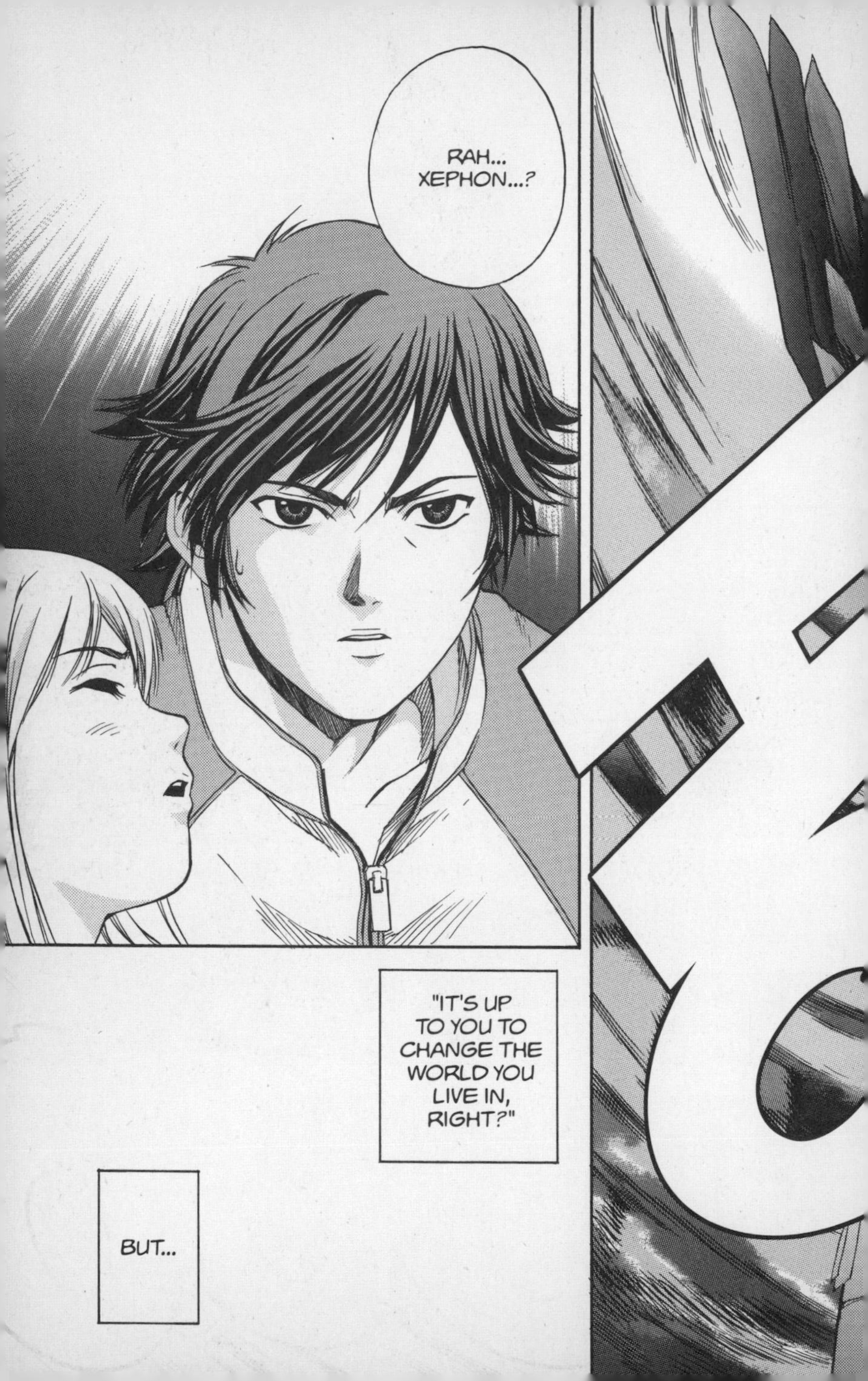
RAH... XEPHON...?
"IT'S UP TO YOU TO CHANGE THE WORLD YOU LIVE IN, RIGHT?"
BUT...

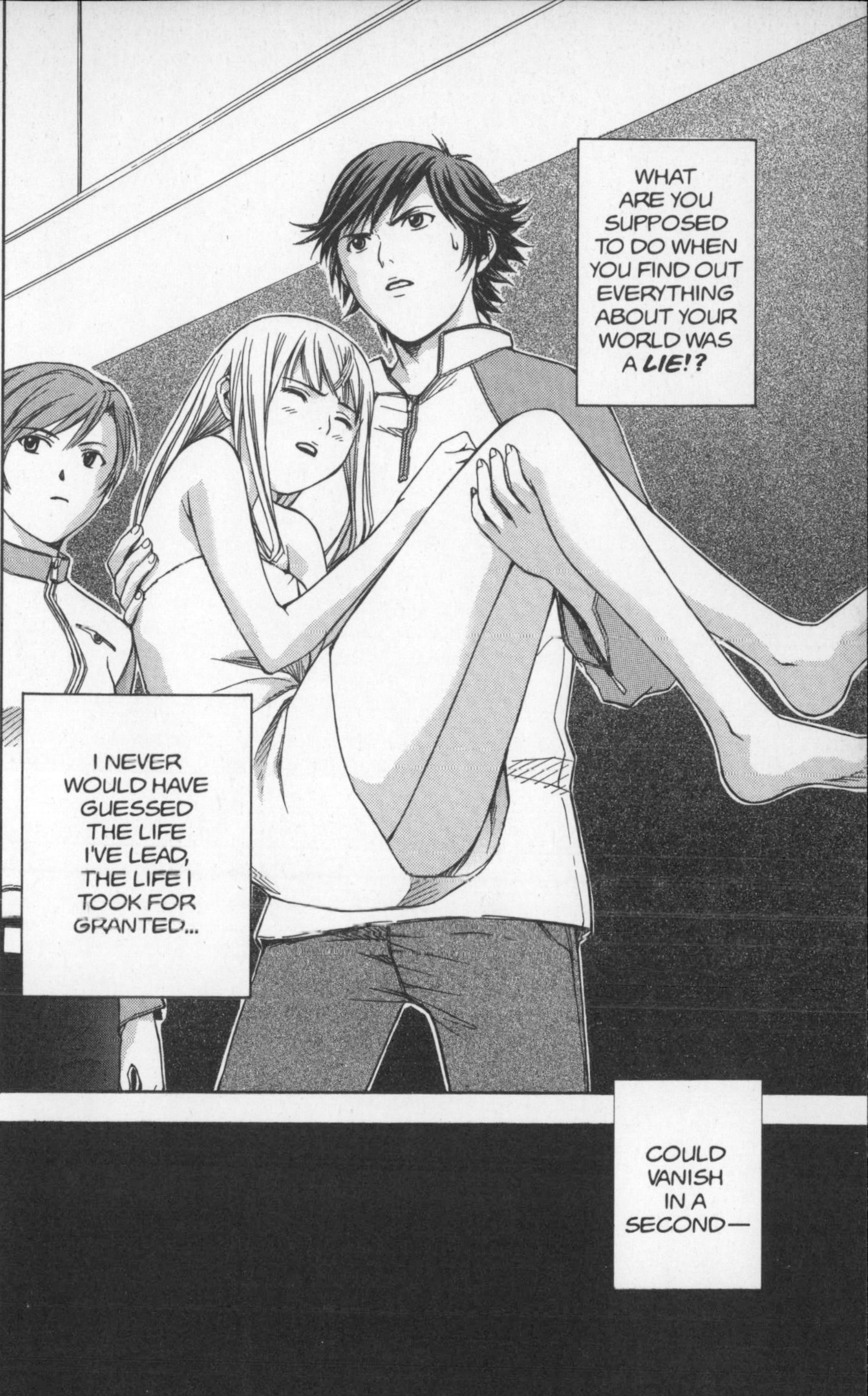
WHAT ARE YOU SUPPOSED TO DO WHEN YOU FIND OUT EVERYTHING ABOUT YOUR WORLD WAS A LIE!?
I NEVER WOULD HAVE GUESSED THE LIFE I'VE LEAD, THE LIFE I TOOK FOR GRANTED...
COULD VANISH IN A SECOND—

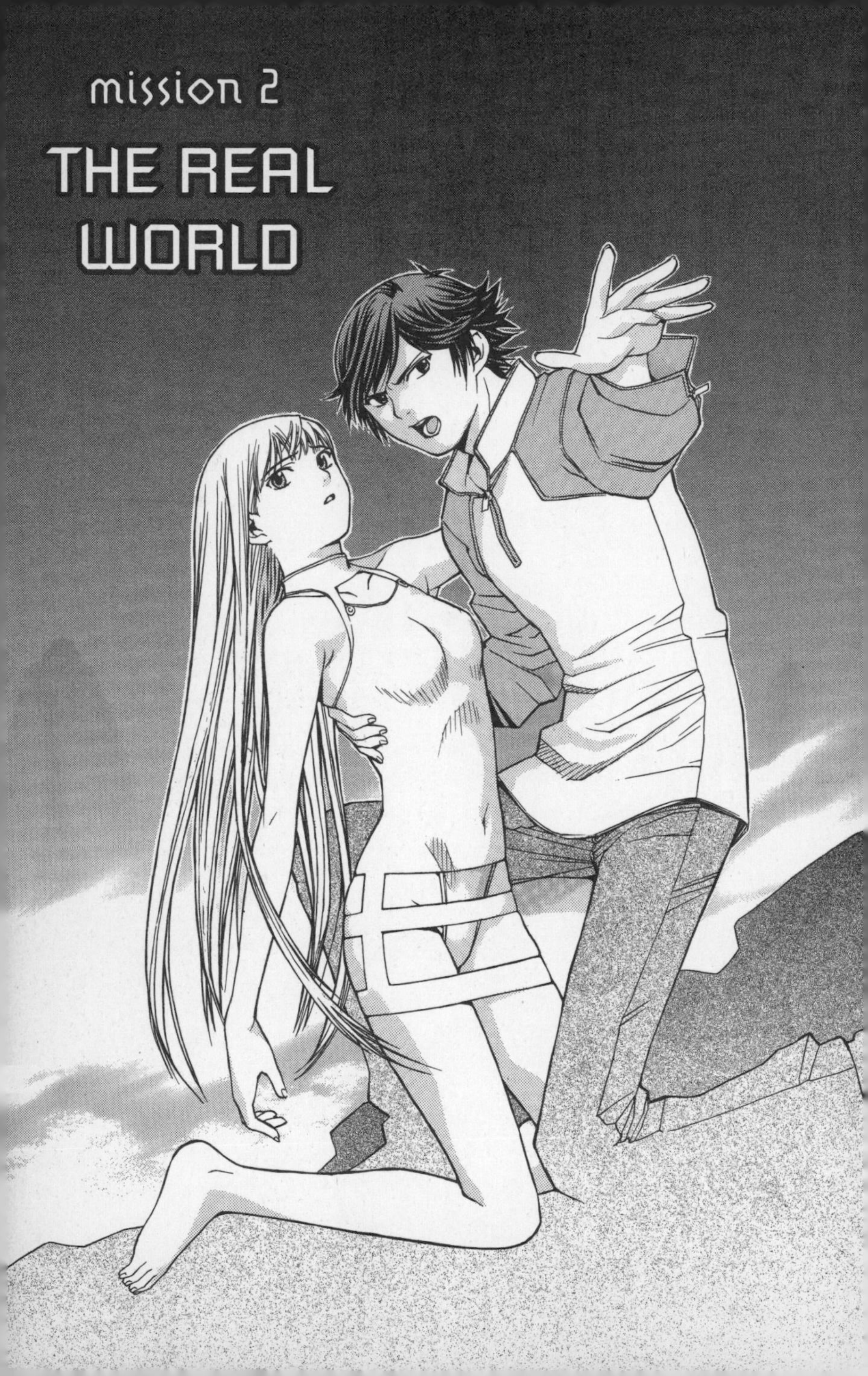
mission 2
THE REAL WORLD

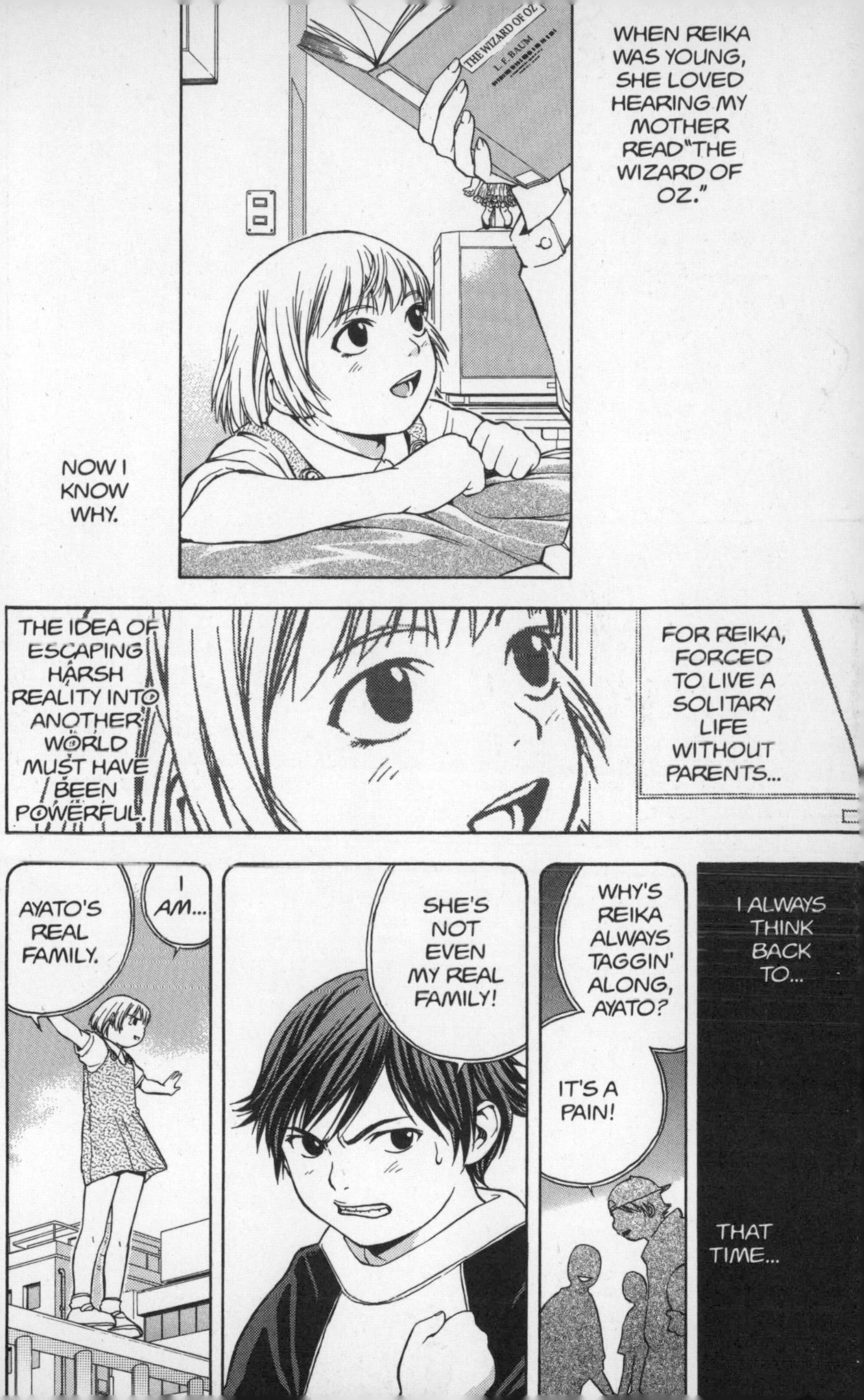
WHEN REIKA WAS YOUNG, SHE LOVED HEARING MY MOTHER READ "THE WIZARD OF OZ."
NOW I KNOW WHY.
FOR REIKA, FORCED TO LIVE A SOLITARY LIFE WITHOUT PARENTS...
THE IDEA OF ESCAPING HARSH REALITY INTO ANOTHER WORLD MUST HAVE BEEN POWERFUL.
I ALWAYS THINK BACK TO...
THAT TIME...
WHY'S REIKA ALWAYS TAGGIN' ALONG, AYATO?
IT'S A PAIN!
SHE'S NOT EVEN MY REAL FAMILY!
I AM...
AYATO'S REAL FAMILY.

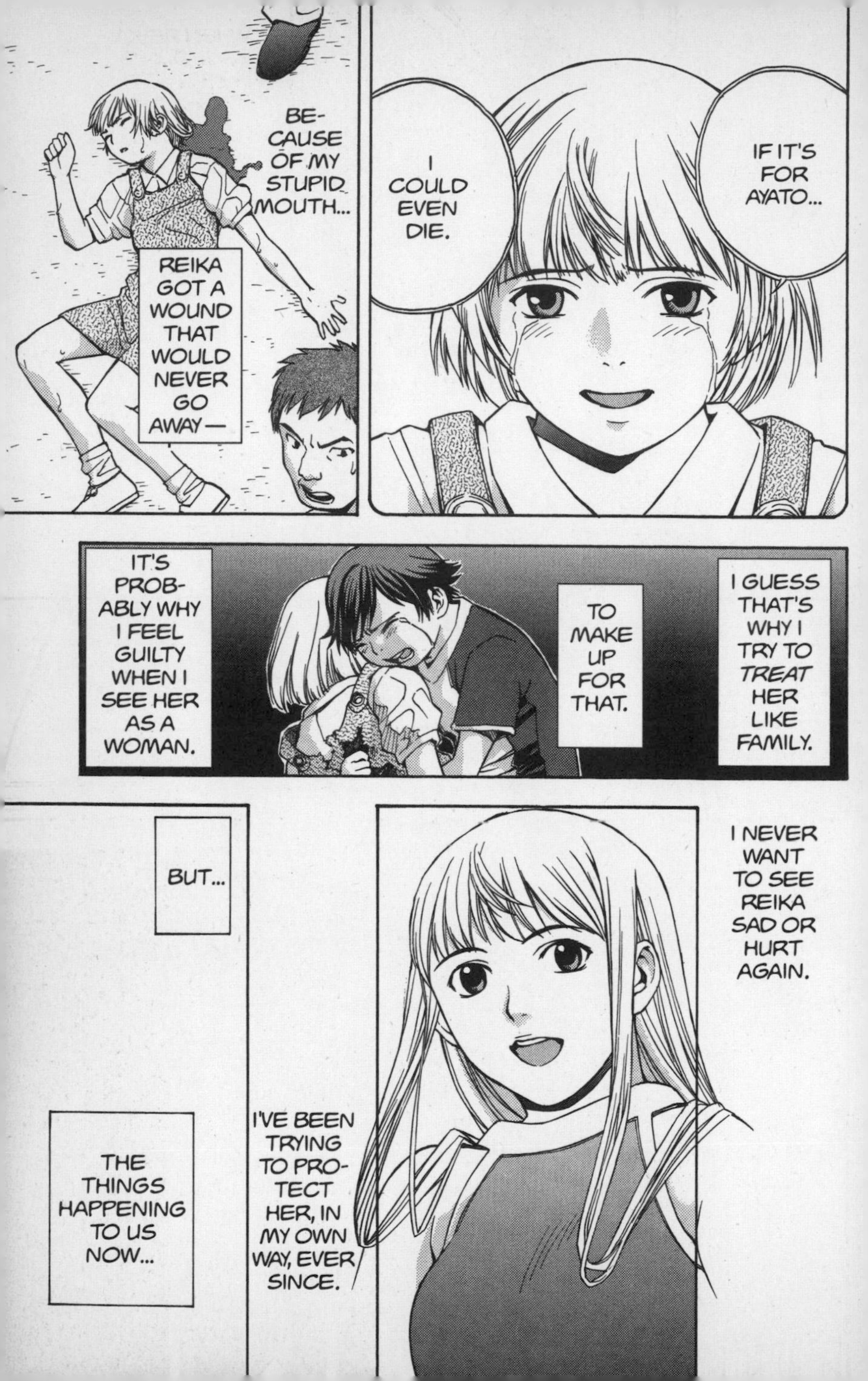
IF IT'S FOR AYATO...
I COULD EVEN DIE.
BECAUSE OF MY STUPID MOUTH...
REIKA GOT A WOUND THAT WOULD NEVER GO AWAY—
I GUESS THAT'S WHY I TRY TO *TREAT* HER LIKE FAMILY.
TO MAKE UP FOR THAT.
IT'S PROBABLY WHY I FEEL GUILTY WHEN I SEE HER AS A WOMAN.
I NEVER WANT TO SEE REIKA SAD OR HURT AGAIN.
I'VE BEEN TRYING TO PROTECT HER, IN MY OWN WAY, EVER SINCE.
BUT...
THE THINGS HAPPENING TO US NOW...

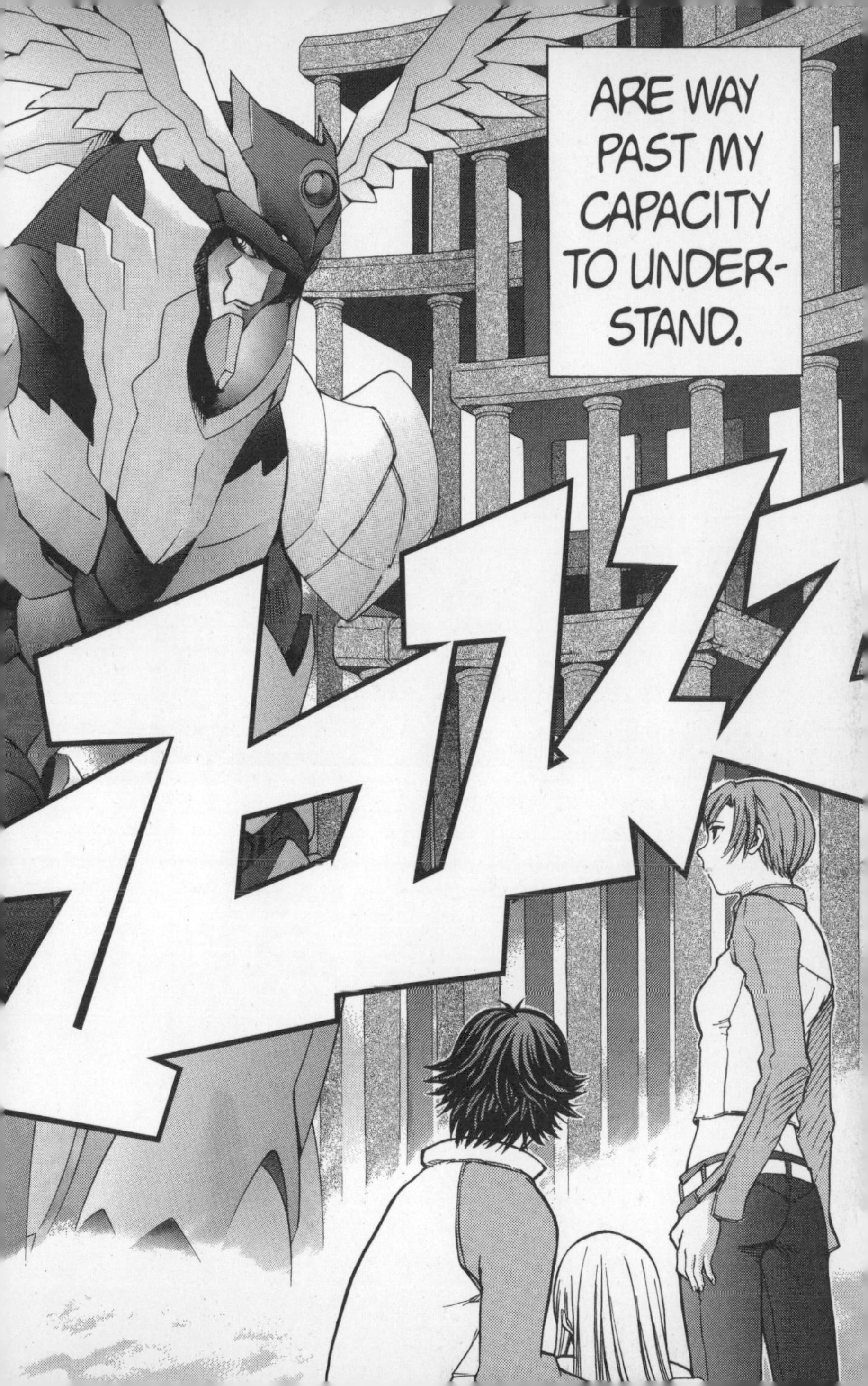
ARE WAY PAST MY CAPACITY TO UNDER-STAND.

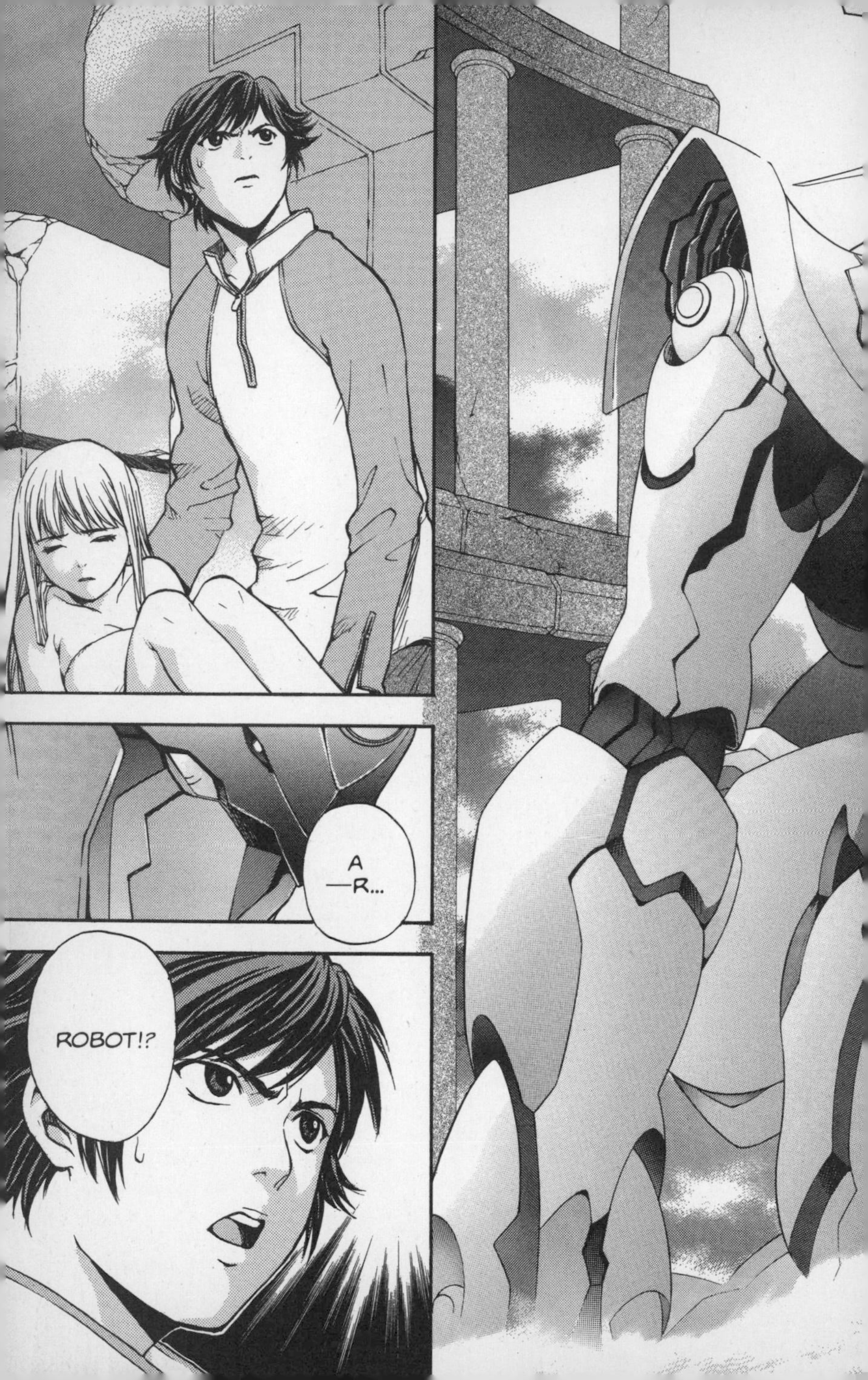
A
—R...
ROBOT!?

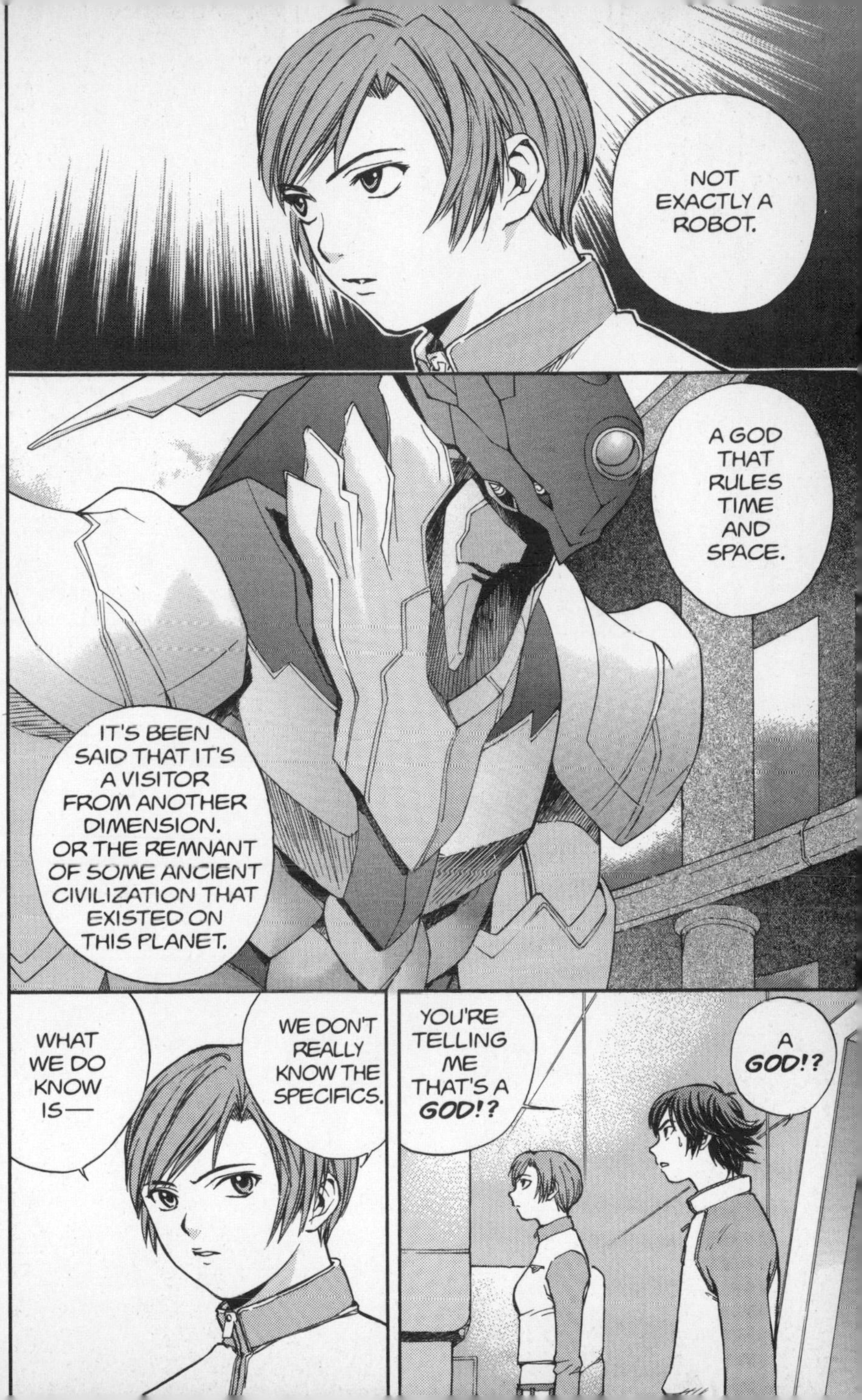
NOT EXACTLY A ROBOT.
A GOD THAT RULES TIME AND SPACE.
IT'S BEEN SAID THAT IT'S A VISITOR FROM ANOTHER DIMENSION. OR THE REMNANT OF SOME ANCIENT CIVILIZATION THAT EXISTED ON THIS PLANET.
A *GOD!?*
YOU'RE TELLING ME THAT'S A *GOD!?*
WE DON'T REALLY KNOW THE SPECIFICS.
WHAT WE DO KNOW IS—

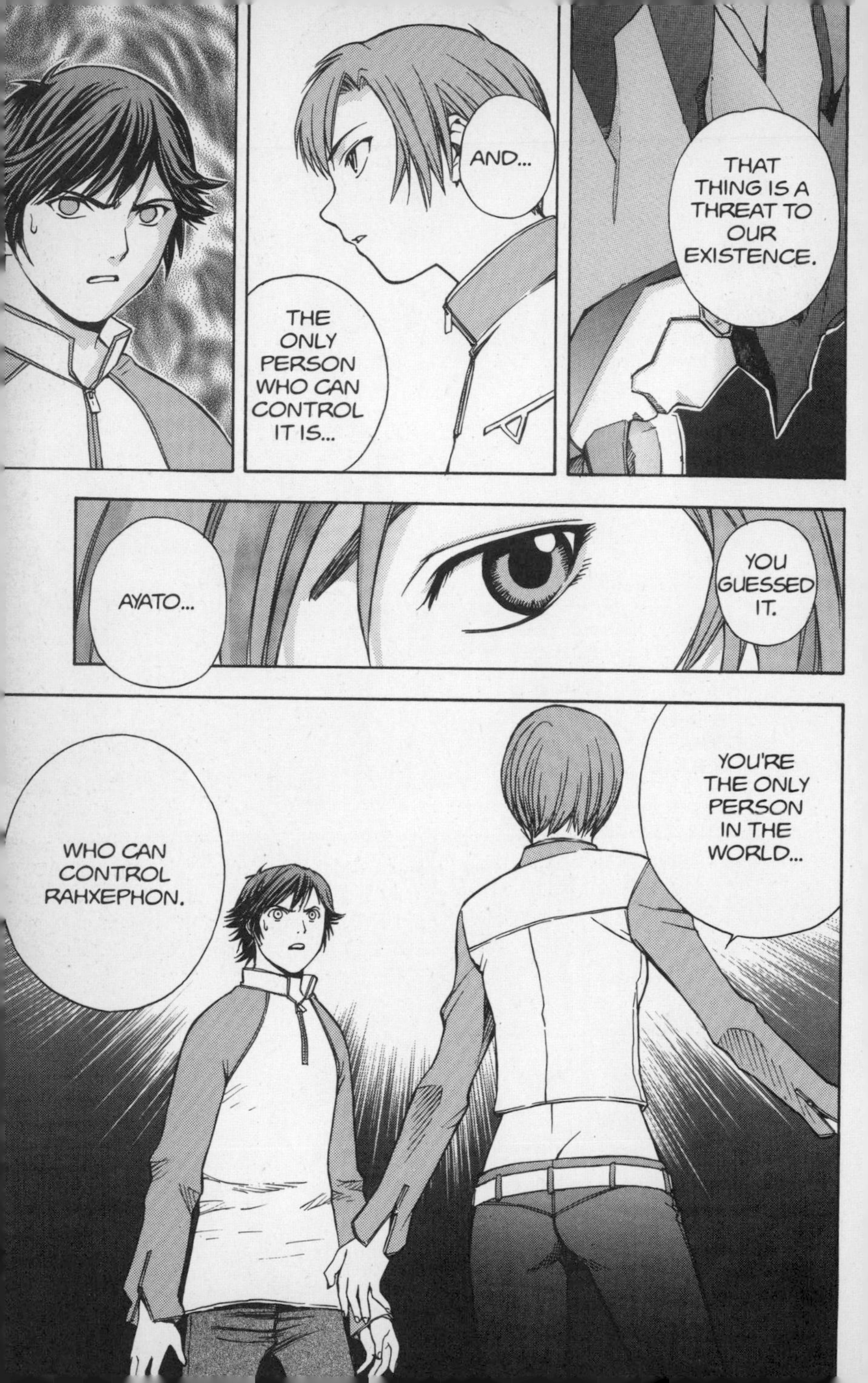
THAT THING IS A THREAT TO OUR EXISTENCE.
AND...
THE ONLY PERSON WHO CAN CONTROL IT IS...
AYATO...
YOU GUESSED IT.
YOU'RE THE ONLY PERSON IN THE WORLD...
WHO CAN CONTROL RAHXEPHON.

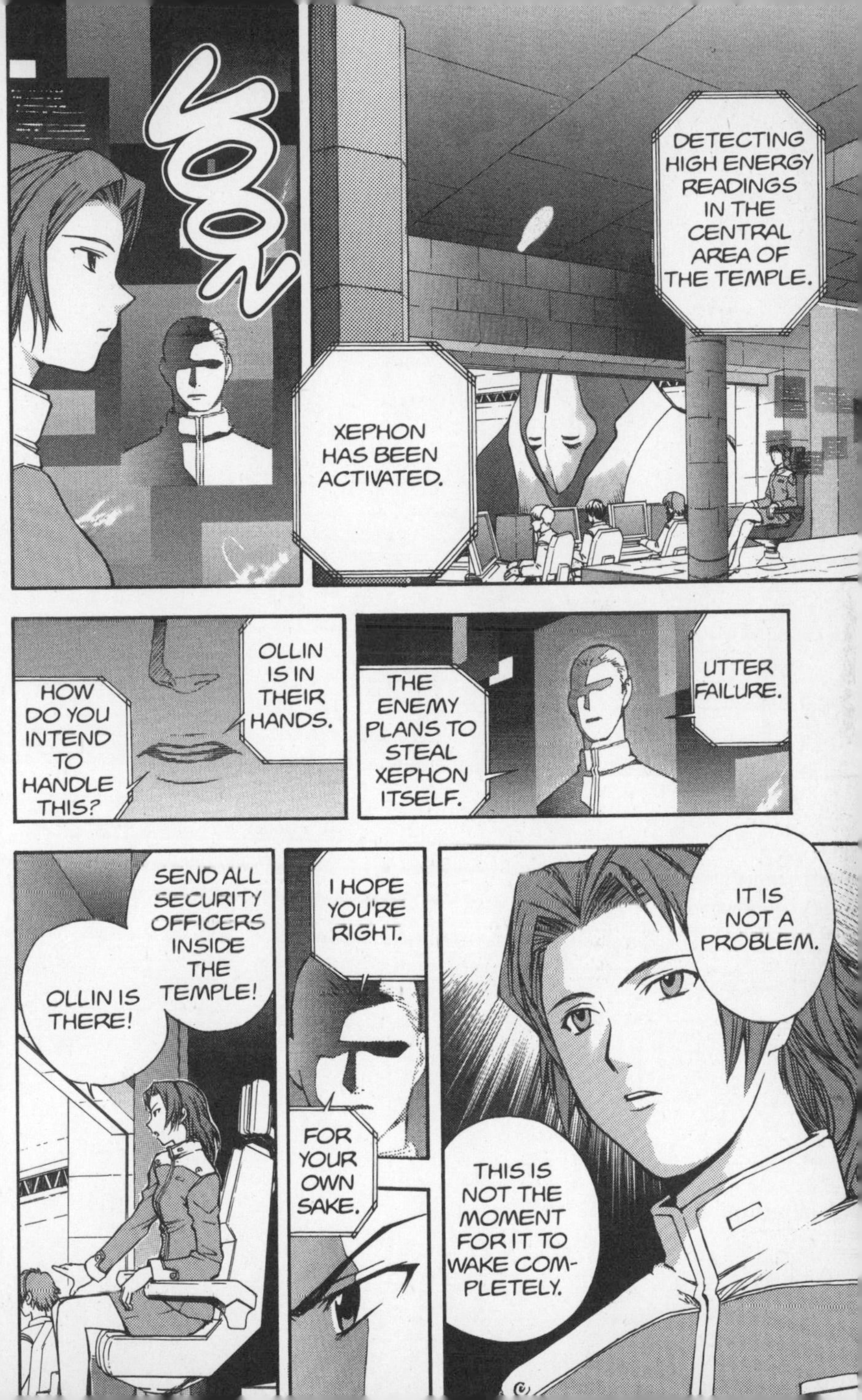
DETECTING HIGH ENERGY READINGS IN THE CENTRAL AREA OF THE TEMPLE.
XEPHON HAS BEEN ACTIVATED.
VOON
UTTER FAILURE.
THE ENEMY PLANS TO STEAL XEPHON ITSELF.
OLLIN IS IN THEIR HANDS.
HOW DO YOU INTEND TO HANDLE THIS?
IT IS NOT A PROBLEM.
THIS IS NOT THE MOMENT FOR IT TO WAKE COM-PLETELY.
I HOPE YOU'RE RIGHT.
FOR YOUR OWN SAKE.
SEND ALL SECURITY OFFICERS INSIDE THE TEMPLE!
OLLIN IS THERE!

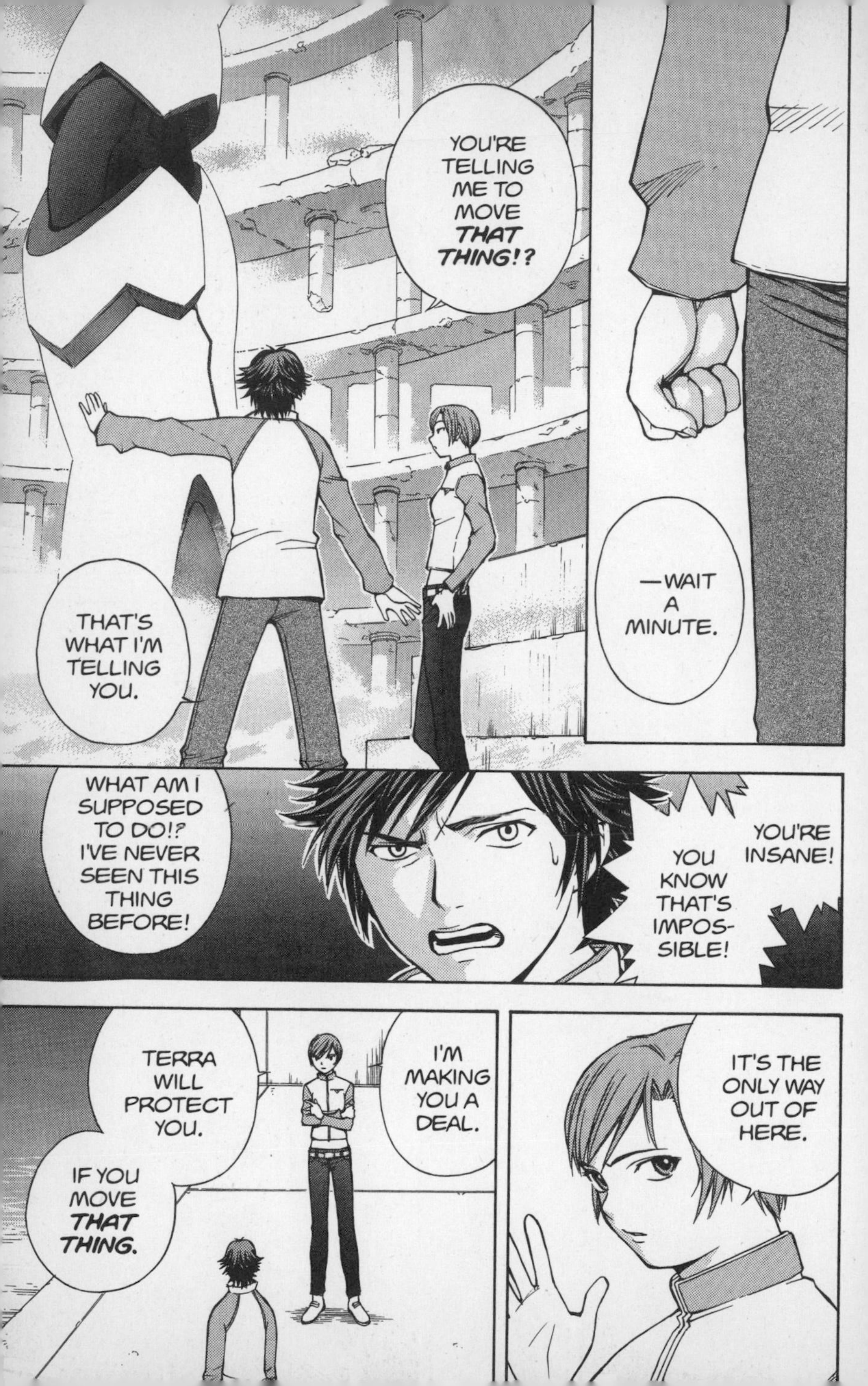
—WAIT A MINUTE.
YOU'RE TELLING ME TO MOVE *THAT THING!?*
THAT'S WHAT I'M TELLING YOU.
YOU'RE INSANE!
YOU KNOW THAT'S IMPOS-SIBLE!
WHAT AM I SUPPOSED TO DO!? I'VE NEVER SEEN THIS THING BEFORE!
IT'S THE ONLY WAY OUT OF HERE.
I'M MAKING YOU A DEAL.
TERRA WILL PROTECT YOU.
IF YOU MOVE *THAT THING.*

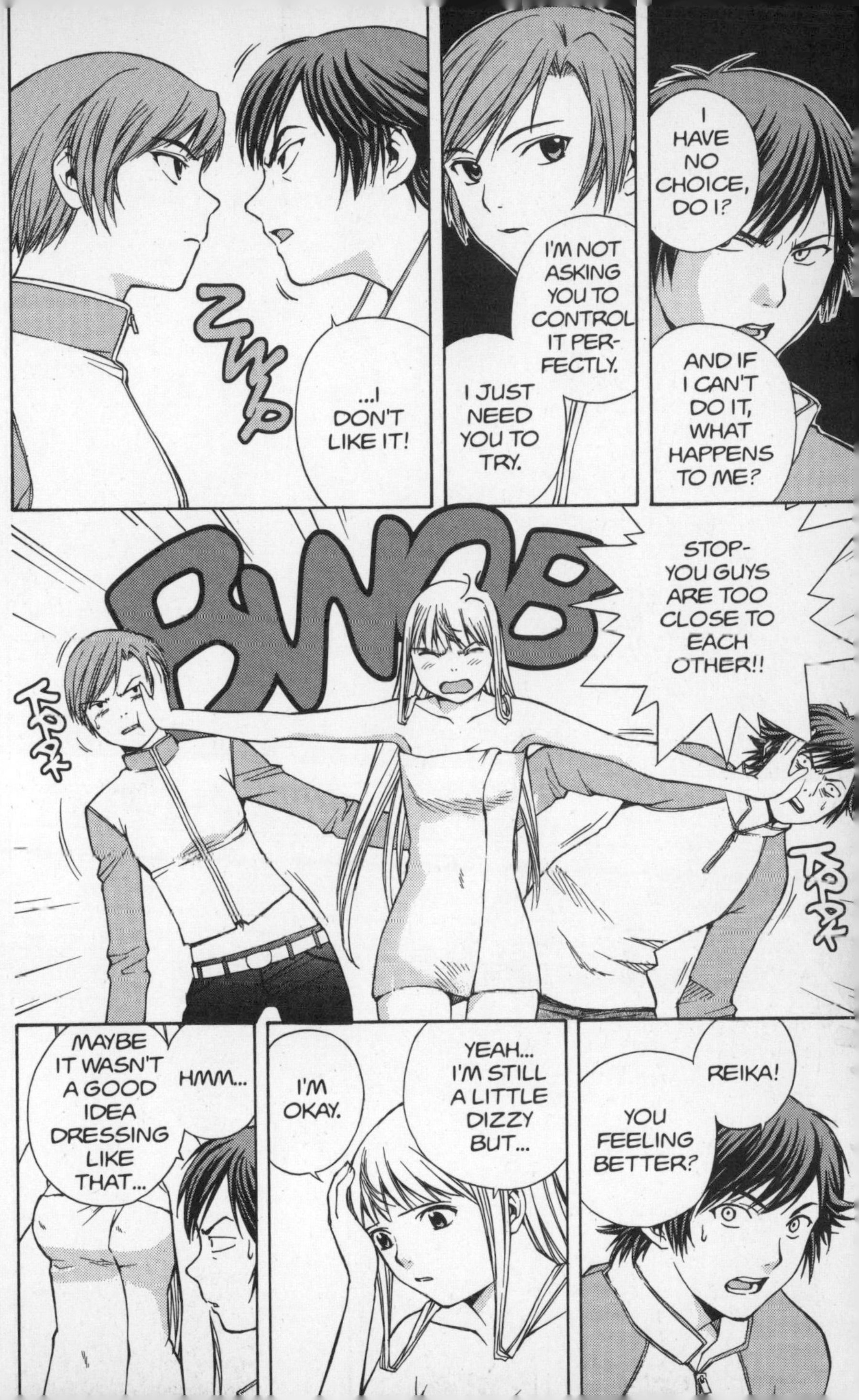
I HAVE NO CHOICE, DO I?
AND IF I CAN'T DO IT, WHAT HAPPENS TO ME?
I'M NOT ASKING YOU TO CONTROL IT PERFECTLY.
I JUST NEED YOU TO TRY.
...I DON'T LIKE IT!
STOP- YOU GUYS ARE TOO CLOSE TO EACH OTHER!!
REIKA!
YOU FEELING BETTER?
YEAH... I'M STILL A LITTLE DIZZY BUT...
I'M OKAY.
HMM...
MAYBE IT WASN'T A GOOD IDEA DRESSING LIKE THAT...

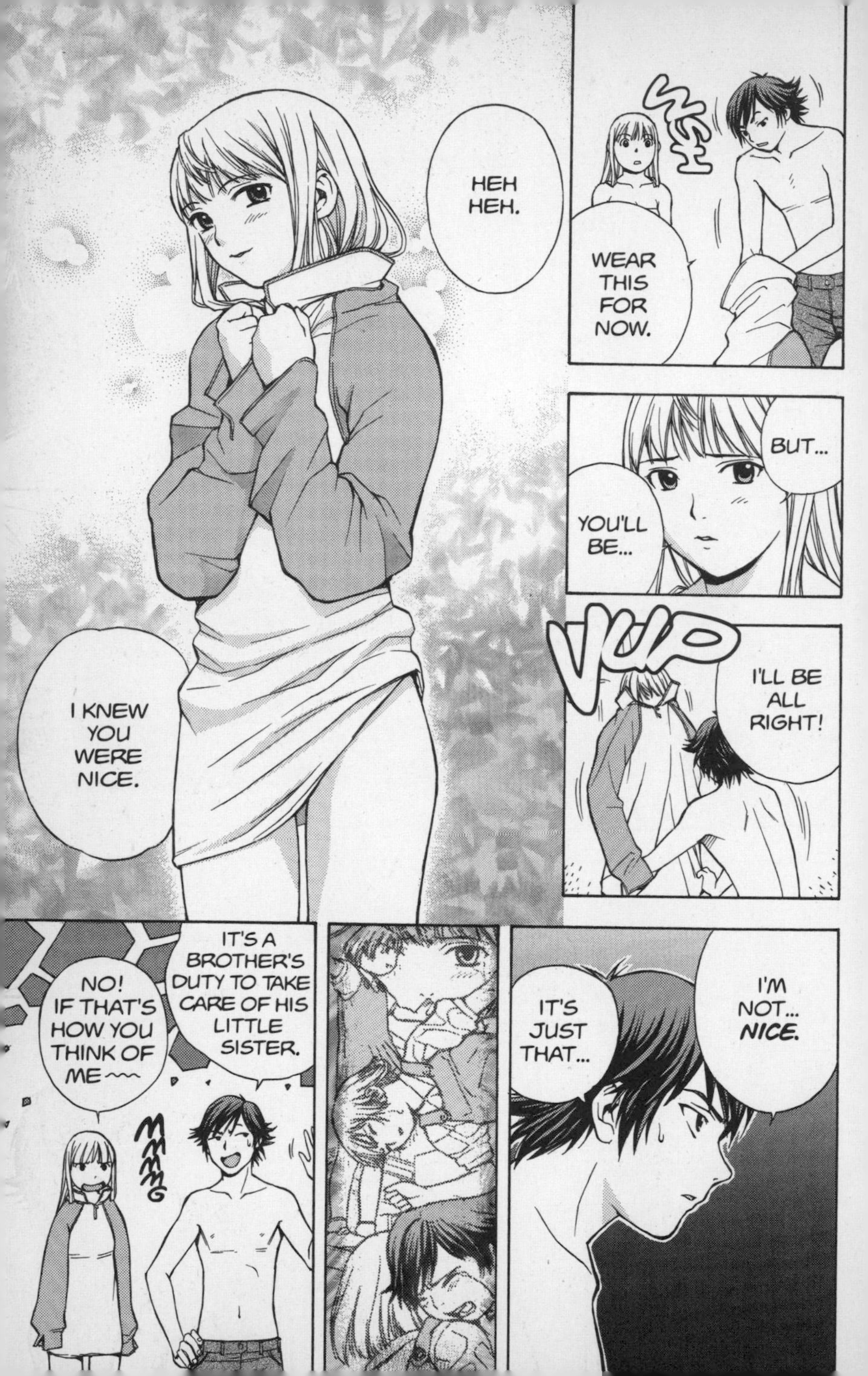
WEAR THIS FOR NOW.
BUT...
YOU'LL BE...
VUP
I'LL BE ALL RIGHT!
HEH HEH.
I KNEW YOU WERE NICE.
I'M NOT... **NICE.**
IT'S JUST THAT...
IT'S A BROTHER'S DUTY TO TAKE CARE OF HIS LITTLE SISTER.
NO! IF THAT'S HOW YOU THINK OF ME~~
MMMMG

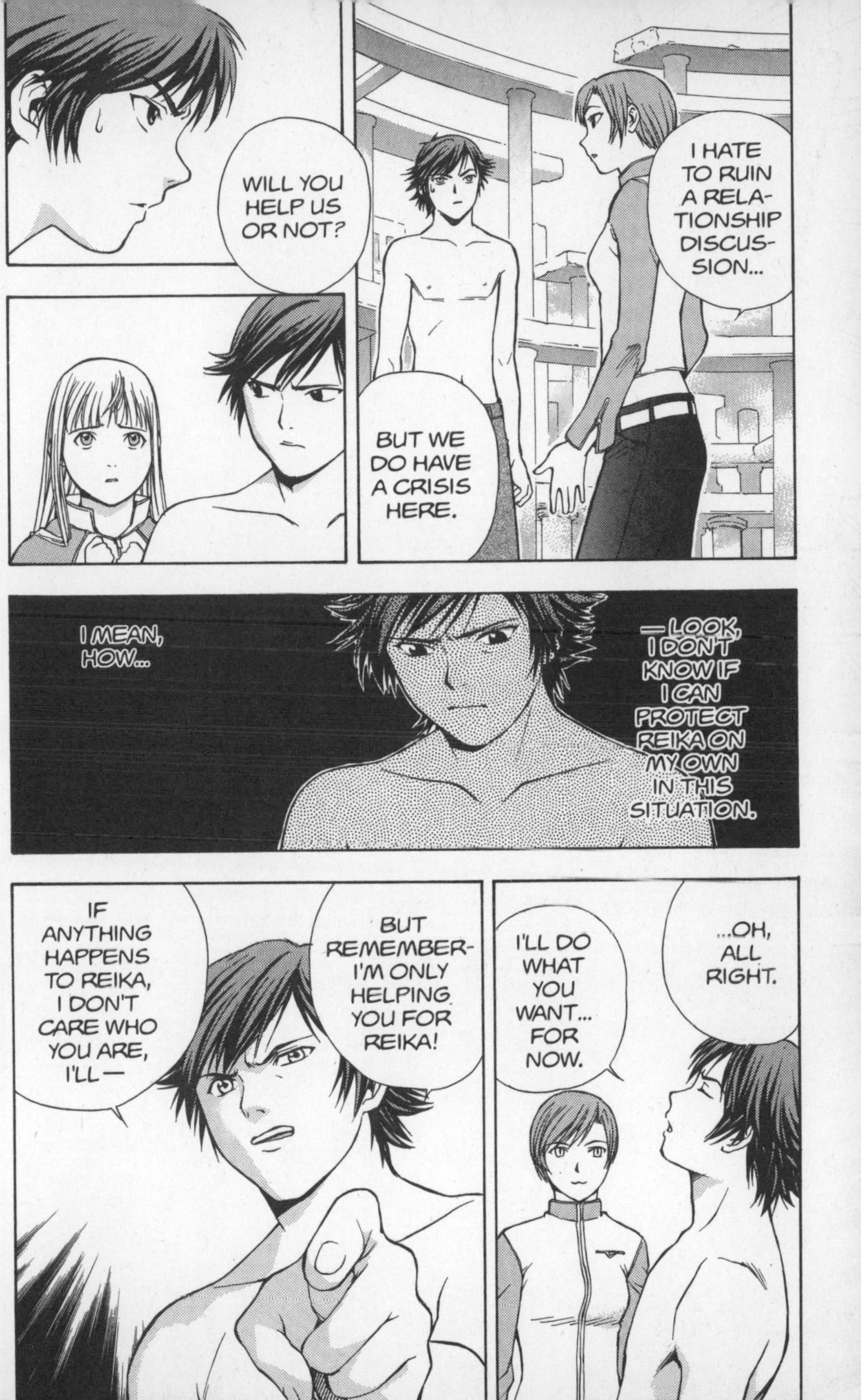
I HATE TO RUIN A RELATIONSHIP DISCUSSION...
BUT WE DO HAVE A CRISIS HERE.
WILL YOU HELP US OR NOT?
—LOOK, I DON'T KNOW IF I CAN PROTECT REIKA ON MY OWN IN THIS SITUATION.
I MEAN, HOW...
...OH, ALL RIGHT.
I'LL DO WHAT YOU WANT... FOR NOW.
BUT REMEMBER- I'M ONLY HELPING YOU FOR REIKA!
IF ANYTHING HAPPENS TO REIKA, I DON'T CARE WHO YOU ARE, I'LL—

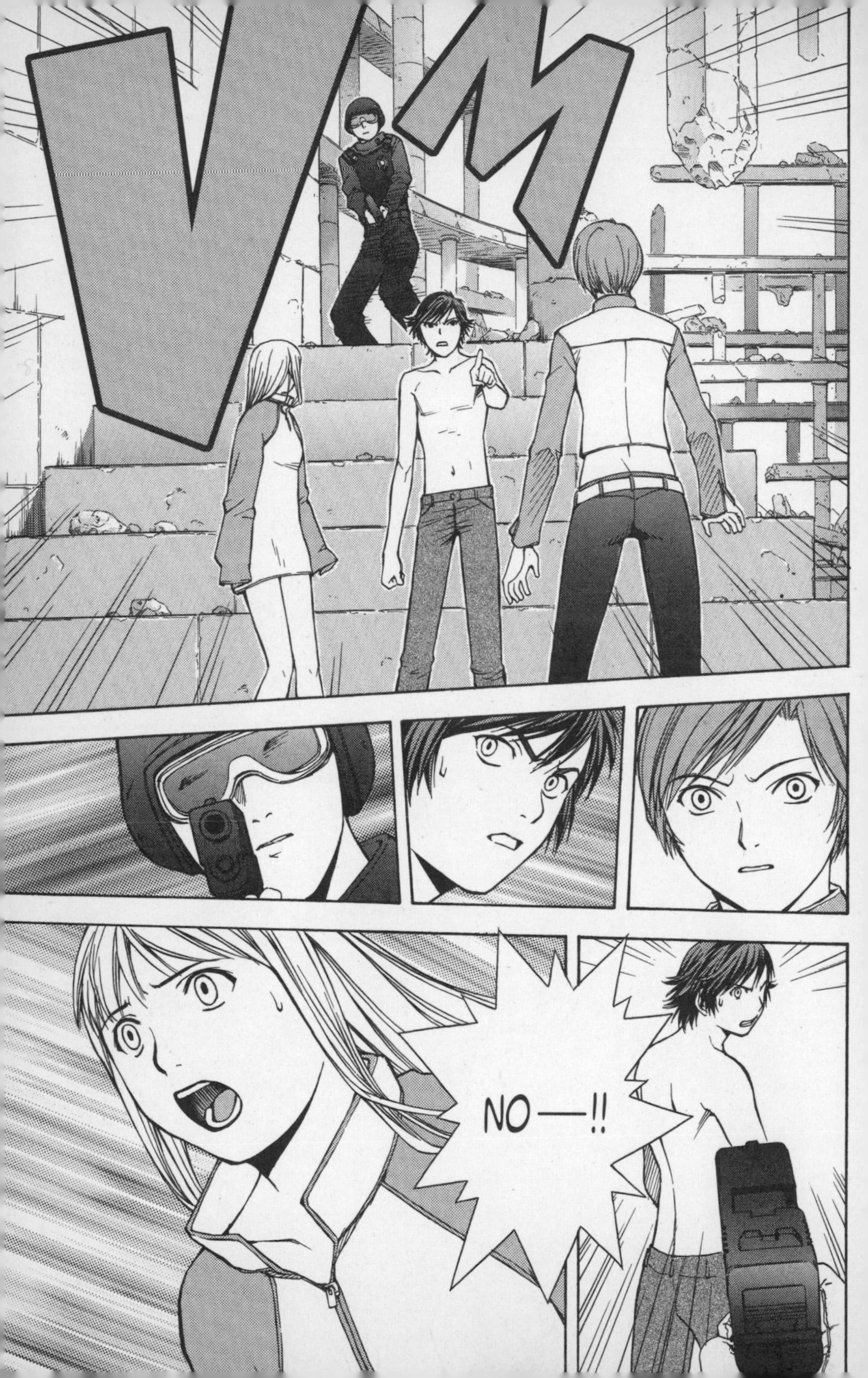
VM
NO—!!

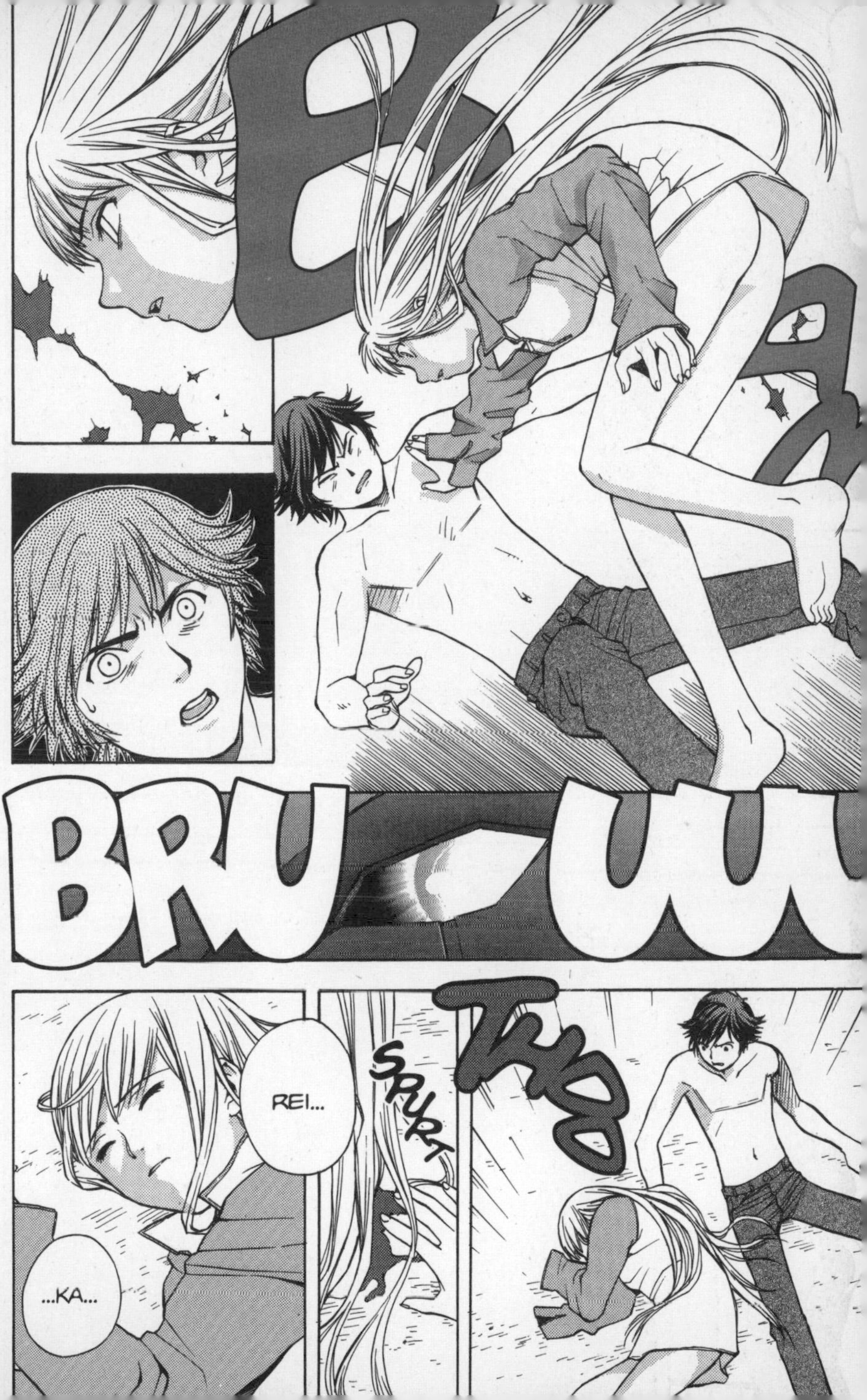
BRU
UUU
SPURT
REI...
...KA...

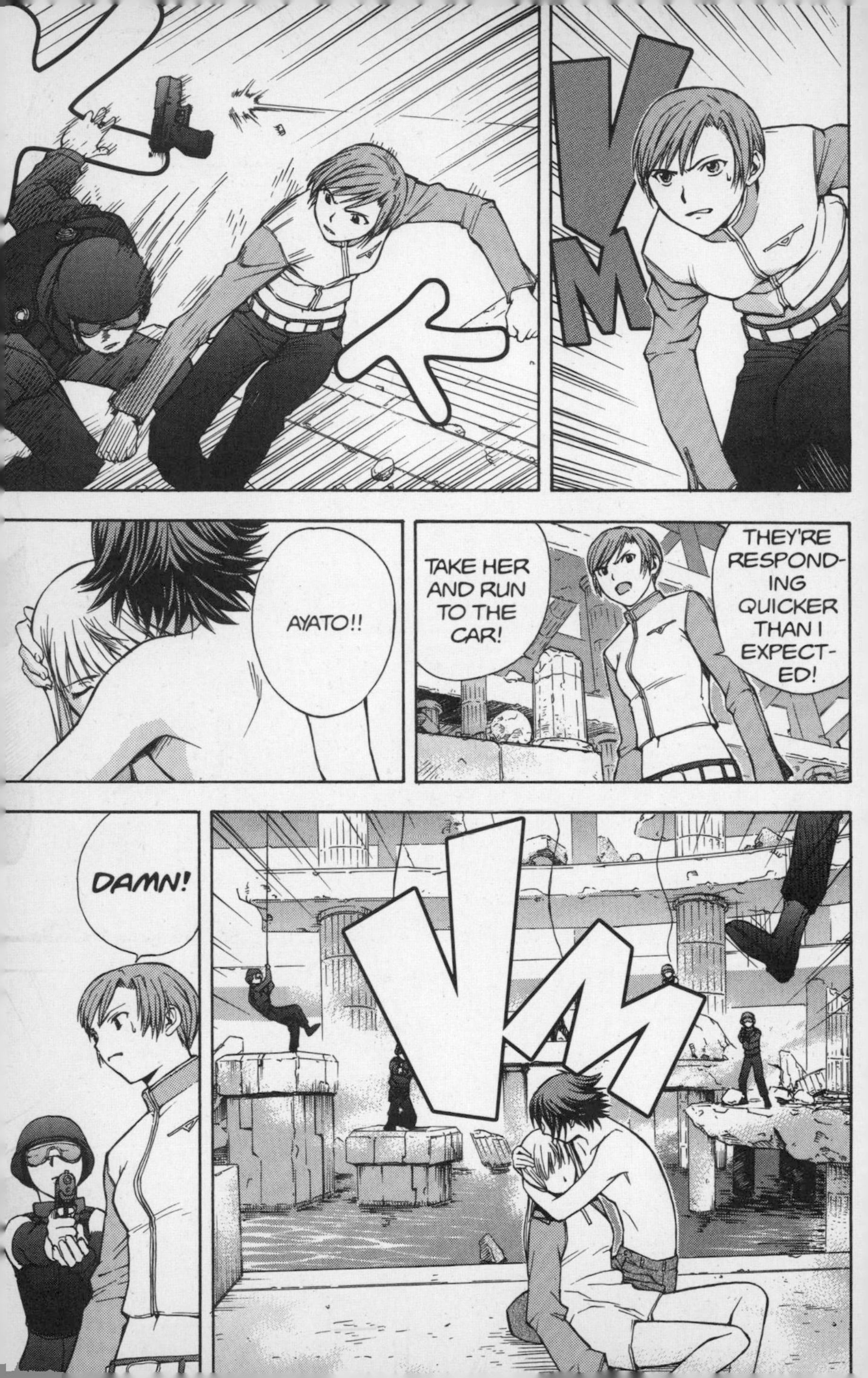
VM
THEY'RE RESPOND-ING QUICKER THAN I EXPECT-ED!
TAKE HER AND RUN TO THE CAR!
AYATO!!
VM
DAMN!

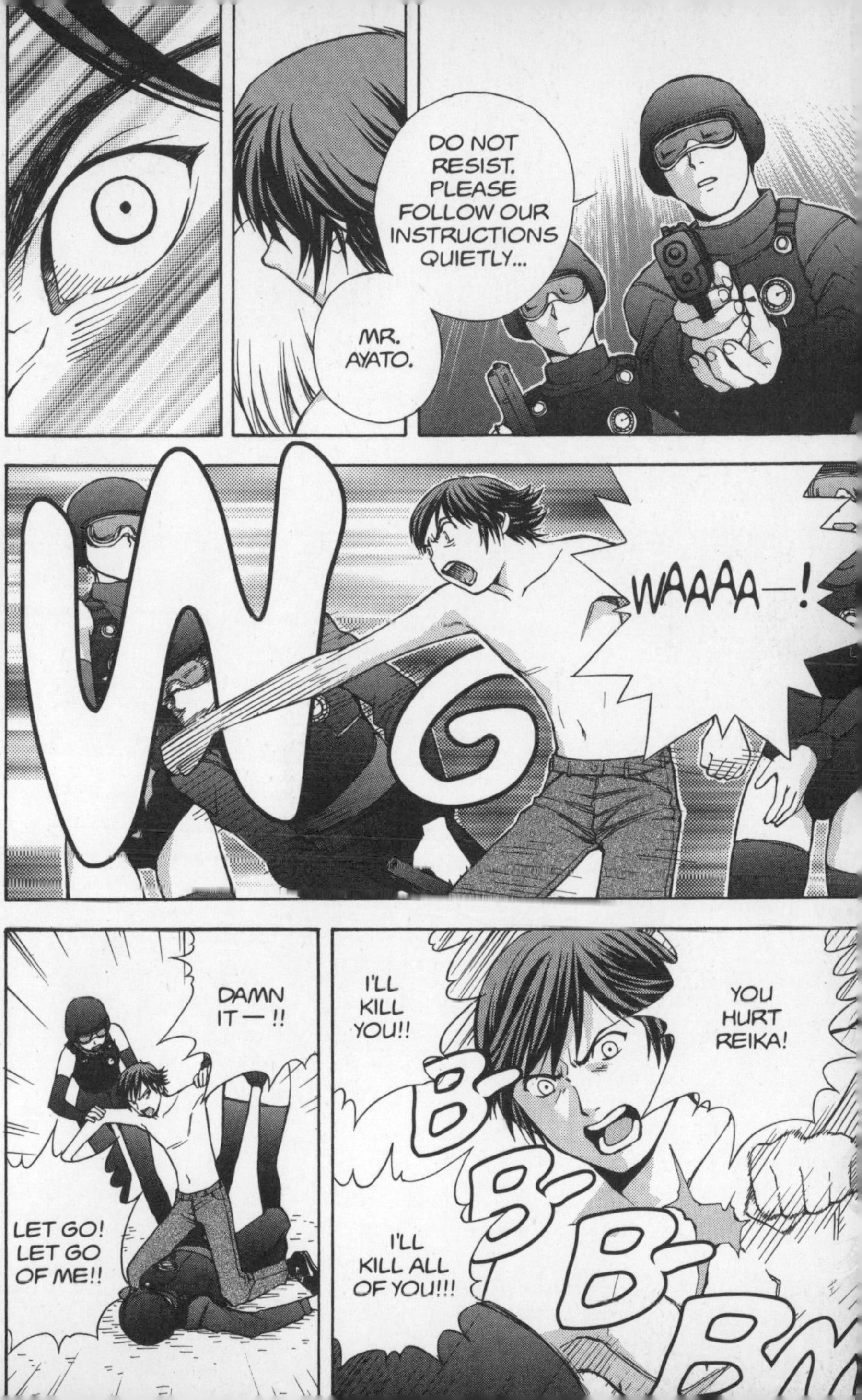
DO NOT RESIST. PLEASE FOLLOW OUR INSTRUCTIONS QUIETLY...
MR. AYATO.
WG
WAAAA—!
YOU HURT REIKA!
I'LL KILL YOU!!
I'LL KILL ALL OF YOU!!!
B- B- B-
DAMN IT—!!
LET GO! LET GO OF ME!!

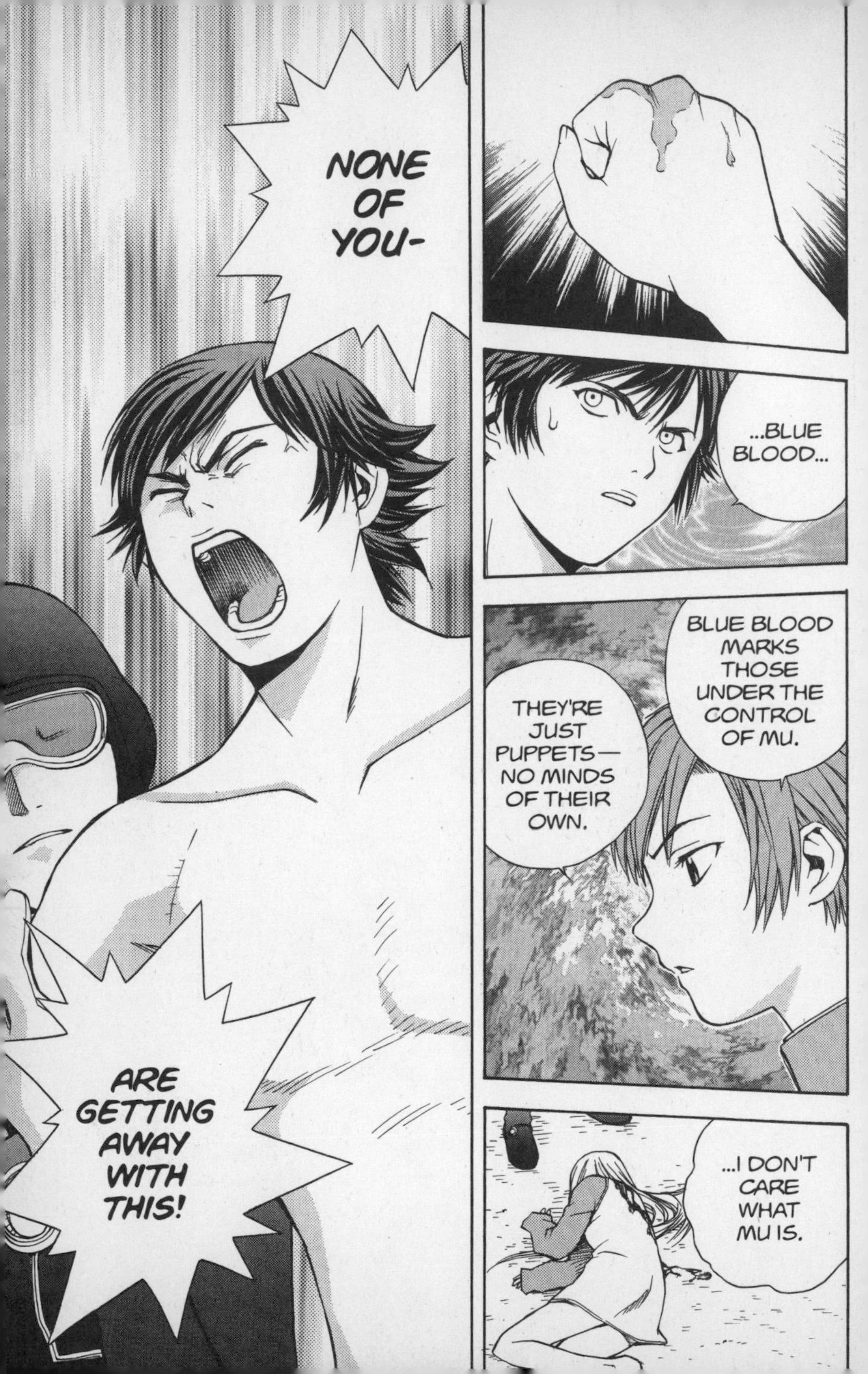
...BLUE BLOOD...
BLUE BLOOD MARKS THOSE UNDER THE CONTROL OF MU.
THEY'RE JUST PUPPETS— NO MINDS OF THEIR OWN.
...I DON'T CARE WHAT MU IS.
NONE OF YOU-
ARE GETTING AWAY WITH THIS!

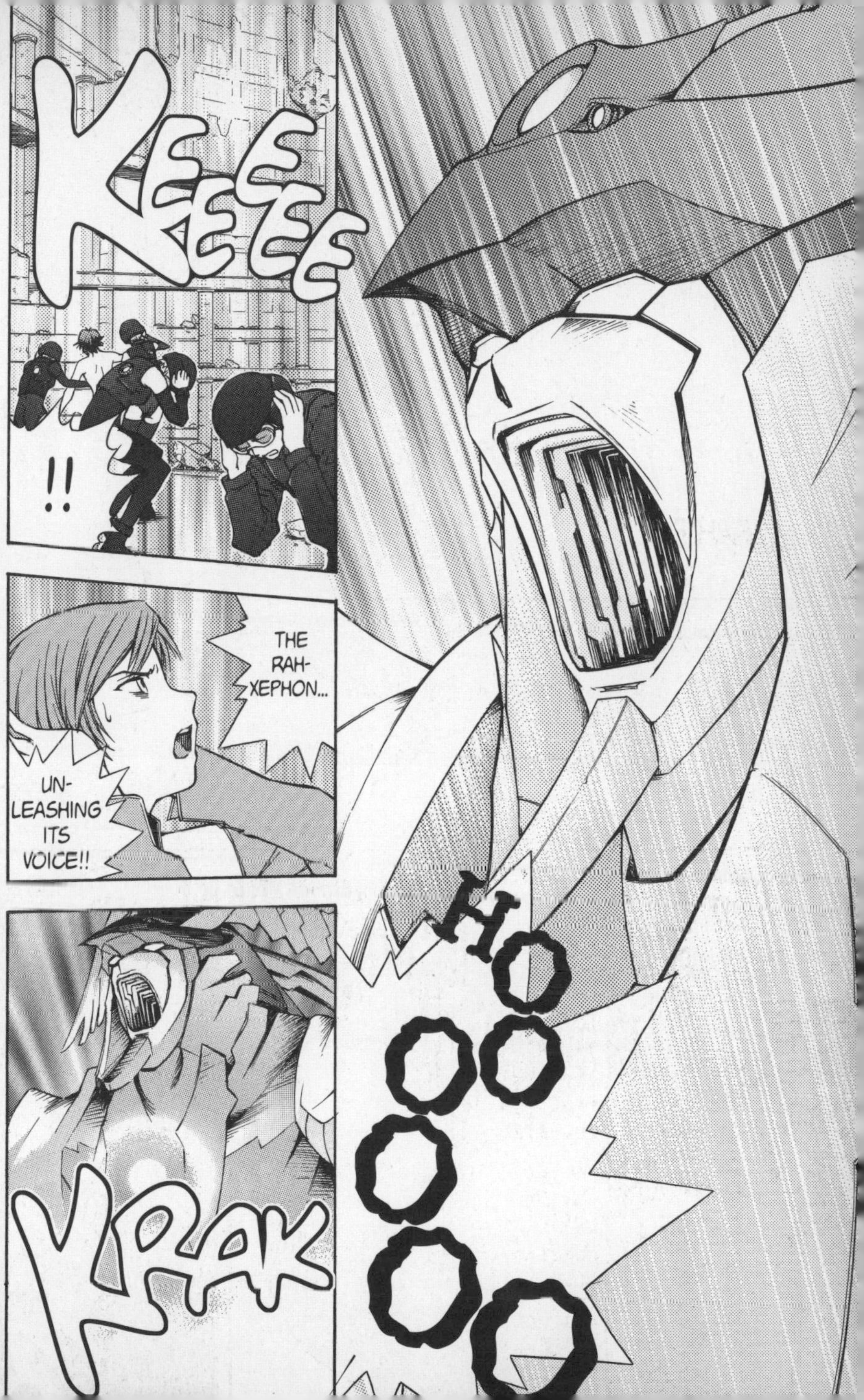
HOOOOOOO
KEEEEE
!!
THE RAH-XEPHON...
UN-LEASHING ITS VOICE!!
KRAK

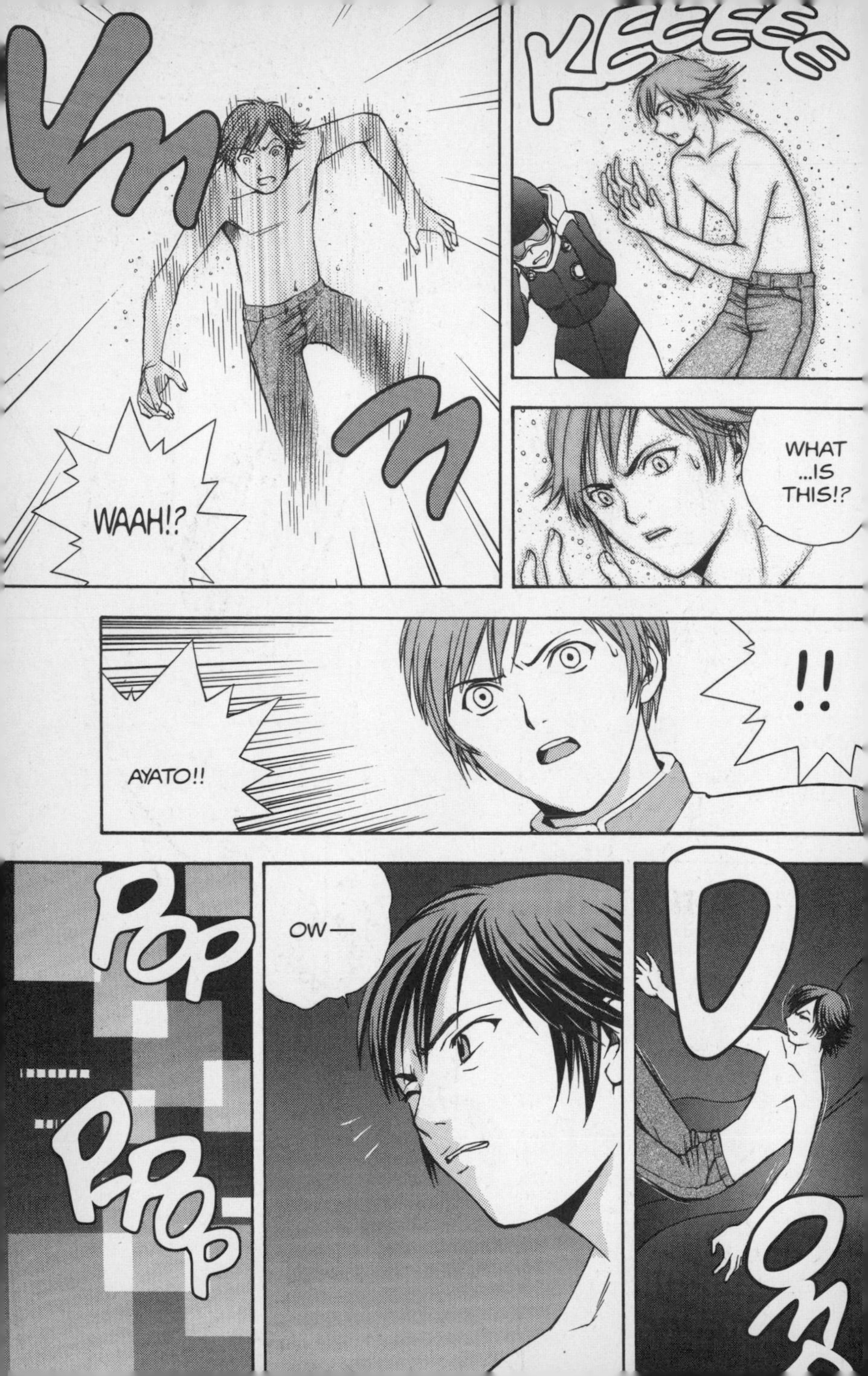
KEEEEE
WHAT ...IS THIS!?
VMM
WAAH!?
!!
AYATO!!
DOM
OW—
POP
……
…
PPOP

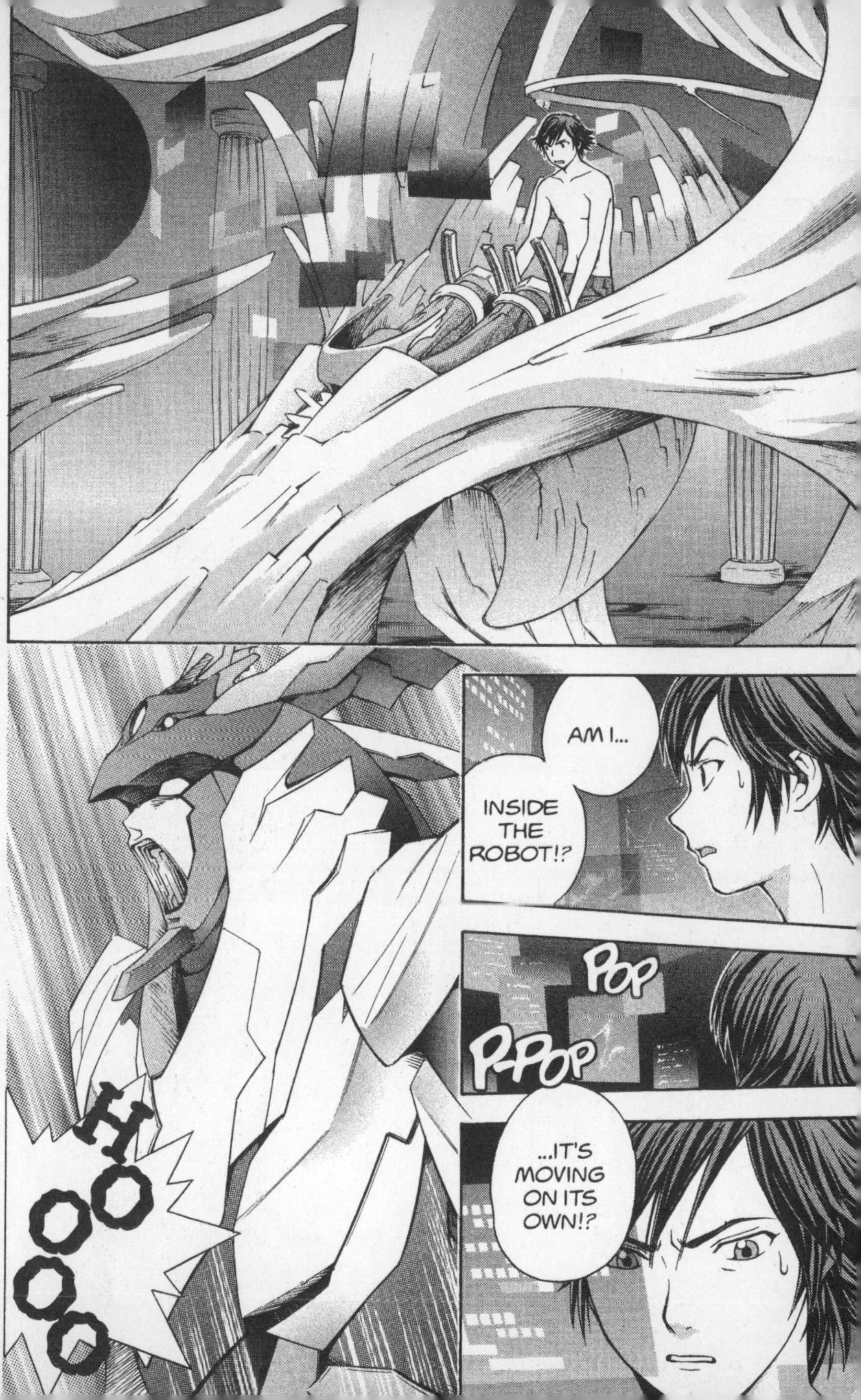
AM I...
INSIDE THE ROBOT!?
POP
P-POP
...IT'S MOVING ON ITS OWN!?
HOOOO

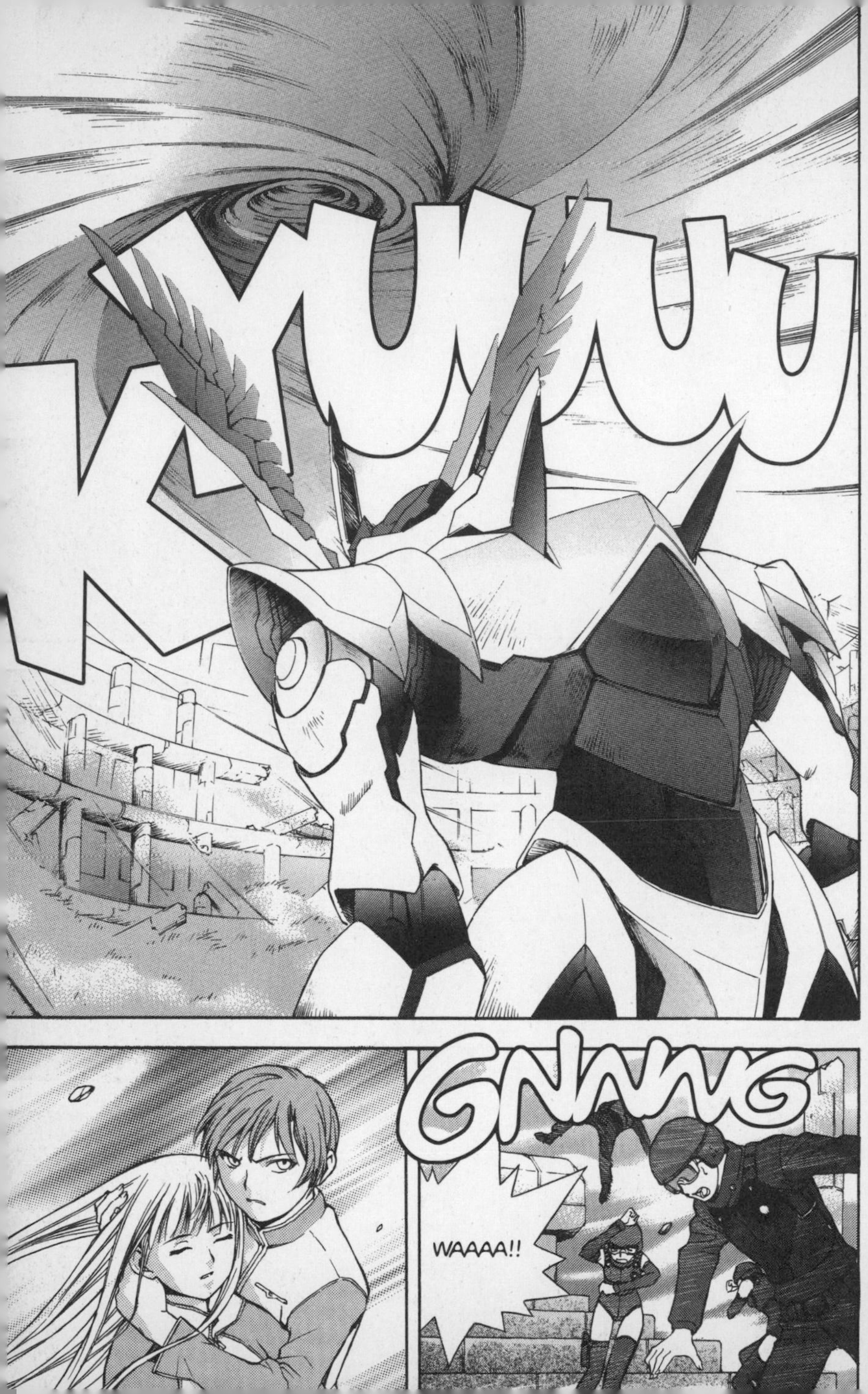
KYUUUU
GNNNG
WAAAA!!

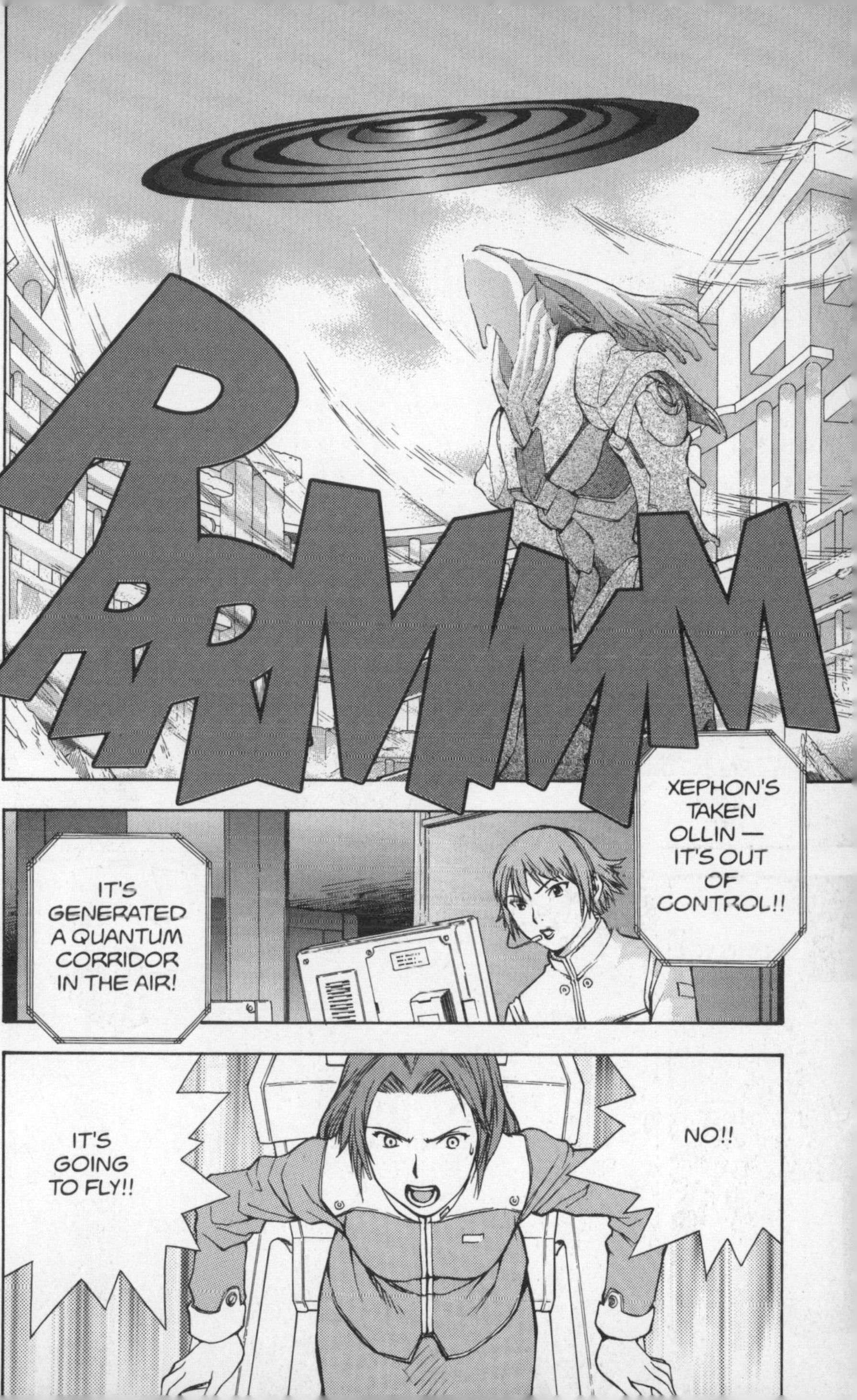
XEPHON'S TAKEN OLLIN — IT'S OUT OF CONTROL!!
IT'S GENERATED A QUANTUM CORRIDOR IN THE AIR!
NO!!
IT'S GOING TO FLY!!

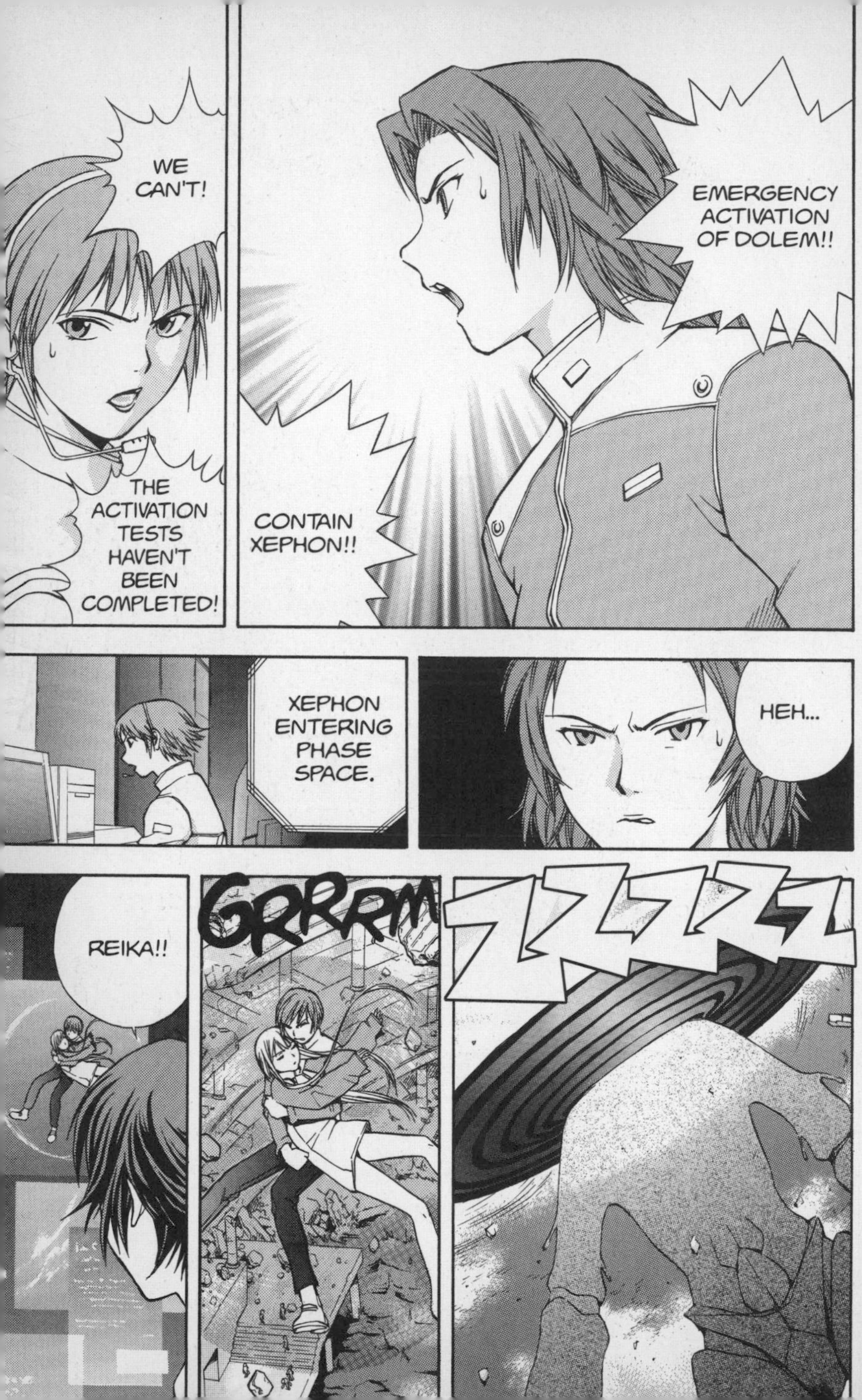
EMERGENCY ACTIVATION OF DOLEM!!
CONTAIN XEPHON!!
WE CAN'T!
THE ACTIVATION TESTS HAVEN'T BEEN COMPLETED!
HEH...
XEPHON ENTERING PHASE SPACE.
ZZZZZ
GRRRM
REIKA!!

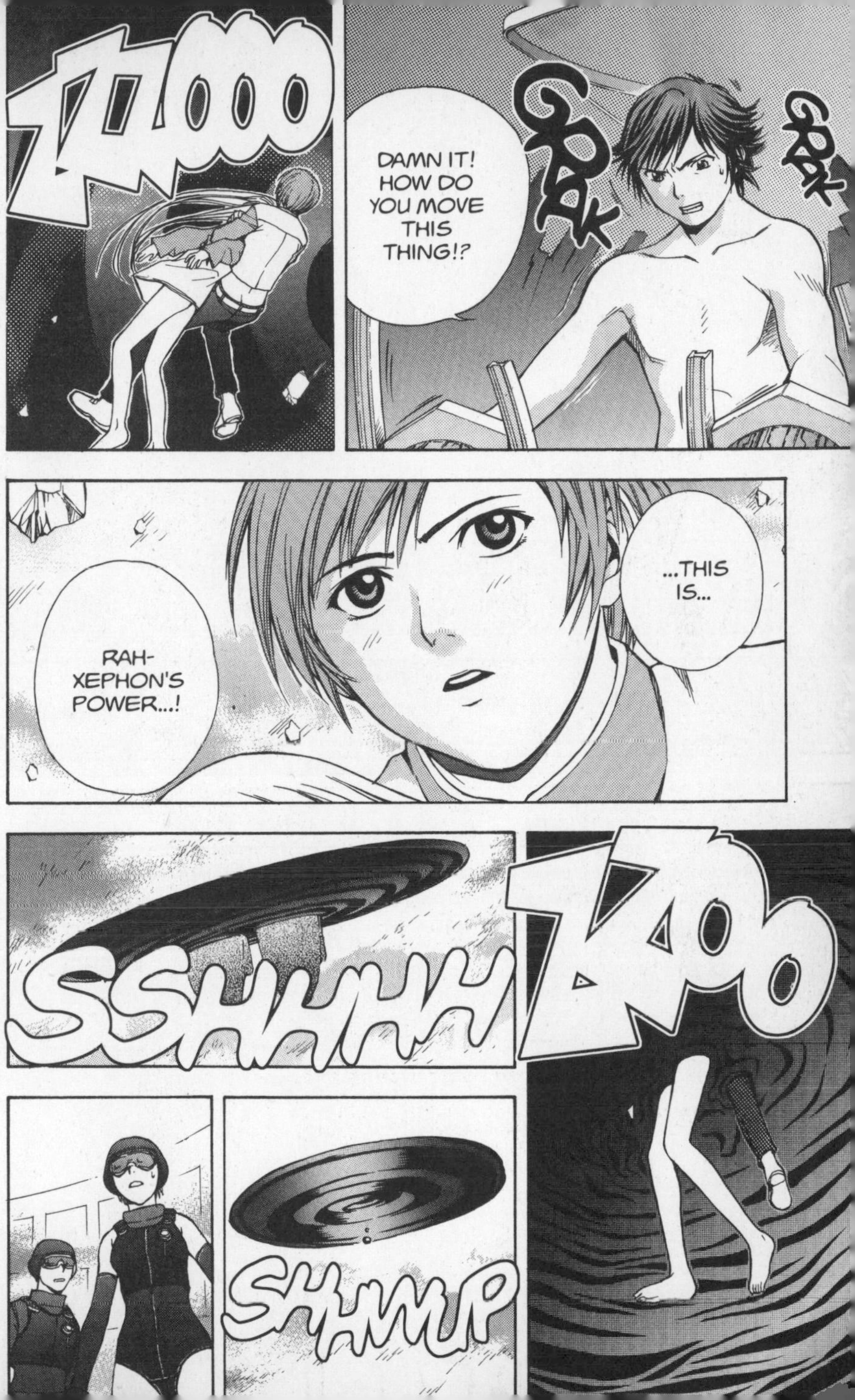
GRAK
GRAK
DAMN IT! HOW DO YOU MOVE THIS THING!?
ZZOOO
...THIS IS...
RAH-XEPHON'S POWER...!
ZOO
SSHHHH
SHMMP

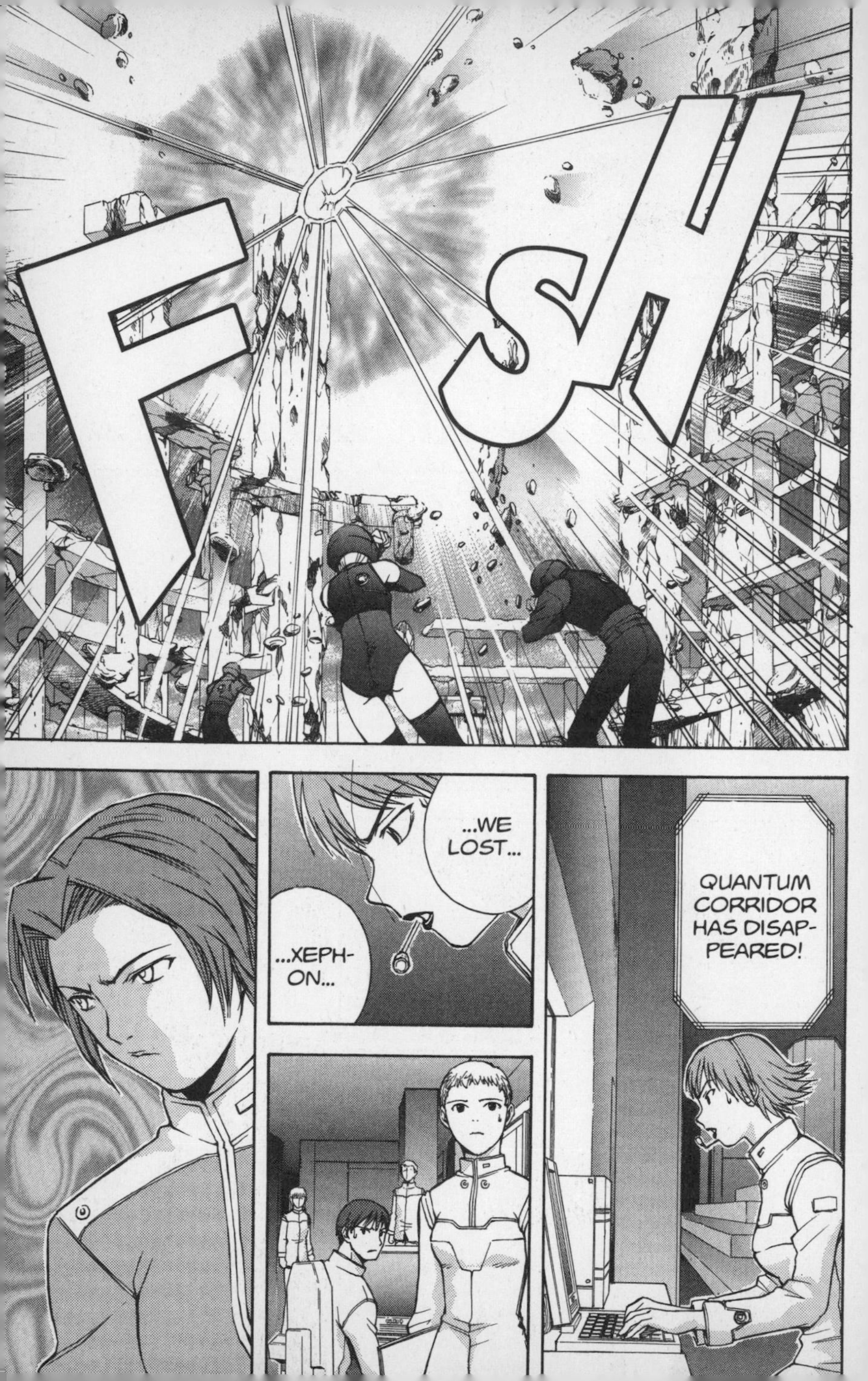
FSH
QUANTUM CORRIDOR HAS DISAP-PEARED!
...WE LOST...
...XEPH-ON...

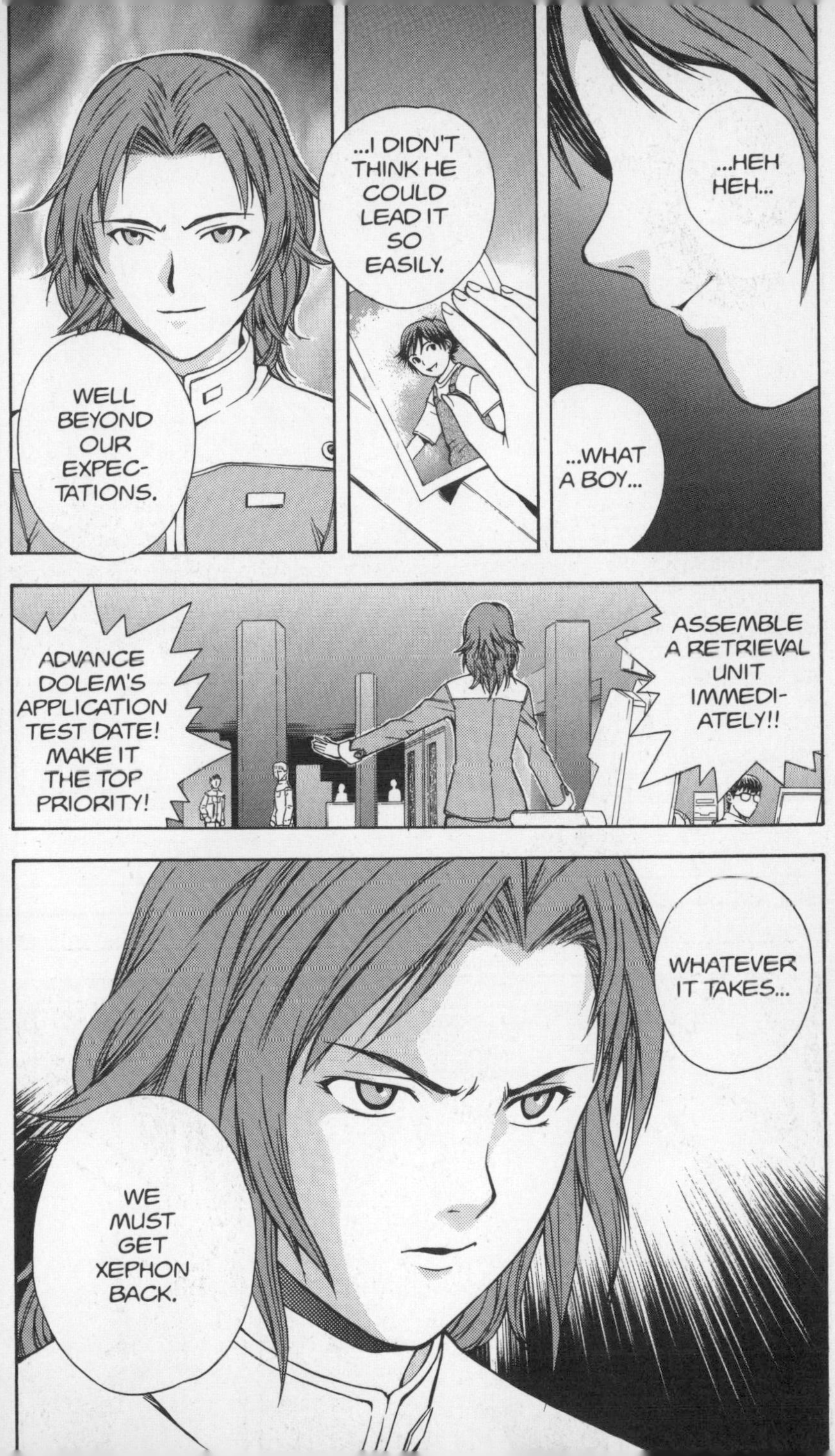
...HEH HEH...
...WHAT A BOY...
...I DIDN'T THINK HE COULD LEAD IT SO EASILY.
WELL BEYOND OUR EXPECTATIONS.
ASSEMBLE A RETRIEVAL UNIT IMMEDIATELY!!
ADVANCE DOLEM'S APPLICATION TEST DATE! MAKE IT THE TOP PRIORITY!
WHATEVER IT TAKES...
WE MUST GET XEPHON BACK.

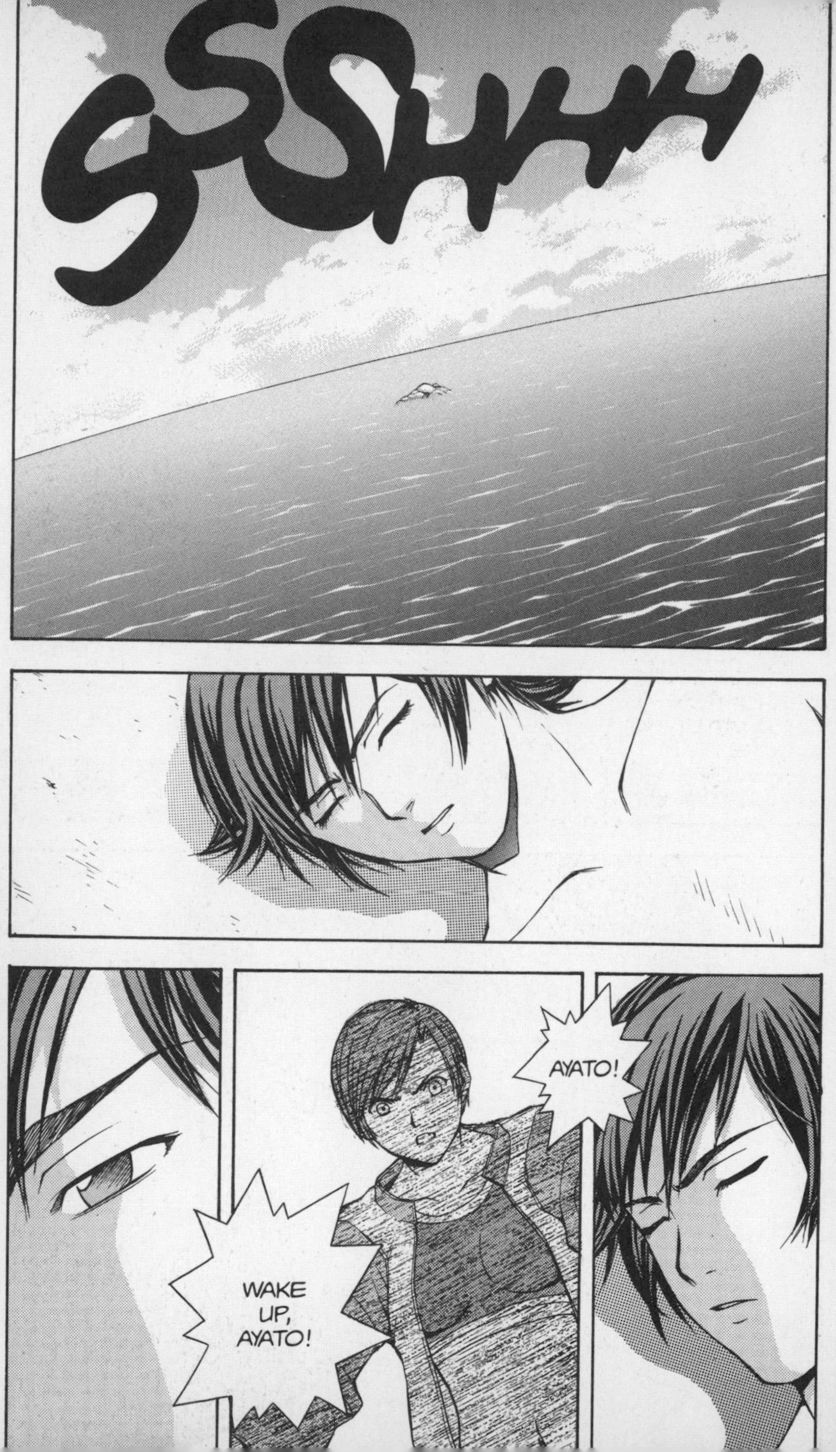
SSSHHH
AYATO!
WAKE UP, AYATO!

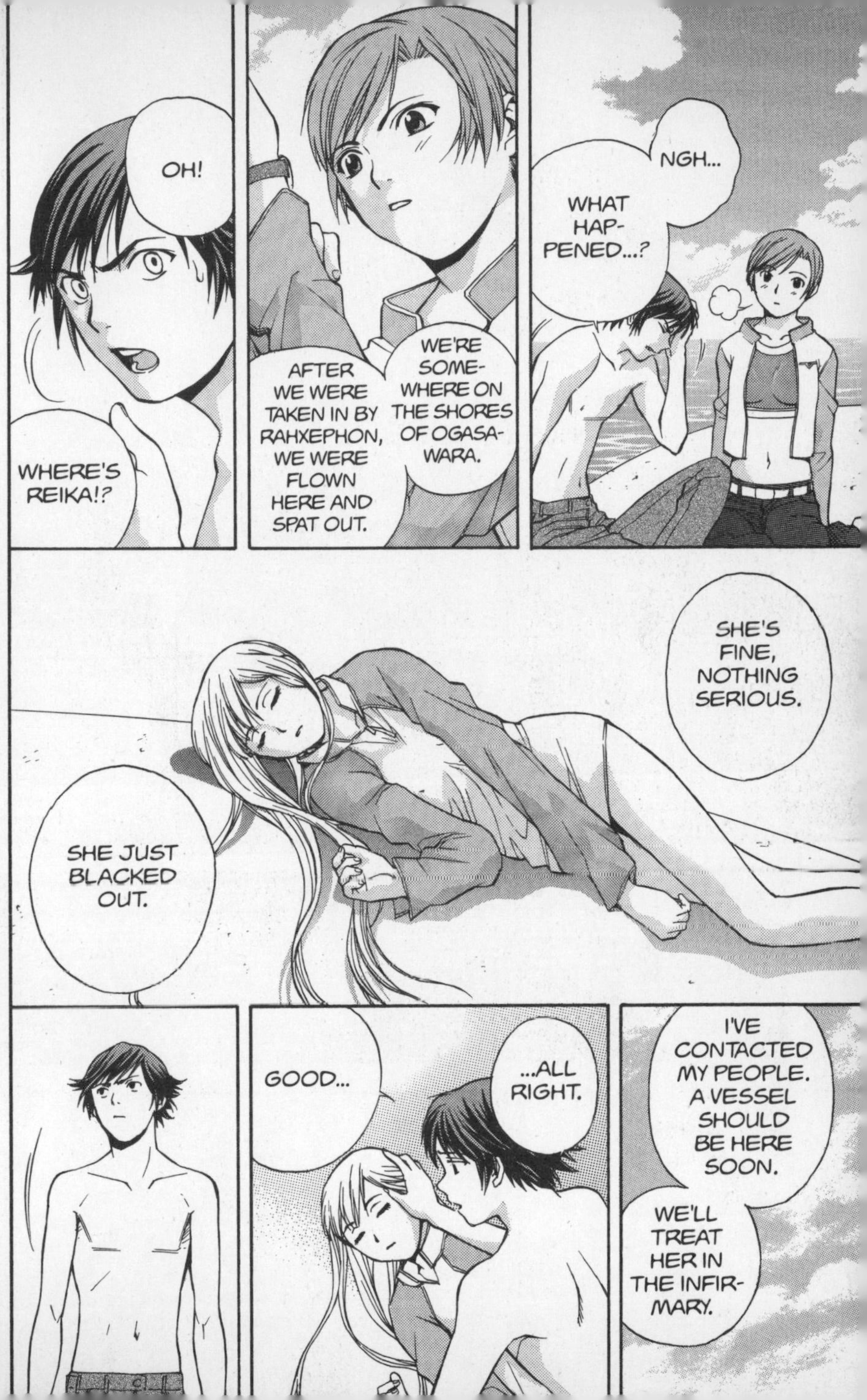
NGH...
WHAT HAP-PENED...?
WE'RE SOME-WHERE ON THE SHORES OF OGASA-WARA.
AFTER WE WERE TAKEN IN BY RAHXEPHON, WE WERE FLOWN HERE AND SPAT OUT.
OH!
WHERE'S REIKA!?
SHE'S FINE, NOTHING SERIOUS.
SHE JUST BLACKED OUT.
I'VE CONTACTED MY PEOPLE. A VESSEL SHOULD BE HERE SOON.
WE'LL TREAT HER IN THE INFIR-MARY.
...ALL RIGHT.
GOOD...

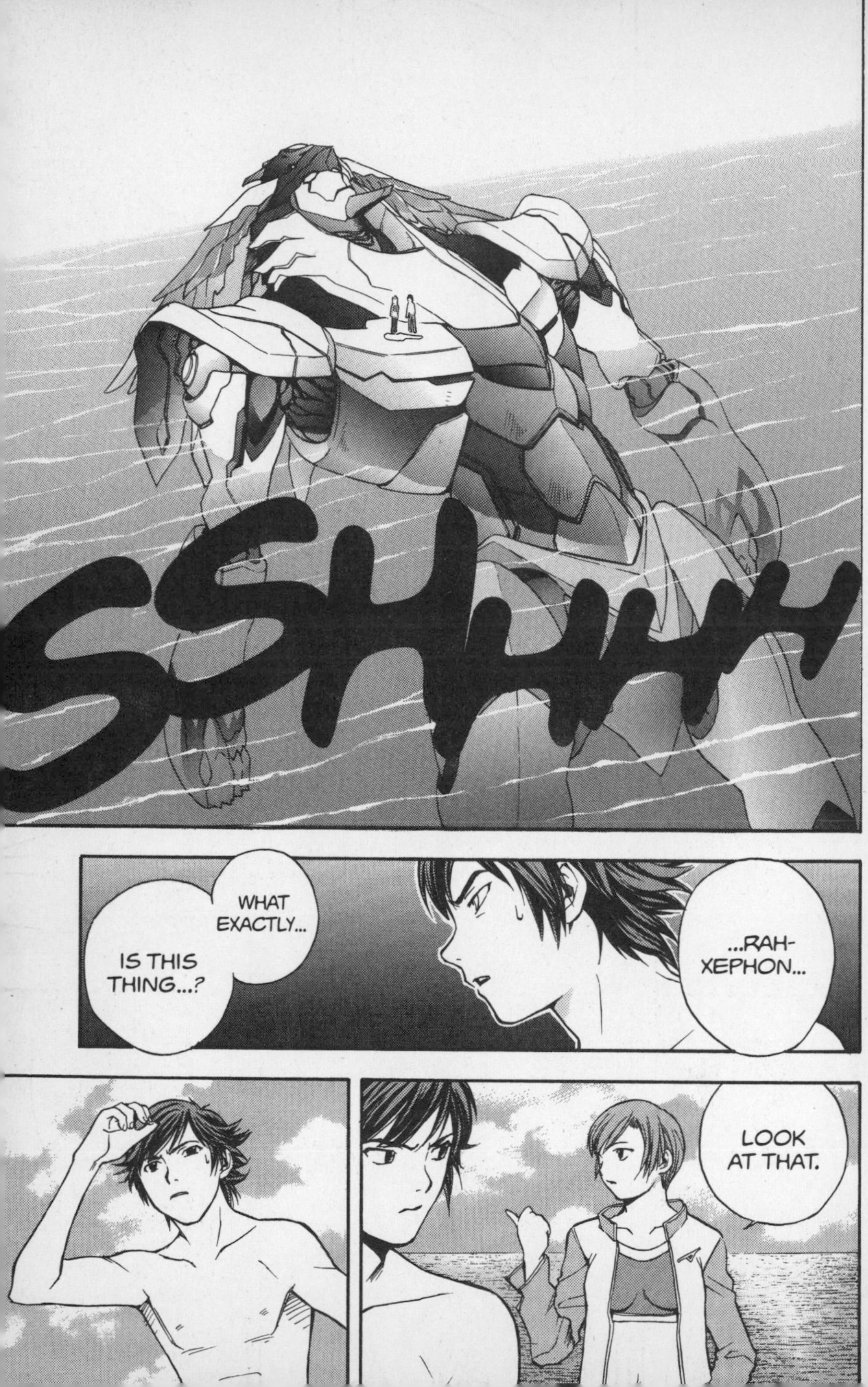
SSHHH
...RAH-XEPHON...
WHAT EXACTLY... IS THIS THING...?
LOOK AT THAT.

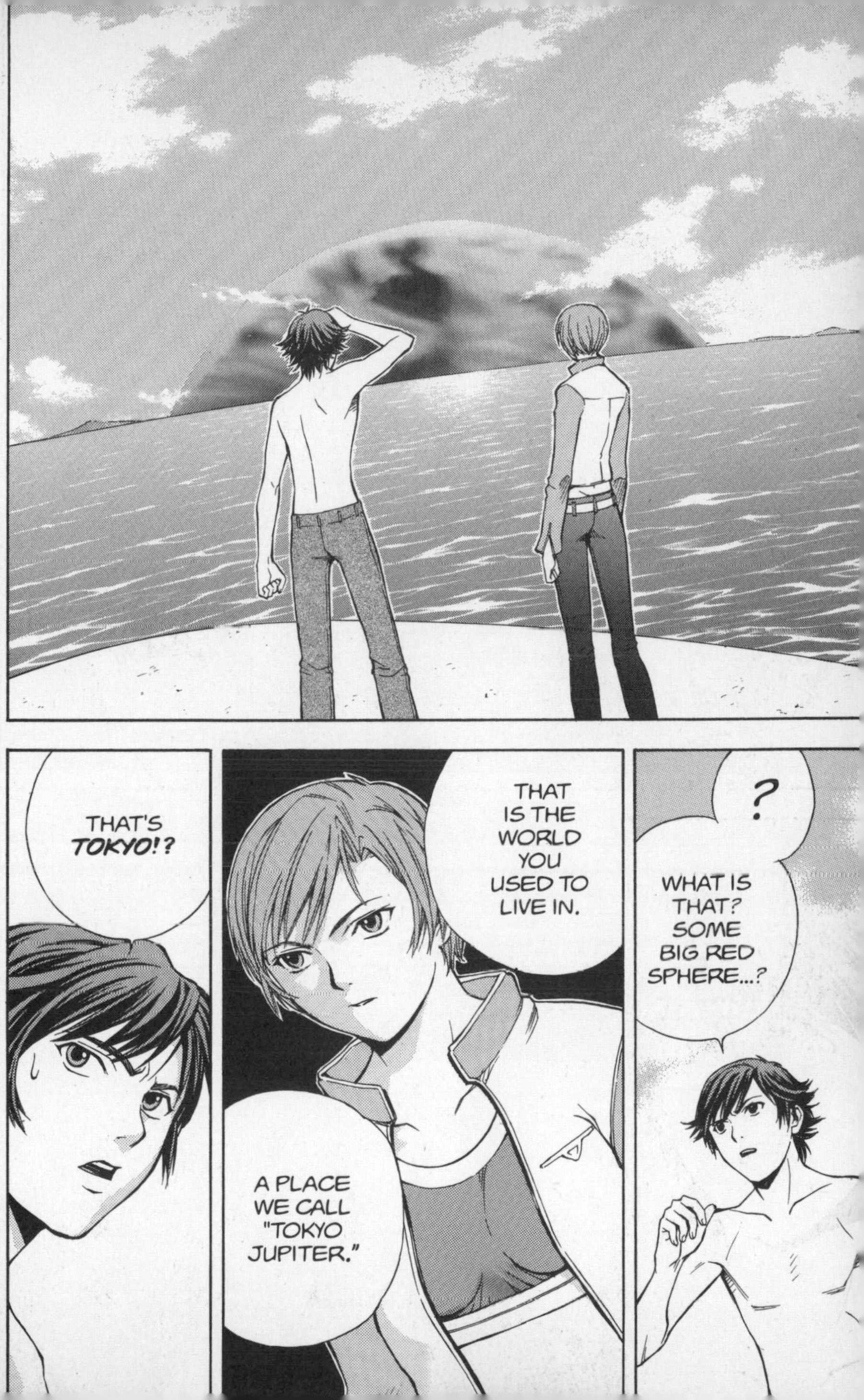
?
WHAT IS THAT? SOME BIG RED SPHERE...?
THAT IS THE WORLD YOU USED TO LIVE IN.
A PLACE WE CALL "TOKYO JUPITER."
THAT'S *TOKYO*!?

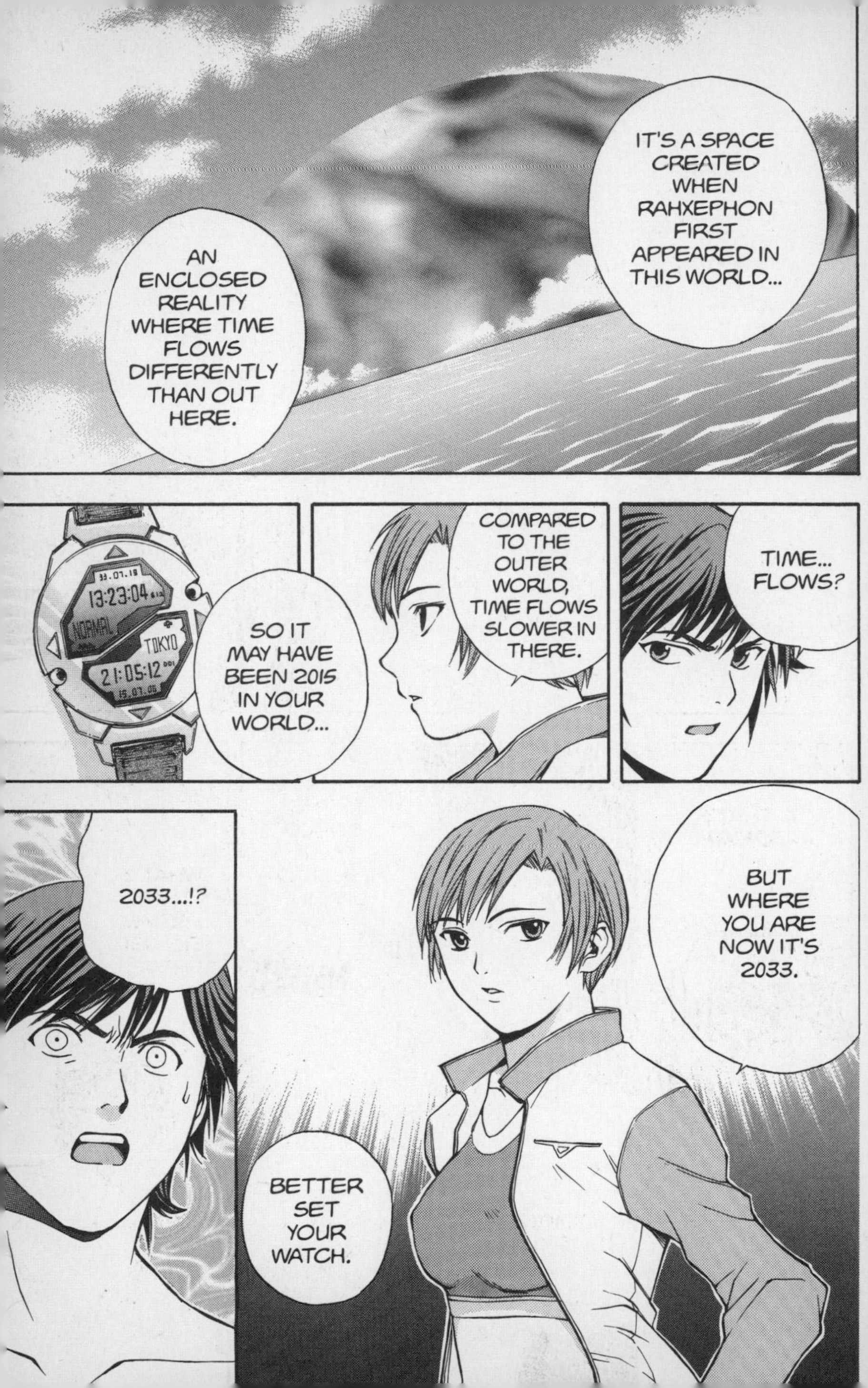
IT'S A SPACE CREATED WHEN RAHXEPHON FIRST APPEARED IN THIS WORLD...
AN ENCLOSED REALITY WHERE TIME FLOWS DIFFERENTLY THAN OUT HERE.
TIME... FLOWS?
COMPARED TO THE OUTER WORLD, TIME FLOWS SLOWER IN THERE.
13:23:04
NORMAL
TOKYO
21:05:12
SO IT MAY HAVE BEEN 2015 IN YOUR WORLD...
BUT WHERE YOU ARE NOW IT'S 2033.
2033...!?
BETTER SET YOUR WATCH.

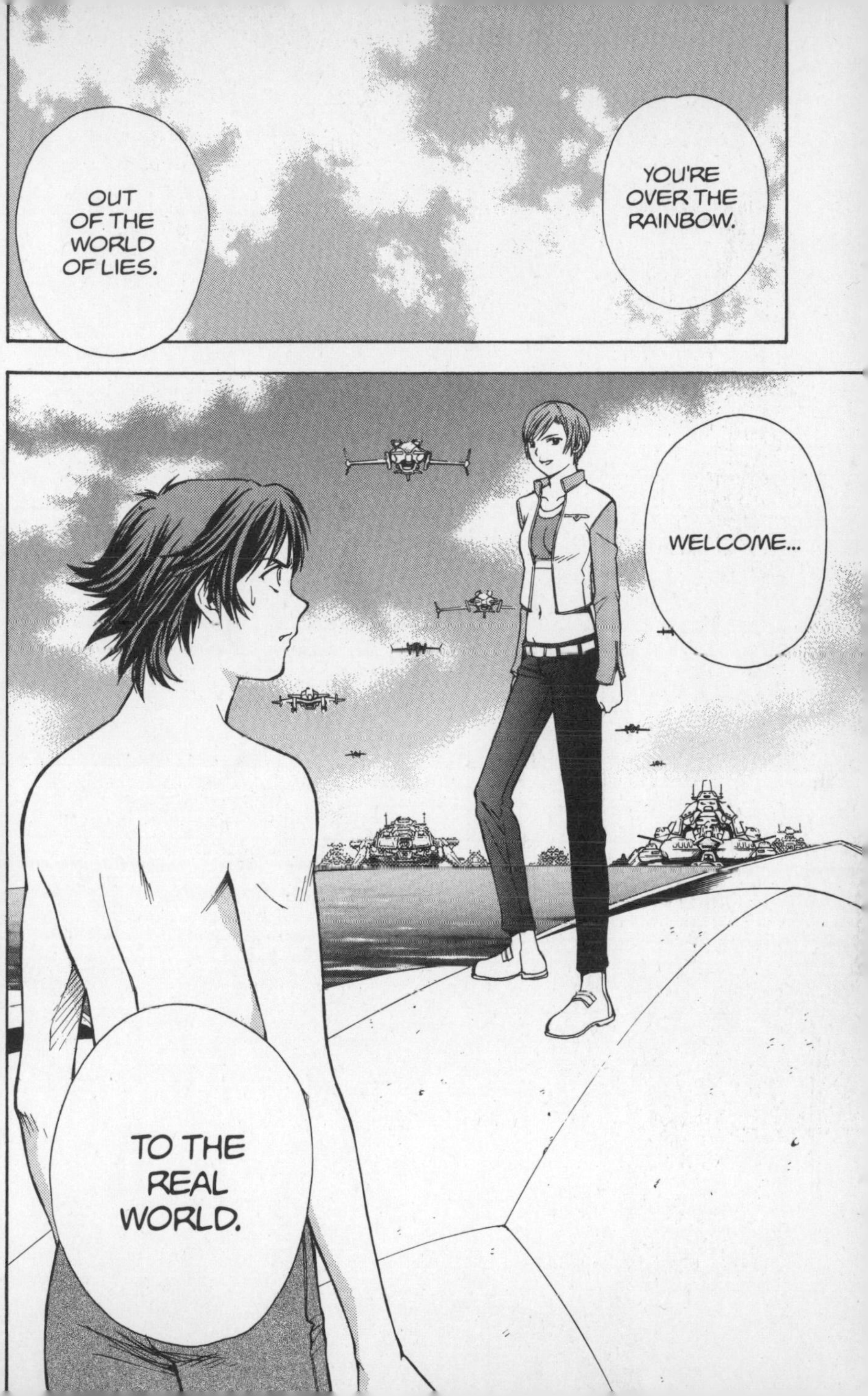
YOU'RE OVER THE RAINBOW.
OUT OF THE WORLD OF LIES.
WELCOME...
TO THE REAL WORLD.

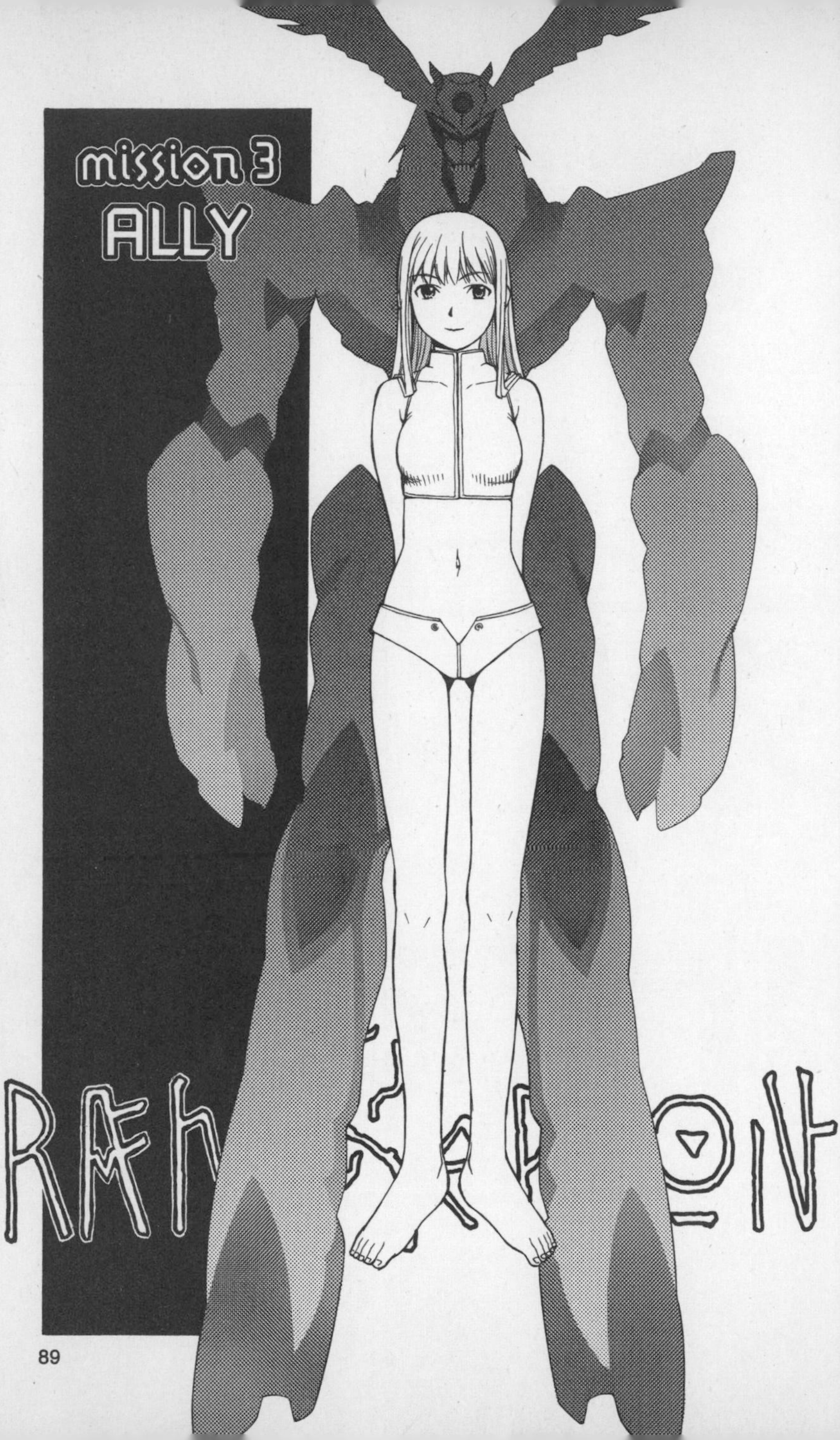
mission 3
ALLY

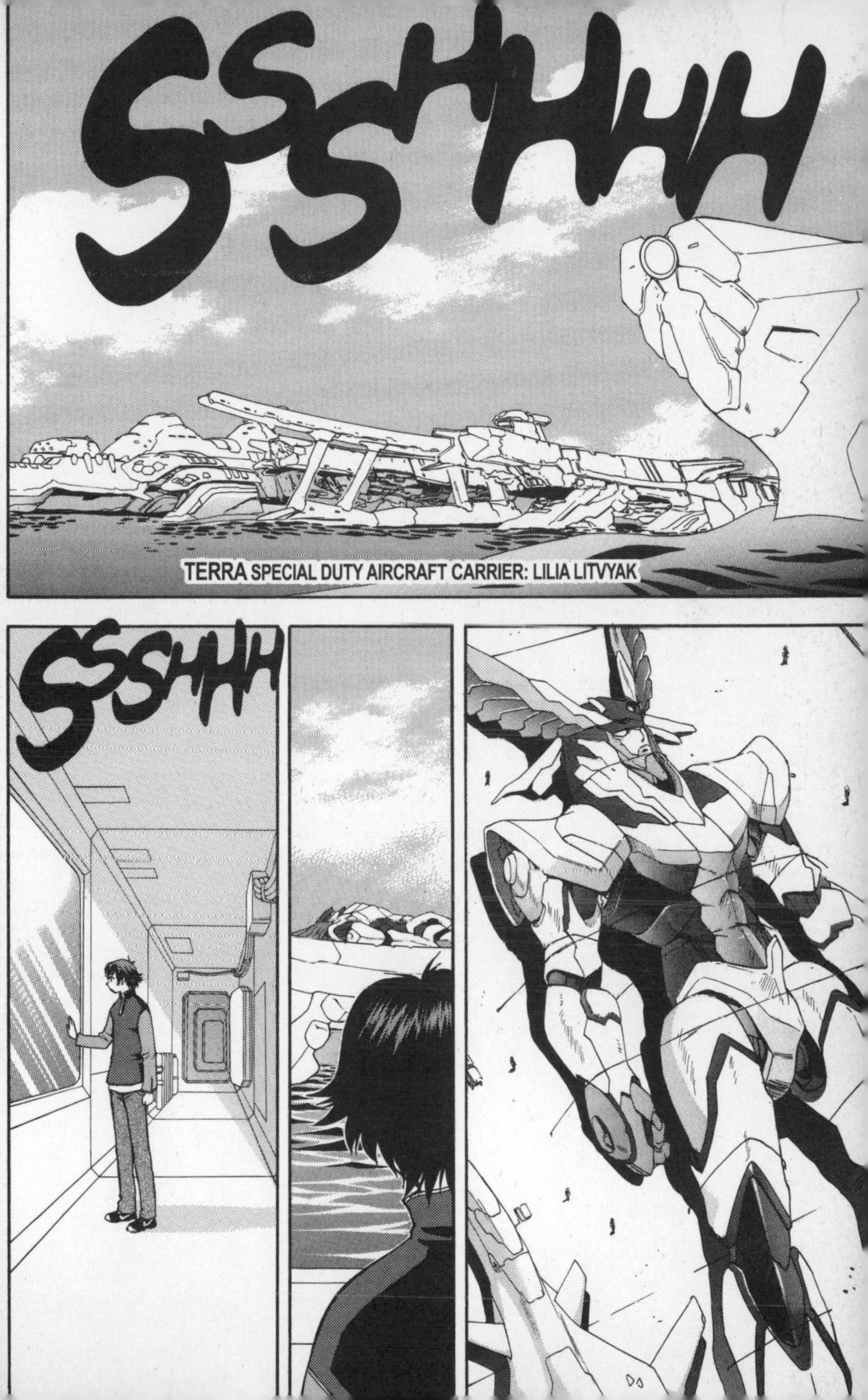
SSSHHHH
TERRA SPECIAL DUTY AIRCRAFT CARRIER: LILIA LITVYAK
SSHHH

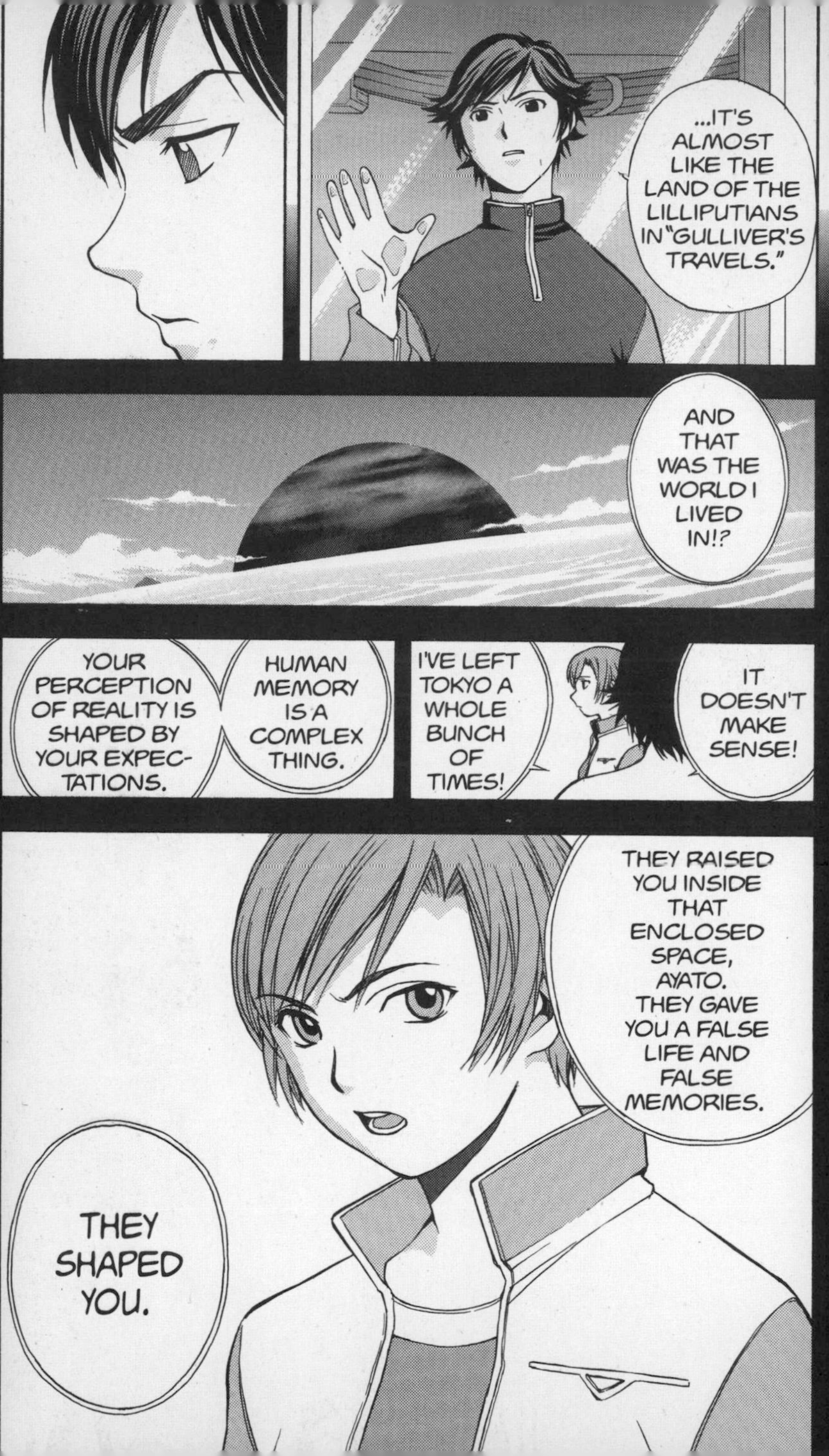
...IT'S ALMOST LIKE THE LAND OF THE LILLIPUTIANS IN "GULLIVER'S TRAVELS."
AND THAT WAS THE WORLD I LIVED IN!?
IT DOESN'T MAKE SENSE!
I'VE LEFT TOKYO A WHOLE BUNCH OF TIMES!
HUMAN MEMORY IS A COMPLEX THING.
YOUR PERCEPTION OF REALITY IS SHAPED BY YOUR EXPECTATIONS.
THEY RAISED YOU INSIDE THAT ENCLOSED SPACE, AYATO. THEY GAVE YOU A FALSE LIFE AND FALSE MEMORIES.
THEY SHAPED YOU.

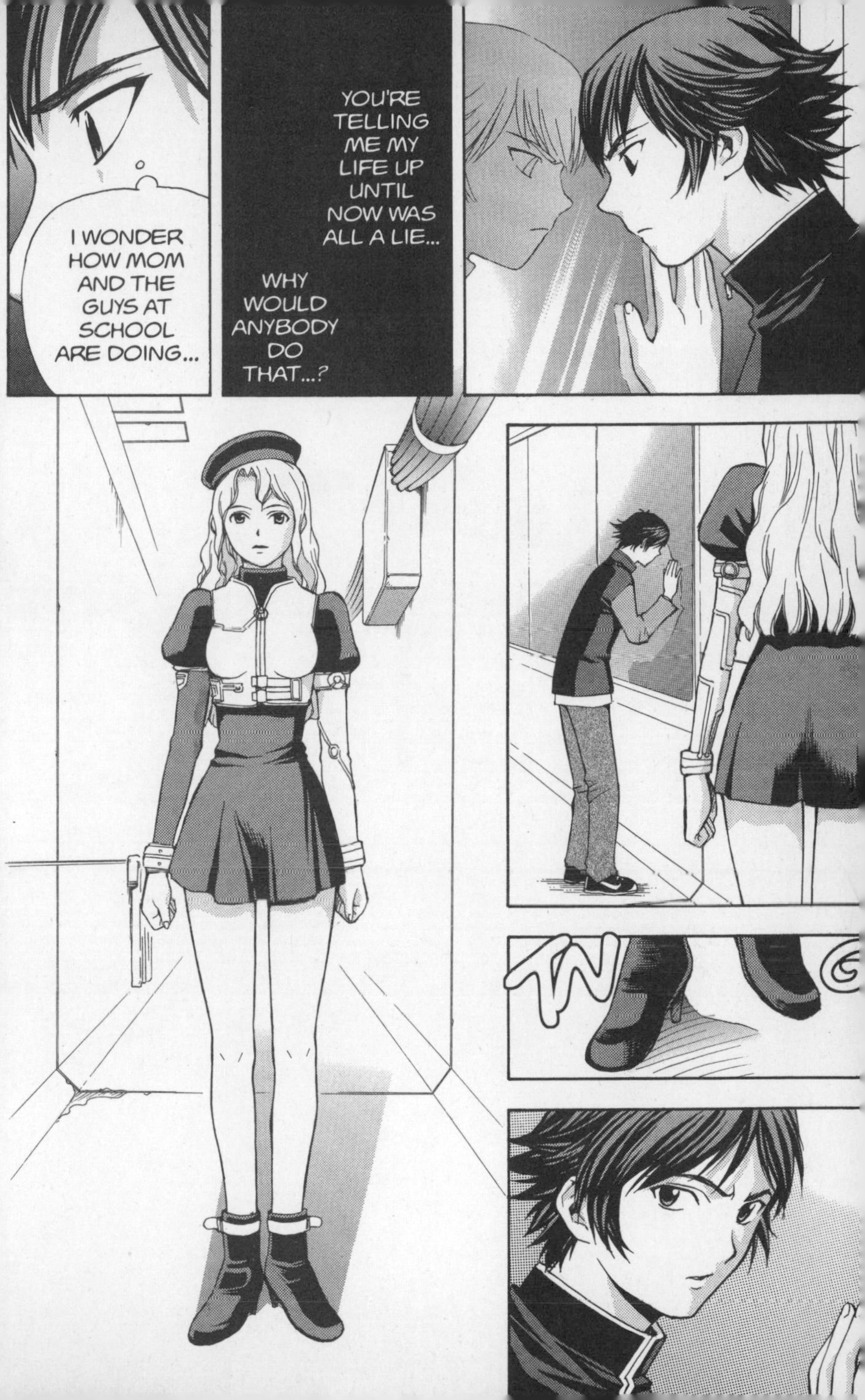
YOU'RE TELLING ME MY LIFE UP UNTIL NOW WAS ALL A LIE...
WHY WOULD ANYBODY DO THAT...?
I WONDER HOW MOM AND THE GUYS AT SCHOOL ARE DOING...
TN

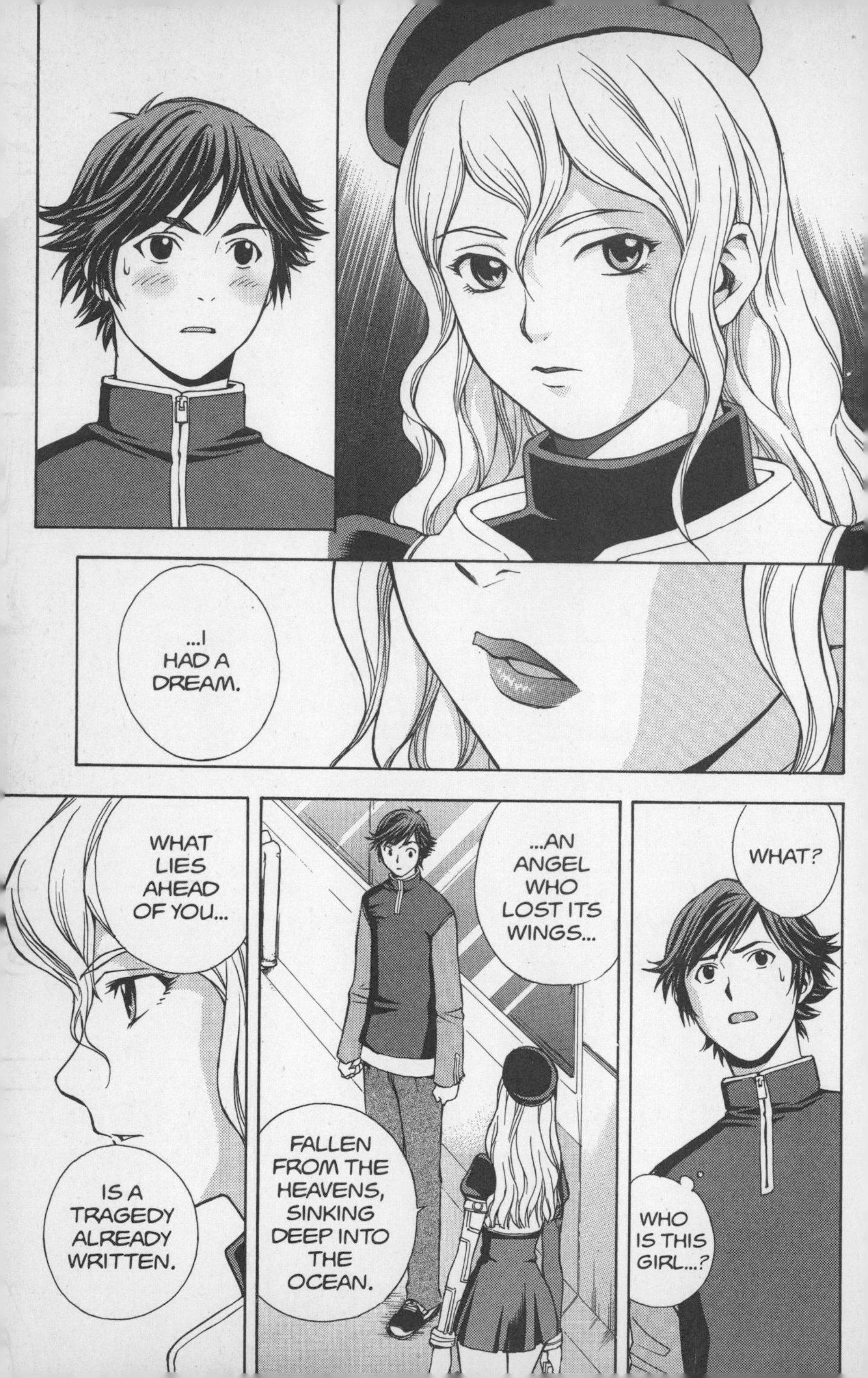
...I HAD A DREAM.
WHAT LIES AHEAD OF YOU...
IS A TRAGEDY ALREADY WRITTEN.
...AN ANGEL WHO LOST ITS WINGS...
FALLEN FROM THE HEAVENS, SINKING DEEP INTO THE OCEAN.
WHAT?
WHO IS THIS GIRL...?

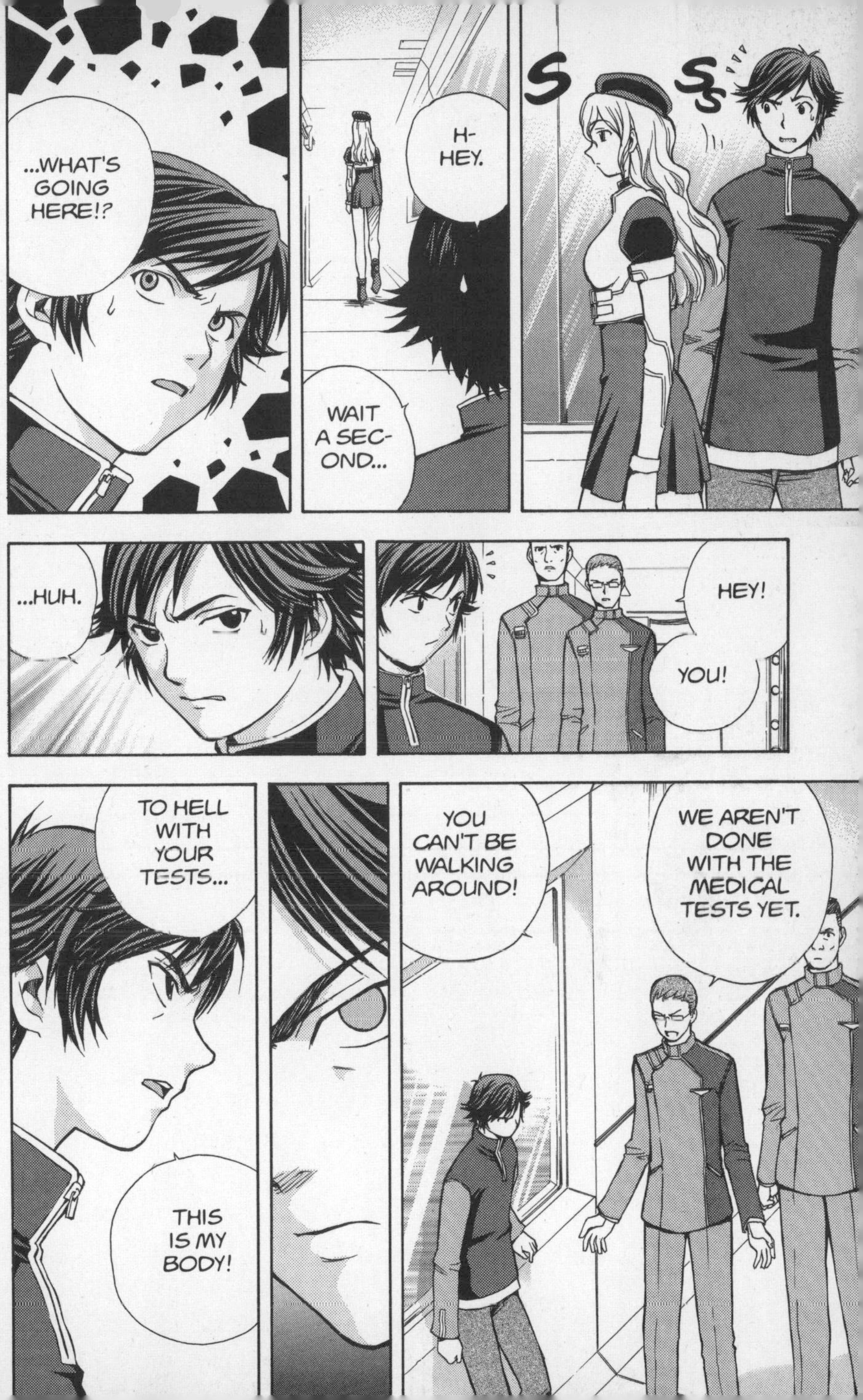
S
SS
H- HEY.
WAIT A SEC- OND...
...WHAT'S GOING HERE!?
HEY!
YOU!
...HUH.
WE AREN'T DONE WITH THE MEDICAL TESTS YET.
YOU CAN'T BE WALKING AROUND!
TO HELL WITH YOUR TESTS...
THIS IS MY BODY!

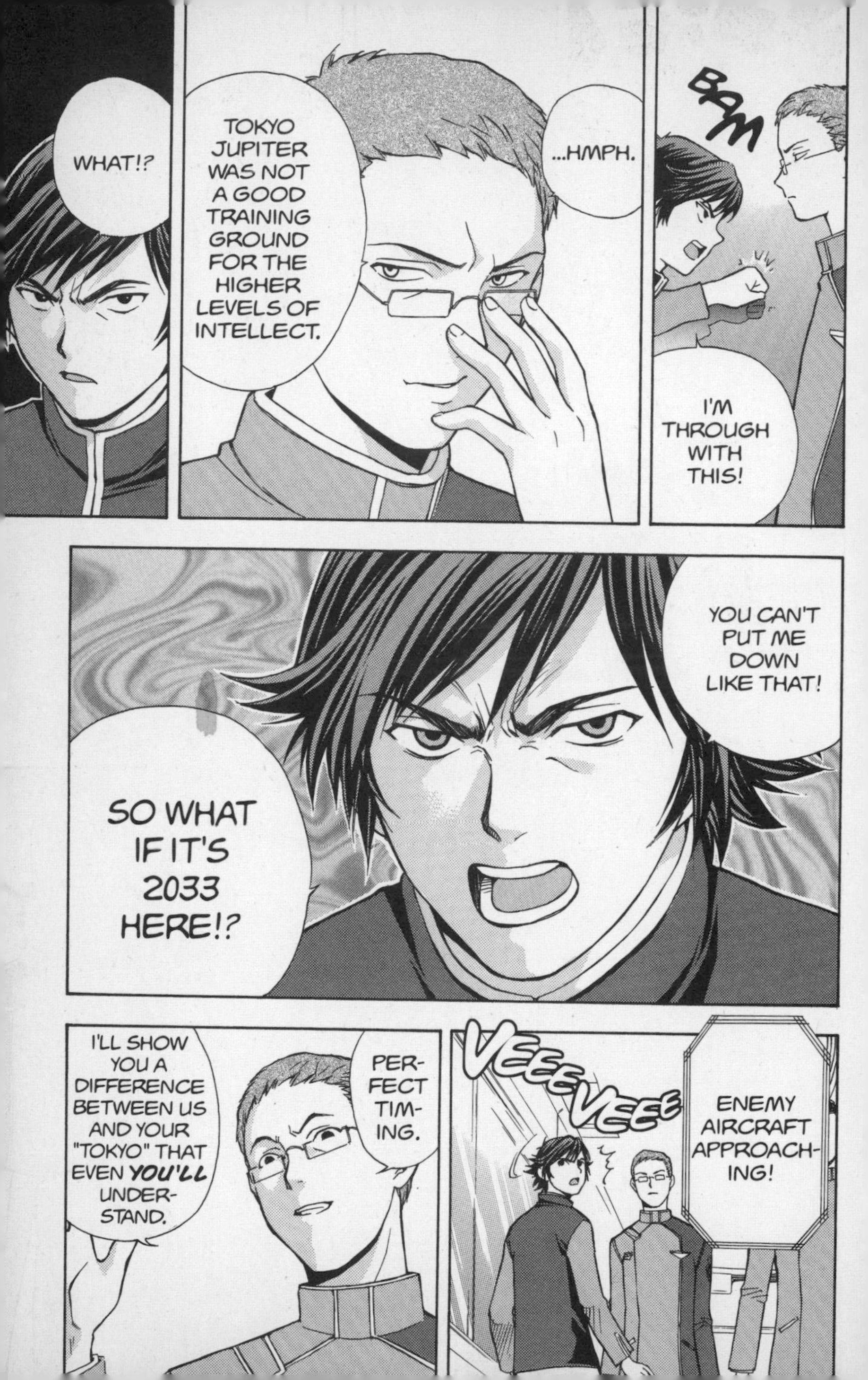
WHAT!?
TOKYO JUPITER WAS NOT A GOOD TRAINING GROUND FOR THE HIGHER LEVELS OF INTELLECT.
...HMPH.
BAM
I'M THROUGH WITH THIS!
YOU CAN'T PUT ME DOWN LIKE THAT!
SO WHAT IF IT'S 2033 HERE!?
I'LL SHOW YOU A DIFFERENCE BETWEEN US AND YOUR "TOKYO" THAT EVEN YOU'LL UNDERSTAND.
PER-FECT TIM-ING.
VEEE VEEE
ENEMY AIRCRAFT APPROACH-ING!

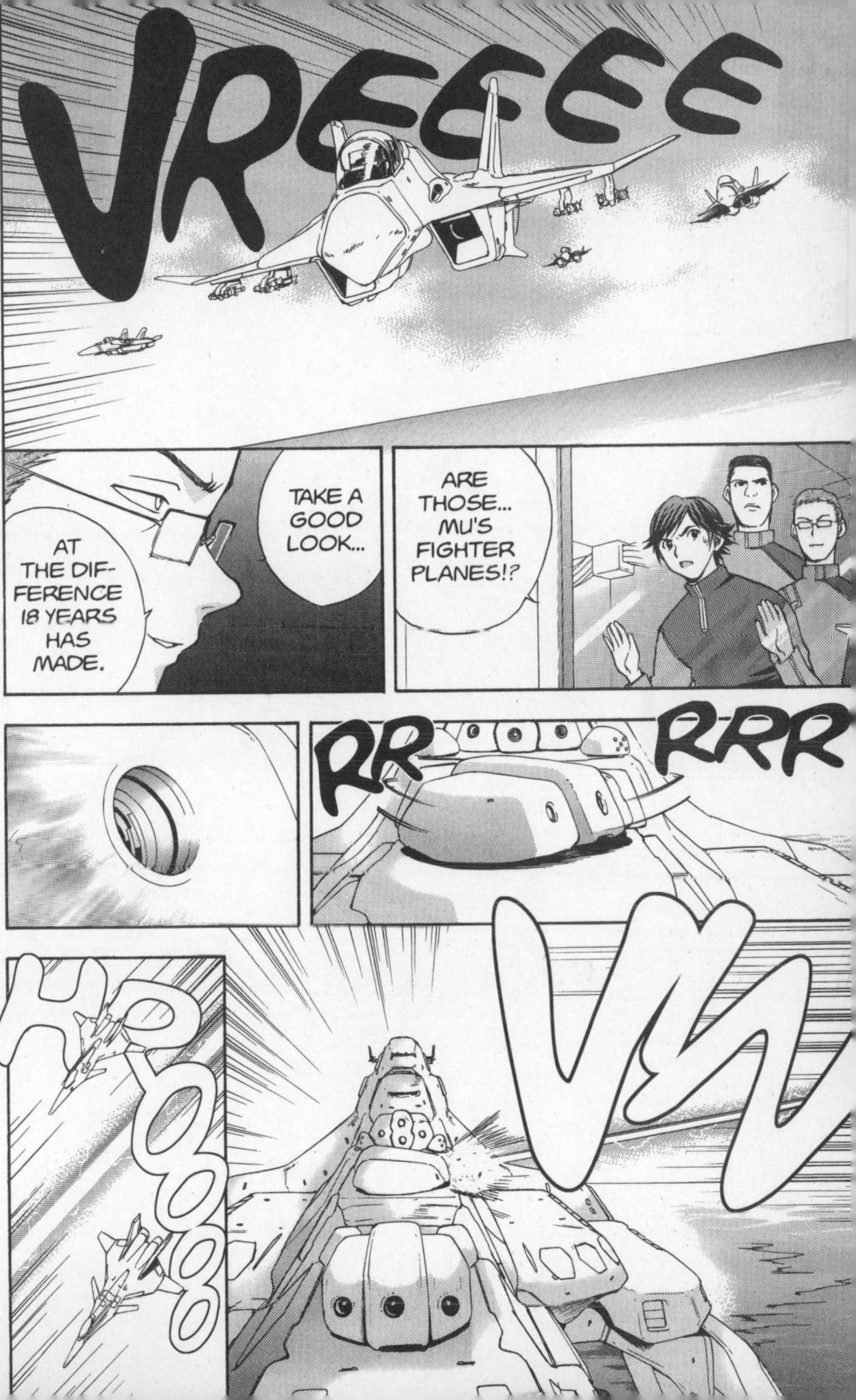
VREEEE
ARE THOSE... MU'S FIGHTER PLANES!?
TAKE A GOOD LOOK...
AT THE DIF-FERENCE 18 YEARS HAS MADE.
RR
RRR
VM
HOOOO

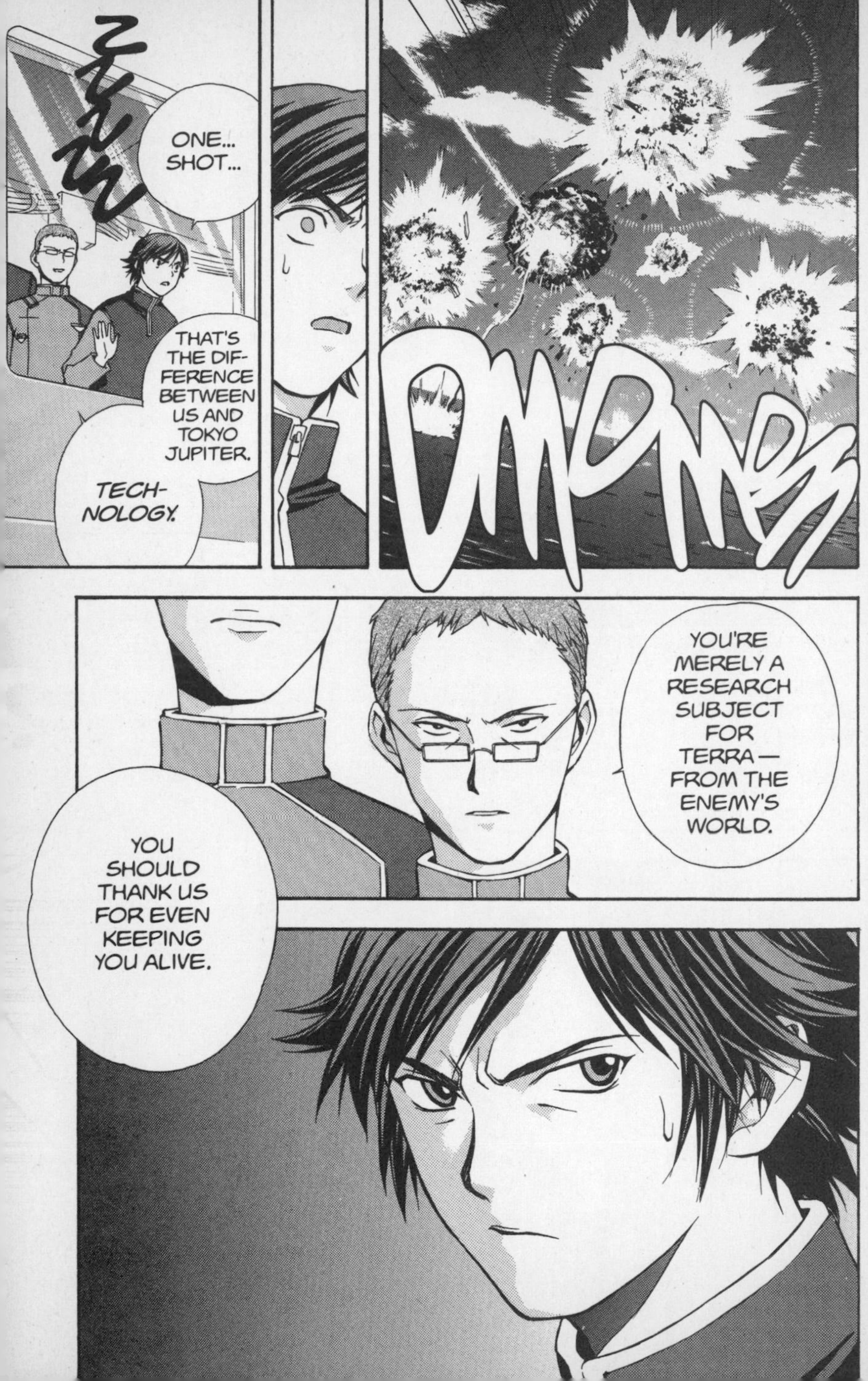
ONE... SHOT...
THAT'S THE DIFFERENCE BETWEEN US AND TOKYO JUPITER.
TECHNOLOGY.
YOU'RE MERELY A RESEARCH SUBJECT FOR TERRA— FROM THE ENEMY'S WORLD.
YOU SHOULD THANK US FOR EVEN KEEPING YOU ALIVE.

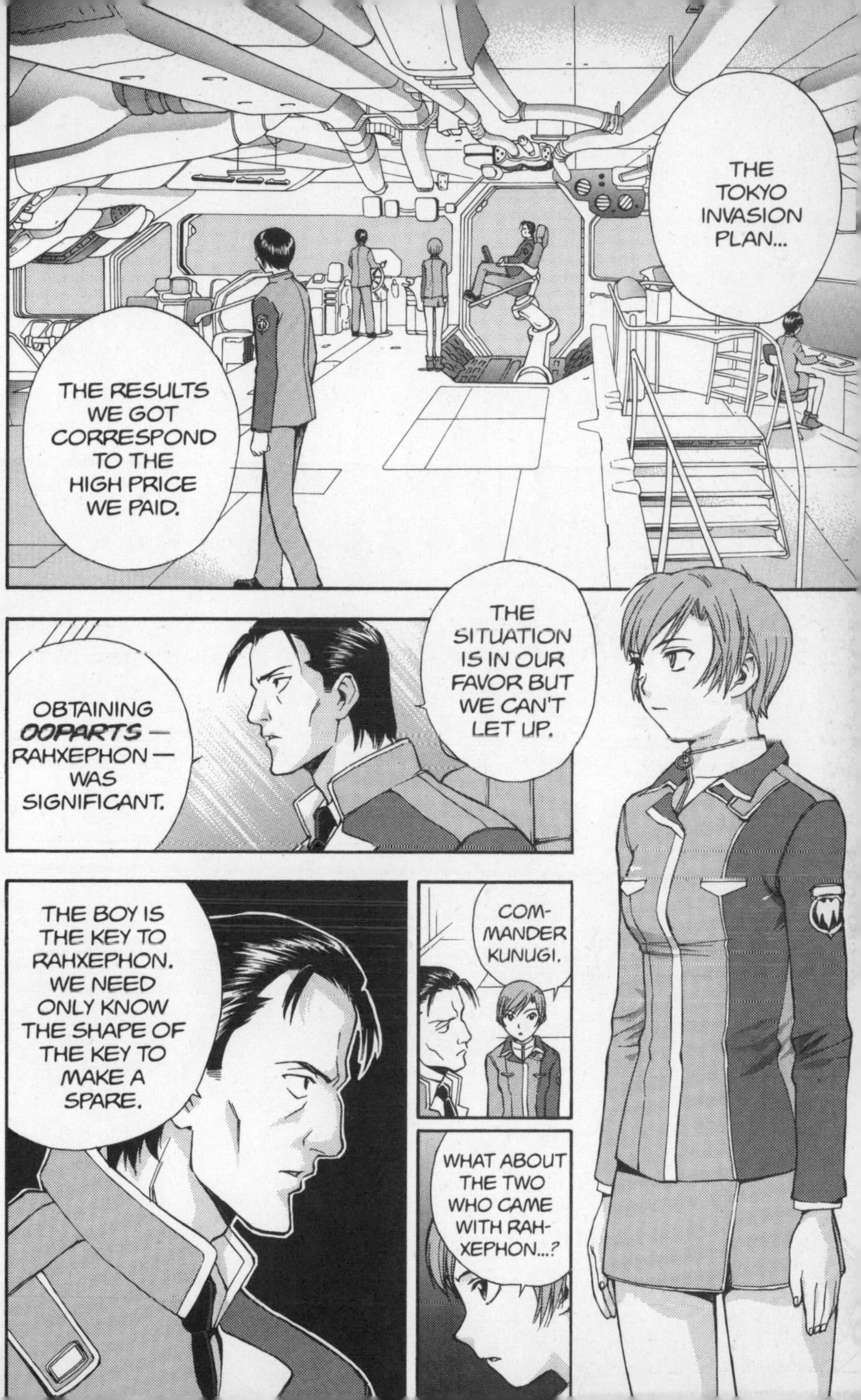
THE TOKYO INVASION PLAN...
THE RESULTS WE GOT CORRESPOND TO THE HIGH PRICE WE PAID.
THE SITUATION IS IN OUR FAVOR BUT WE CAN'T LET UP.
OBTAINING OOPARTS — RAHXEPHON — WAS SIGNIFICANT.
COM-MANDER KUNUGI.
WHAT ABOUT THE TWO WHO CAME WITH RAH-XEPHON...?
THE BOY IS THE KEY TO RAHXEPHON. WE NEED ONLY KNOW THE SHAPE OF THE KEY TO MAKE A SPARE.

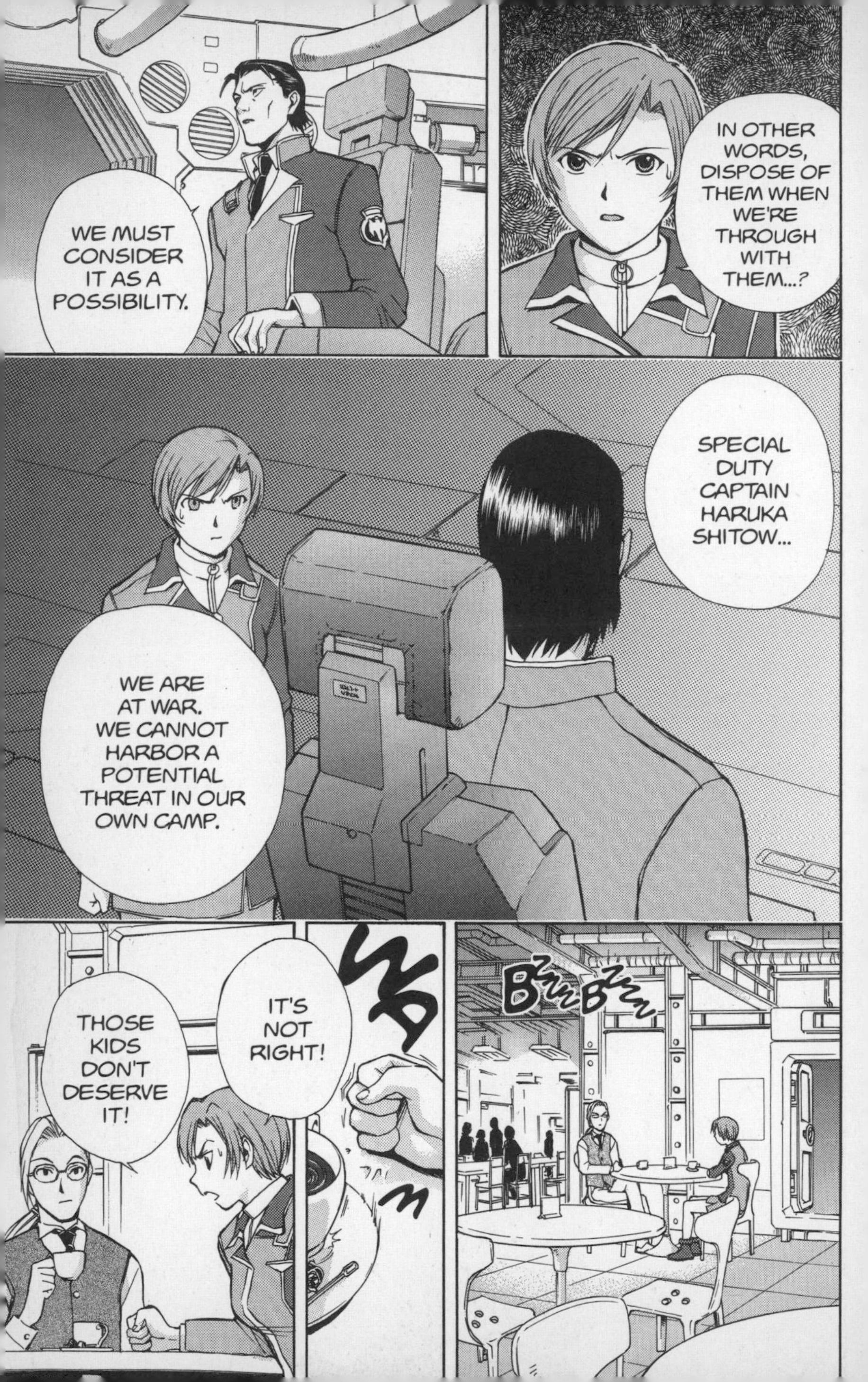
IN OTHER WORDS, DISPOSE OF THEM WHEN WE'RE THROUGH WITH THEM...?
WE MUST CONSIDER IT AS A POSSIBILITY.
SPECIAL DUTY CAPTAIN HARUKA SHITOW...
WE ARE AT WAR. WE CANNOT HARBOR A POTENTIAL THREAT IN OUR OWN CAMP.
BZZZ BZZZZ
WA
IT'S NOT RIGHT!
THOSE KIDS DON'T DESERVE IT!

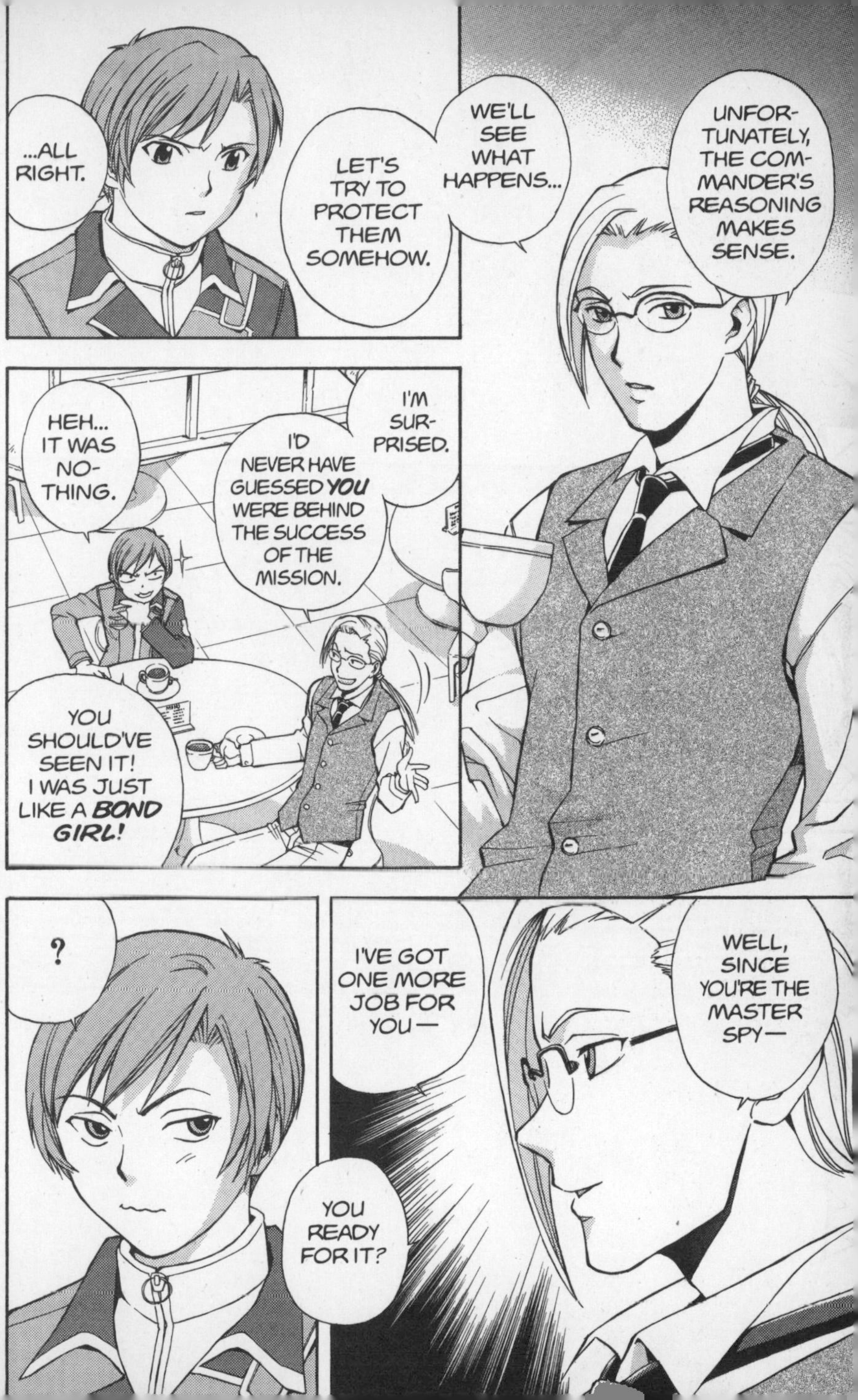
UNFORTUNATELY, THE COMMANDER'S REASONING MAKES SENSE.
WE'LL SEE WHAT HAPPENS...
LET'S TRY TO PROTECT THEM SOMEHOW.
...ALL RIGHT.
I'M SURPRISED.
I'D NEVER HAVE GUESSED ***YOU*** WERE BEHIND THE SUCCESS OF THE MISSION.
HEH... IT WAS NOTHING.
YOU SHOULD'VE SEEN IT! I WAS JUST LIKE A ***BOND GIRL!***
WELL, SINCE YOU'RE THE MASTER SPY—
I'VE GOT ONE MORE JOB FOR YOU—
YOU READY FOR IT?
?

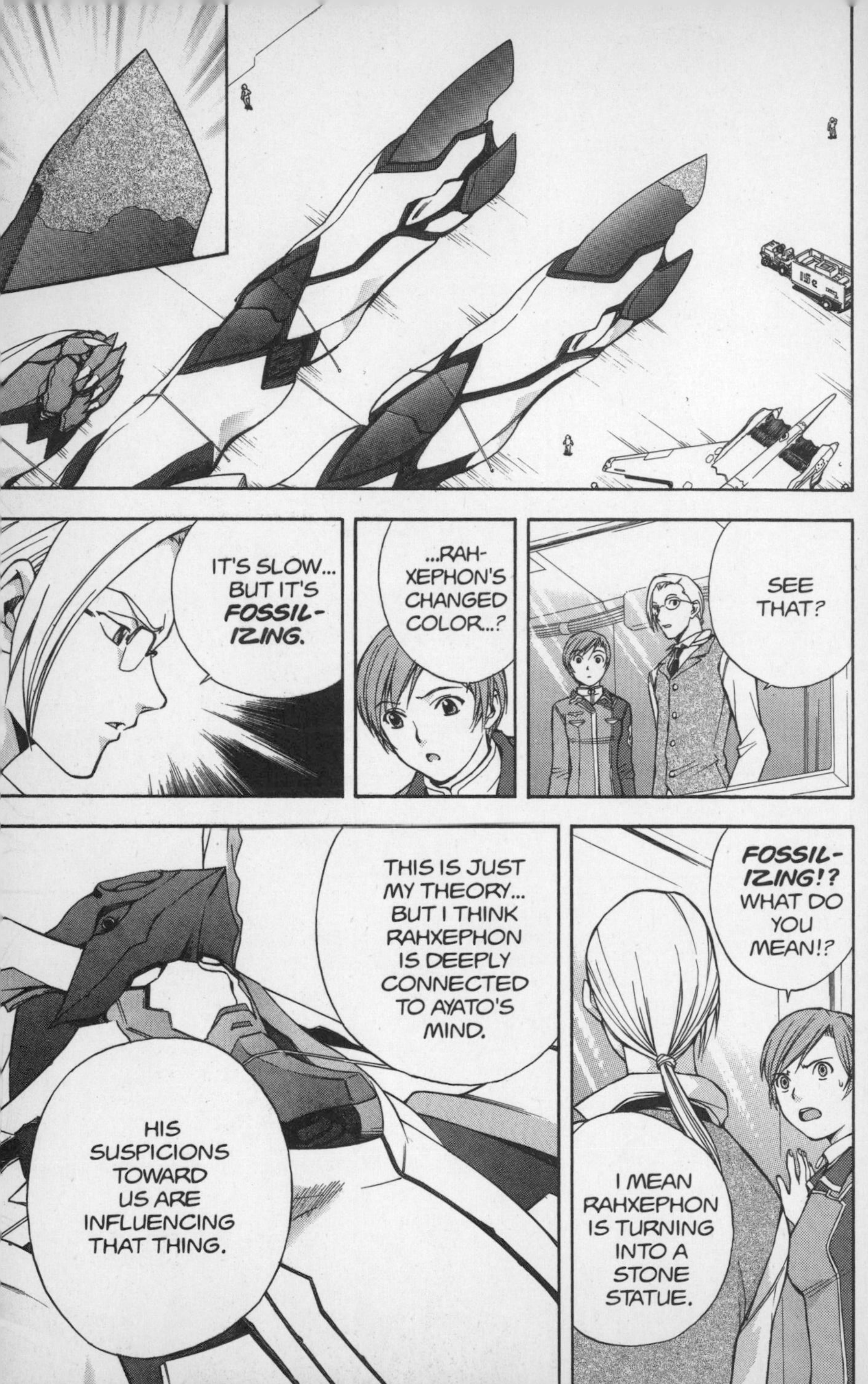
SEE THAT?
...RAH-XEPHON'S CHANGED COLOR...?
IT'S SLOW... BUT IT'S FOSSIL-IZING.
FOSSIL-IZING!? WHAT DO YOU MEAN!?
I MEAN RAHXEPHON IS TURNING INTO A STONE STATUE.
THIS IS JUST MY THEORY... BUT I THINK RAHXEPHON IS DEEPLY CONNECTED TO AYATO'S MIND.
HIS SUSPICIONS TOWARD US ARE INFLUENCING THAT THING.

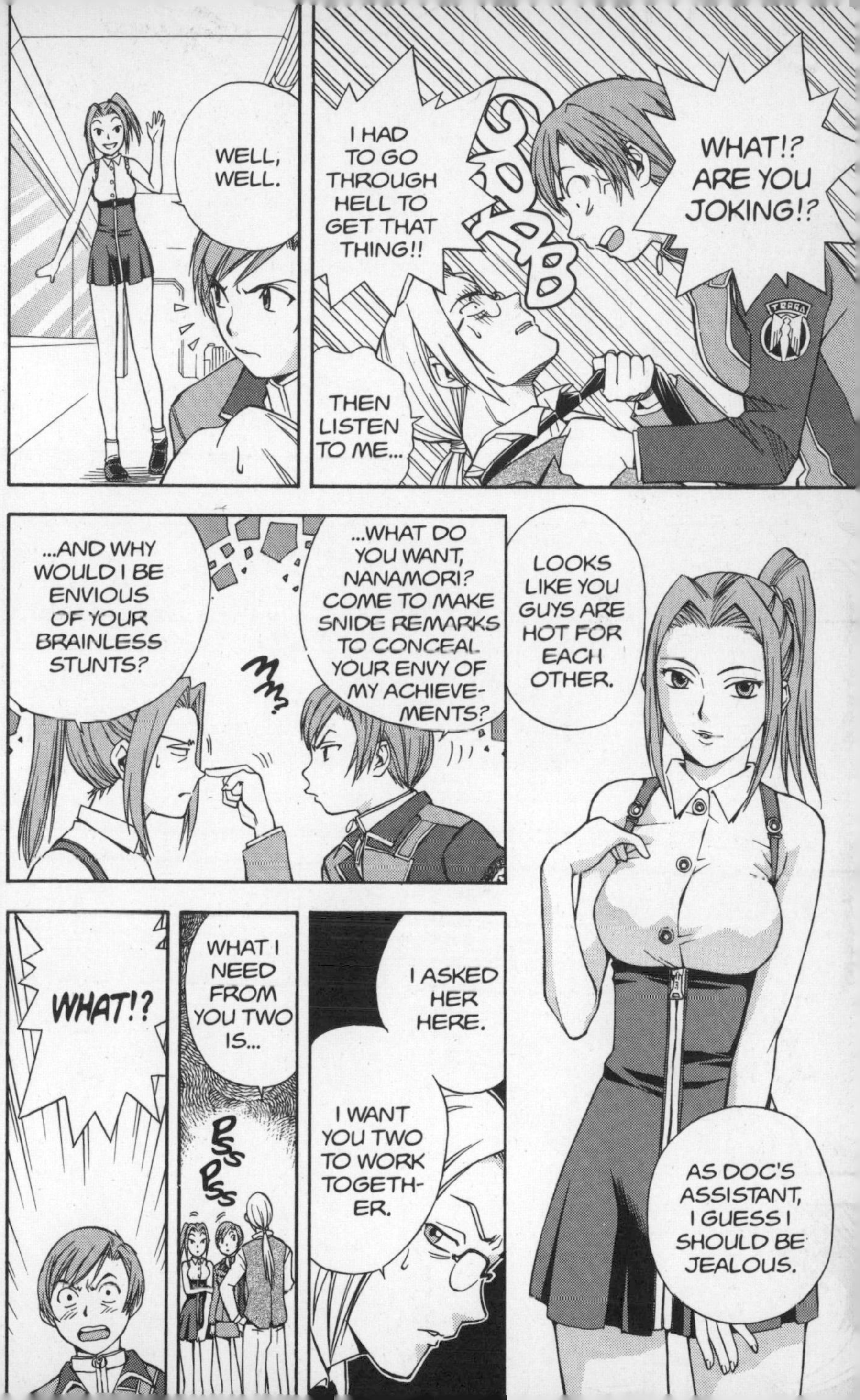
WHAT!? ARE YOU JOKING!?
GRAB
I HAD TO GO THROUGH HELL TO GET THAT THING!!
THEN LISTEN TO ME...
WELL, WELL.
LOOKS LIKE YOU GUYS ARE HOT FOR EACH OTHER.
AS DOC'S ASSISTANT, I GUESS I SHOULD BE JEALOUS.
...WHAT DO YOU WANT, NANAMORI? COME TO MAKE SNIDE REMARKS TO CONCEAL YOUR ENVY OF MY ACHIEVEMENTS?
...AND WHY WOULD I BE ENVIOUS OF YOUR BRAINLESS STUNTS?
I ASKED HER HERE.
I WANT YOU TWO TO WORK TOGETHER.
WHAT I NEED FROM YOU TWO IS...
PSS PSS
WHAT!?

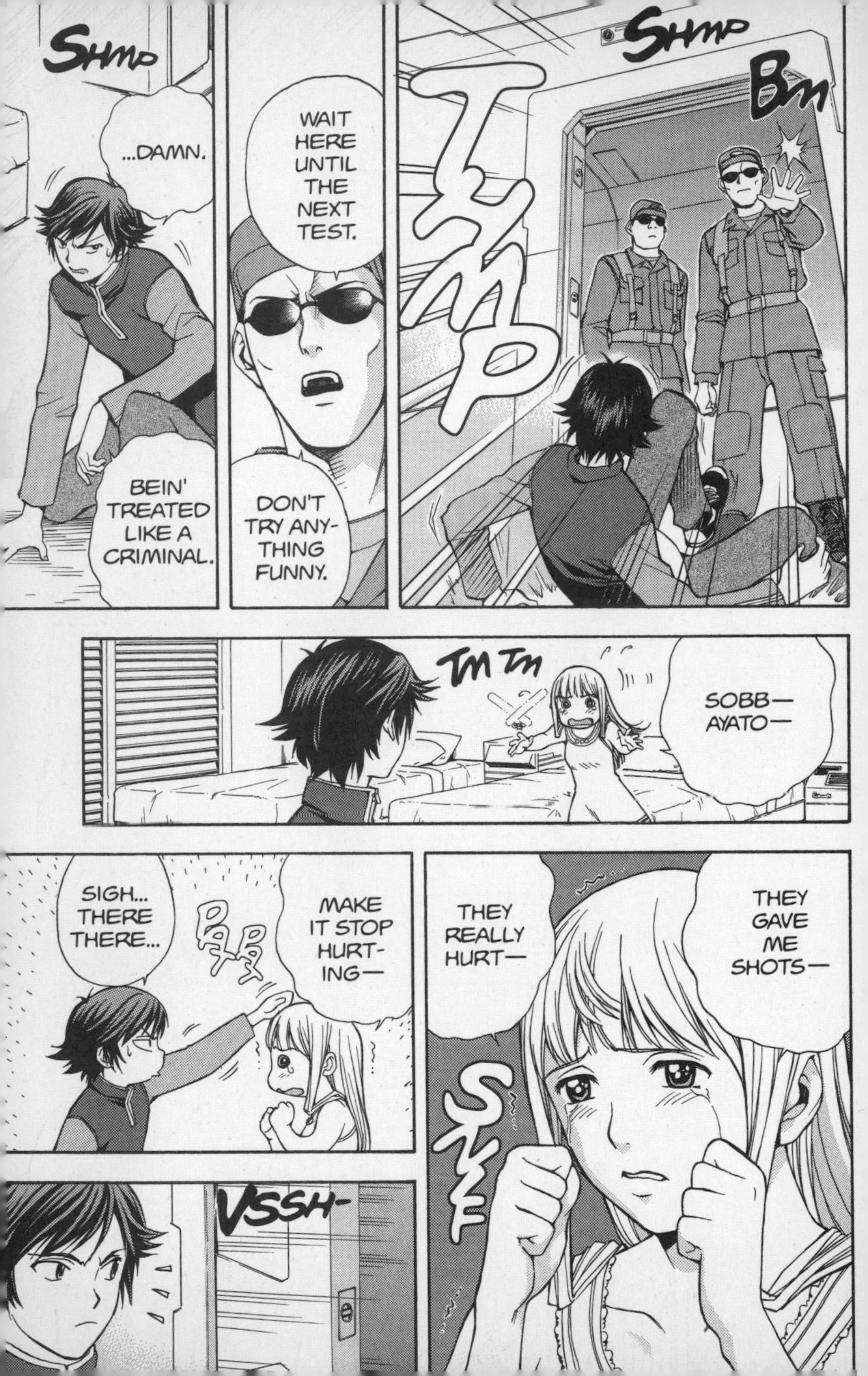
SHMP
BM
TMP
WAIT HERE UNTIL THE NEXT TEST.
DON'T TRY ANY-THING FUNNY.
SHMP
...DAMN.
BEIN' TREATED LIKE A CRIMINAL.
TM TM
SOBB— AYATO—
THEY GAVE ME SHOTS—
THEY REALLY HURT—
MAKE IT STOP HURT-ING—
SIGH... THERE THERE...
VSSH-

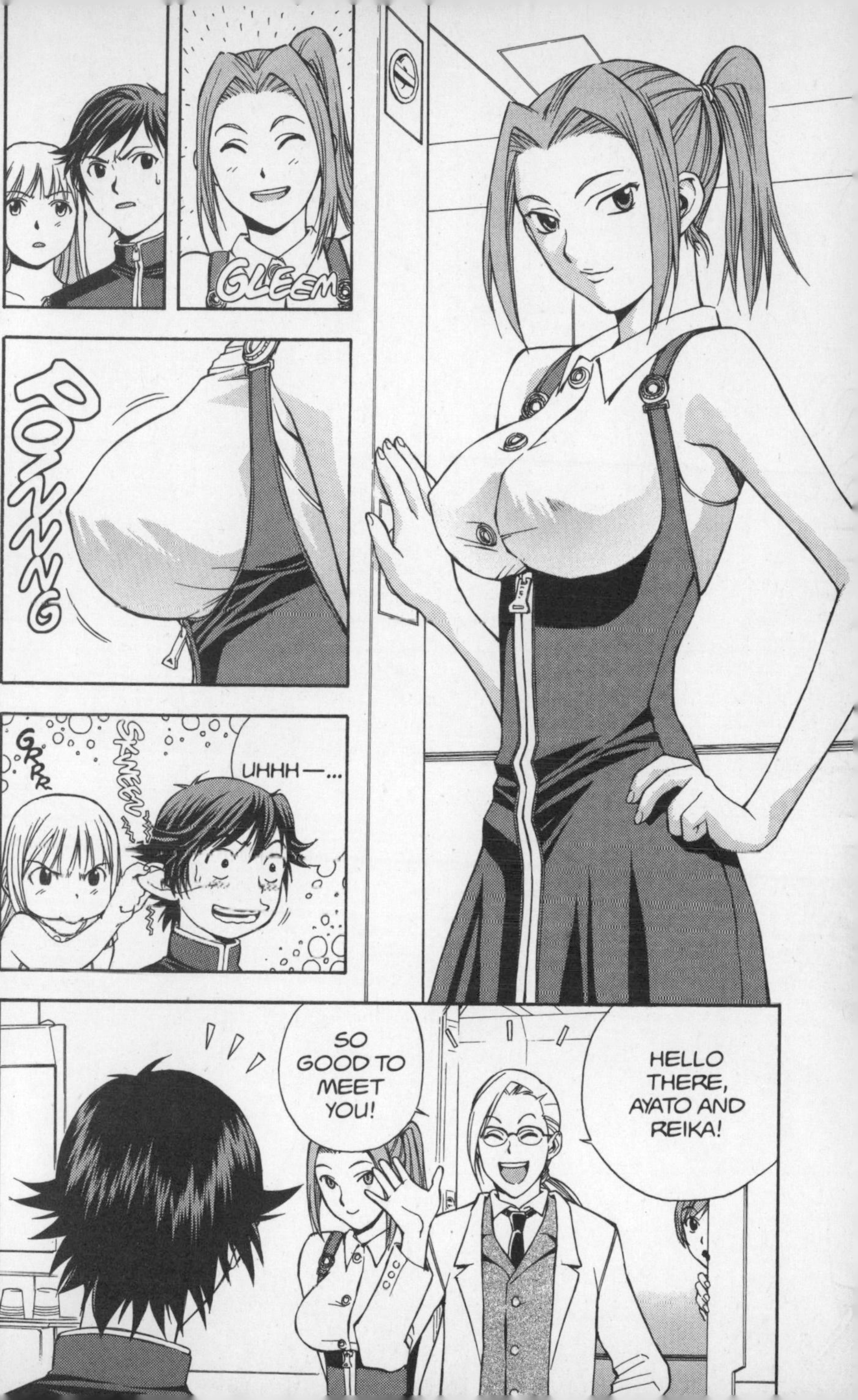
GLEEM
POINNNG
UHHH—...
GRRR
SKWEEZE
HELLO THERE, AYATO AND REIKA!
SO GOOD TO MEET YOU!

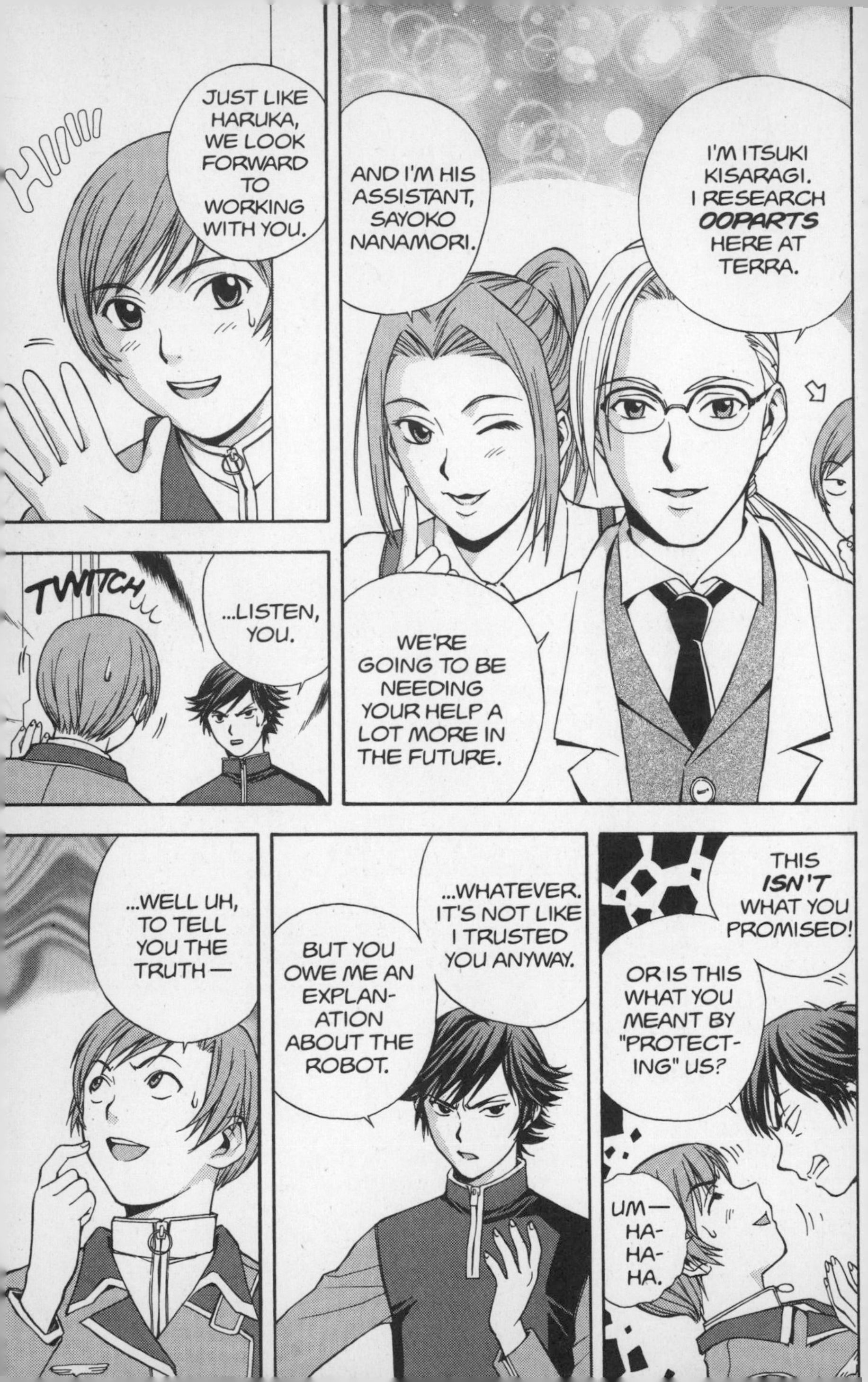
I'M ITSUKI KISARAGI. I RESEARCH OOPARTS HERE AT TERRA.
AND I'M HIS ASSISTANT, SAYOKO NANAMORI.
WE'RE GOING TO BE NEEDING YOUR HELP A LOT MORE IN THE FUTURE.
JUST LIKE HARUKA, WE LOOK FORWARD TO WORKING WITH YOU.
TWITCH
...LISTEN, YOU.
THIS ISN'T WHAT YOU PROMISED!
OR IS THIS WHAT YOU MEANT BY "PROTECTING" US?
UM— HA-HA-HA.
...WHATEVER. IT'S NOT LIKE I TRUSTED YOU ANYWAY.
BUT YOU OWE ME AN EXPLANATION ABOUT THE ROBOT.
...WELL UH, TO TELL YOU THE TRUTH—

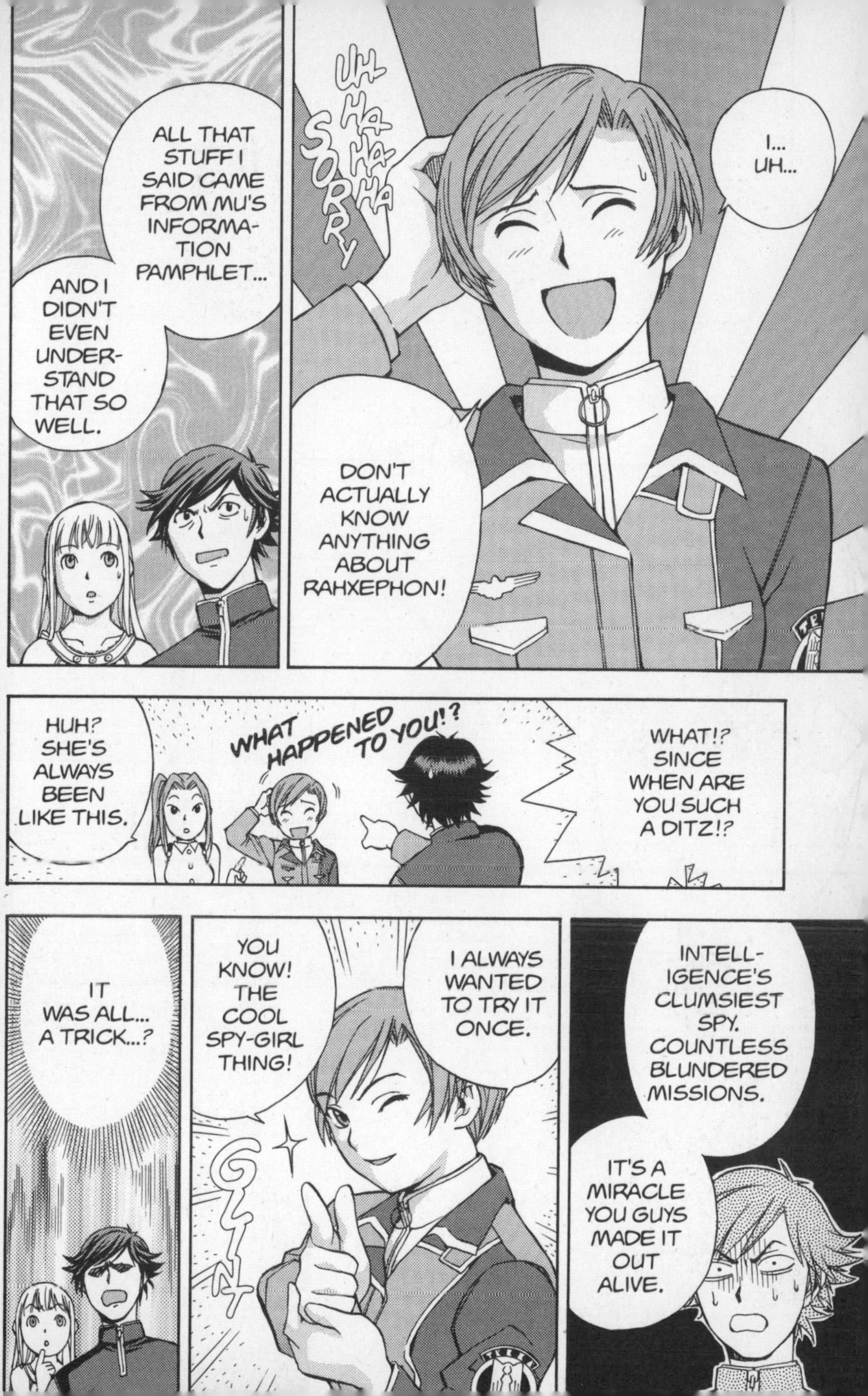

I... UH...
UH HA HA HA
SORRY
DON'T ACTUALLY KNOW ANYTHING ABOUT RAHXEPHON!
ALL THAT STUFF I SAID CAME FROM MU'S INFORMATION PAMPHLET...
AND I DIDN'T EVEN UNDERSTAND THAT SO WELL.
WHAT!? SINCE WHEN ARE YOU SUCH A DITZ!?
WHAT HAPPENED TO YOU!?
HUH? SHE'S ALWAYS BEEN LIKE THIS.
INTELLIGENCE'S CLUMSIEST SPY. COUNTLESS BLUNDERED MISSIONS.
IT'S A MIRACLE YOU GUYS MADE IT OUT ALIVE.
I ALWAYS WANTED TO TRY IT ONCE.
YOU KNOW! THE COOL SPY-GIRL THING!
GLINT
IT WAS ALL... A TRICK...?

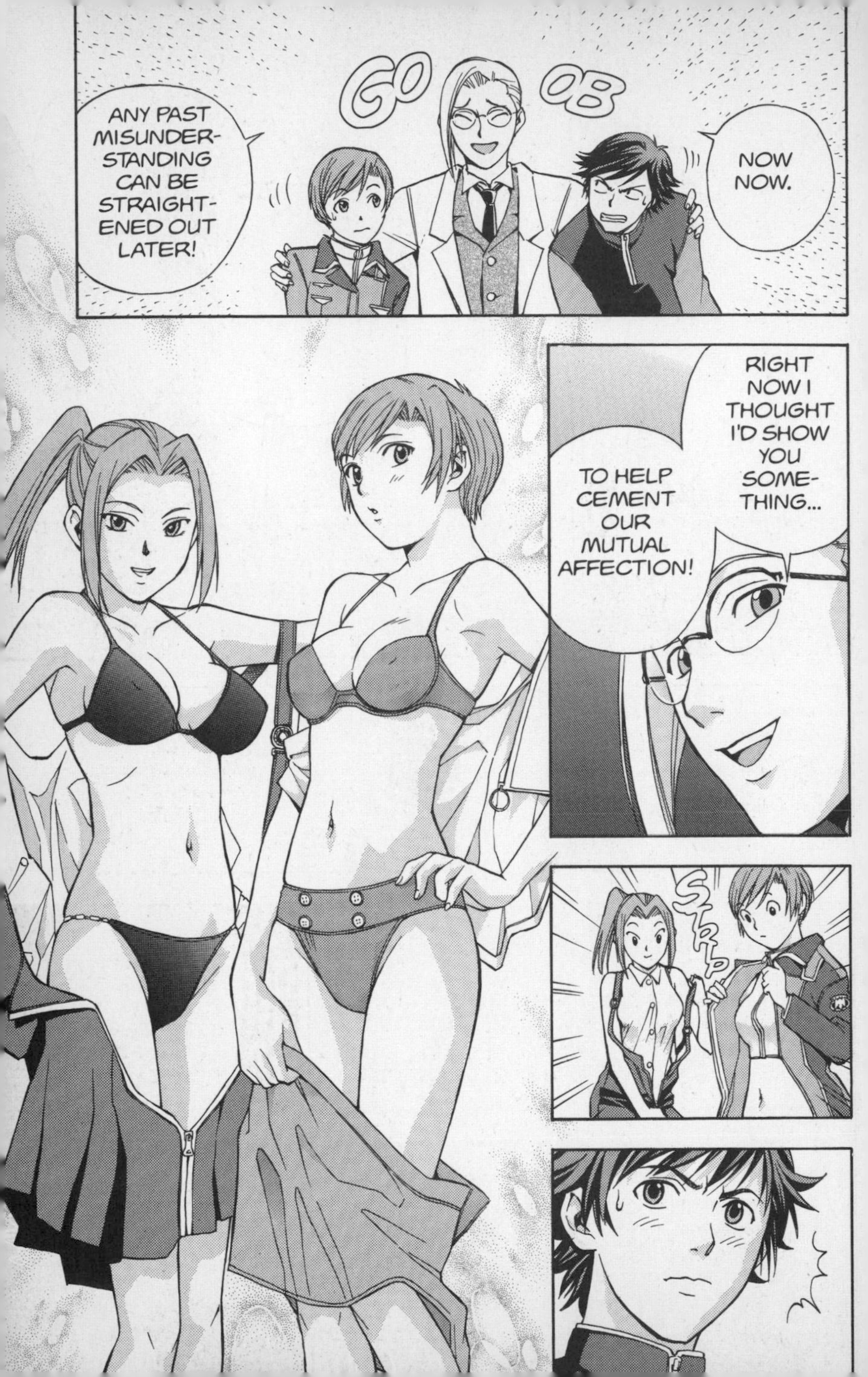
NOW NOW.
GO OB
ANY PAST MISUNDER-STANDING CAN BE STRAIGHT-ENED OUT LATER!
RIGHT NOW I THOUGHT I'D SHOW YOU SOME-THING...
TO HELP CEMENT OUR MUTUAL AFFECTION!
STRIP

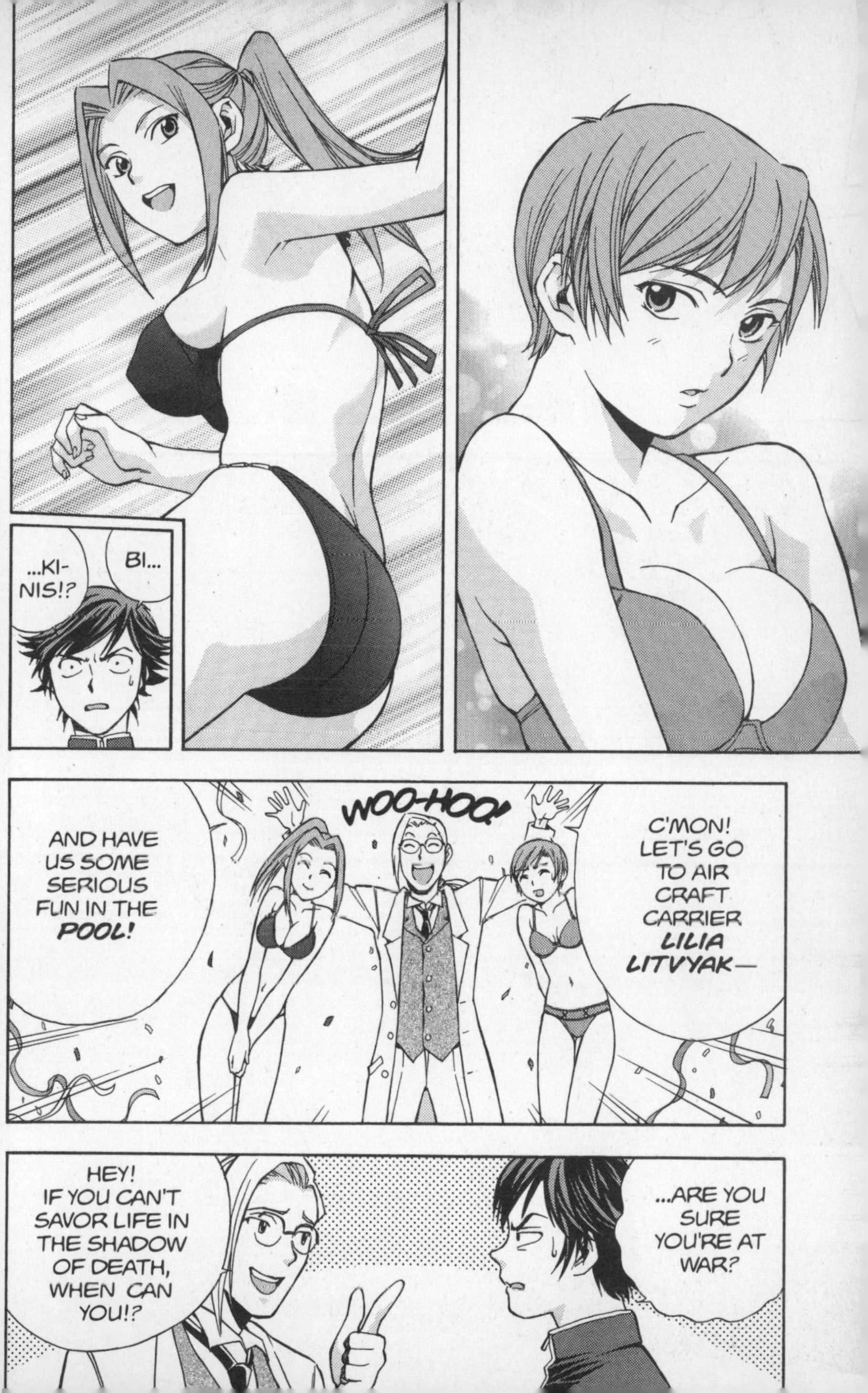
BI...
...KI-NIS!?
C'MON! LET'S GO TO AIR CRAFT CARRIER *LILIA LITVYAK*—
WOO-HOO!
AND HAVE US SOME SERIOUS FUN IN THE *POOL!*
...ARE YOU SURE YOU'RE AT WAR?
HEY! IF YOU CAN'T SAVOR LIFE IN THE SHADOW OF DEATH, WHEN CAN YOU!?

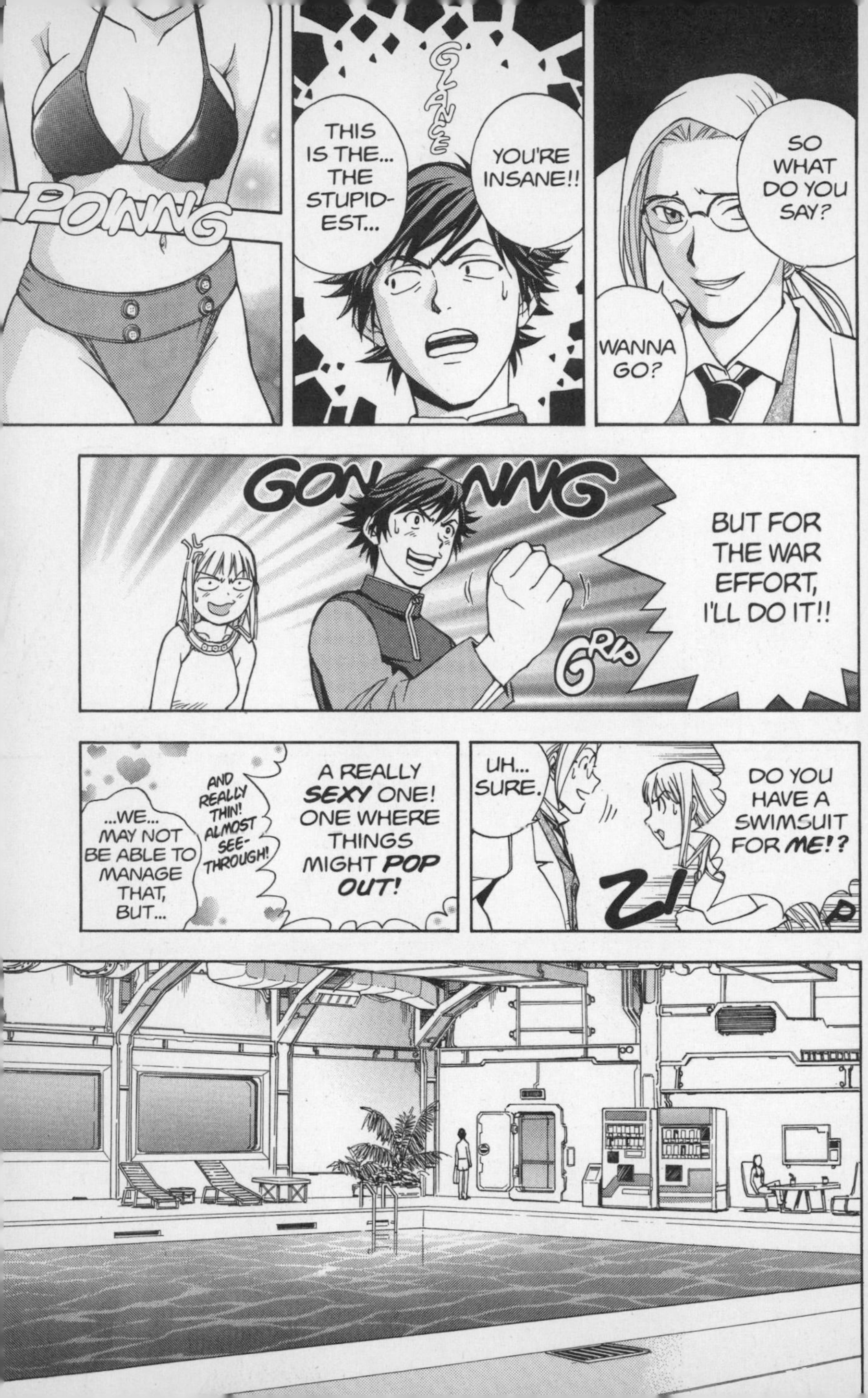
SO WHAT DO YOU SAY?
WANNA GO?
GLANCE
YOU'RE INSANE!!
THIS IS THE... THE STUPID-EST...
POINNG
BUT FOR THE WAR EFFORT, I'LL DO IT!!
GRIP
DO YOU HAVE A SWIMSUIT FOR ME!?
UH... SURE.
A REALLY SEXY ONE! ONE WHERE THINGS MIGHT POP OUT!
AND REALLY THIN! ALMOST SEE-THROUGH!
...WE... MAY NOT BE ABLE TO MANAGE THAT, BUT...

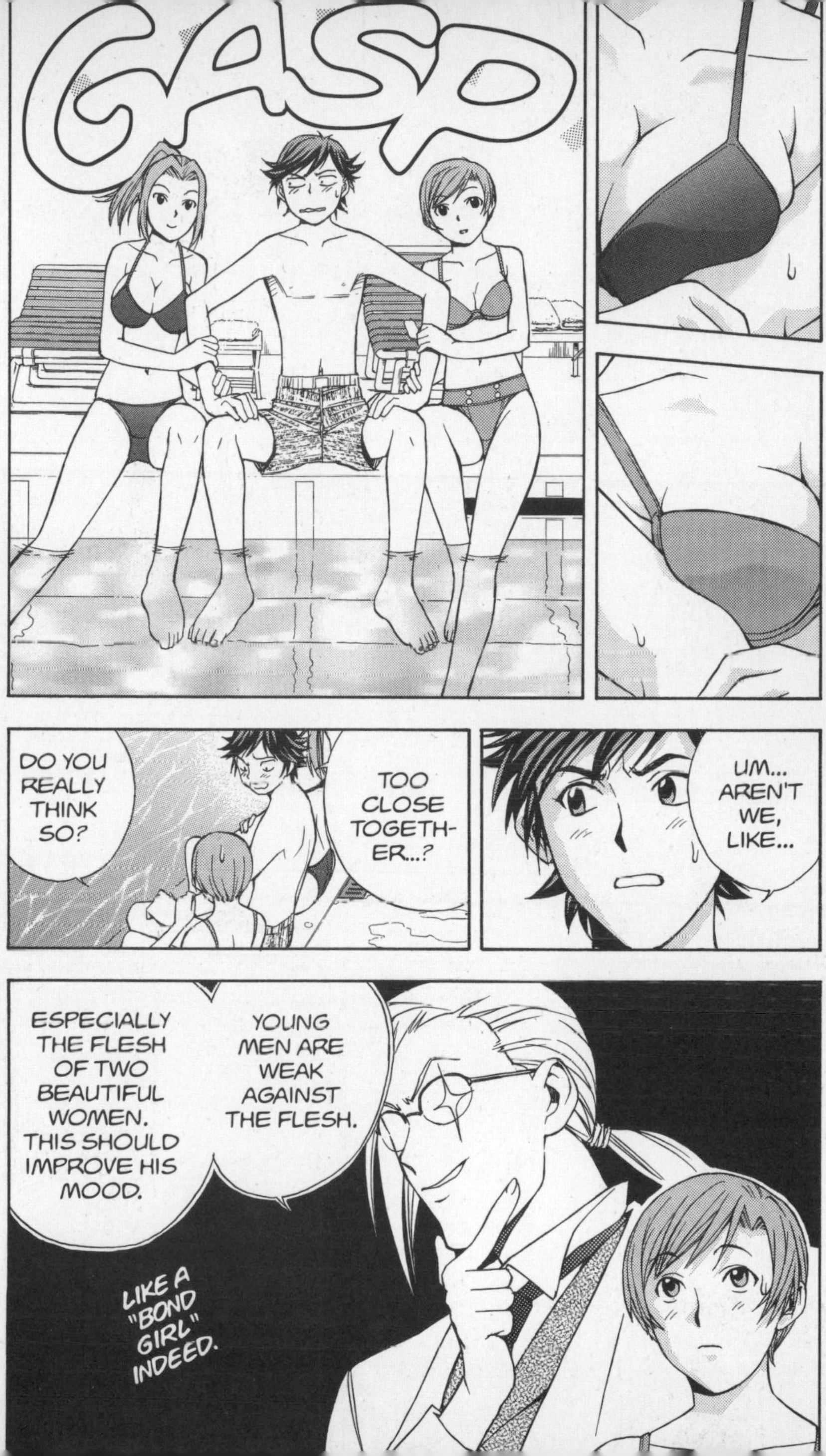
GASP
UM... AREN'T WE, LIKE...
TOO CLOSE TOGETH-ER...?
DO YOU REALLY THINK SO?
YOUNG MEN ARE WEAK AGAINST THE FLESH.
ESPECIALLY THE FLESH OF TWO BEAUTIFUL WOMEN. THIS SHOULD IMPROVE HIS MOOD.
LIKE A "BOND GIRL" INDEED.

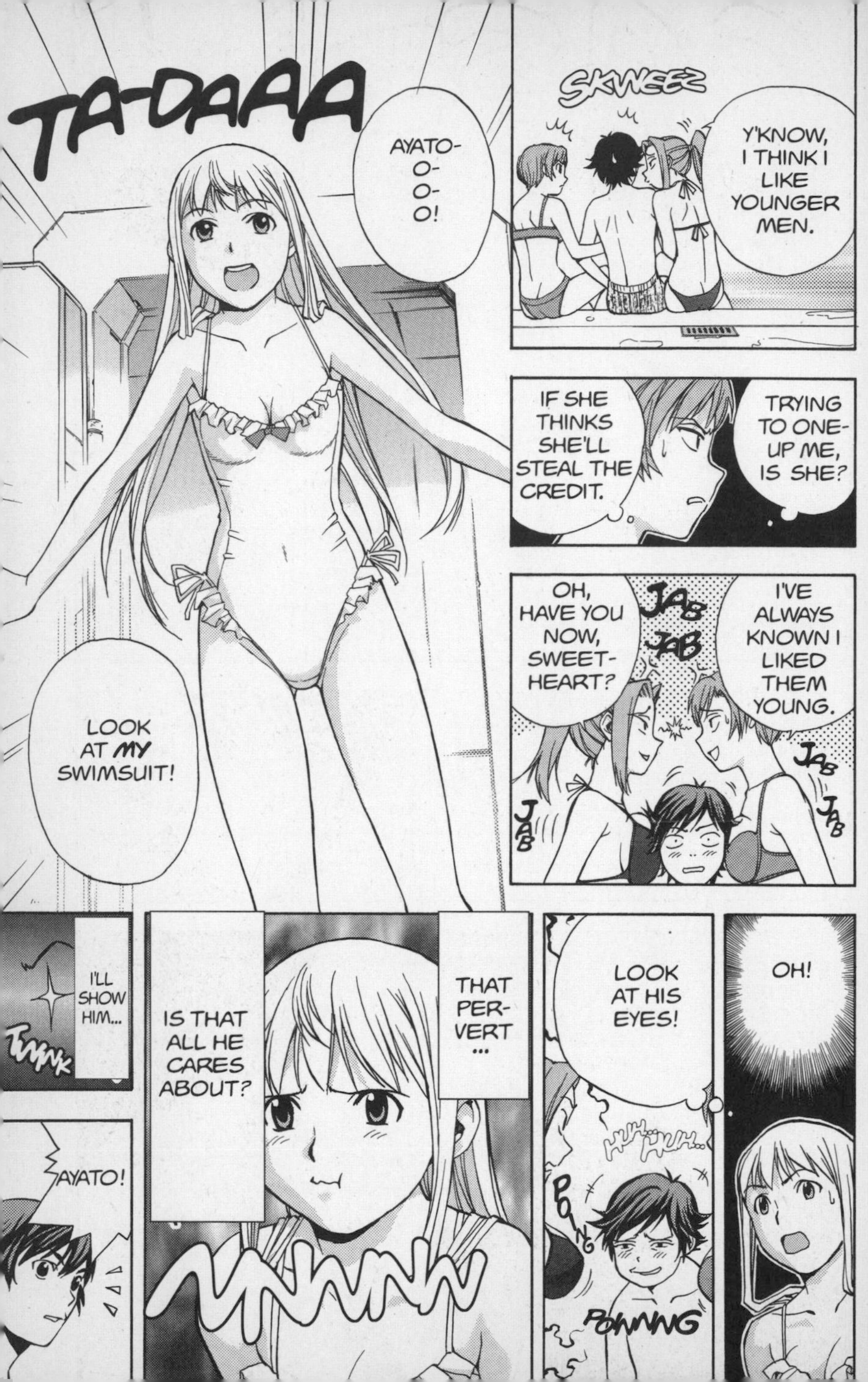
SKWEEZ
Y'KNOW, I THINK I LIKE YOUNGER MEN.
TRYING TO ONE-UP ME, IS SHE?
IF SHE THINKS SHE'LL STEAL THE CREDIT.
I'VE ALWAYS KNOWN I LIKED THEM YOUNG.
JAB JAB
OH, HAVE YOU NOW, SWEET-HEART?
JAB JAB
JAB
TA-DAAA
AYATO-O-O-O-O!
LOOK AT *MY* SWIMSUIT!
OH!
LOOK AT HIS EYES!
HUH... HUH...
POING
POINNG
THAT PER-VERT...
IS THAT ALL HE CARES ABOUT?
MNNN
I'LL SHOW HIM...
TWINK
AYATO!

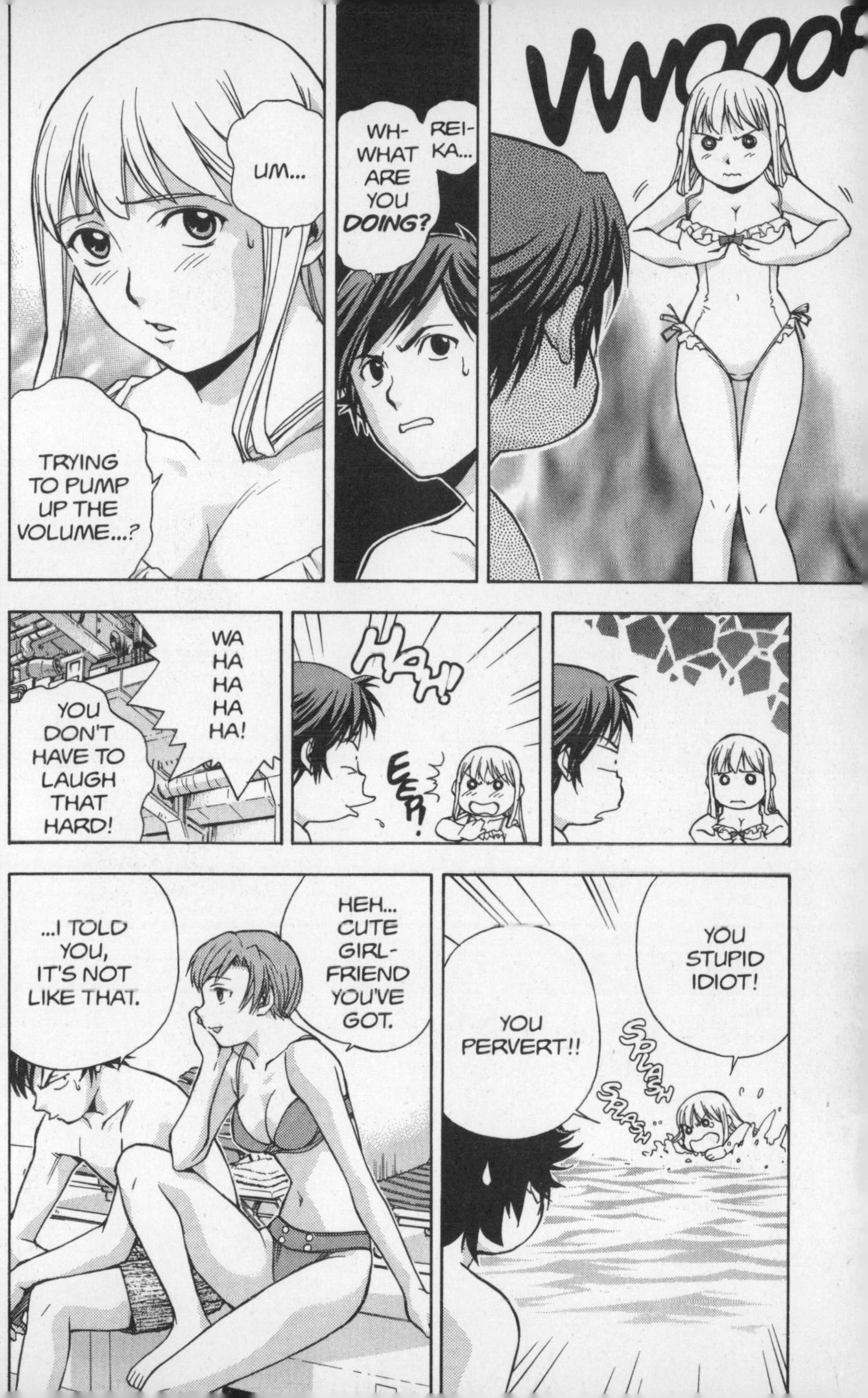
VWOOOF
REI-KA...
WH-WHAT ARE YOU DOING?
UM...
TRYING TO PUMP UP THE VOLUME...?
HAH!
EEER!
WA HA HA HA HA!
YOU DON'T HAVE TO LAUGH THAT HARD!
YOU STUPID IDIOT!
YOU PERVERT!!
SPLASH
SPLASH
HEH... CUTE GIRL-FRIEND YOU'VE GOT.
...I TOLD YOU, IT'S NOT LIKE THAT.

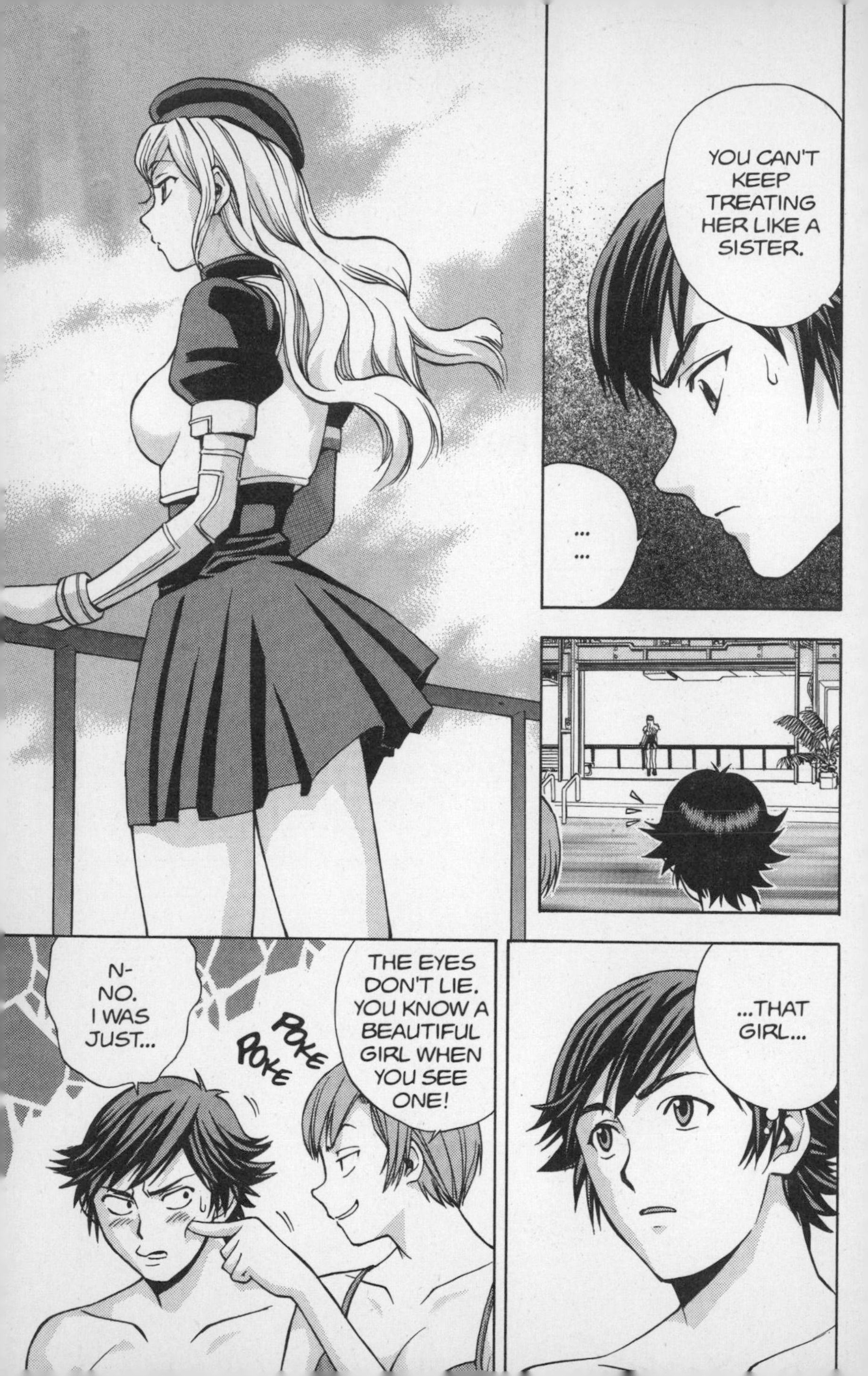
YOU CAN'T KEEP TREATING HER LIKE A SISTER.
......
...THAT GIRL...
THE EYES DON'T LIE. YOU KNOW A BEAUTIFUL GIRL WHEN YOU SEE ONE!
POKE POKE
N- NO. I WAS JUST...

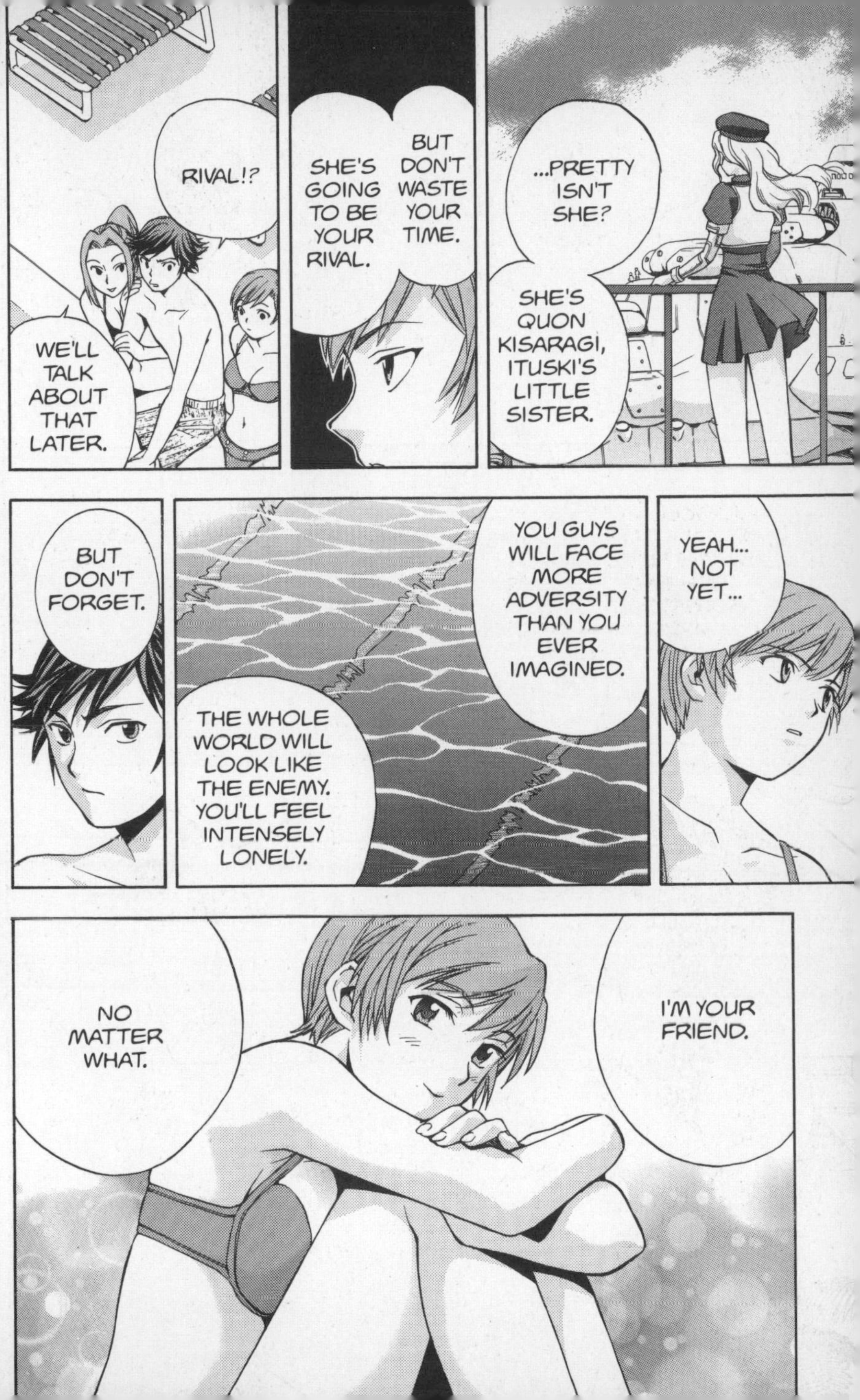
...PRETTY ISN'T SHE?
SHE'S QUON KISARAGI, ITUSKI'S LITTLE SISTER.
BUT DON'T WASTE YOUR TIME.
SHE'S GOING TO BE YOUR RIVAL.
RIVAL!?
WE'LL TALK ABOUT THAT LATER.
YEAH... NOT YET...
YOU GUYS WILL FACE MORE ADVERSITY THAN YOU EVER IMAGINED.
THE WHOLE WORLD WILL LOOK LIKE THE ENEMY. YOU'LL FEEL INTENSELY LONELY.
BUT DON'T FORGET.
I'M YOUR FRIEND.
NO MATTER WHAT.

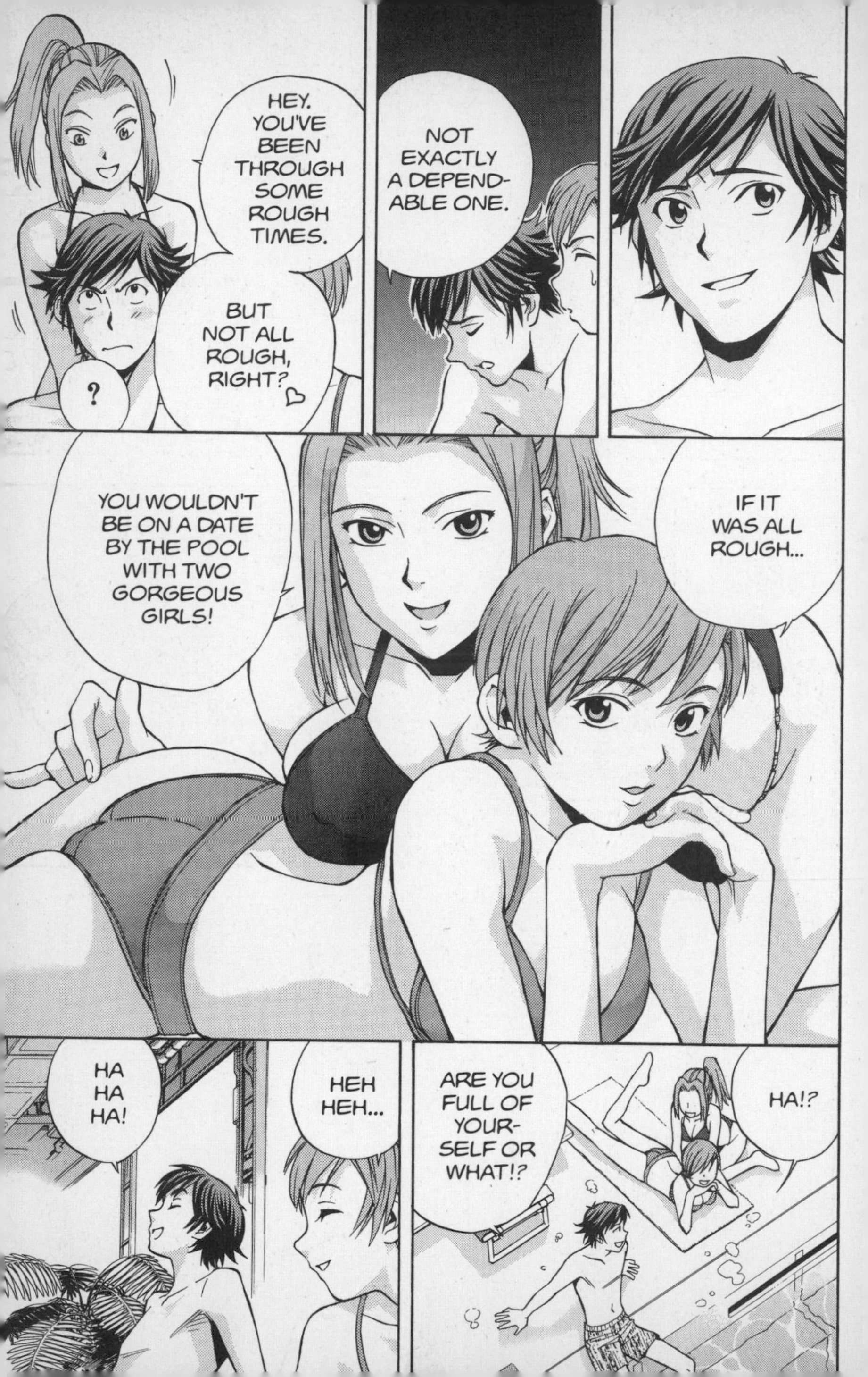
NOT EXACTLY A DEPENDABLE ONE.
HEY. YOU'VE BEEN THROUGH SOME ROUGH TIMES.
BUT NOT ALL ROUGH, RIGHT? ♡
?
IF IT WAS ALL ROUGH...
YOU WOULDN'T BE ON A DATE BY THE POOL WITH TWO GORGEOUS GIRLS!
HA!?
ARE YOU FULL OF YOURSELF OR WHAT!?
HEH HEH...
HA HA HA!

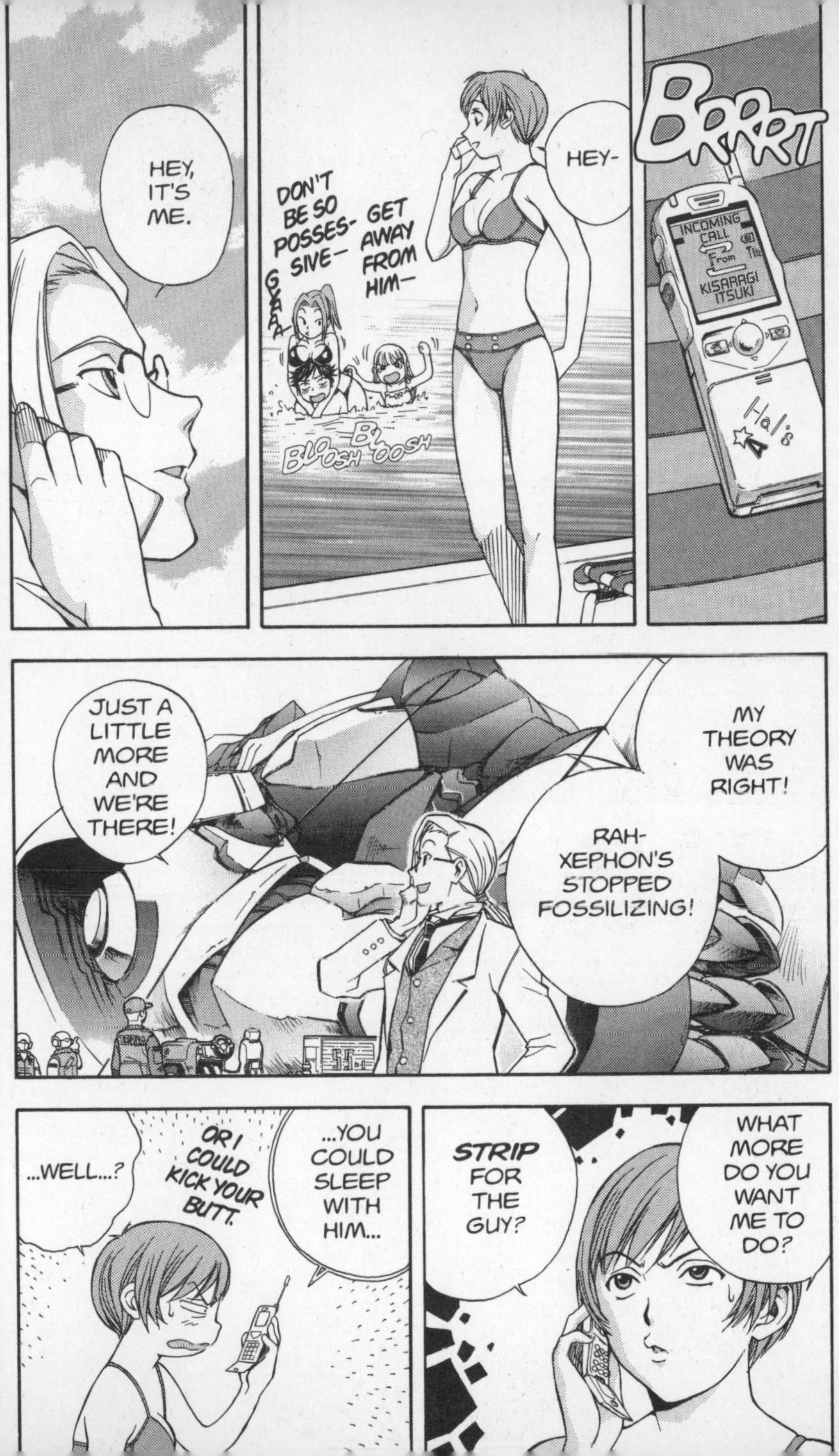
BRRRT
INCOMING CALL From KISARAGI ITSUKI
Hal's
HEY-
DON'T BE SO POSSES-SIVE-
GET AWAY FROM HIM-
BLOOSH BLOOSH
HEY, IT'S ME.
MY THEORY WAS RIGHT!
RAH-XEPHON'S STOPPED FOSSILIZING!
JUST A LITTLE MORE AND WE'RE THERE!
WHAT MORE DO YOU WANT ME TO DO?
STRIP FOR THE GUY?
...YOU COULD SLEEP WITH HIM...
OR I COULD KICK YOUR BUTT.
...WELL...?

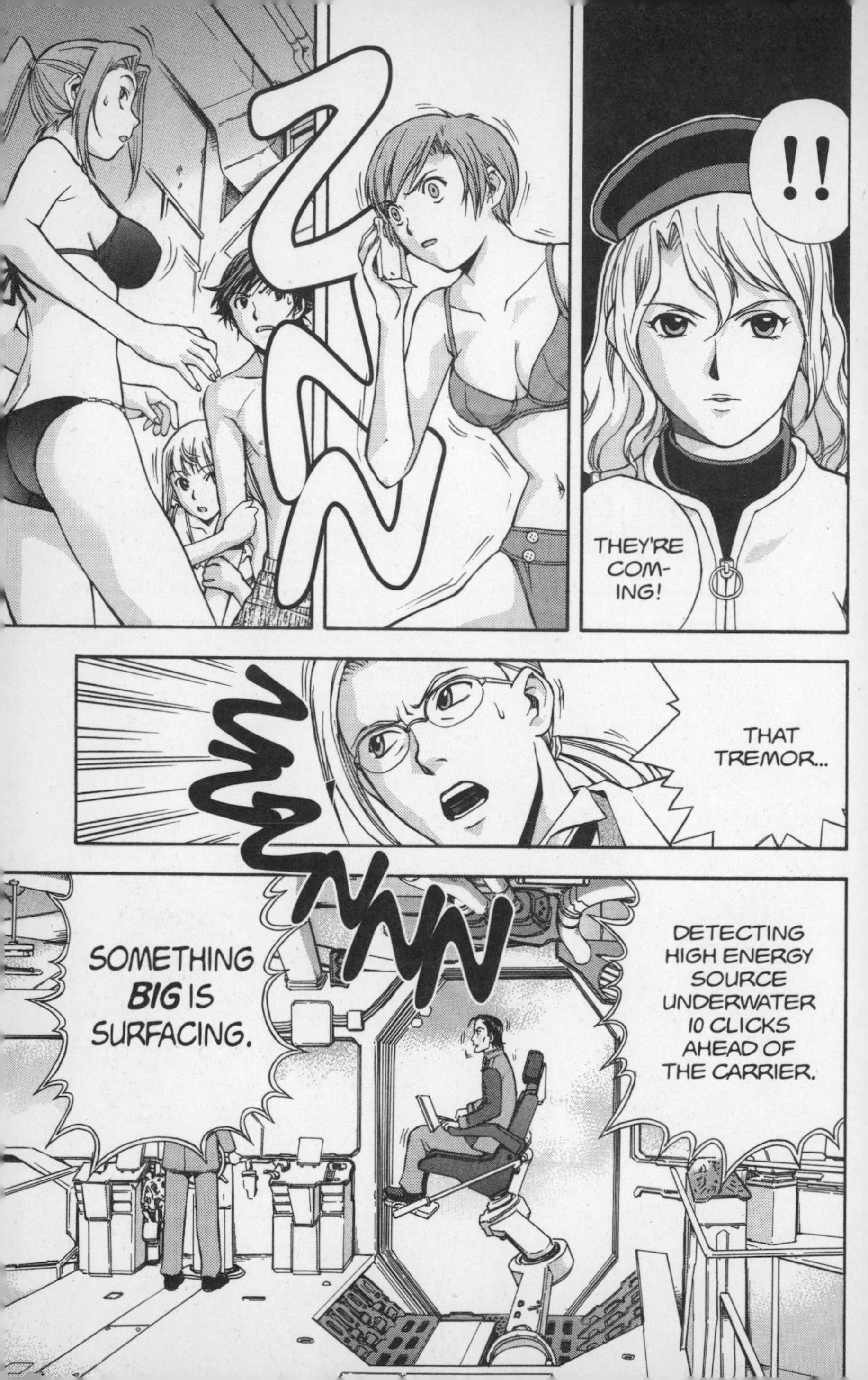
!!
THEY'RE COM-ING!
THAT TREMOR...
DETECTING HIGH ENERGY SOURCE UNDERWATER 10 CLICKS AHEAD OF THE CARRIER.
SOMETHING BIG IS SURFACING.

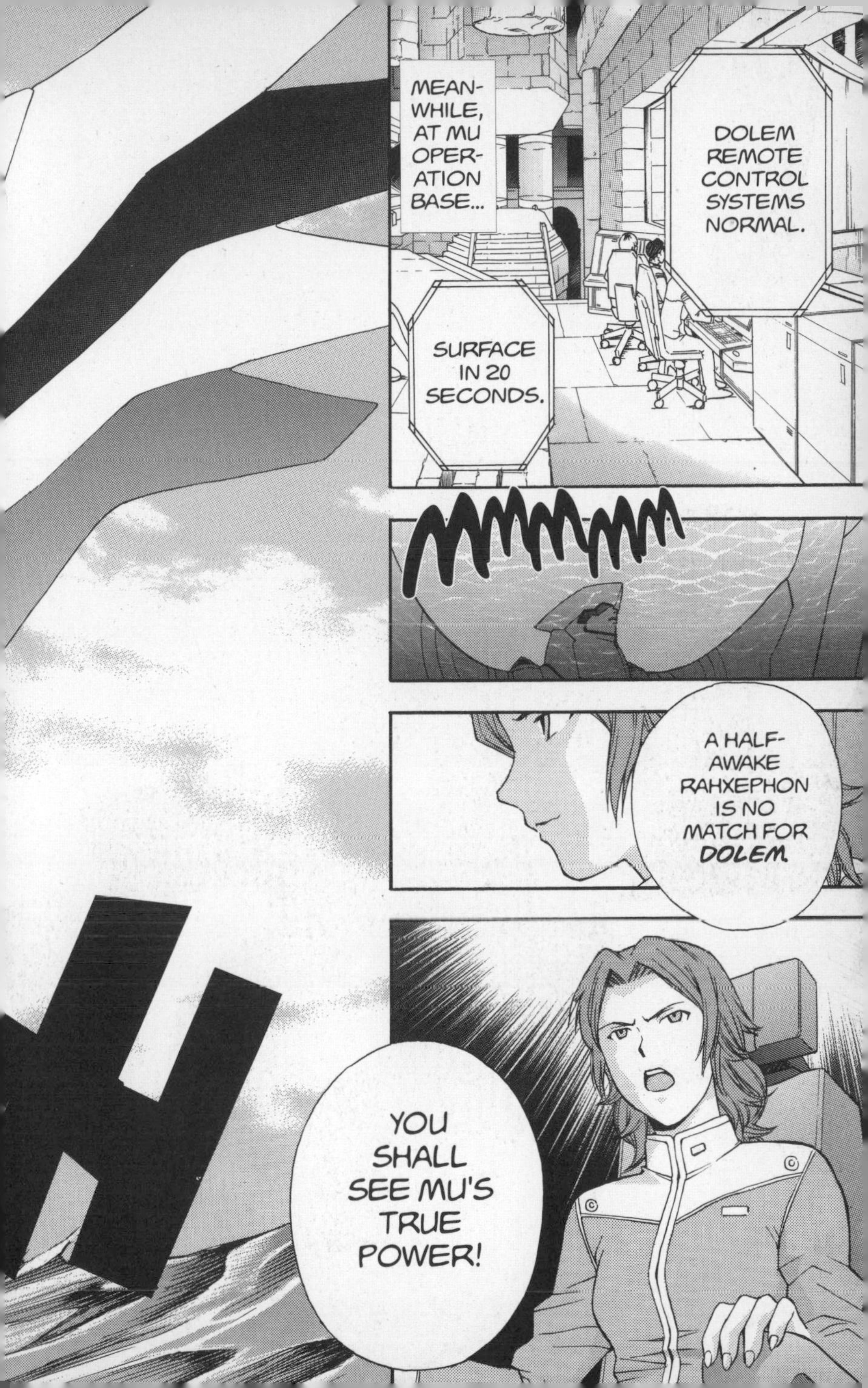
MEAN-WHILE, AT MU OPER-ATION BASE...
DOLEM REMOTE CONTROL SYSTEMS NORMAL.
SURFACE IN 20 SECONDS.
A HALF-AWAKE RAHXEPHON IS NO MATCH FOR **DOLEM**.
YOU SHALL SEE MU'S TRUE POWER!

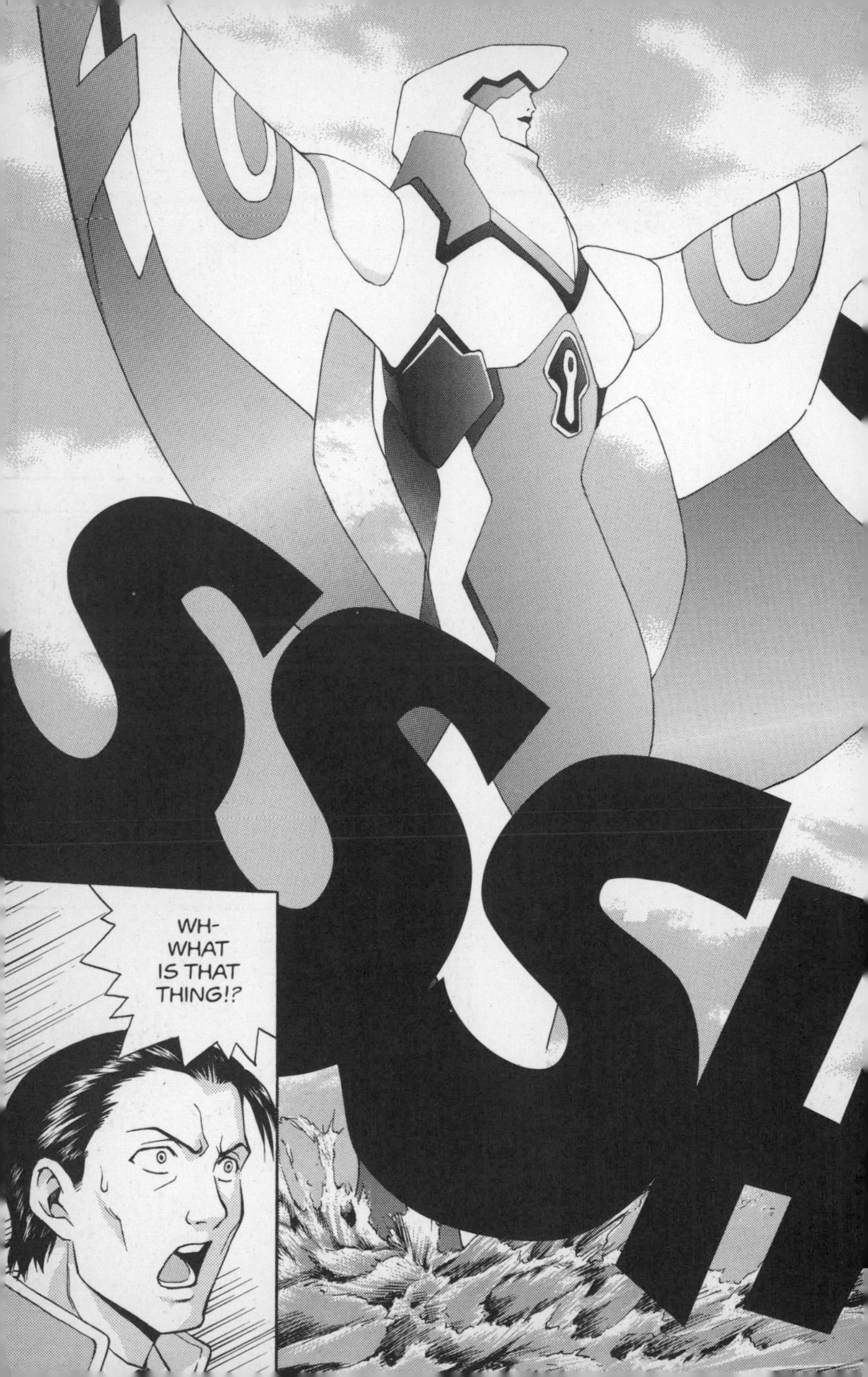
SSSH
WH- WHAT IS THAT THING!?

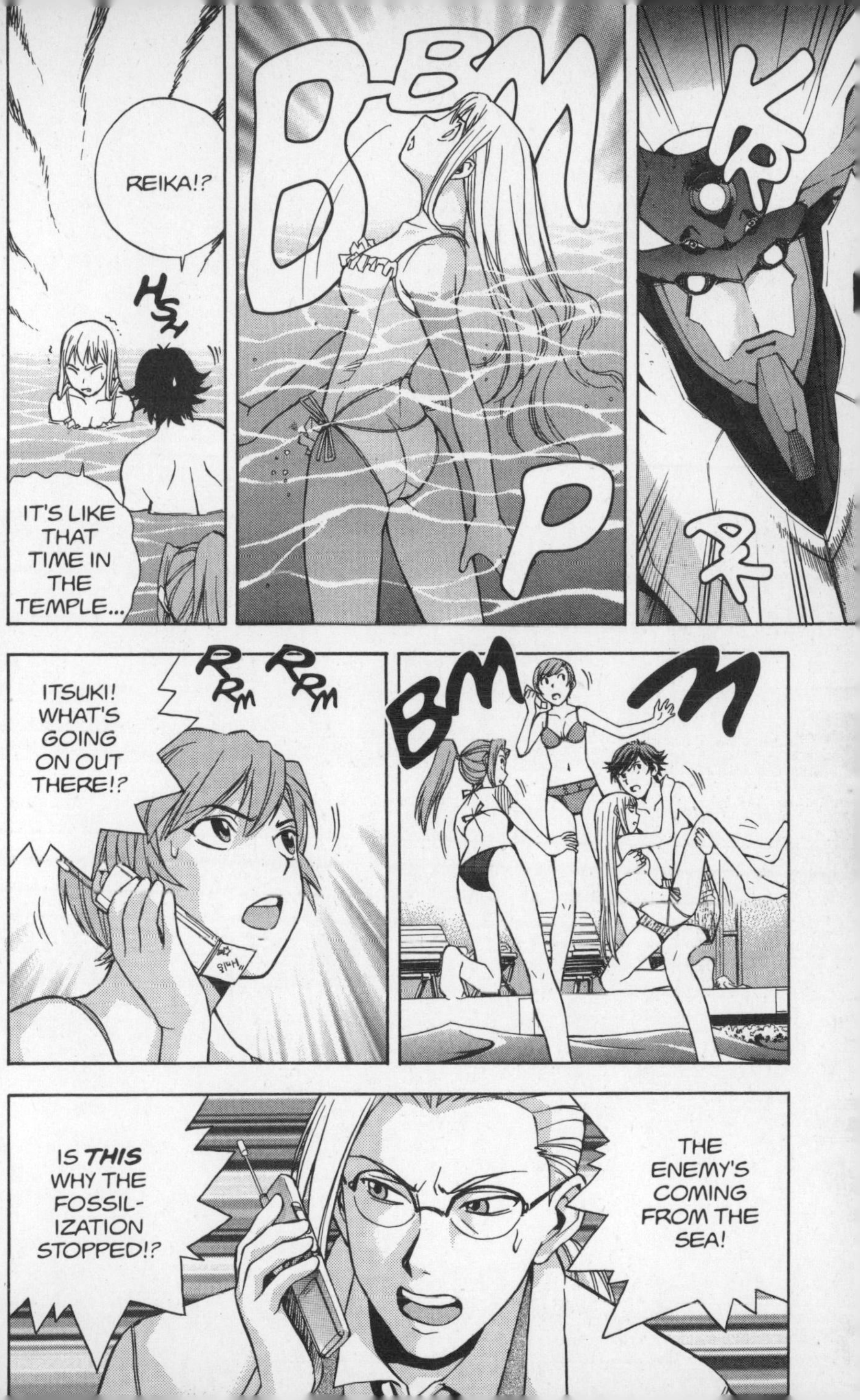

KRK
D-BM
P
REIKA!?
HSH
IT'S LIKE THAT TIME IN THE TEMPLE...
BM
M
ITSUKI! WHAT'S GOING ON OUT THERE!?
RRM RRM
THE ENEMY'S COMING FROM THE SEA!
IS THIS WHY THE FOSSIL-IZATION STOPPED!?

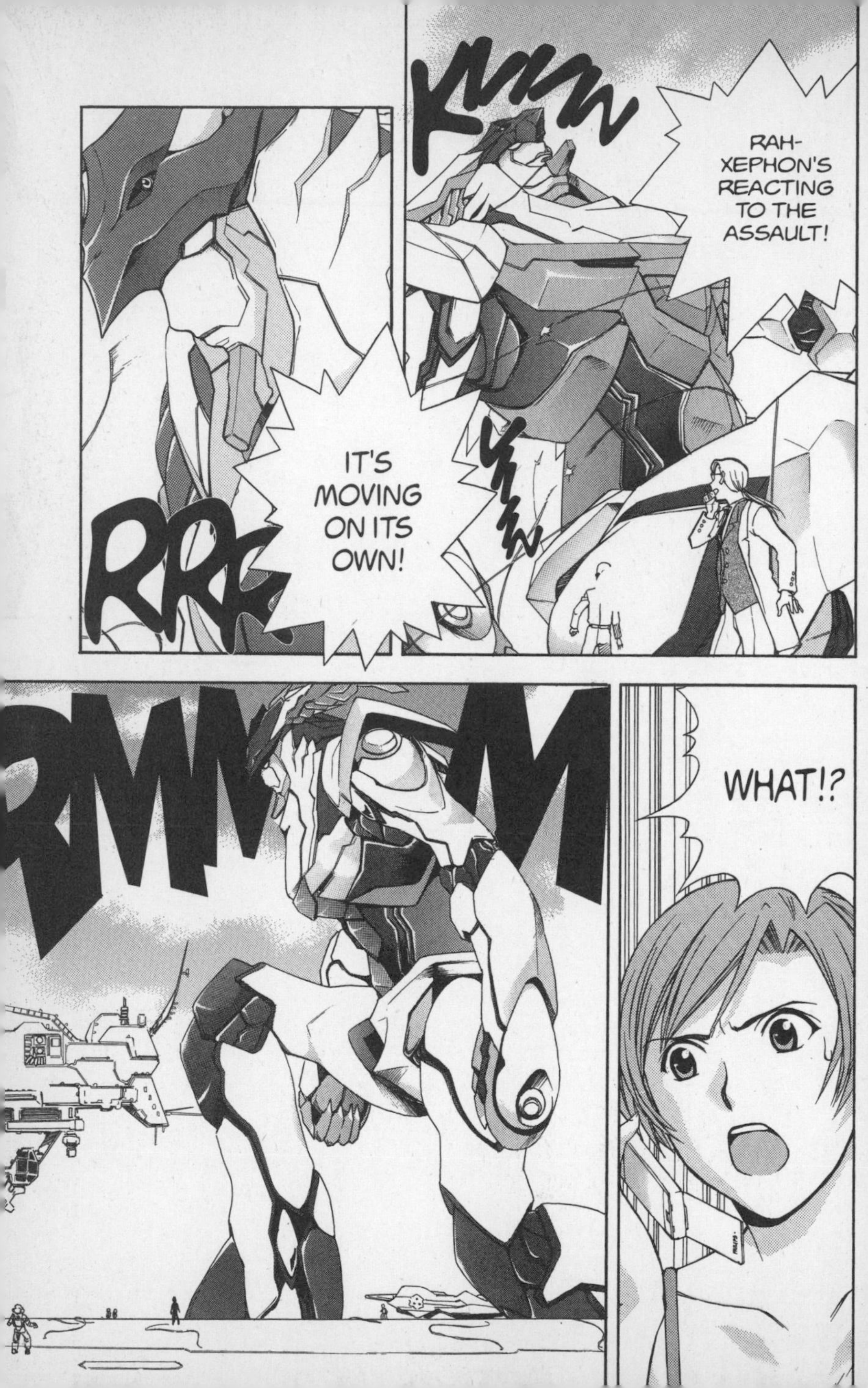
RAH-XEPHON'S REACTING TO THE ASSAULT!
IT'S MOVING ON ITS OWN!
WHAT!?

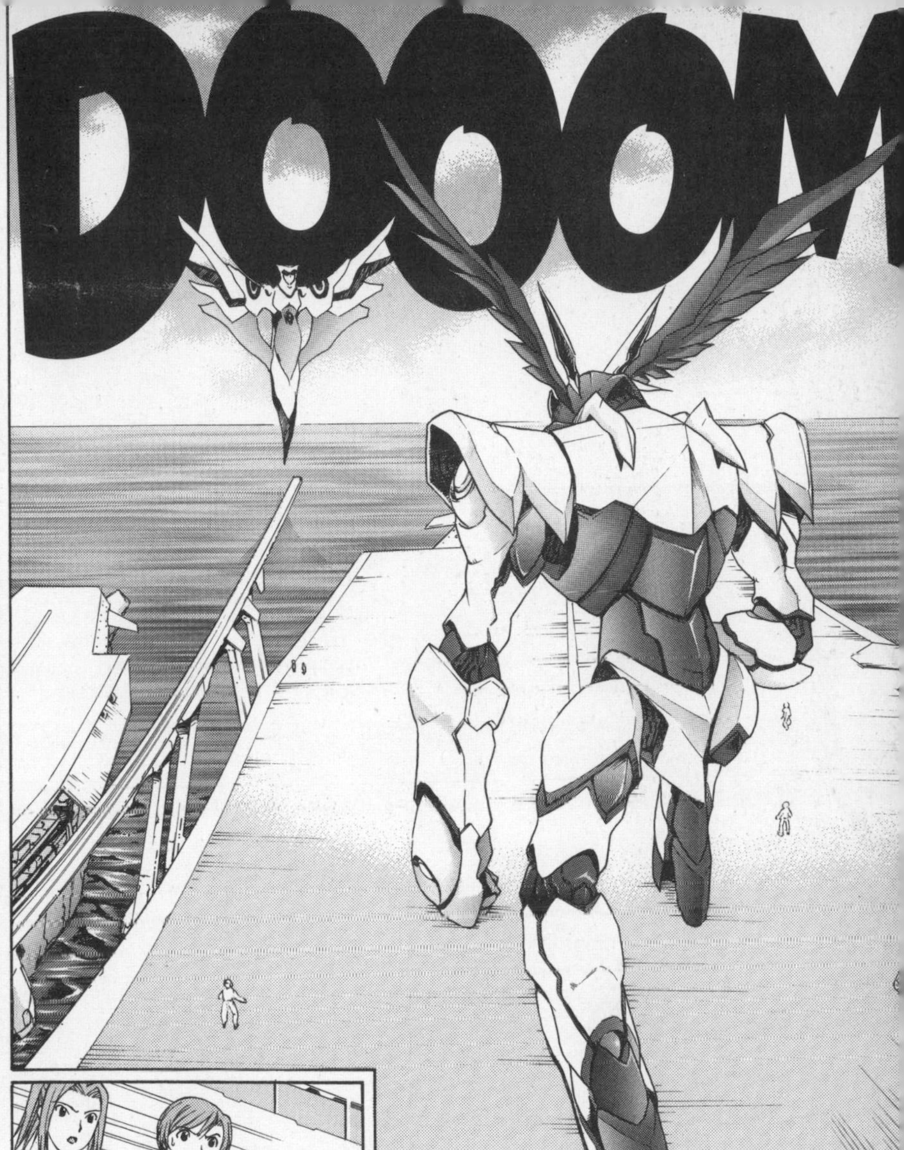
DOOOM
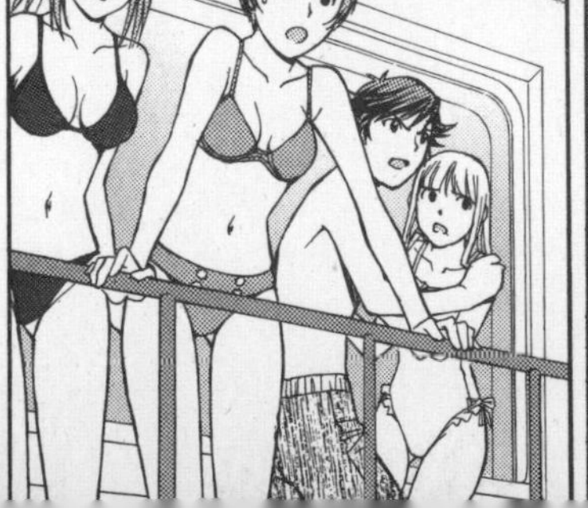

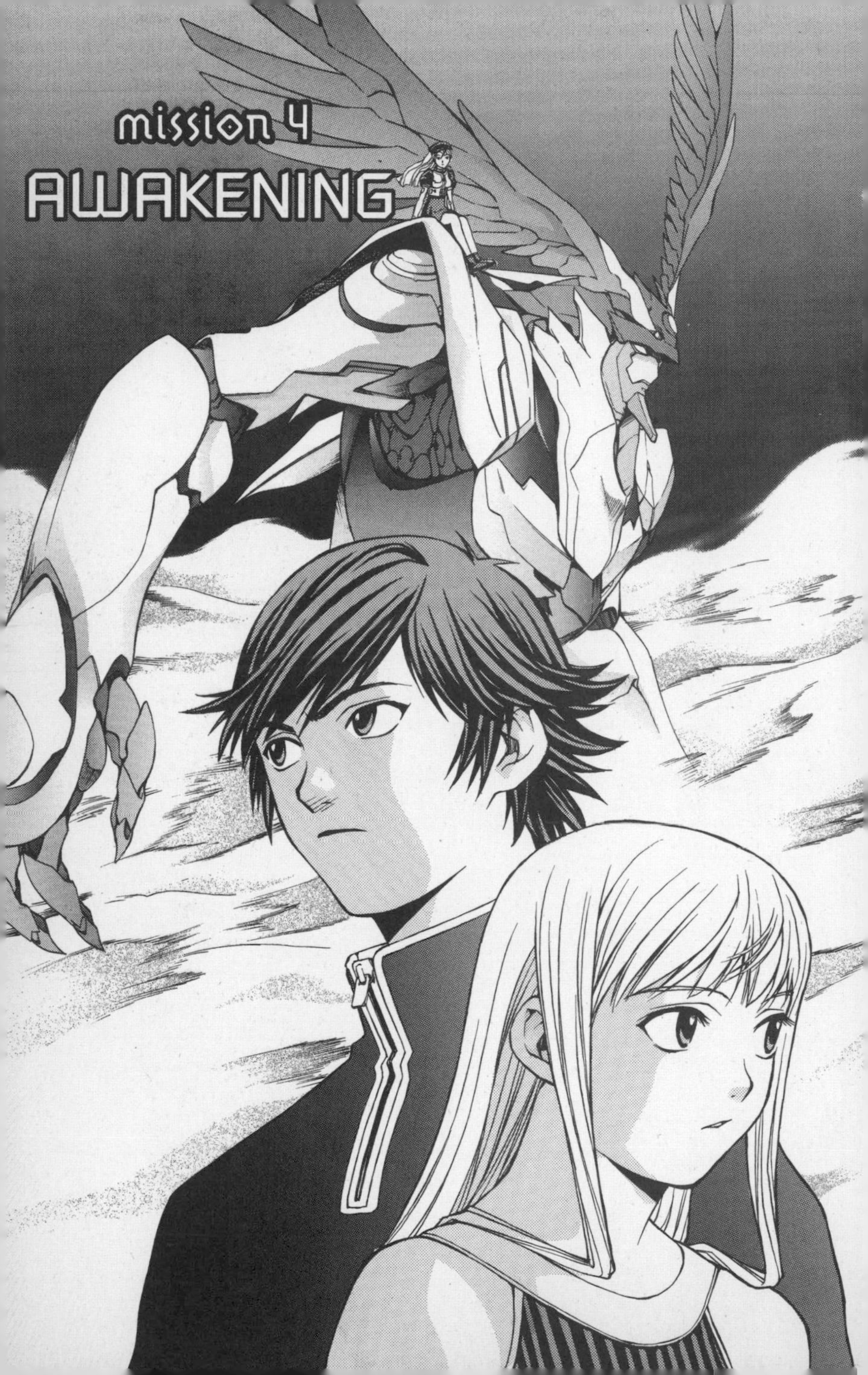
mission 4
AWAKENING

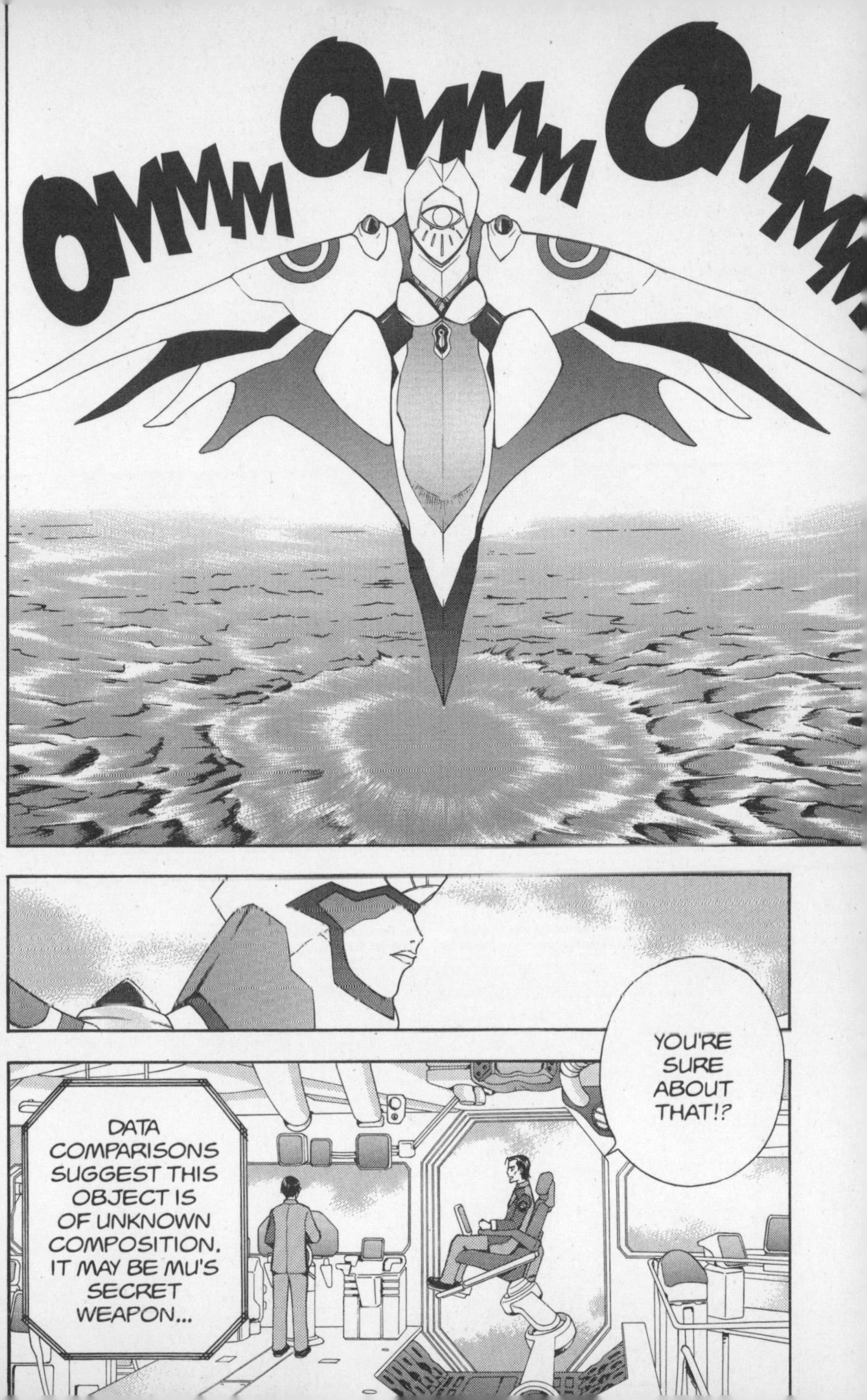
OMMM OMMM OMMM
DATA COMPARISONS SUGGEST THIS OBJECT IS OF UNKNOWN COMPOSITION. IT MAY BE MU'S SECRET WEAPON...
YOU'RE SURE ABOUT THAT!?

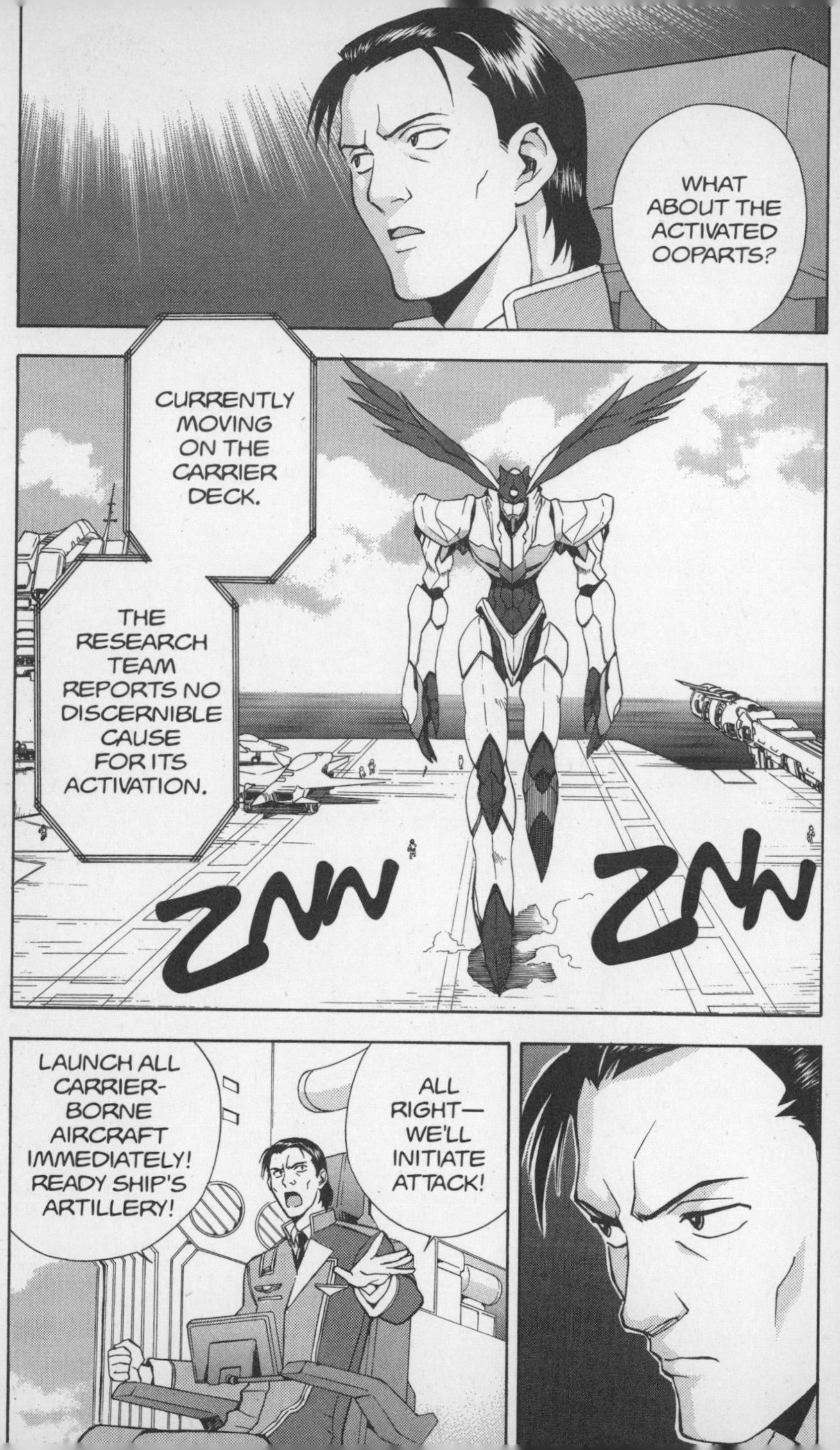
WHAT ABOUT THE ACTIVATED OOPARTS?
CURRENTLY MOVING ON THE CARRIER DECK.
THE RESEARCH TEAM REPORTS NO DISCERNIBLE CAUSE FOR ITS ACTIVATION.
ALL RIGHT— WE'LL INITIATE ATTACK!
LAUNCH ALL CARRIER-BORNE AIRCRAFT IMMEDIATELY! READY SHIP'S ARTILLERY!

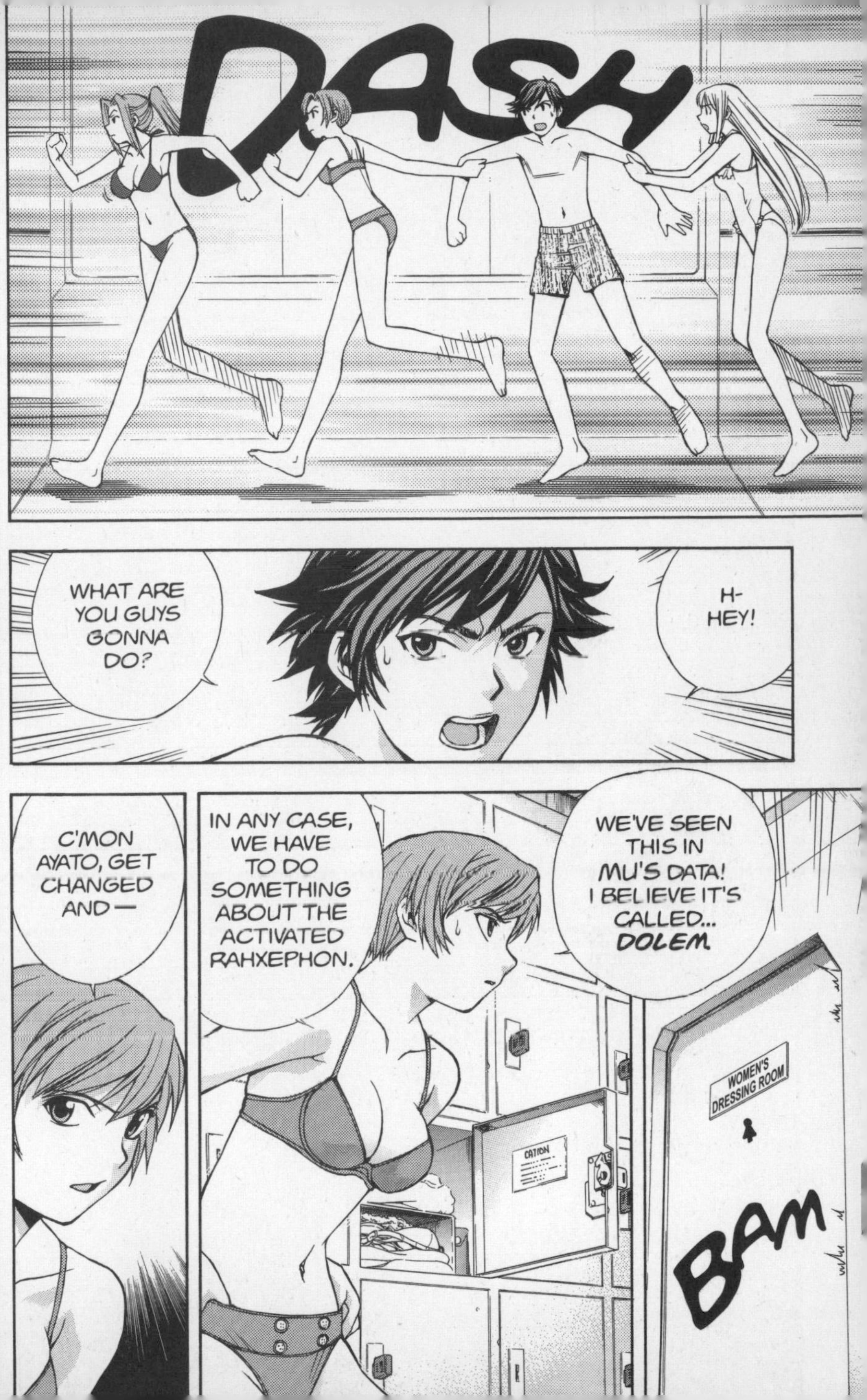
DASH
H- HEY!
WHAT ARE YOU GUYS GONNA DO?
WE'VE SEEN THIS IN MU'S DATA! I BELIEVE IT'S CALLED... **DOLEM**
IN ANY CASE, WE HAVE TO DO SOMETHING ABOUT THE ACTIVATED RAHXEPHON.
WOMEN'S DRESSING ROOM
CATION
BAM
C'MON AYATO, GET CHANGED AND—

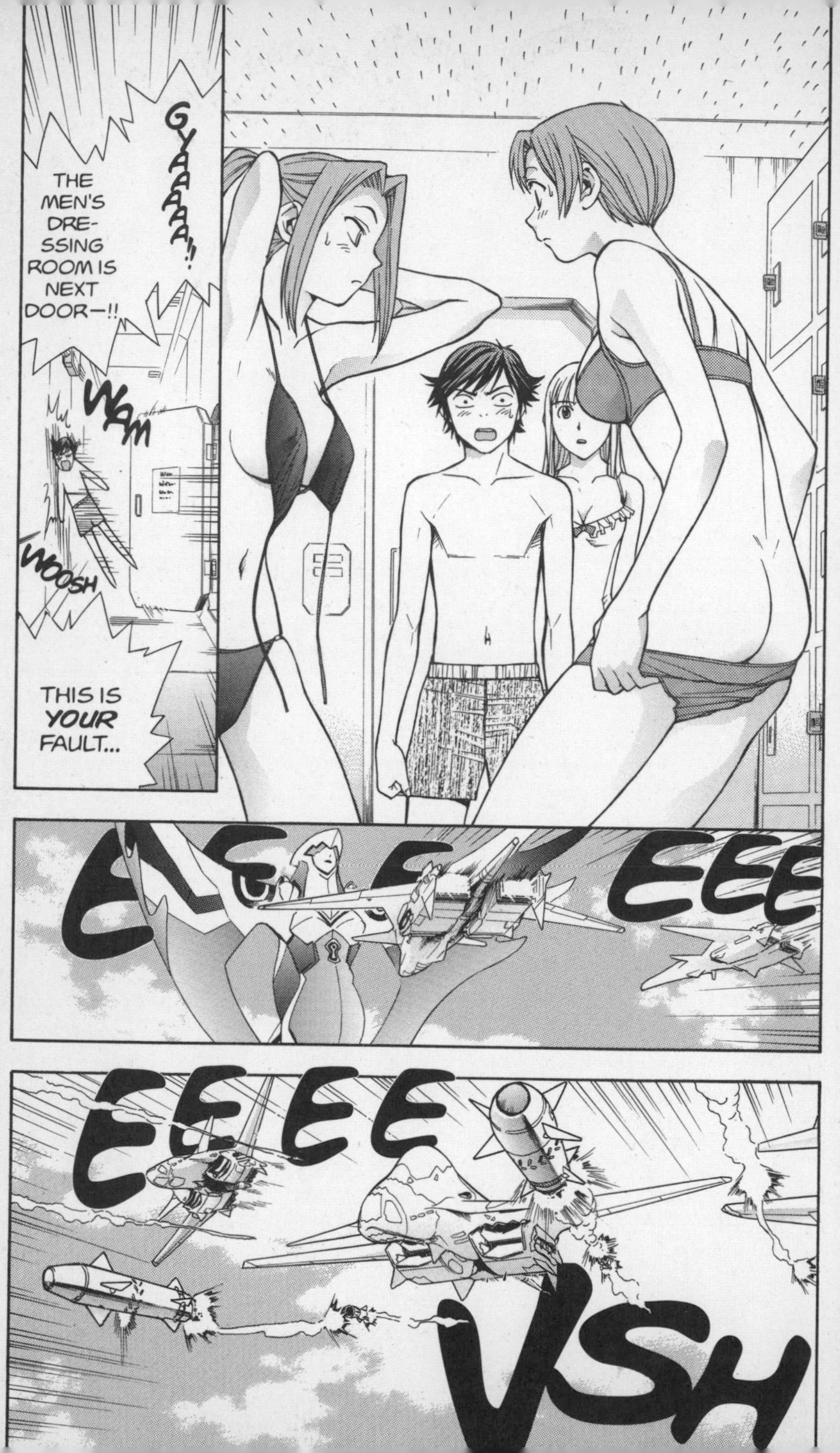
GYAAAAA!!
THE MEN'S DRE-SSING ROOM IS NEXT DOOR—!!
WAM
WOOSH
THIS IS *YOUR* FAULT...
EEEEEEE
EEEE
VSH

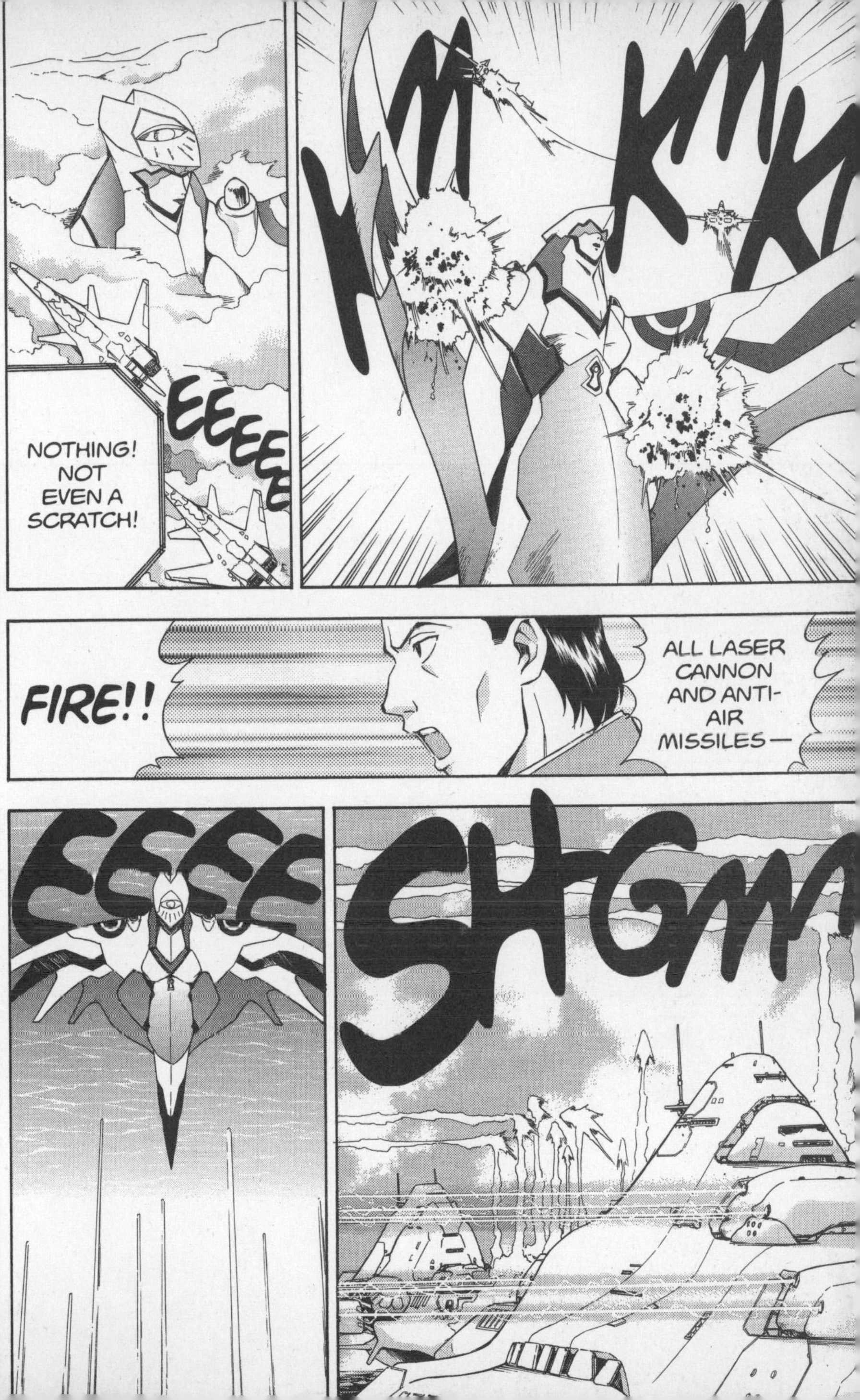
NOTHING! NOT EVEN A SCRATCH!
ALL LASER CANNON AND ANTI-AIR MISSILES—
FIRE!!

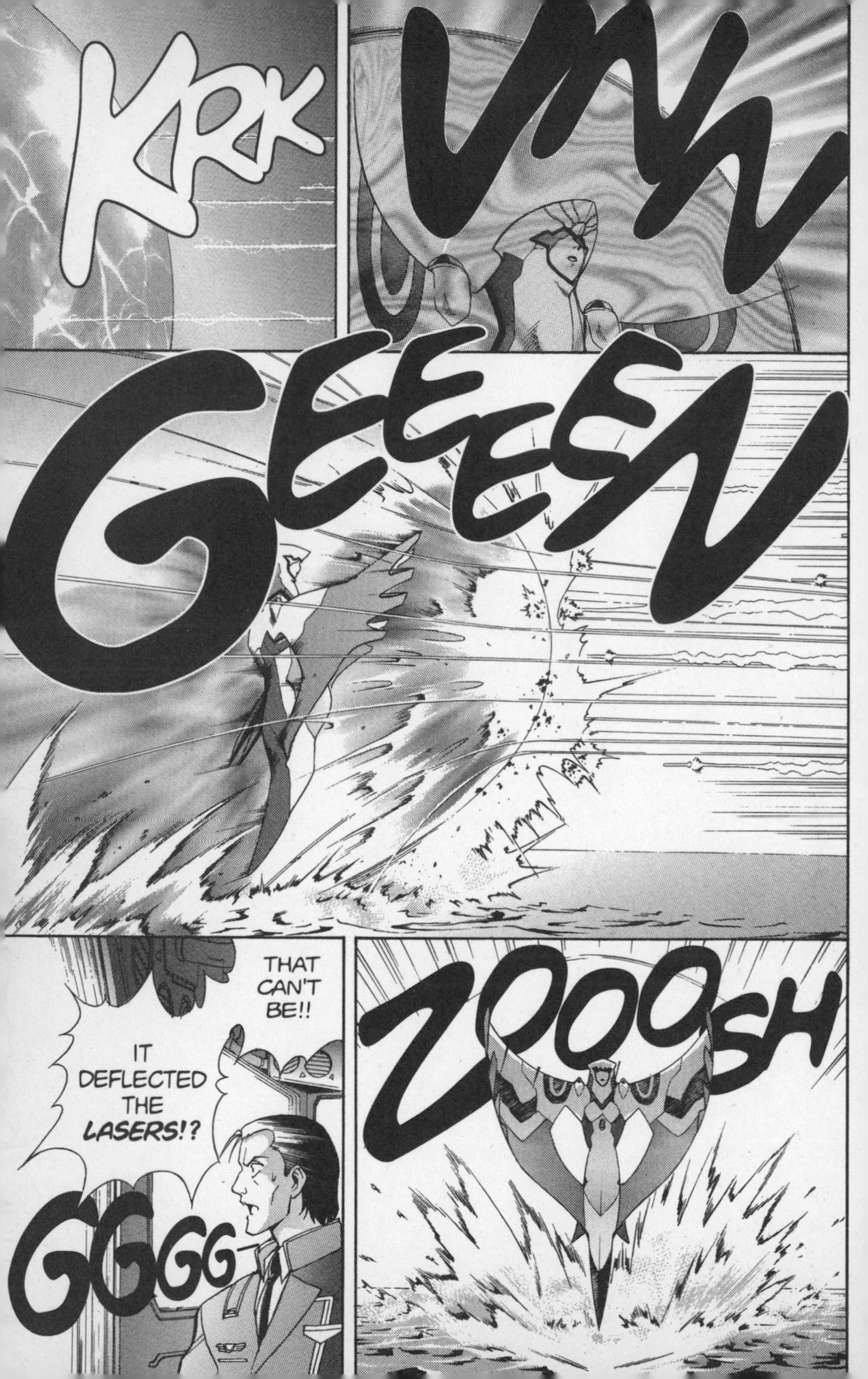

VNN
KRK
GEEEN
ZOOOSH
THAT CAN'T BE!!
IT DEFLECTED THE *LASERS!?*
GGGG

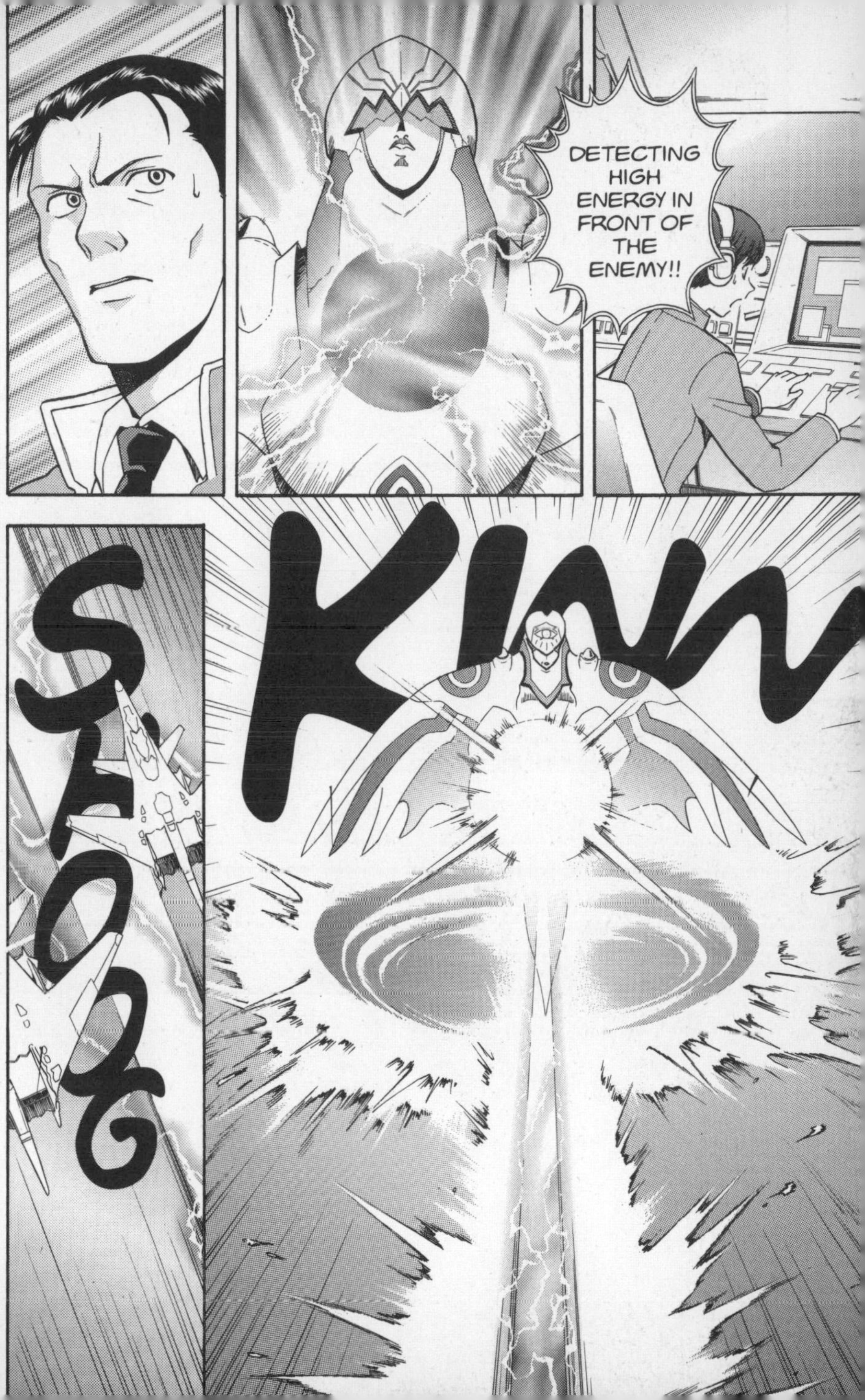
DETECTING HIGH ENERGY IN FRONT OF THE ENEMY!!
KINN
SHOOG

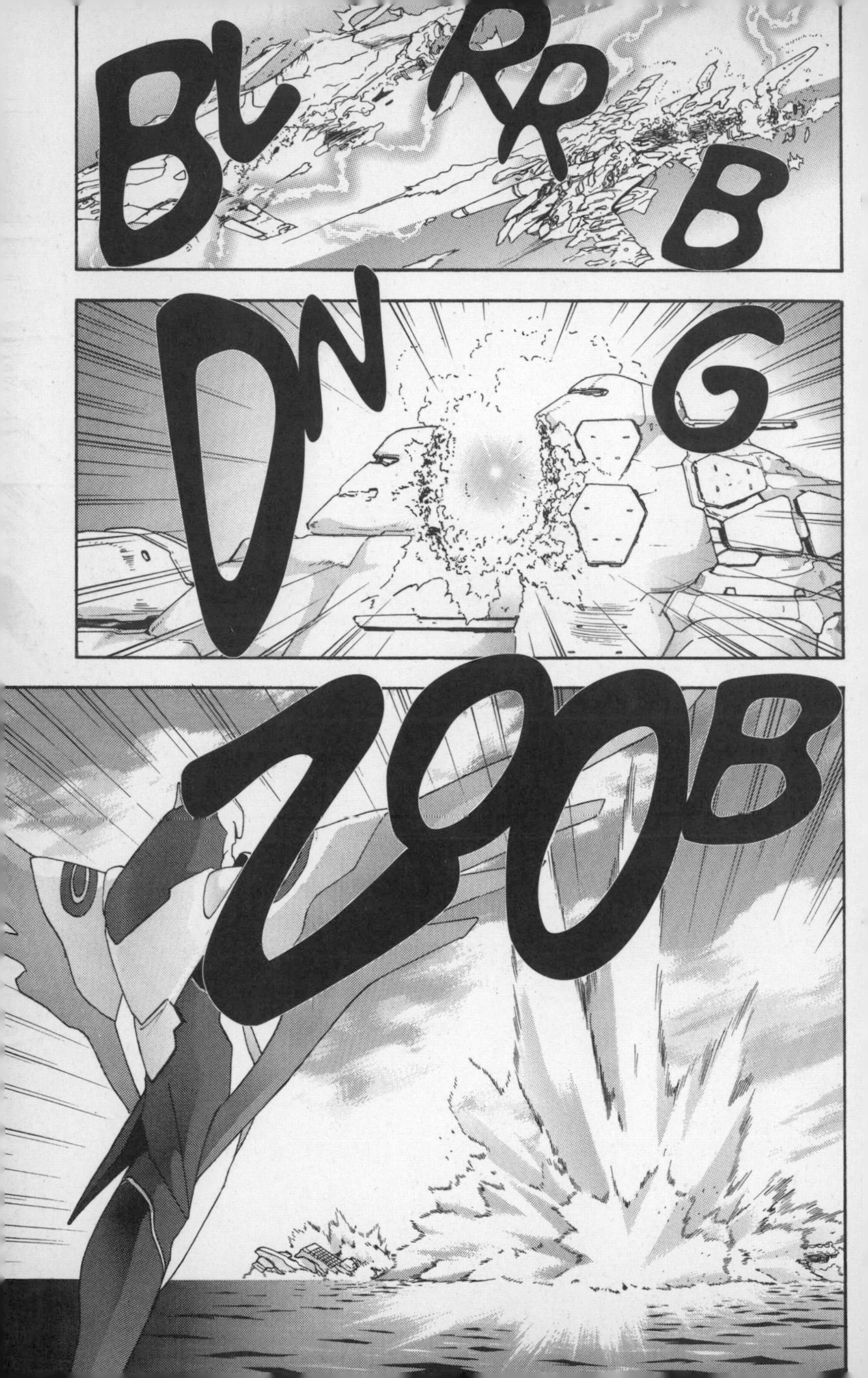
BLRRB
DNG
ZOOB

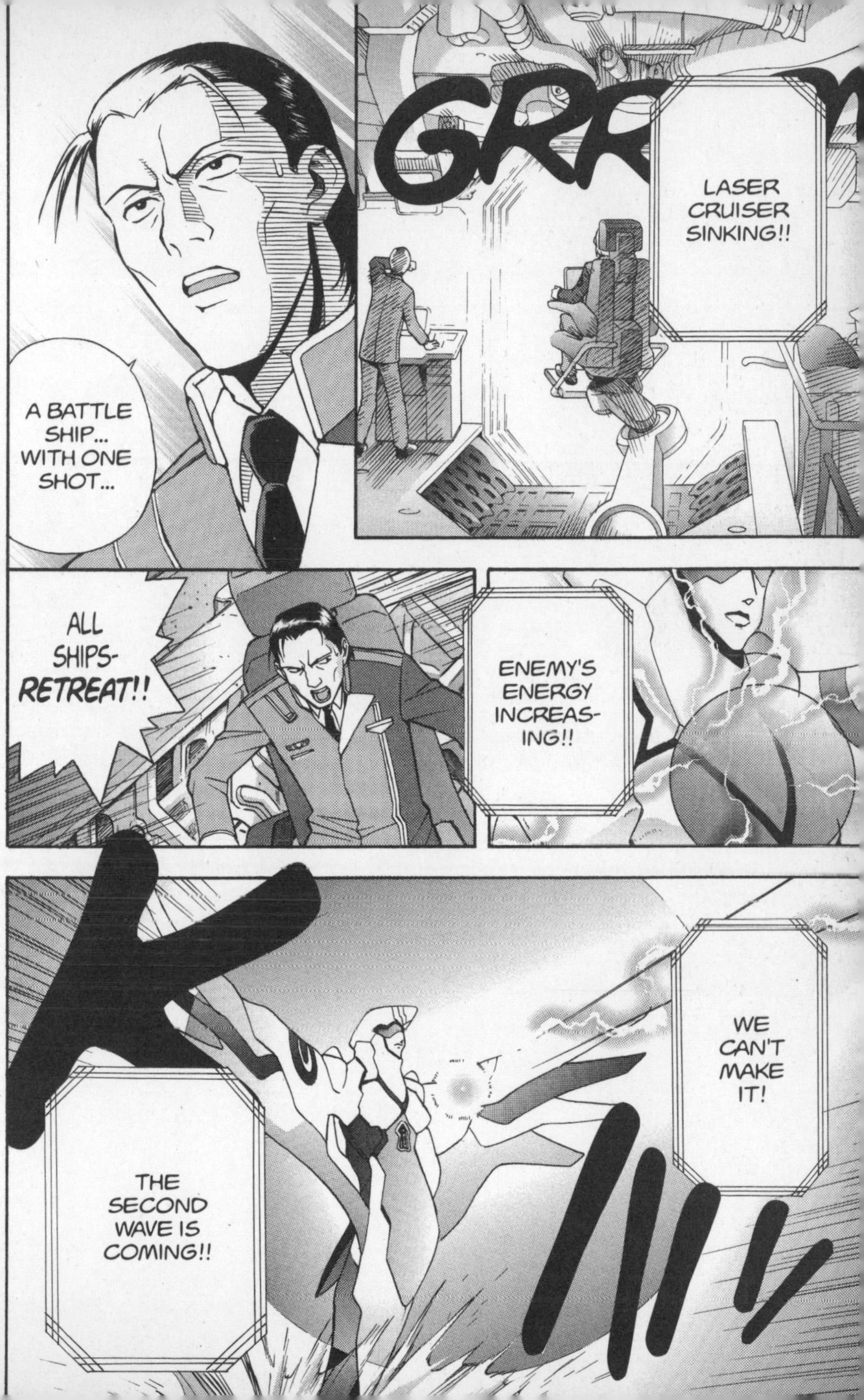
GRR
LASER CRUISER SINKING!!
A BATTLE SHIP... WITH ONE SHOT...
ENEMY'S ENERGY INCREAS-ING!!
ALL SHIPS- RETREAT!!
WE CAN'T MAKE IT!
THE SECOND WAVE IS COMING!!

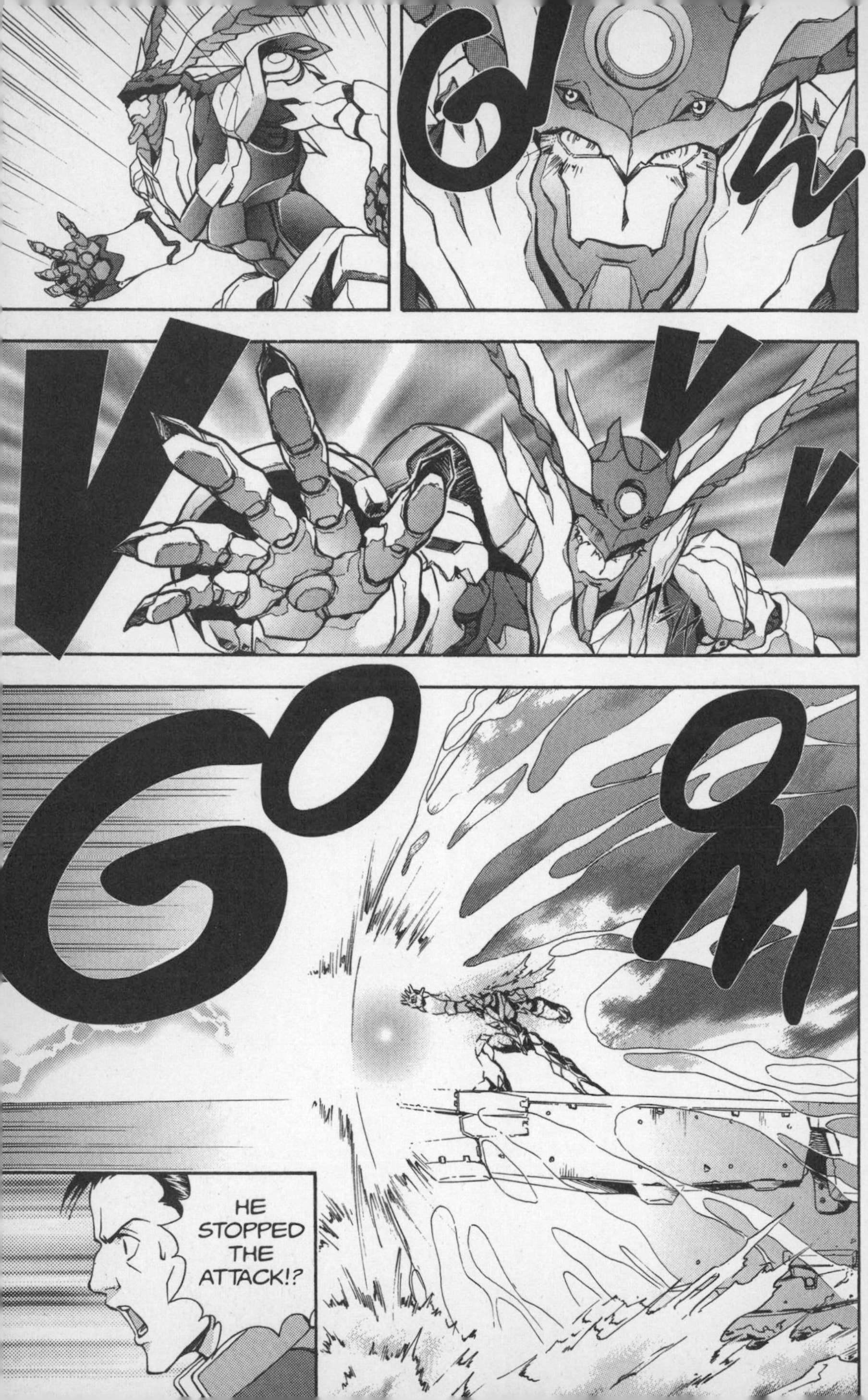
HE STOPPED THE ATTACK!?

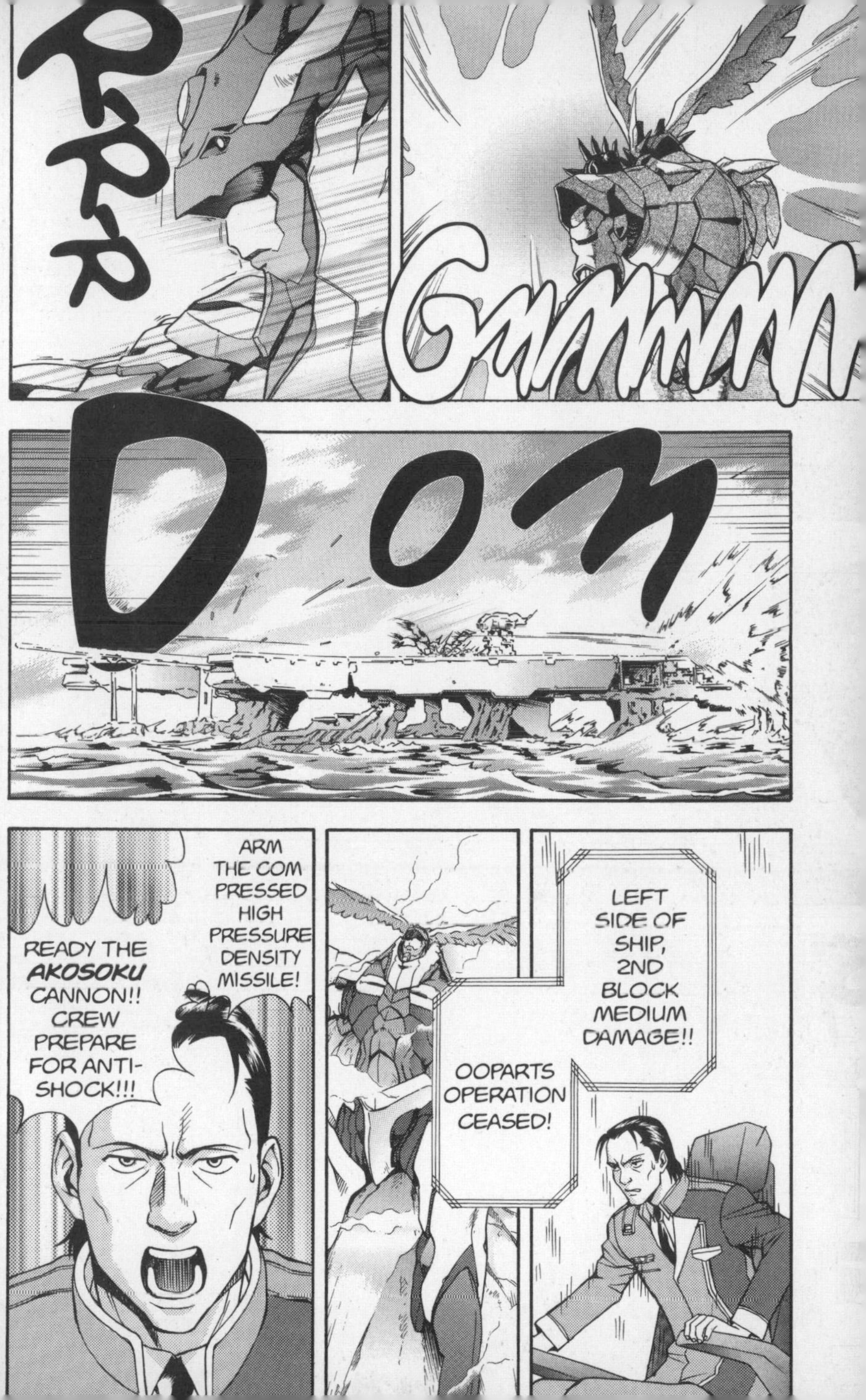
GMMMM
PRRR
DOM
LEFT SIDE OF SHIP, 2ND BLOCK MEDIUM DAMAGE!!
OOPARTS OPERATION CEASED!
ARM THE COM PRESSED HIGH PRESSURE DENSITY MISSILE!
READY THE **AKOSOKU** CANNON!! CREW PREPARE FOR ANTI-SHOCK!!!

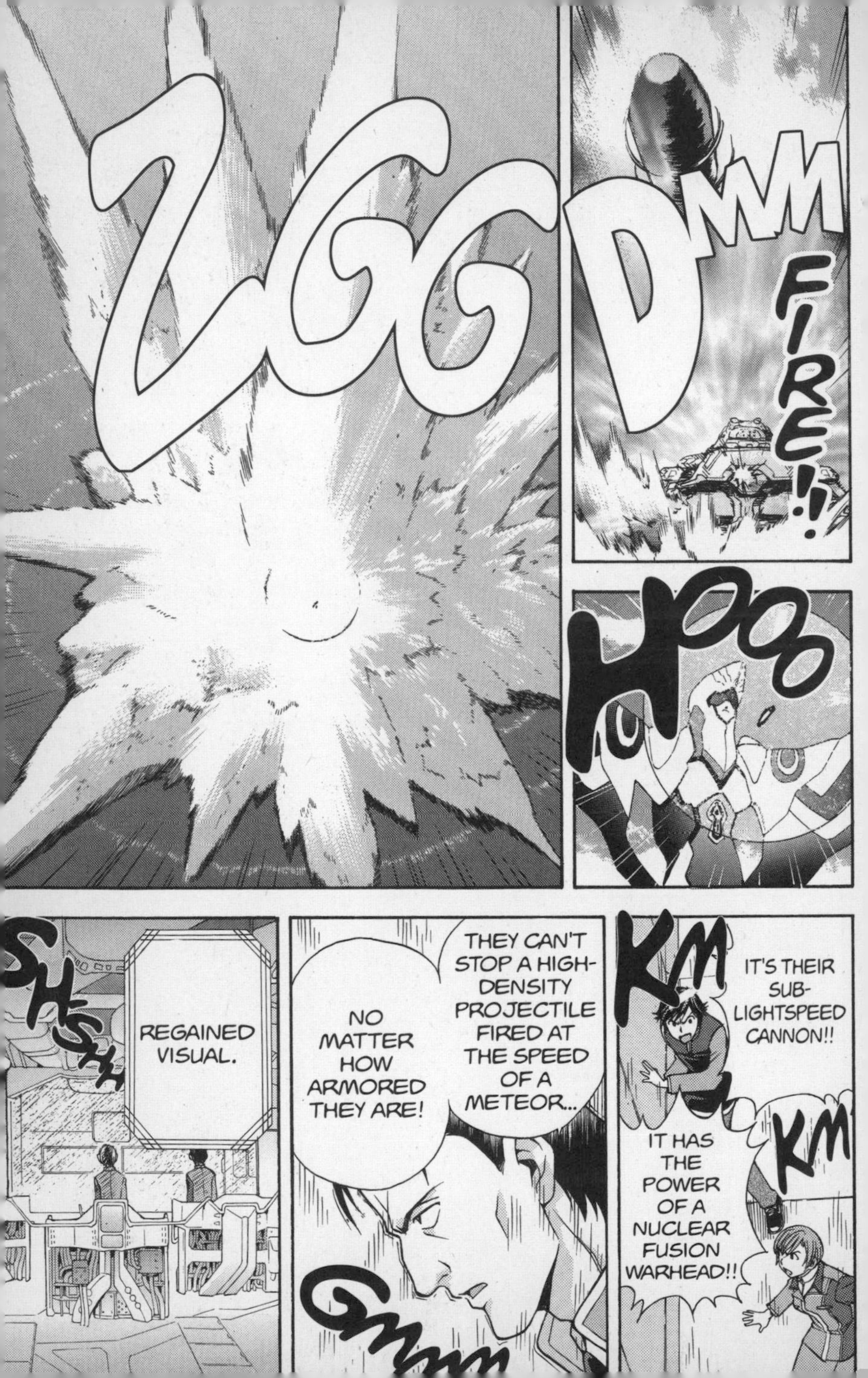
ZGGDMMM
FIRE!!
HOOOO
KM
IT'S THEIR SUB-LIGHTSPEED CANNON!!
KM
IT HAS THE POWER OF A NUCLEAR FUSION WARHEAD!!
THEY CAN'T STOP A HIGH-DENSITY PROJECTILE FIRED AT THE SPEED OF A METEOR...
NO MATTER HOW ARMORED THEY ARE!
GMMM
SHSHH
REGAINED VISUAL.

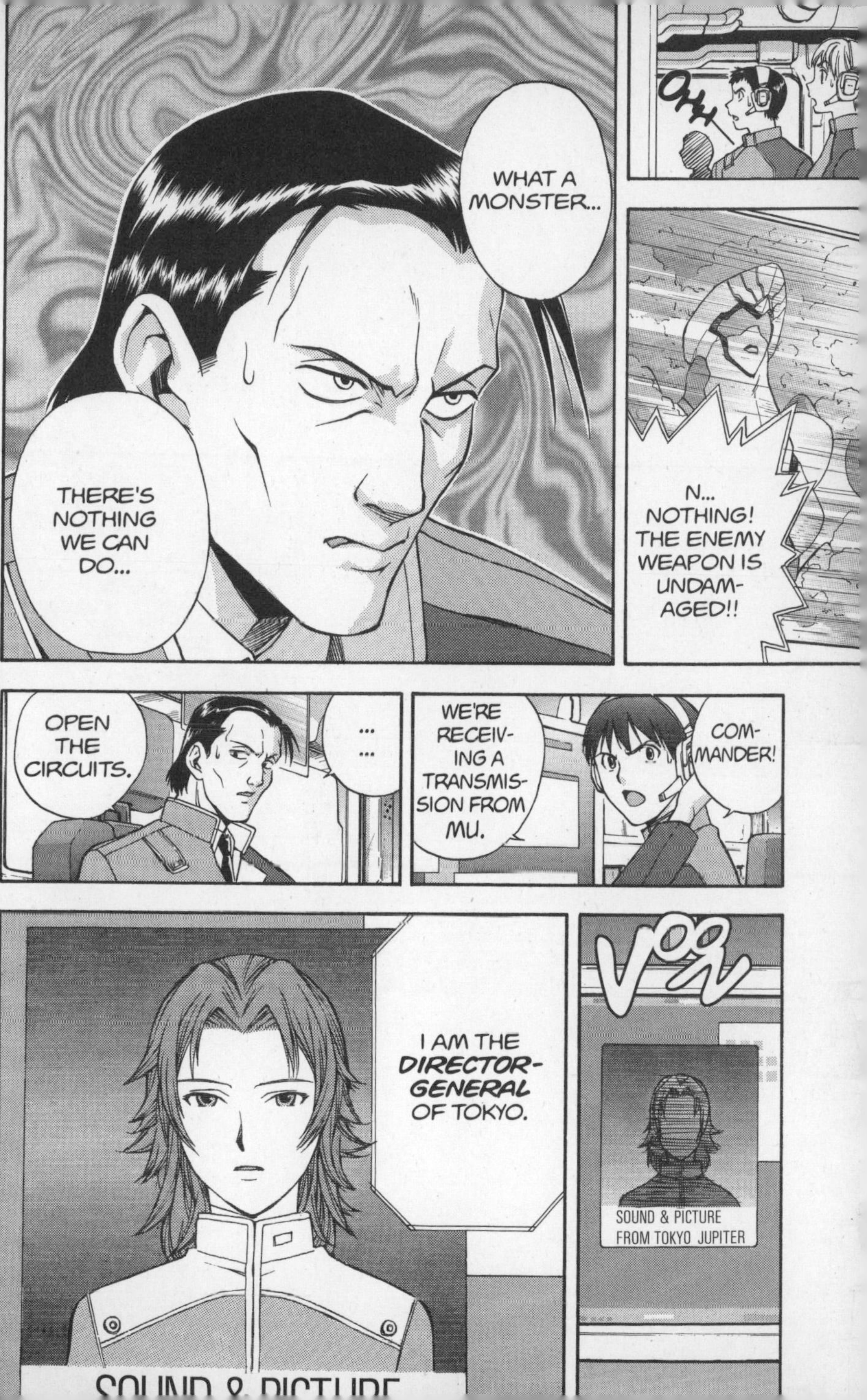
N... NOTHING! THE ENEMY WEAPON IS UNDAMAGED!!
WHAT A MONSTER...
THERE'S NOTHING WE CAN DO...
COMMANDER!
WE'RE RECEIVING A TRANSMISSION FROM MU.
......
OPEN THE CIRCUITS.
SOUND & PICTURE FROM TOKYO JUPITER
I AM THE DIRECTOR-GENERAL OF TOKYO.

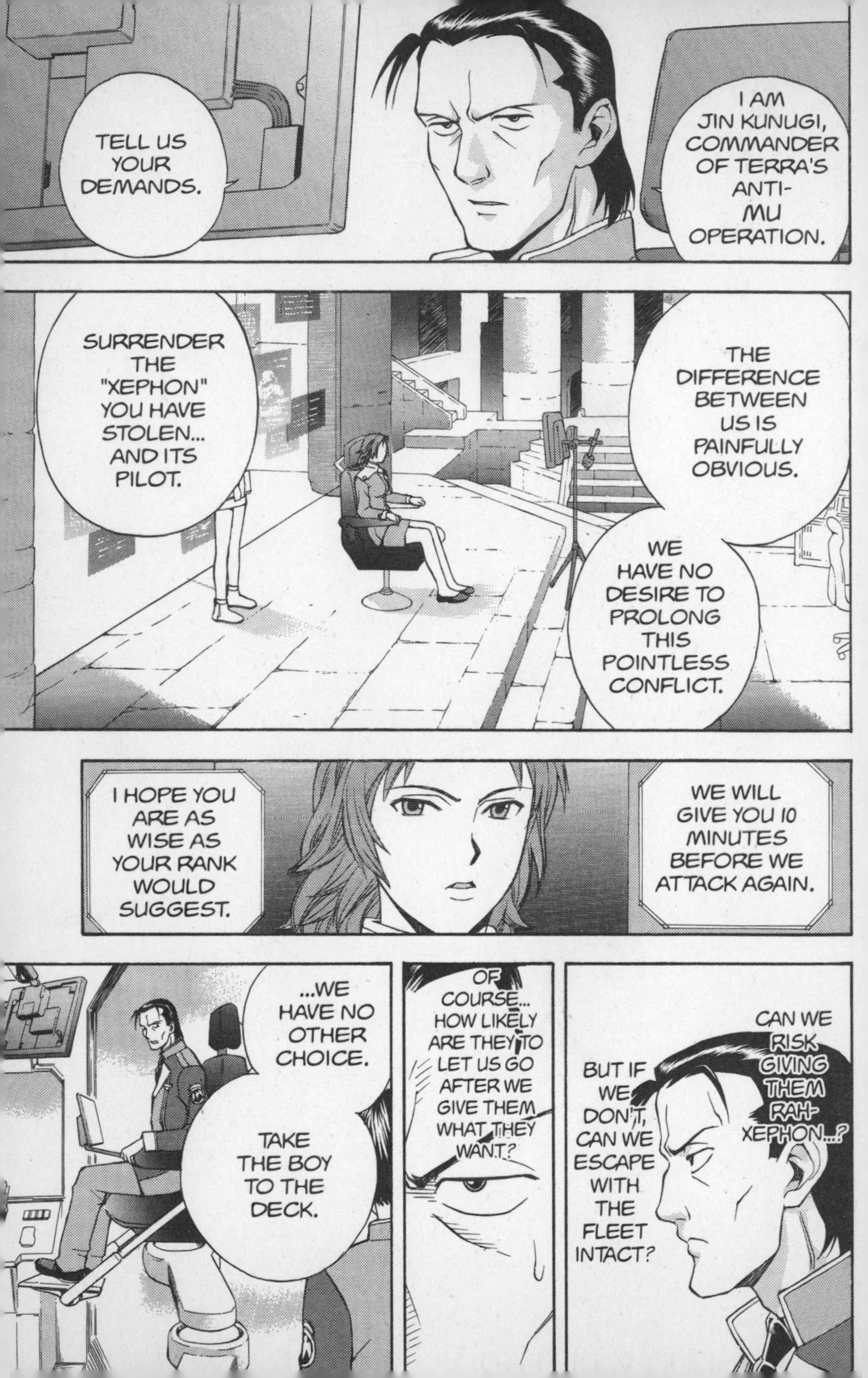
I AM JIN KUNUGI, COMMANDER OF TERRA'S ANTI-MU OPERATION.
TELL US YOUR DEMANDS.
THE DIFFERENCE BETWEEN US IS PAINFULLY OBVIOUS.
WE HAVE NO DESIRE TO PROLONG THIS POINTLESS CONFLICT.
SURRENDER THE "XEPHON" YOU HAVE STOLEN... AND ITS PILOT.
WE WILL GIVE YOU 10 MINUTES BEFORE WE ATTACK AGAIN.
I HOPE YOU ARE AS WISE AS YOUR RANK WOULD SUGGEST.
CAN WE RISK GIVING THEM RAH-XEPHON...?
BUT IF WE DON'T, CAN WE ESCAPE WITH THE FLEET INTACT?
OF COURSE... HOW LIKELY ARE THEY TO LET US GO AFTER WE GIVE THEM WHAT THEY WANT?
...WE HAVE NO OTHER CHOICE.
TAKE THE BOY TO THE DECK.

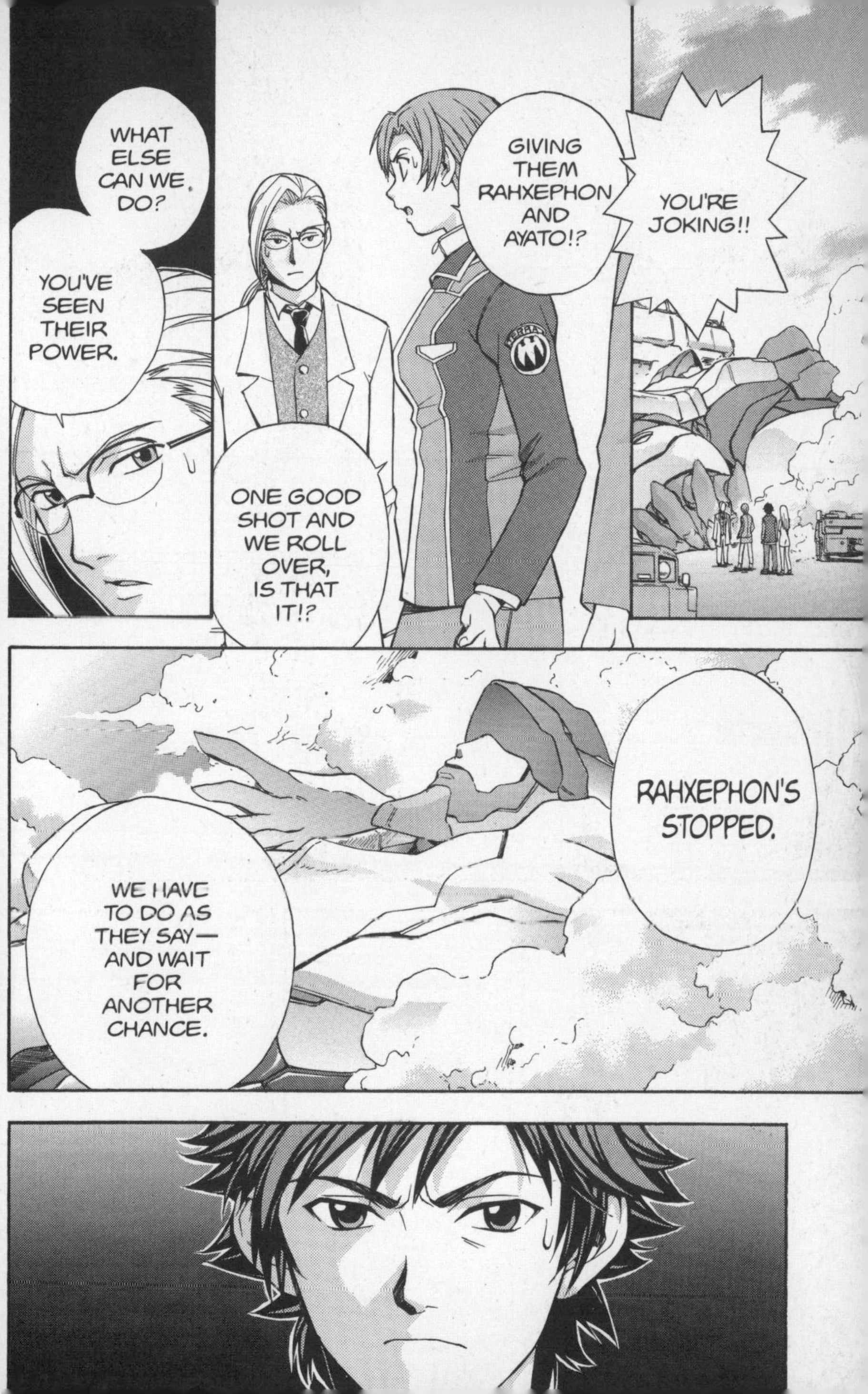
YOU'RE JOKING!!
GIVING THEM RAHXEPHON AND AYATO!?
WHAT ELSE CAN WE DO?
YOU'VE SEEN THEIR POWER.
ONE GOOD SHOT AND WE ROLL OVER, IS THAT IT!?
RAHXEPHON'S STOPPED.
WE HAVE TO DO AS THEY SAY— AND WAIT FOR ANOTHER CHANCE.

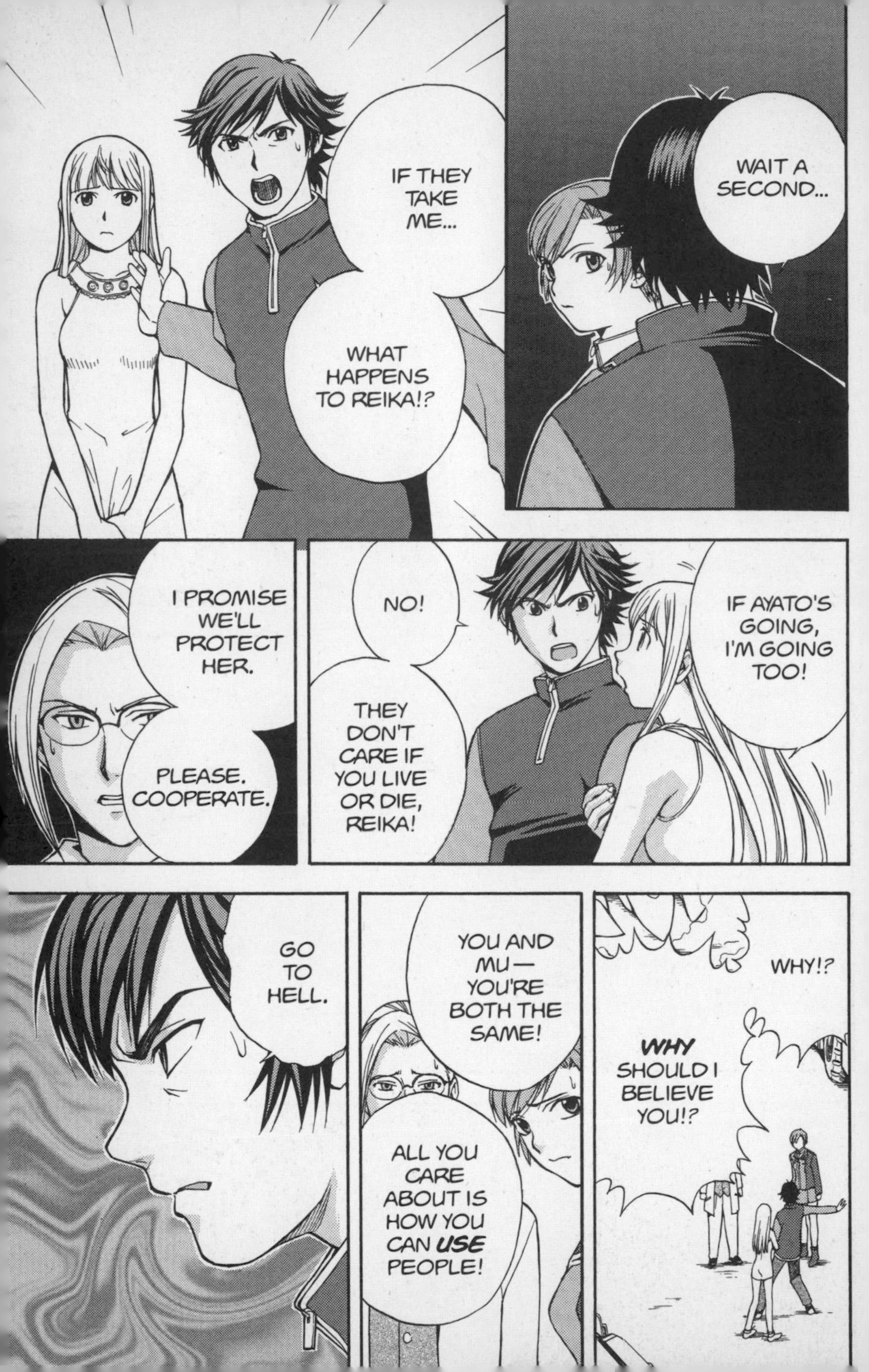
WAIT A SECOND...
IF THEY TAKE ME...
WHAT HAPPENS TO REIKA!?
IF AYATO'S GOING, I'M GOING TOO!
NO!
THEY DON'T CARE IF YOU LIVE OR DIE, REIKA!
I PROMISE WE'LL PROTECT HER.
PLEASE. COOPERATE.
WHY!?
WHY SHOULD I BELIEVE YOU!?
YOU AND MU— YOU'RE BOTH THE SAME!
ALL YOU CARE ABOUT IS HOW YOU CAN USE PEOPLE!
GO TO HELL.

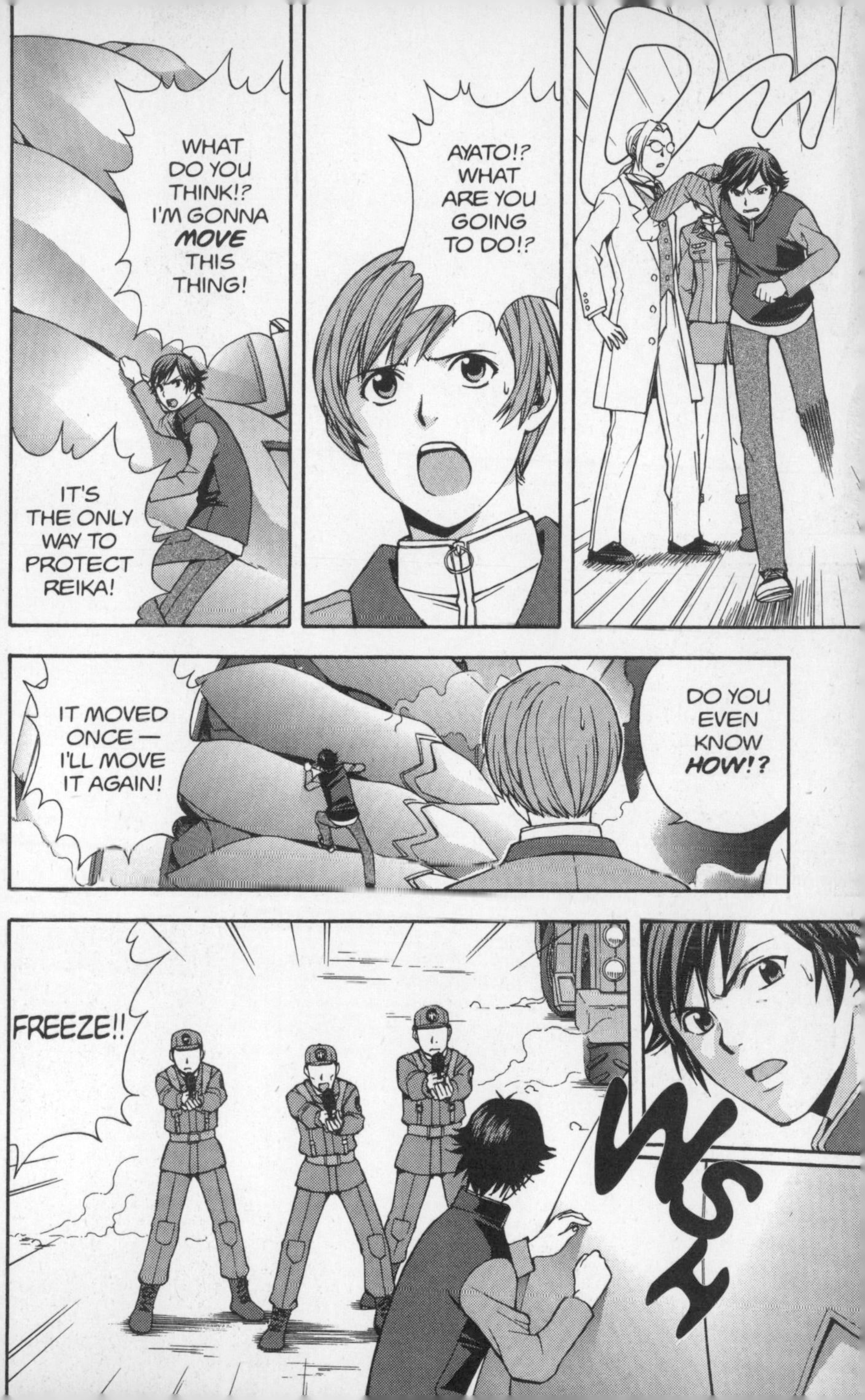
AYATO!? WHAT ARE YOU GOING TO DO!?
WHAT DO YOU THINK!? I'M GONNA **MOVE** THIS THING!
IT'S THE ONLY WAY TO PROTECT REIKA!
DO YOU EVEN KNOW **HOW!?**
IT MOVED ONCE — I'LL MOVE IT AGAIN!
FREEZE!!

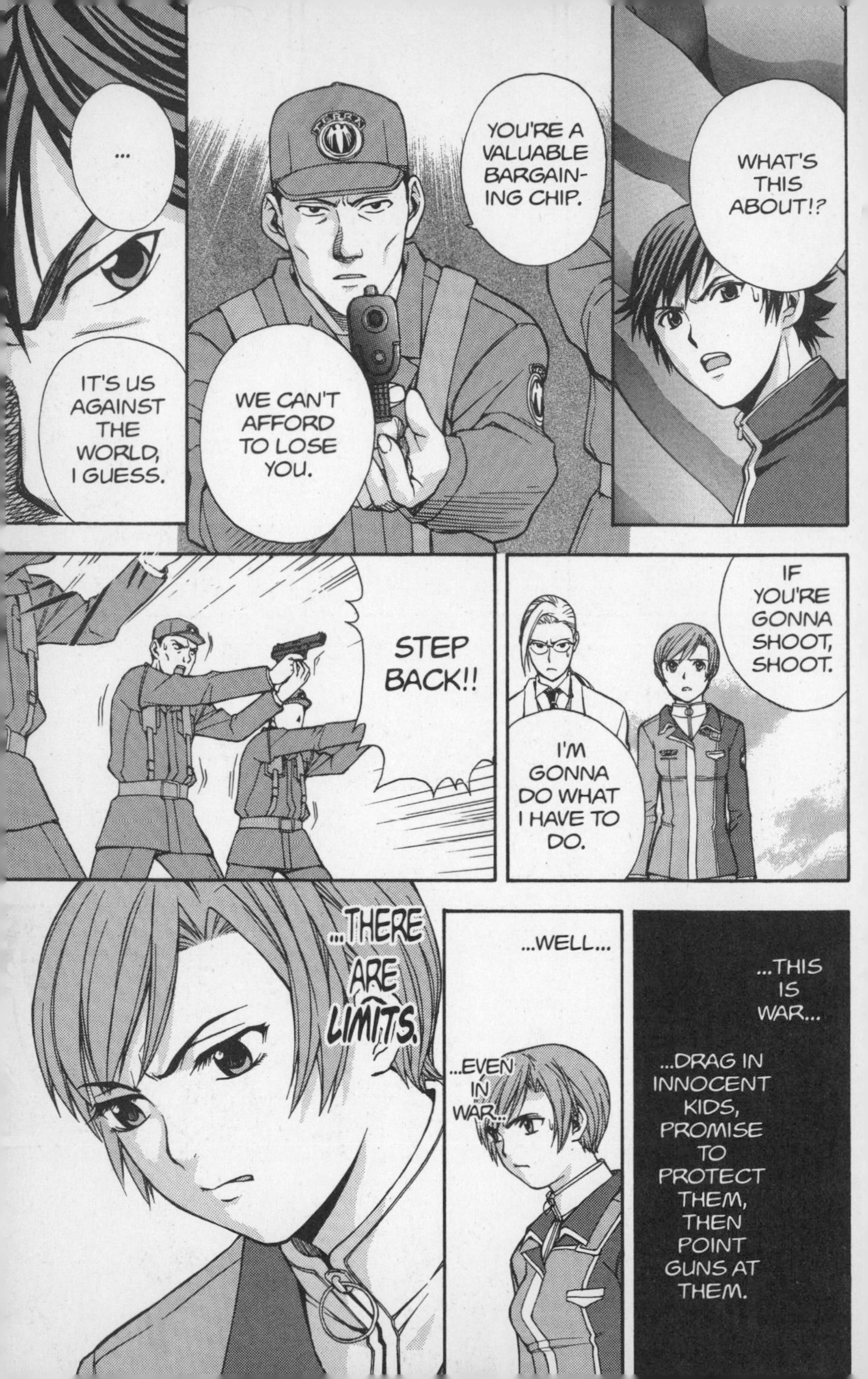
WHAT'S THIS ABOUT!?
YOU'RE A VALUABLE BARGAIN-ING CHIP.
WE CAN'T AFFORD TO LOSE YOU.
...
IT'S US AGAINST THE WORLD, I GUESS.
IF YOU'RE GONNA SHOOT, SHOOT.
I'M GONNA DO WHAT I HAVE TO DO.
STEP BACK!!
...THIS IS WAR...
...DRAG IN INNOCENT KIDS, PROMISE TO PROTECT THEM, THEN POINT GUNS AT THEM.
...WELL...
...EVEN IN WAR...
...THERE ARE LIMITS.

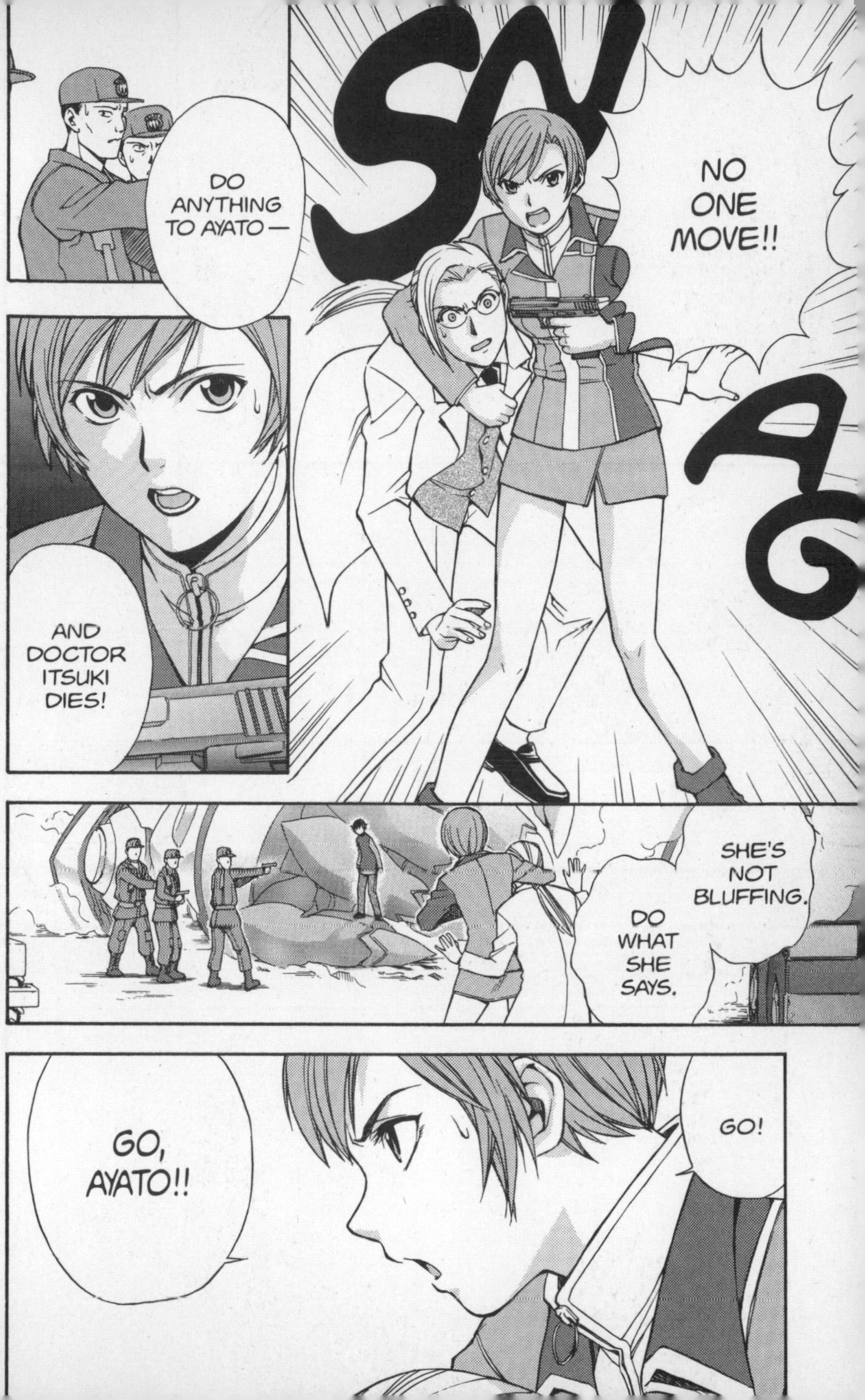
SNAG
NO ONE MOVE!!
DO ANYTHING TO AYATO—
AND DOCTOR ITSUKI DIES!
SHE'S NOT BLUFFING.
DO WHAT SHE SAYS.
GO!
GO, AYATO!!

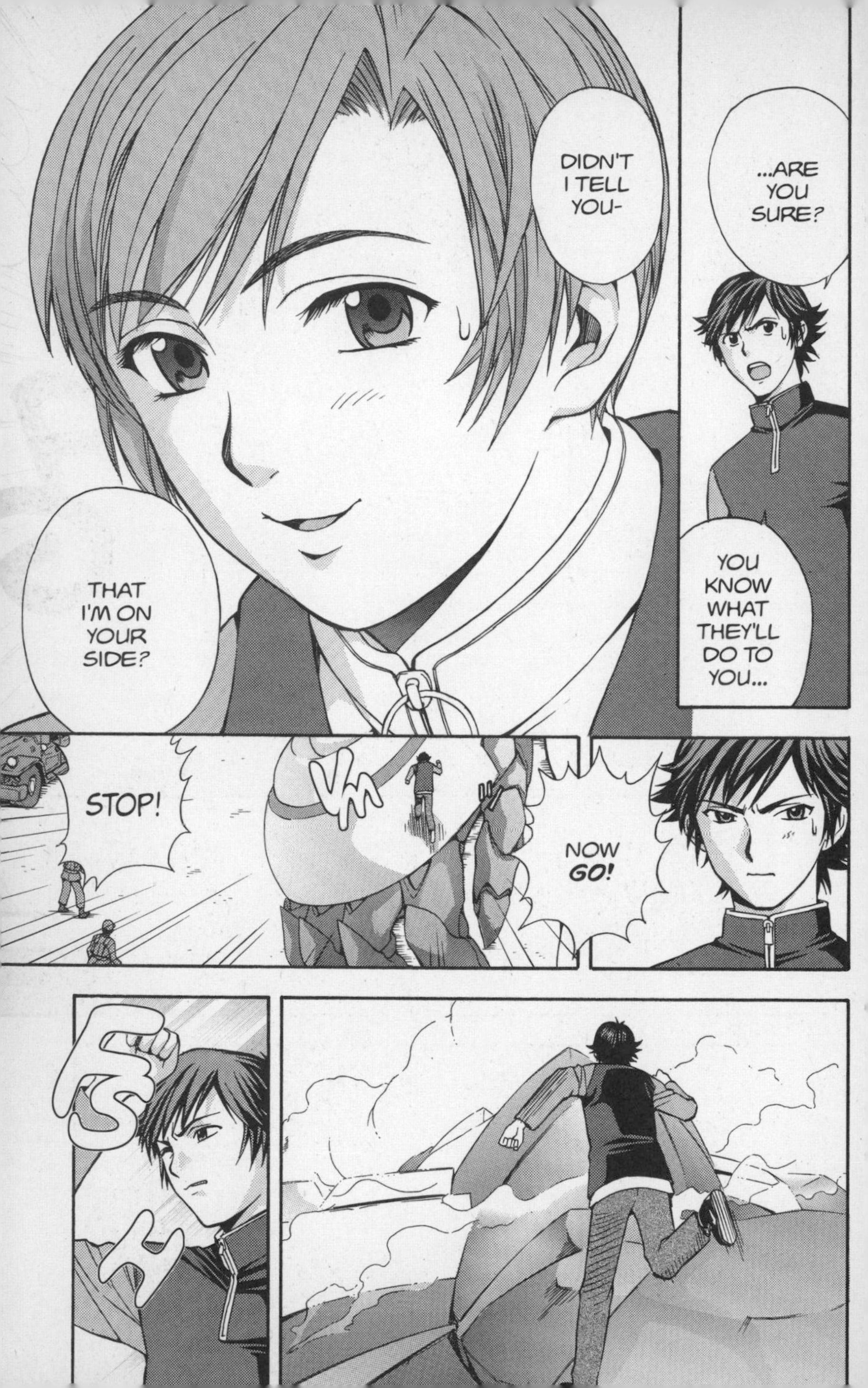
...ARE YOU SURE?
YOU KNOW WHAT THEY'LL DO TO YOU...
DIDN'T I TELL YOU-
THAT I'M ON YOUR SIDE?
NOW GO!
VM
STOP!

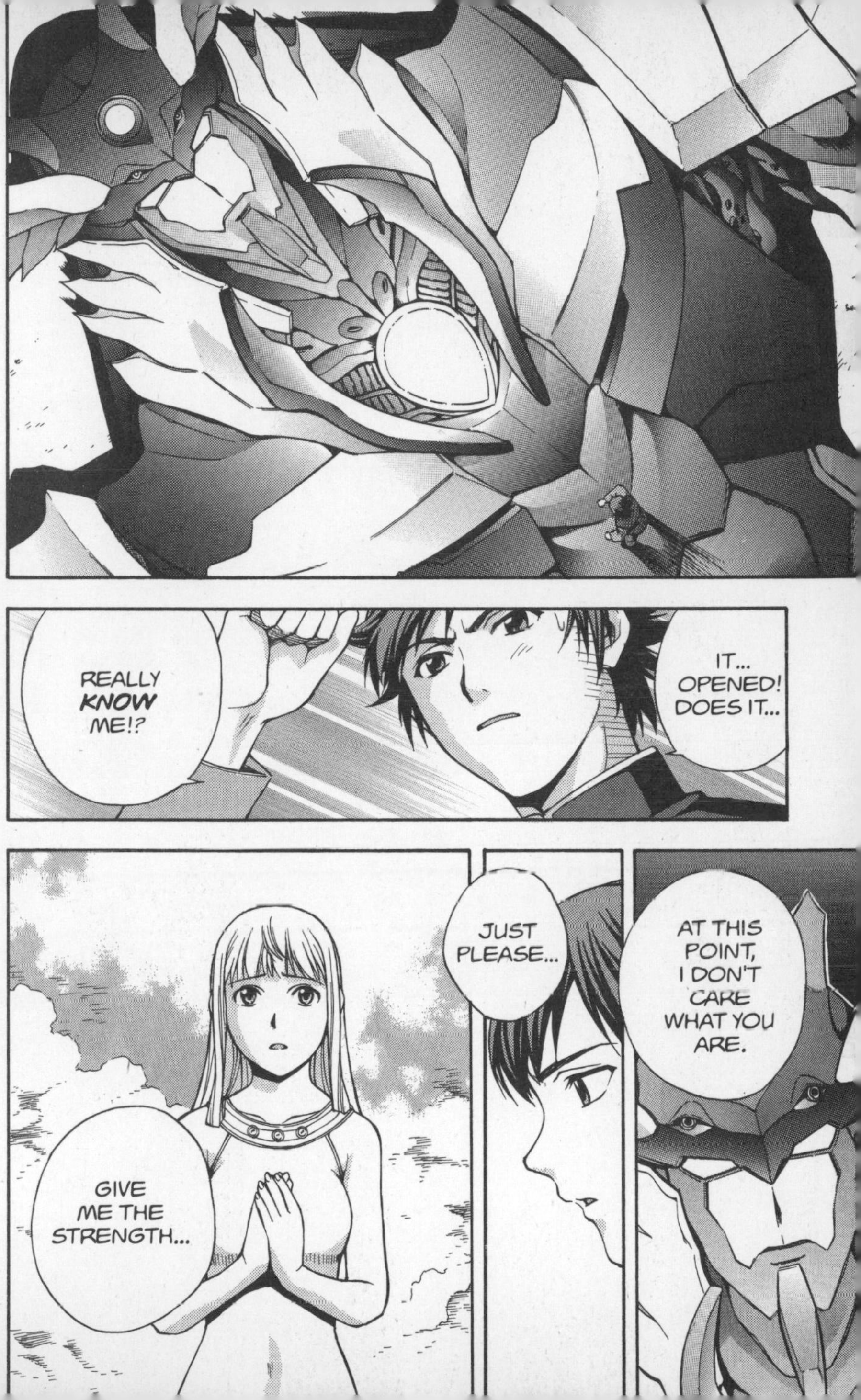
IT... OPENED! DOES IT...
REALLY **KNOW** ME!?
AT THIS POINT, I DON'T CARE WHAT YOU ARE.
JUST PLEASE...
GIVE ME THE STRENGTH...

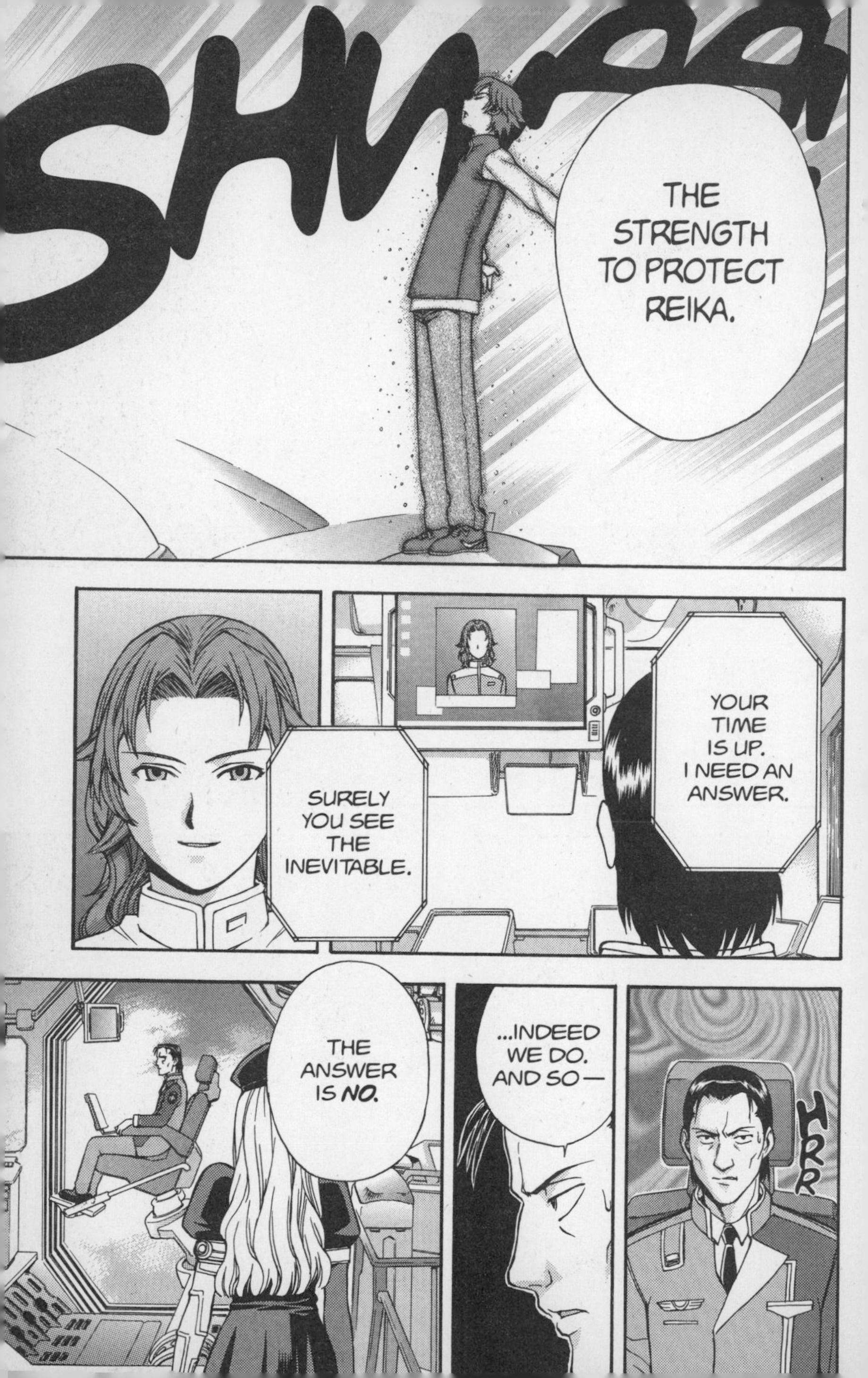
THE STRENGTH TO PROTECT REIKA.
YOUR TIME IS UP. I NEED AN ANSWER.
SURELY YOU SEE THE INEVITABLE.
HRR
...INDEED WE DO. AND SO—
THE ANSWER IS **NO.**

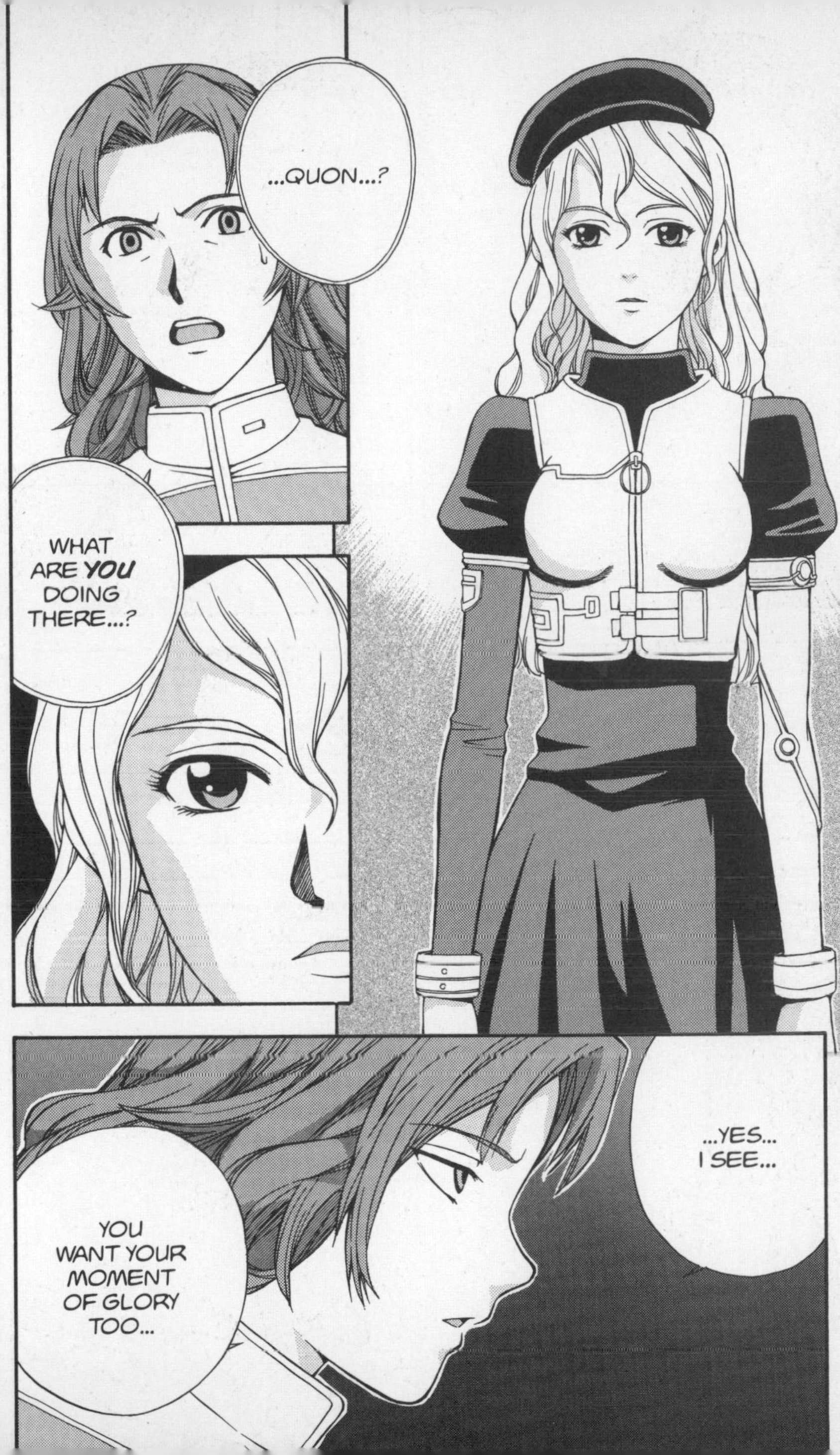
...QUON...?
WHAT ARE ***YOU*** DOING THERE...?
...YES... I SEE...
YOU WANT YOUR MOMENT OF GLORY TOO...

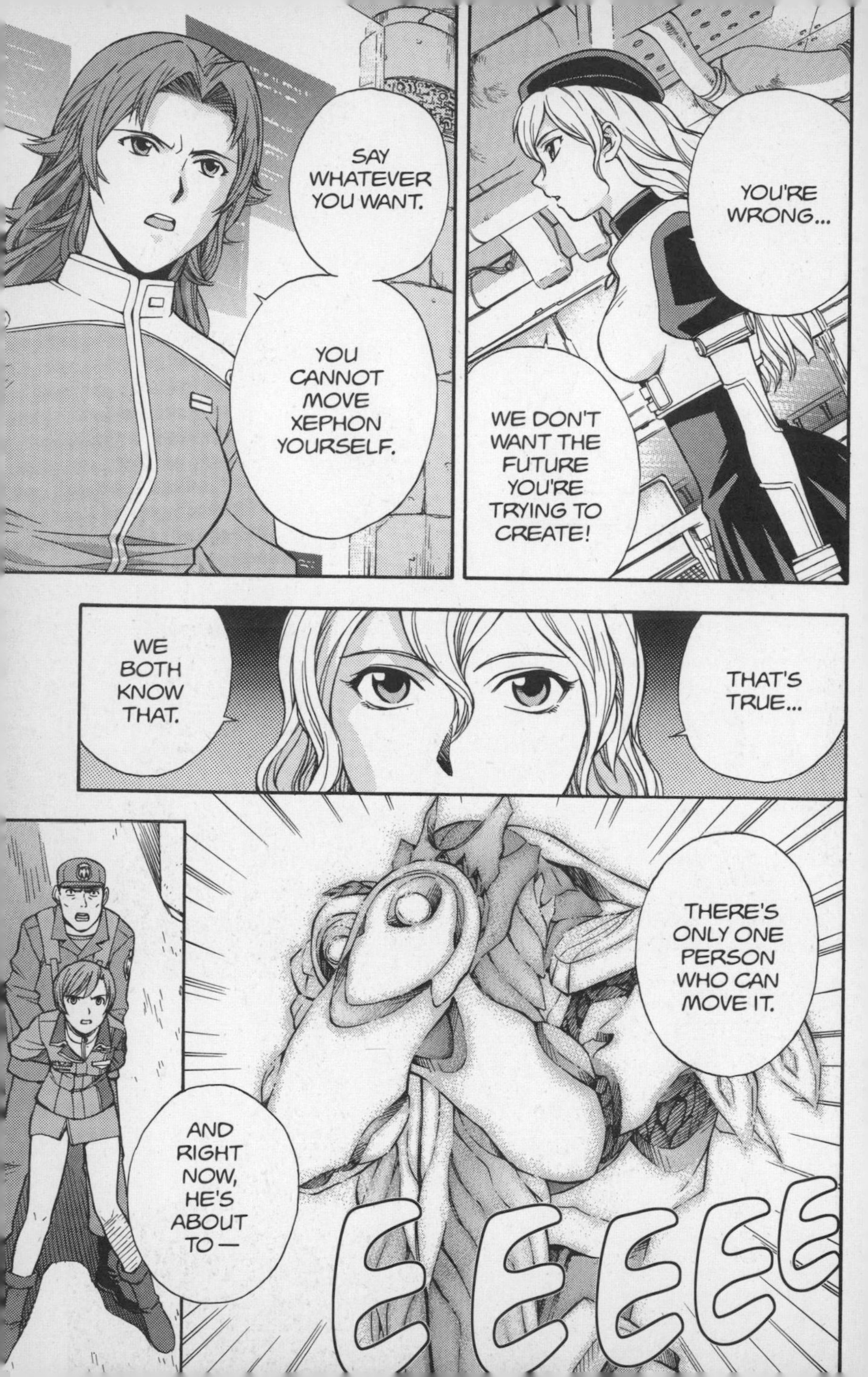
YOU'RE WRONG...
WE DON'T WANT THE FUTURE YOU'RE TRYING TO CREATE!
SAY WHATEVER YOU WANT.
YOU CANNOT MOVE XEPHON YOURSELF.
THAT'S TRUE...
WE BOTH KNOW THAT.
THERE'S ONLY ONE PERSON WHO CAN MOVE IT.
AND RIGHT NOW, HE'S ABOUT TO—
EEEEE

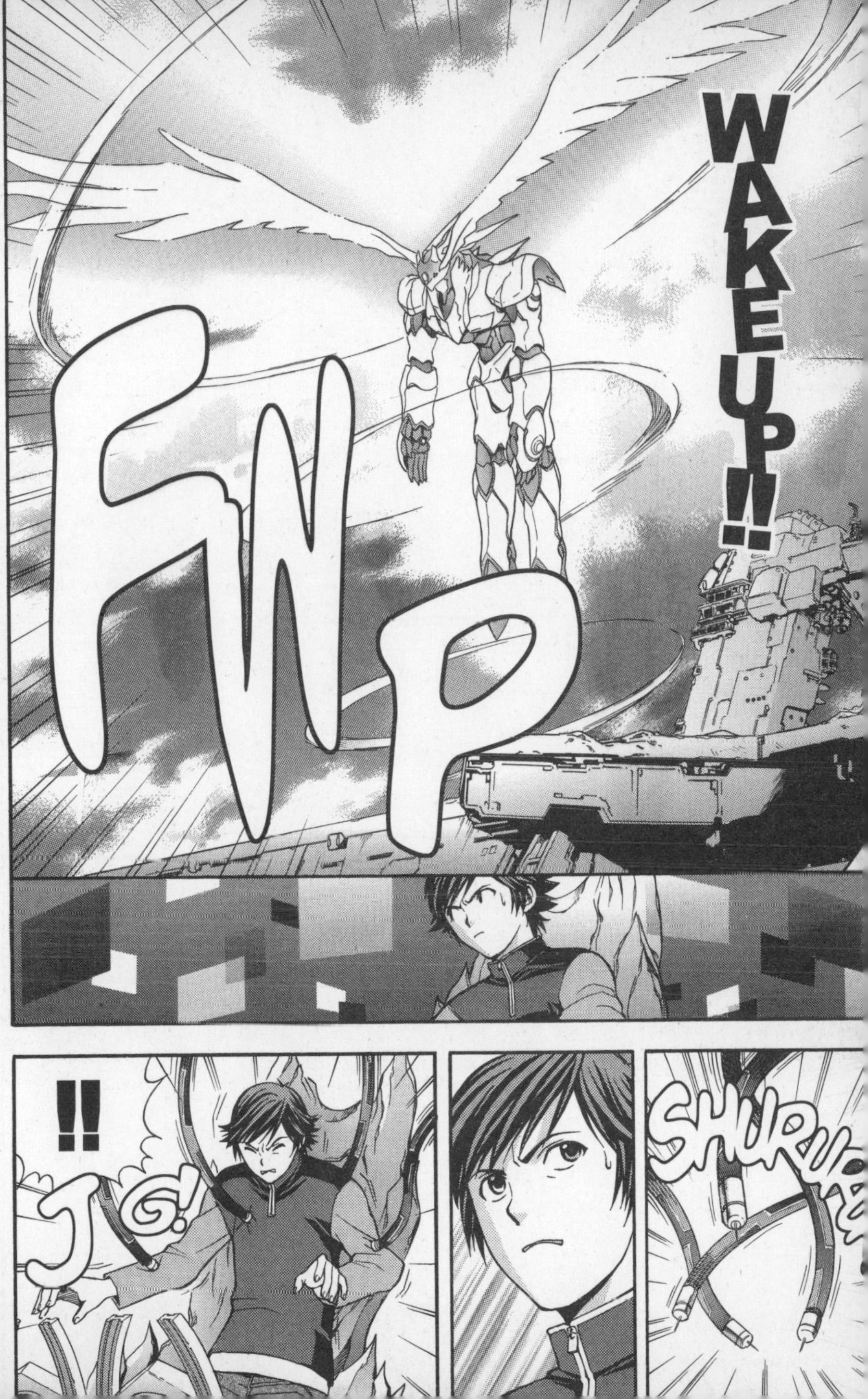
WAKE UP!!
FWP
SHURU
!!
JG!

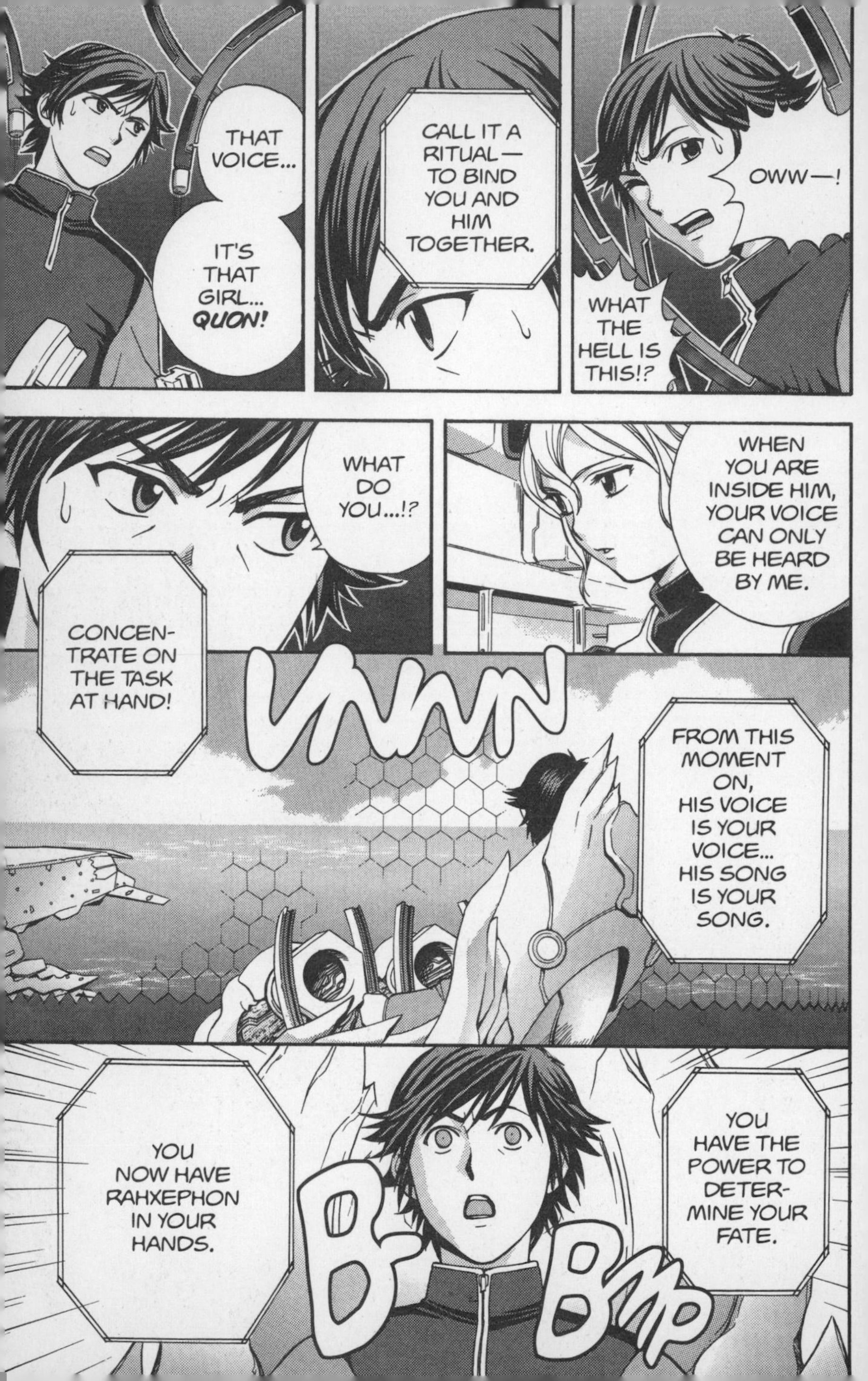

OWW—!
WHAT THE HELL IS THIS!?
CALL IT A RITUAL— TO BIND YOU AND HIM TOGETHER.
THAT VOICE...
IT'S THAT GIRL... **QUON!**
WHEN YOU ARE INSIDE HIM, YOUR VOICE CAN ONLY BE HEARD BY ME.
WHAT DO YOU...!?
CONCENTRATE ON THE TASK AT HAND!
VNNN
FROM THIS MOMENT ON, HIS VOICE IS YOUR VOICE... HIS SONG IS YOUR SONG.
YOU HAVE THE POWER TO DETERMINE YOUR FATE.
YOU NOW HAVE RAHXEPHON IN YOUR HANDS.
B
BMP

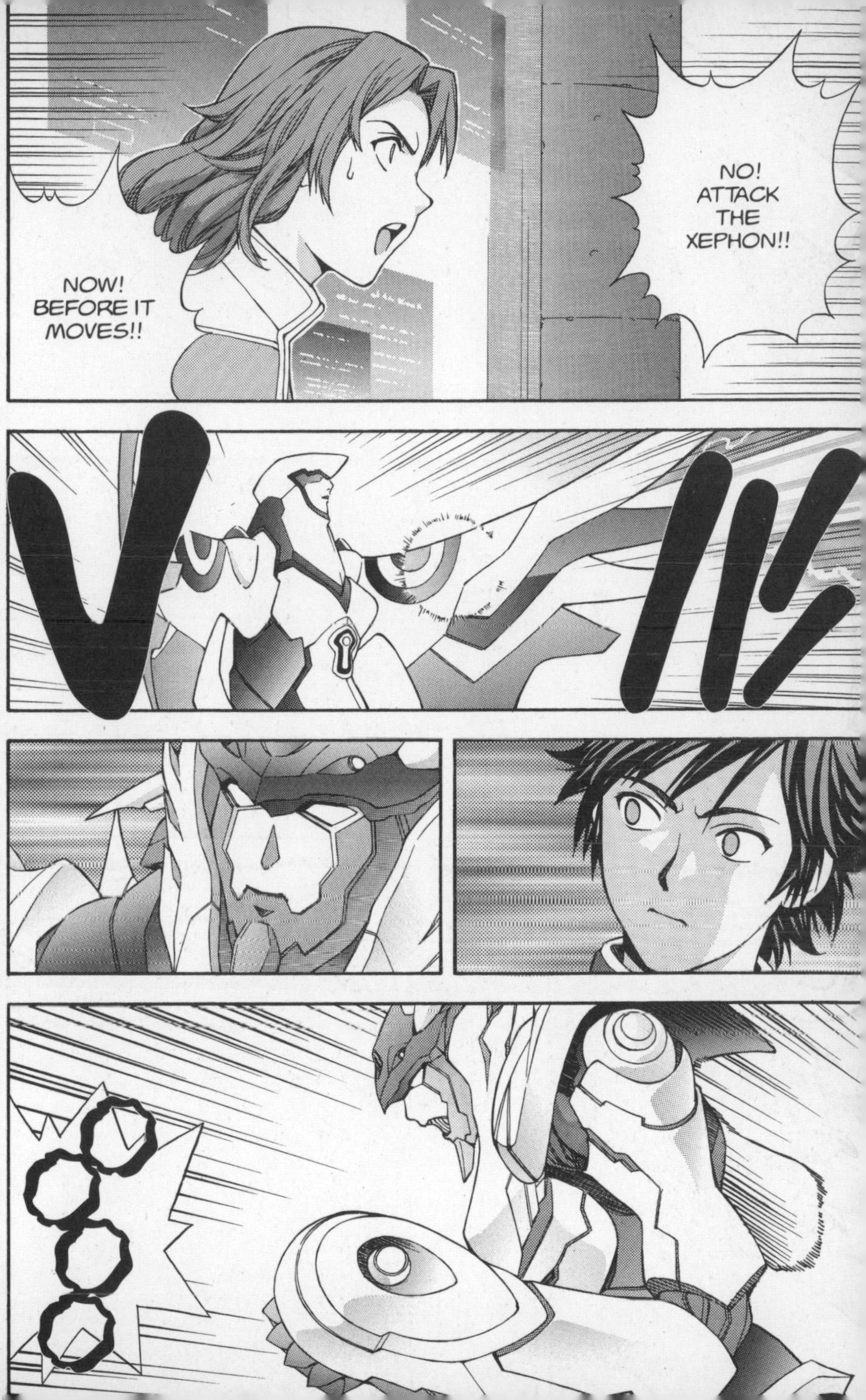
NO! ATTACK THE XEPHON!!
NOW! BEFORE IT MOVES!!

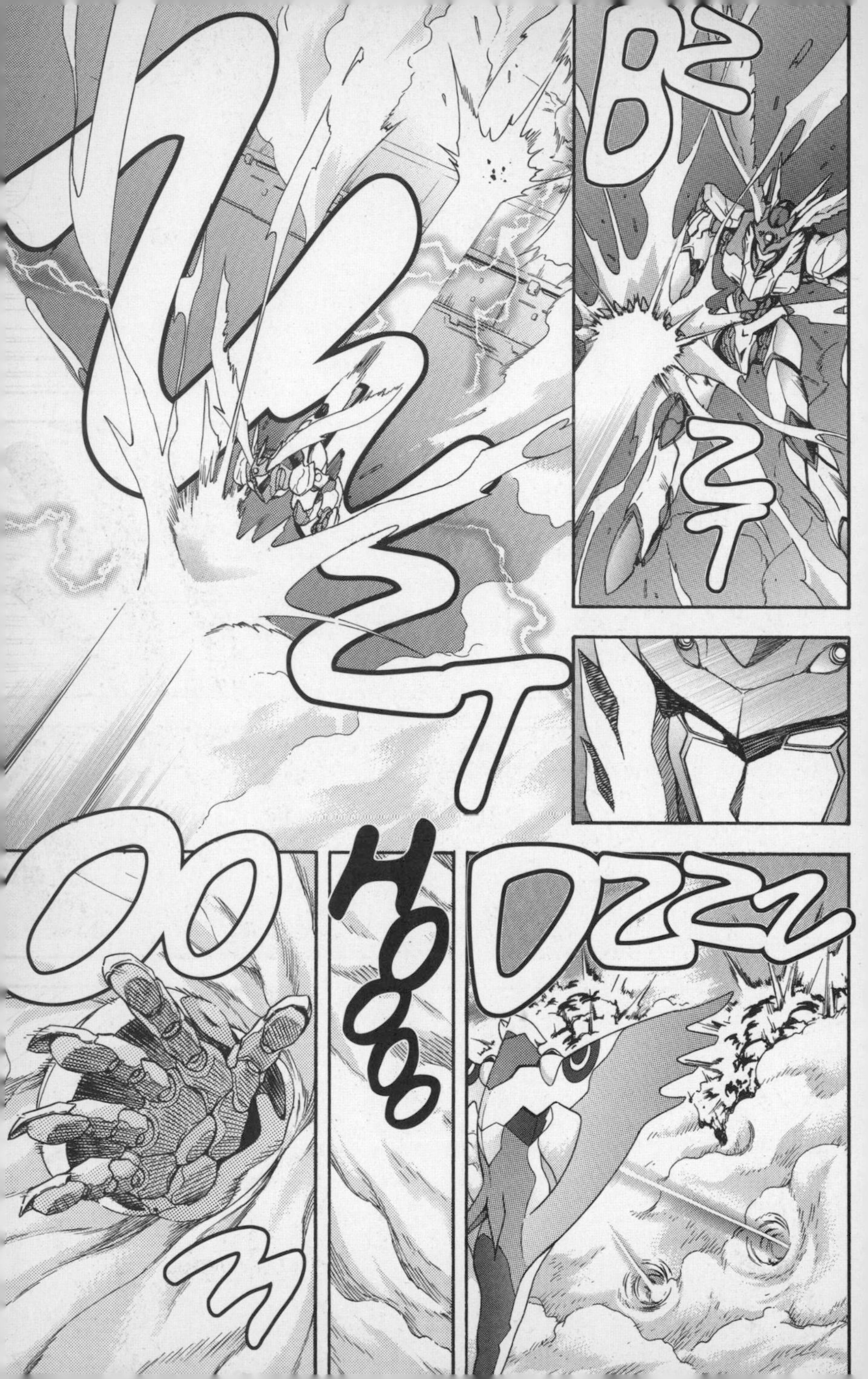
DZZZZ

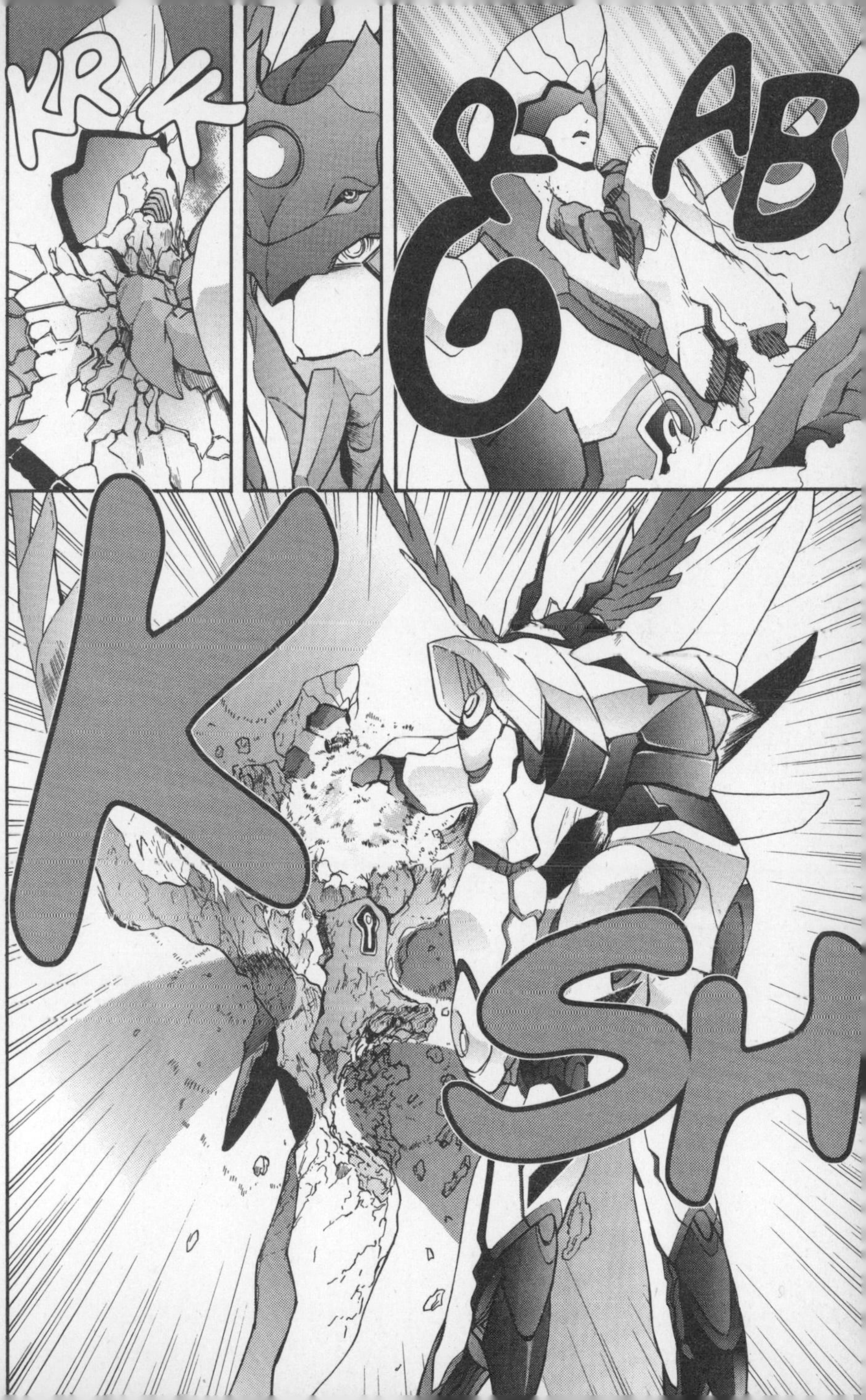
GRAB
KRK
KSH

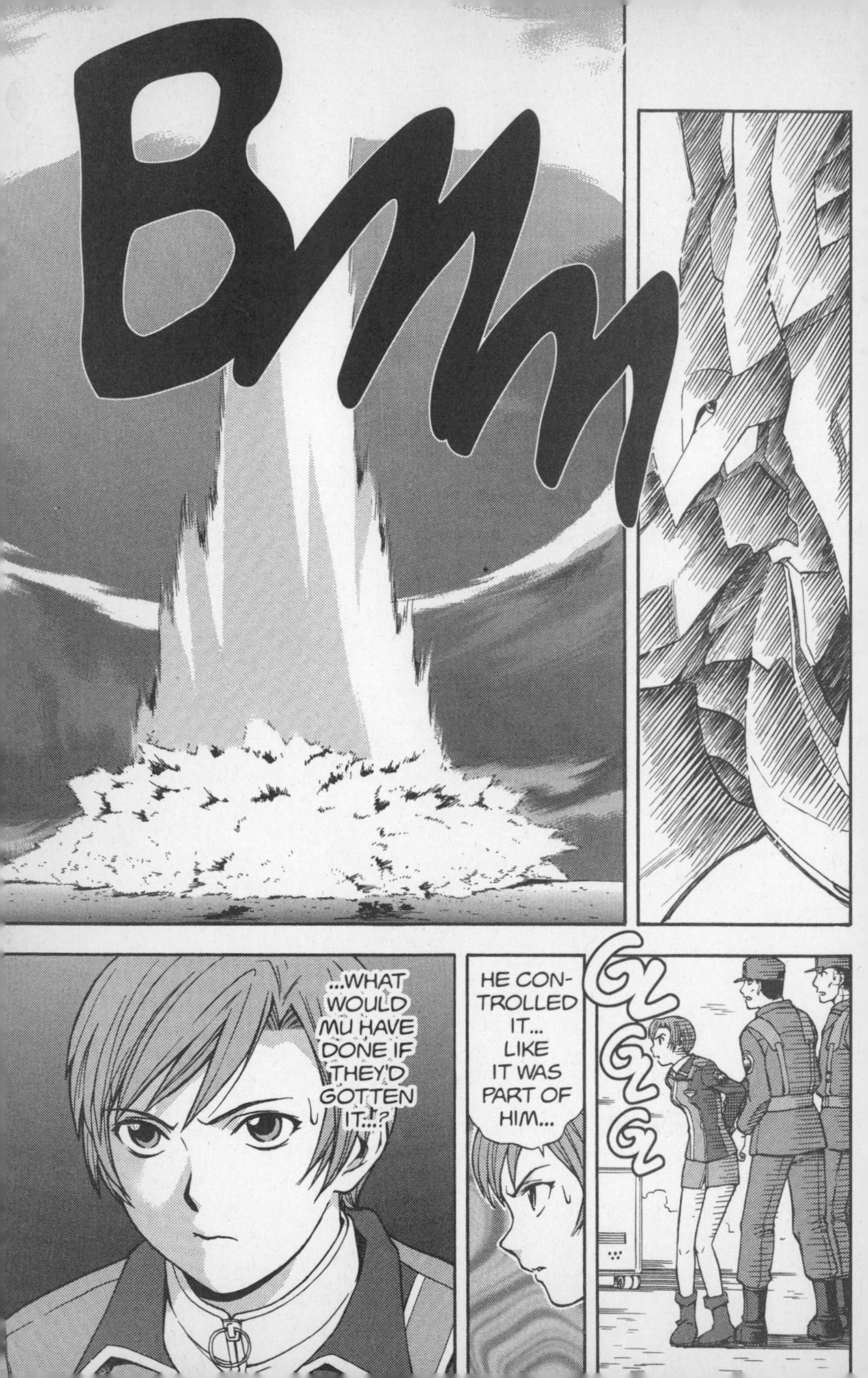
BMM
HE CONTROLLED IT... LIKE IT WAS PART OF HIM...
...WHAT WOULD MU HAVE DONE IF THEY'D GOTTEN IT...?

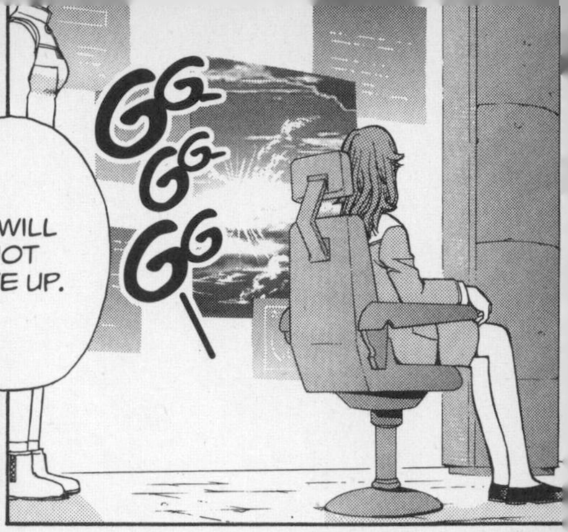
GG GG GG
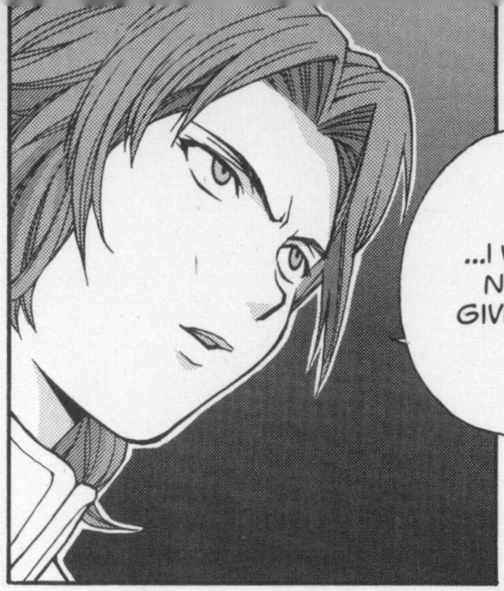
...I WILL NOT GIVE UP.
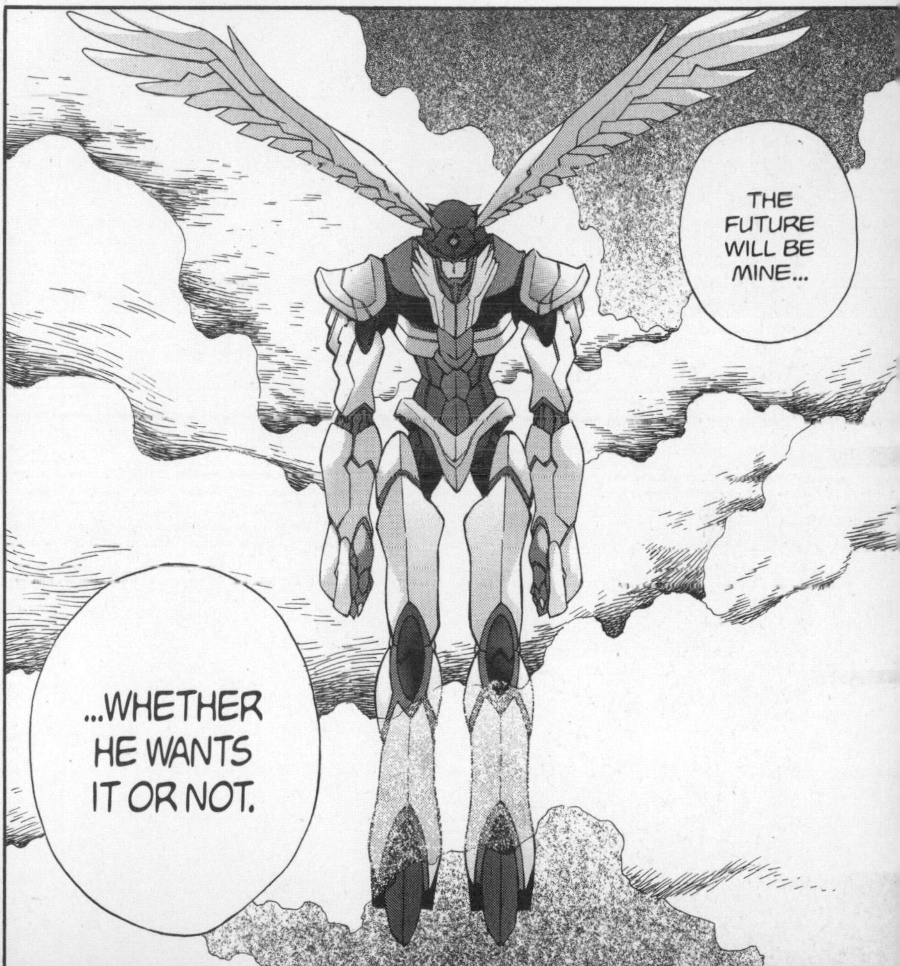
THE FUTURE WILL BE MINE...
...WHETHER HE WANTS IT OR NOT.

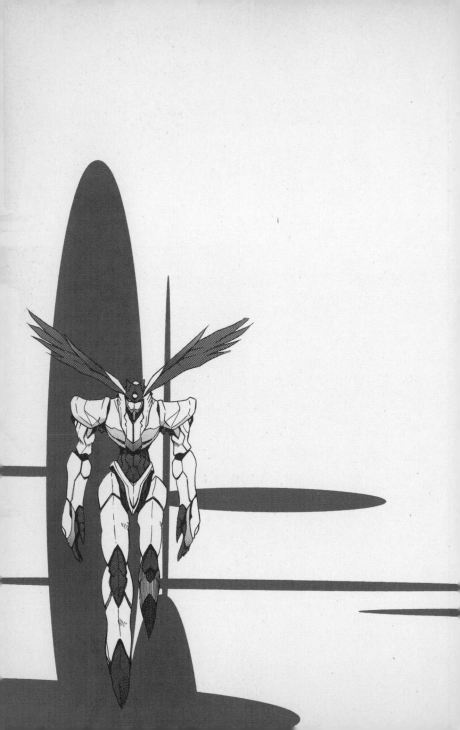

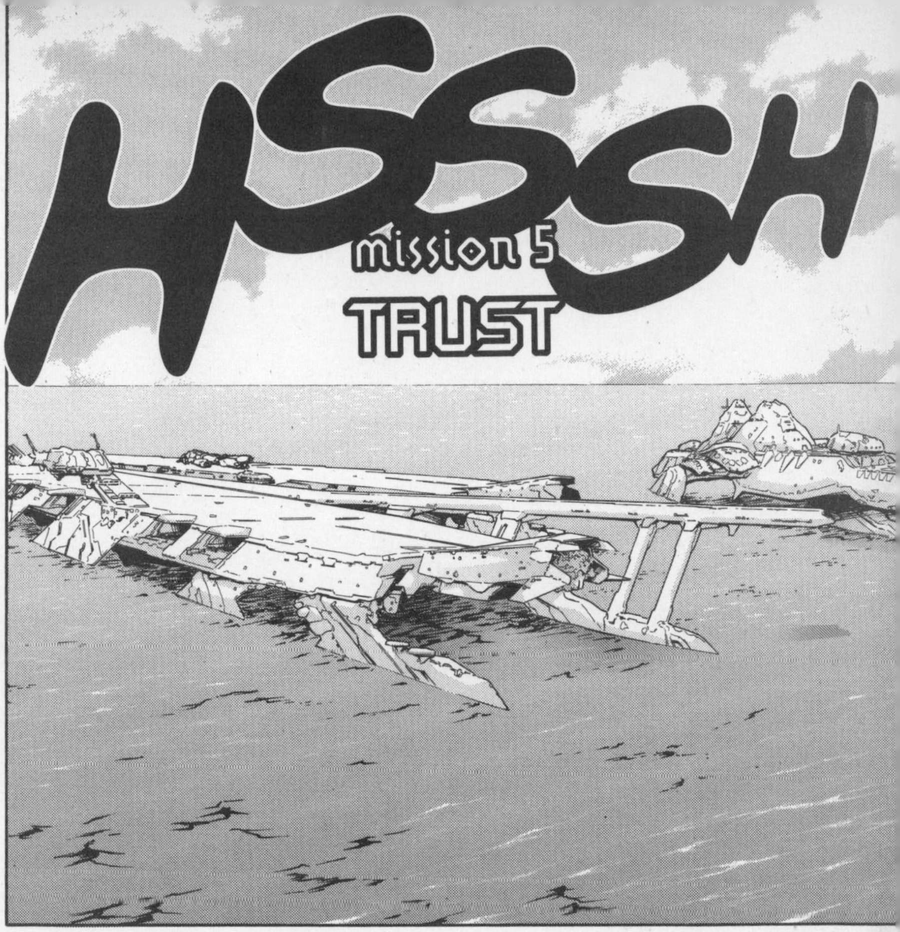
HSSSH
mission 5
TRUST

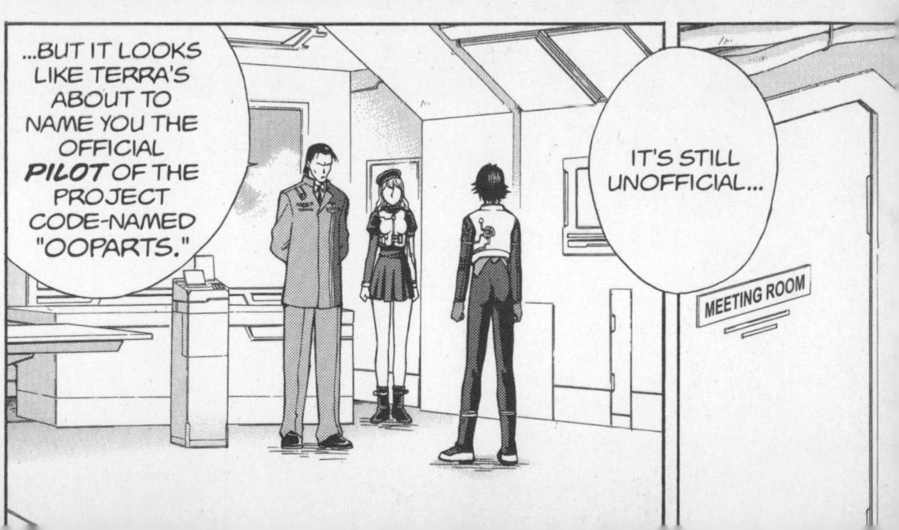
IT'S STILL UNOFFICIAL...
...BUT IT LOOKS LIKE TERRA'S ABOUT TO NAME YOU THE OFFICIAL PILOT OF THE PROJECT CODE-NAMED "OOPARTS."
MEETING ROOM

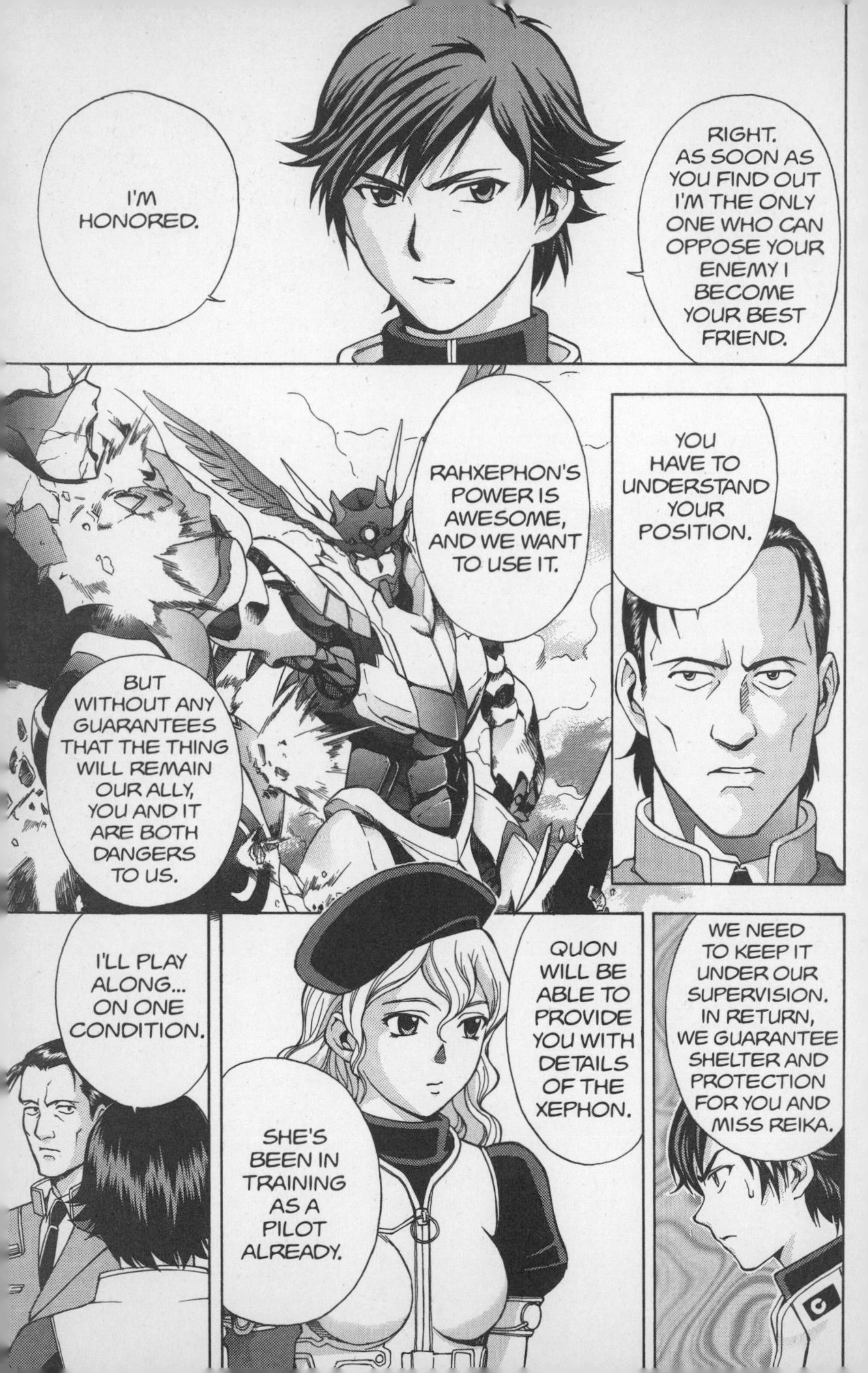
RIGHT. AS SOON AS YOU FIND OUT I'M THE ONLY ONE WHO CAN OPPOSE YOUR ENEMY I BECOME YOUR BEST FRIEND.
I'M HONORED.
YOU HAVE TO UNDERSTAND YOUR POSITION.
RAHXEPHON'S POWER IS AWESOME, AND WE WANT TO USE IT.
BUT WITHOUT ANY GUARANTEES THAT THE THING WILL REMAIN OUR ALLY, YOU AND IT ARE BOTH DANGERS TO US.
WE NEED TO KEEP IT UNDER OUR SUPERVISION. IN RETURN, WE GUARANTEE SHELTER AND PROTECTION FOR YOU AND MISS REIKA.
QUON WILL BE ABLE TO PROVIDE YOU WITH DETAILS OF THE XEPHON.
SHE'S BEEN IN TRAINING AS A PILOT ALREADY.
I'LL PLAY ALONG... ON ONE CONDITION.

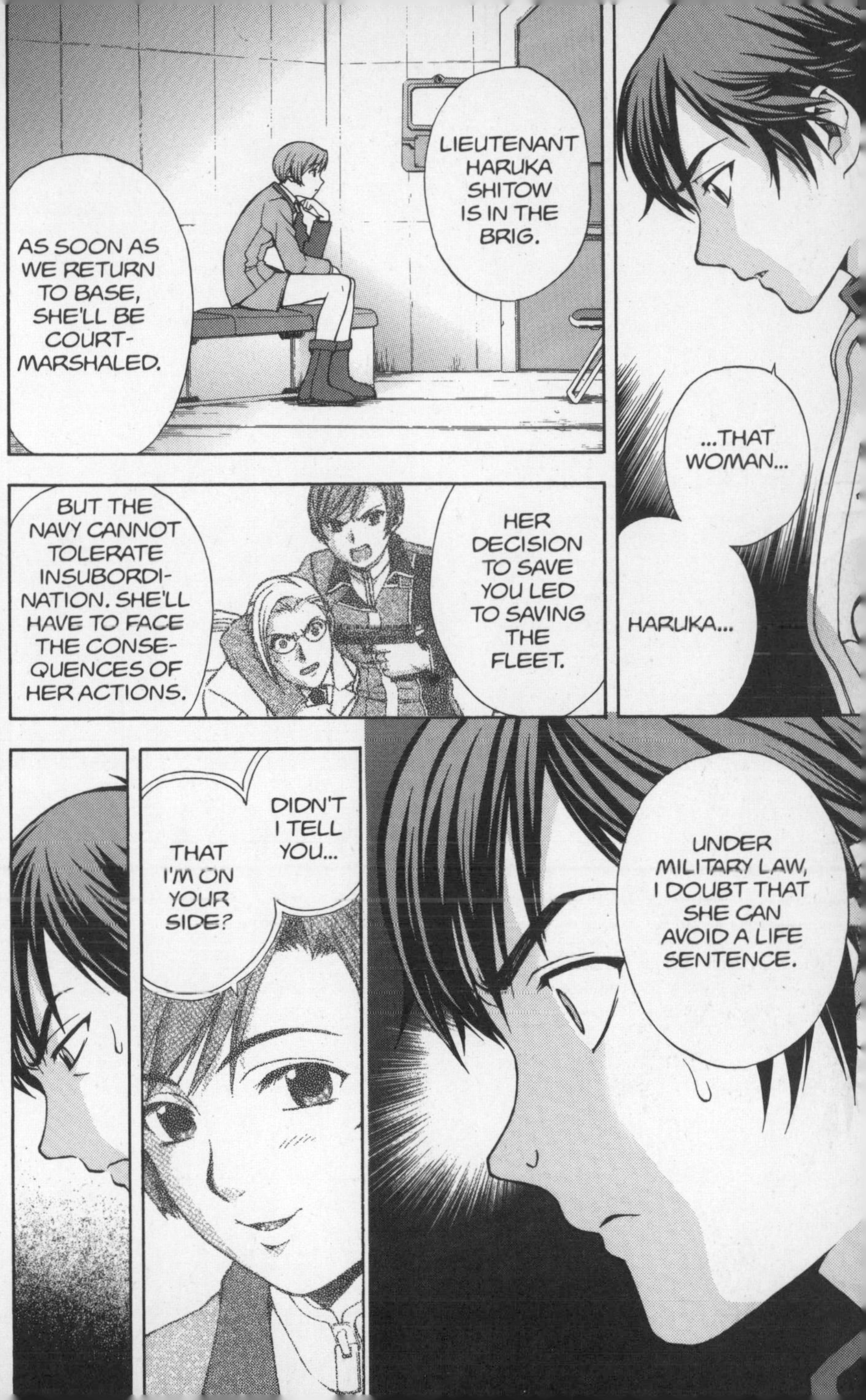
...THAT WOMAN...
HARUKA...
LIEUTENANT HARUKA SHITOW IS IN THE BRIG.
AS SOON AS WE RETURN TO BASE, SHE'LL BE COURT-MARSHALED.
HER DECISION TO SAVE YOU LED TO SAVING THE FLEET.
BUT THE NAVY CANNOT TOLERATE INSUBORDINATION. SHE'LL HAVE TO FACE THE CONSEQUENCES OF HER ACTIONS.
UNDER MILITARY LAW, I DOUBT THAT SHE CAN AVOID A LIFE SENTENCE.
DIDN'T I TELL YOU...
THAT I'M ON YOUR SIDE?

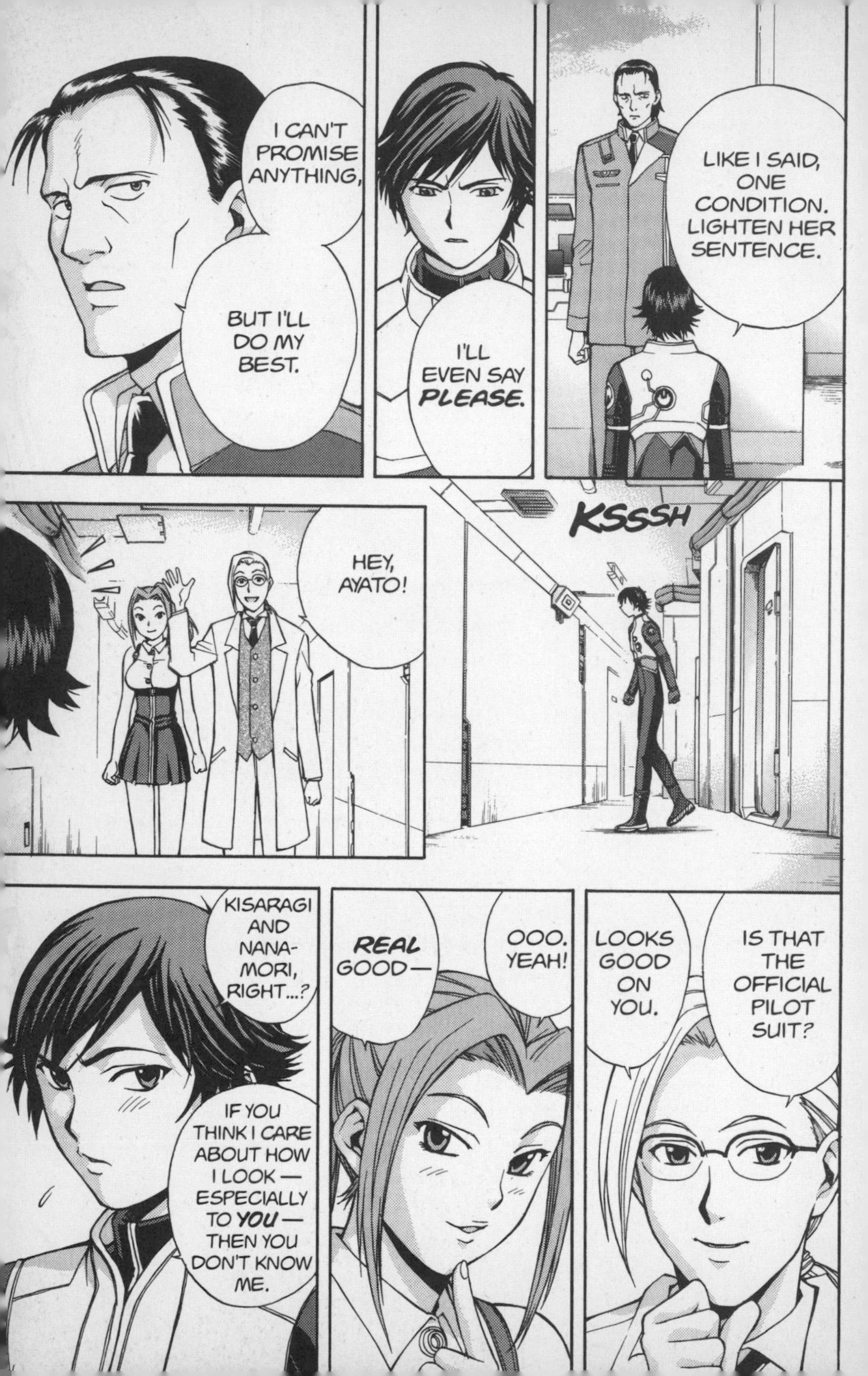
LIKE I SAID, ONE CONDITION. LIGHTEN HER SENTENCE.
I'LL EVEN SAY *PLEASE.*
I CAN'T PROMISE ANYTHING,
BUT I'LL DO MY BEST.
KSSSH
HEY, AYATO!
IS THAT THE OFFICIAL PILOT SUIT?
LOOKS GOOD ON YOU.
OOO. YEAH!
REAL GOOD—
KISARAGI AND NANA-MORI, RIGHT...?
IF YOU THINK I CARE ABOUT HOW I LOOK— ESPECIALLY TO *YOU*— THEN YOU DON'T KNOW ME.

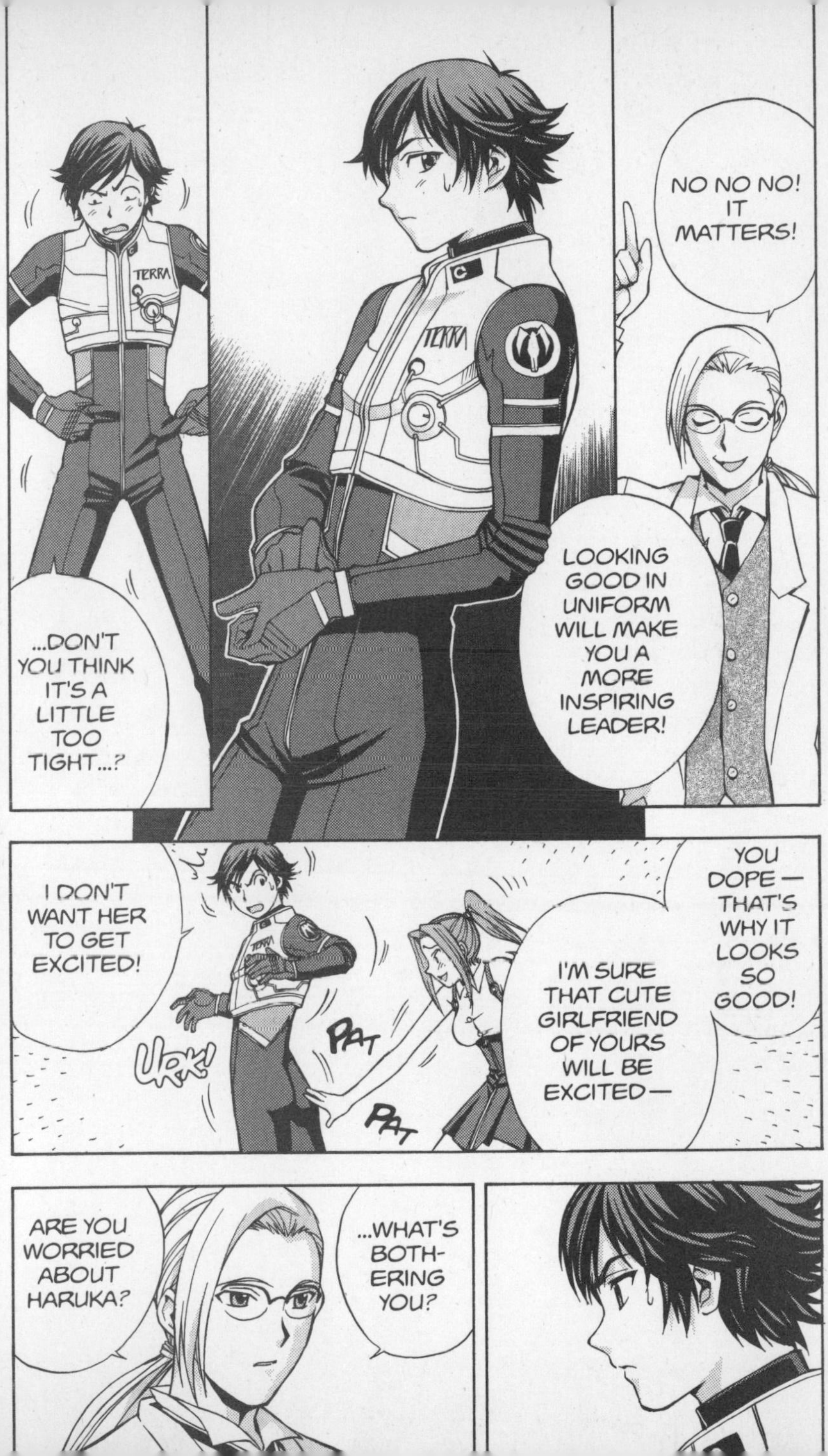
NO NO NO! IT MATTERS!
LOOKING GOOD IN UNIFORM WILL MAKE YOU A MORE INSPIRING LEADER!
...DON'T YOU THINK IT'S A LITTLE TOO TIGHT...?
I'M SURE THAT CUTE GIRLFRIEND OF YOURS WILL BE EXCITED—
PAT
PAT
URK!
I DON'T WANT HER TO GET EXCITED!
YOU DOPE—THAT'S WHY IT LOOKS SO GOOD!
...WHAT'S BOTH-ERING YOU?
ARE YOU WORRIED ABOUT HARUKA?

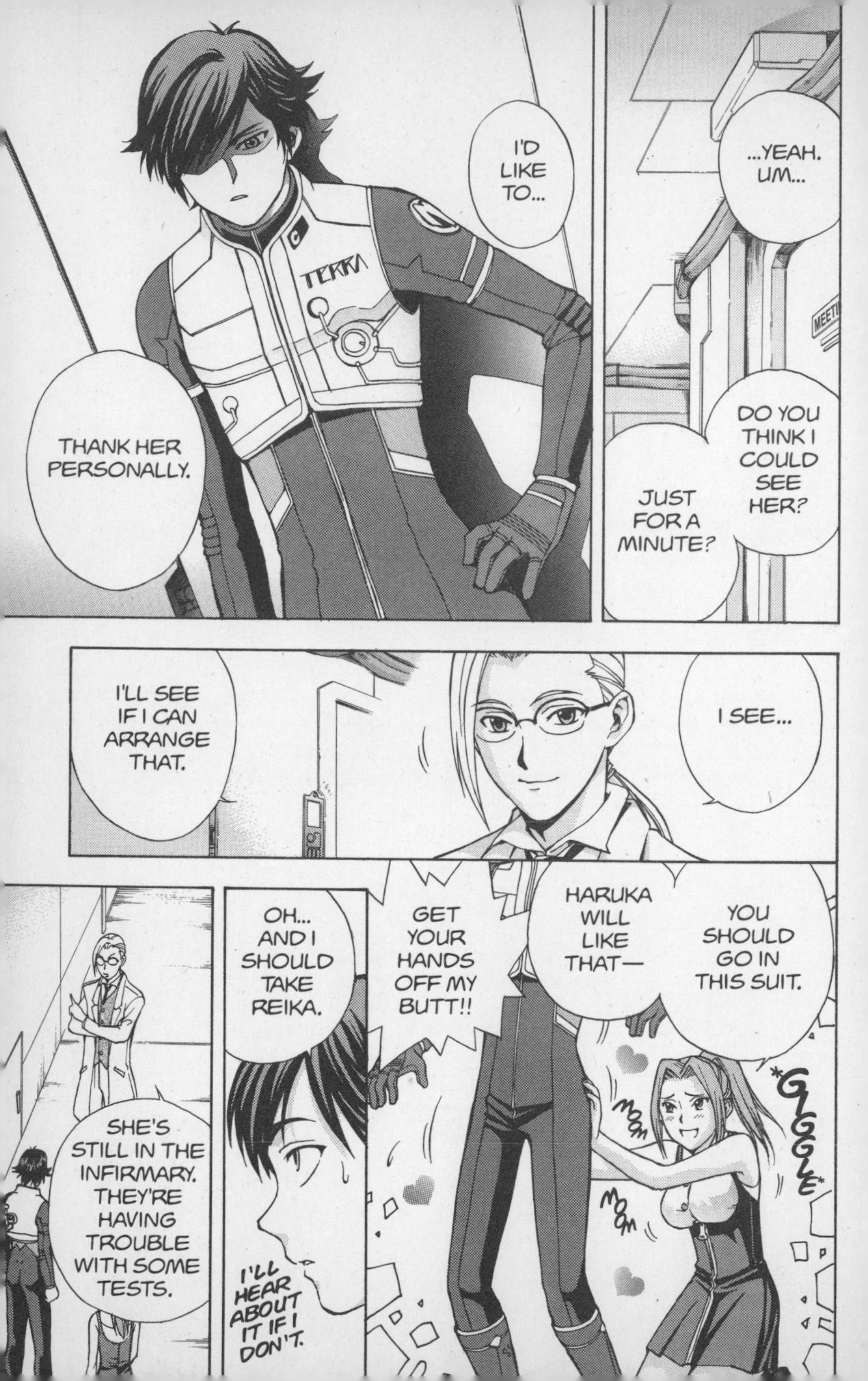
...YEAH. UM...
DO YOU THINK I COULD SEE HER?
JUST FOR A MINUTE?
I'D LIKE TO...
TERRA
THANK HER PERSONALLY.
I SEE...
I'LL SEE IF I CAN ARRANGE THAT.
YOU SHOULD GO IN THIS SUIT.
HARUKA WILL LIKE THAT—
GIGGLE
MOOM
MOOM
GET YOUR HANDS OFF MY BUTT!!
OH... AND I SHOULD TAKE REIKA.
I'LL HEAR ABOUT IT IF I DON'T.
SHE'S STILL IN THE INFIRMARY. THEY'RE HAVING TROUBLE WITH SOME TESTS.

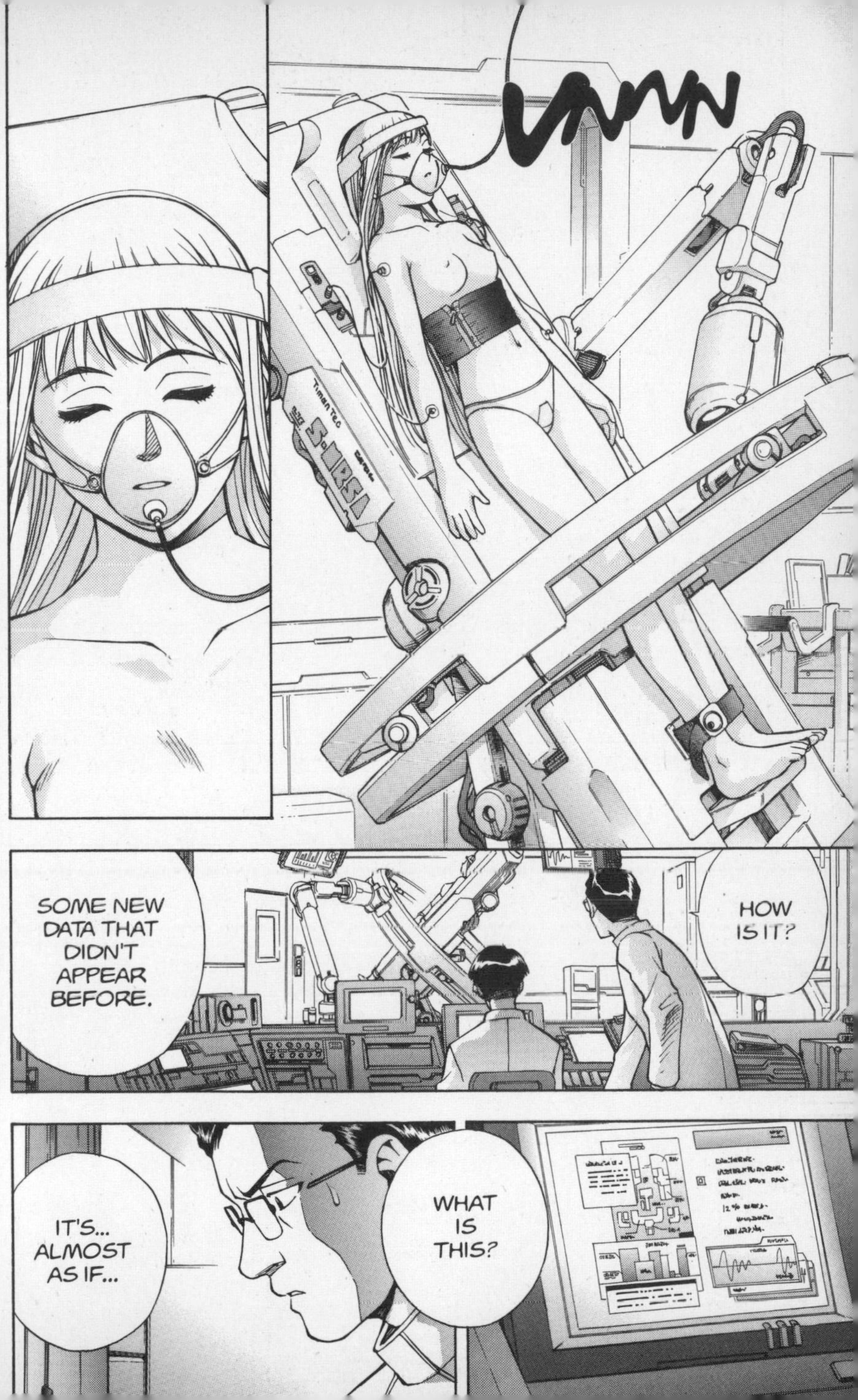
HOW IS IT?
SOME NEW DATA THAT DIDN'T APPEAR BEFORE.
WHAT IS THIS?
IT'S... ALMOST AS IF...

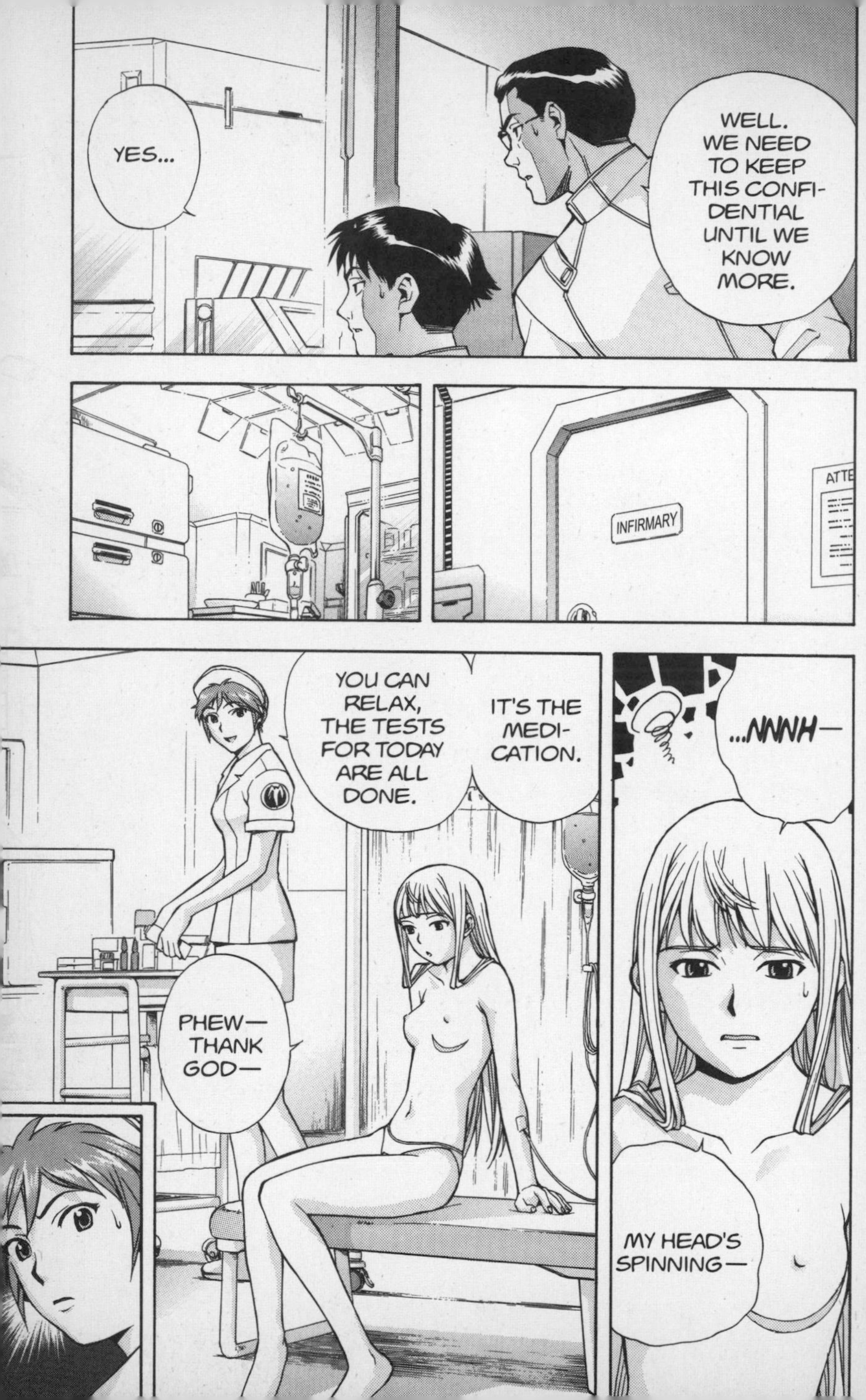
WELL. WE NEED TO KEEP THIS CONFI-DENTIAL UNTIL WE KNOW MORE.
YES...
ATTE
INFIRMARY
...NNNH—
MY HEAD'S SPINNING—
IT'S THE MEDI-CATION.
YOU CAN RELAX, THE TESTS FOR TODAY ARE ALL DONE.
PHEW— THANK GOD—

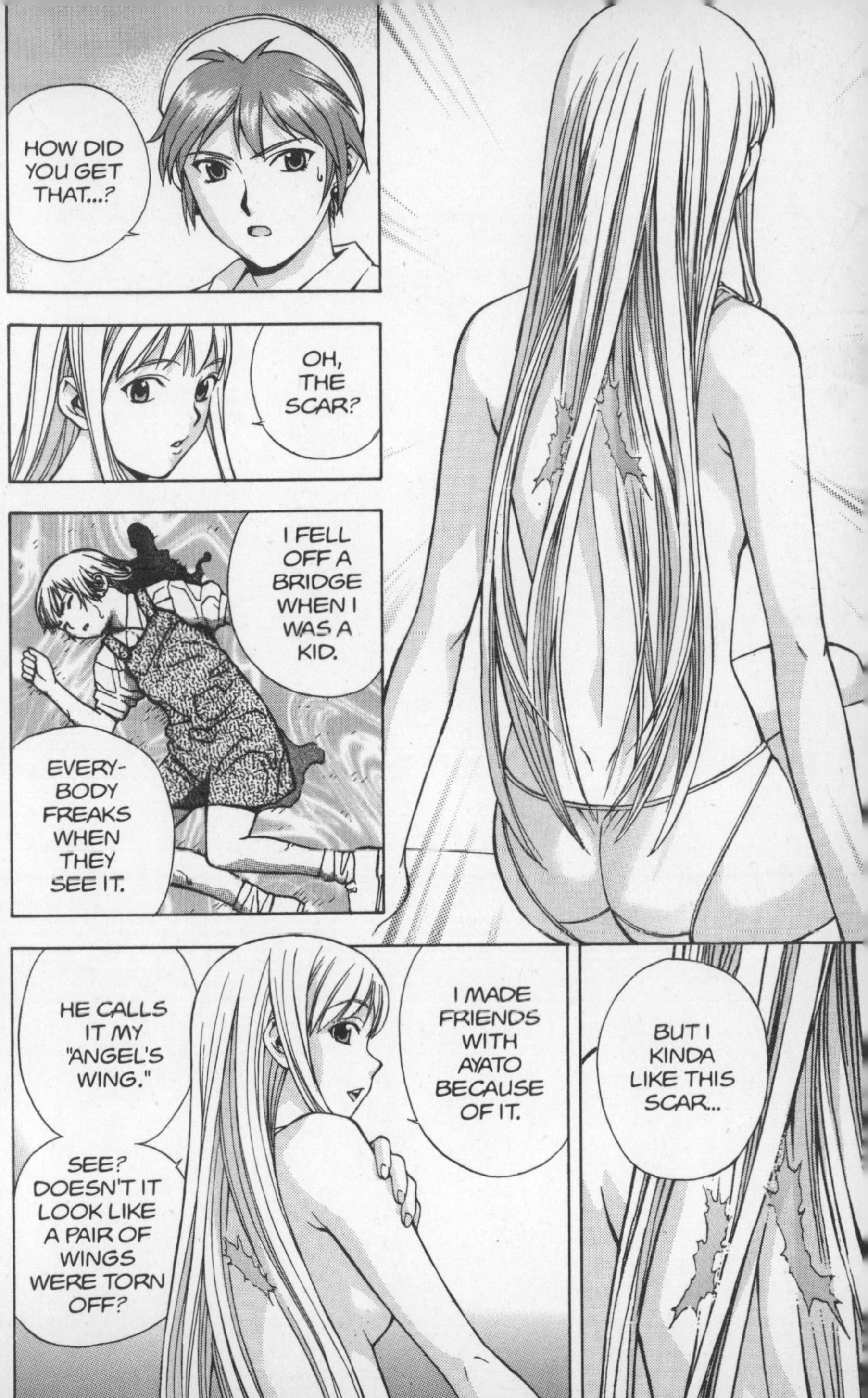
HOW DID YOU GET THAT...?
OH, THE SCAR?
I FELL OFF A BRIDGE WHEN I WAS A KID.
EVERY-BODY FREAKS WHEN THEY SEE IT.
BUT I KINDA LIKE THIS SCAR...
I MADE FRIENDS WITH AYATO BECAUSE OF IT.
HE CALLS IT MY "ANGEL'S WING."
SEE? DOESN'T IT LOOK LIKE A PAIR OF WINGS WERE TORN OFF?

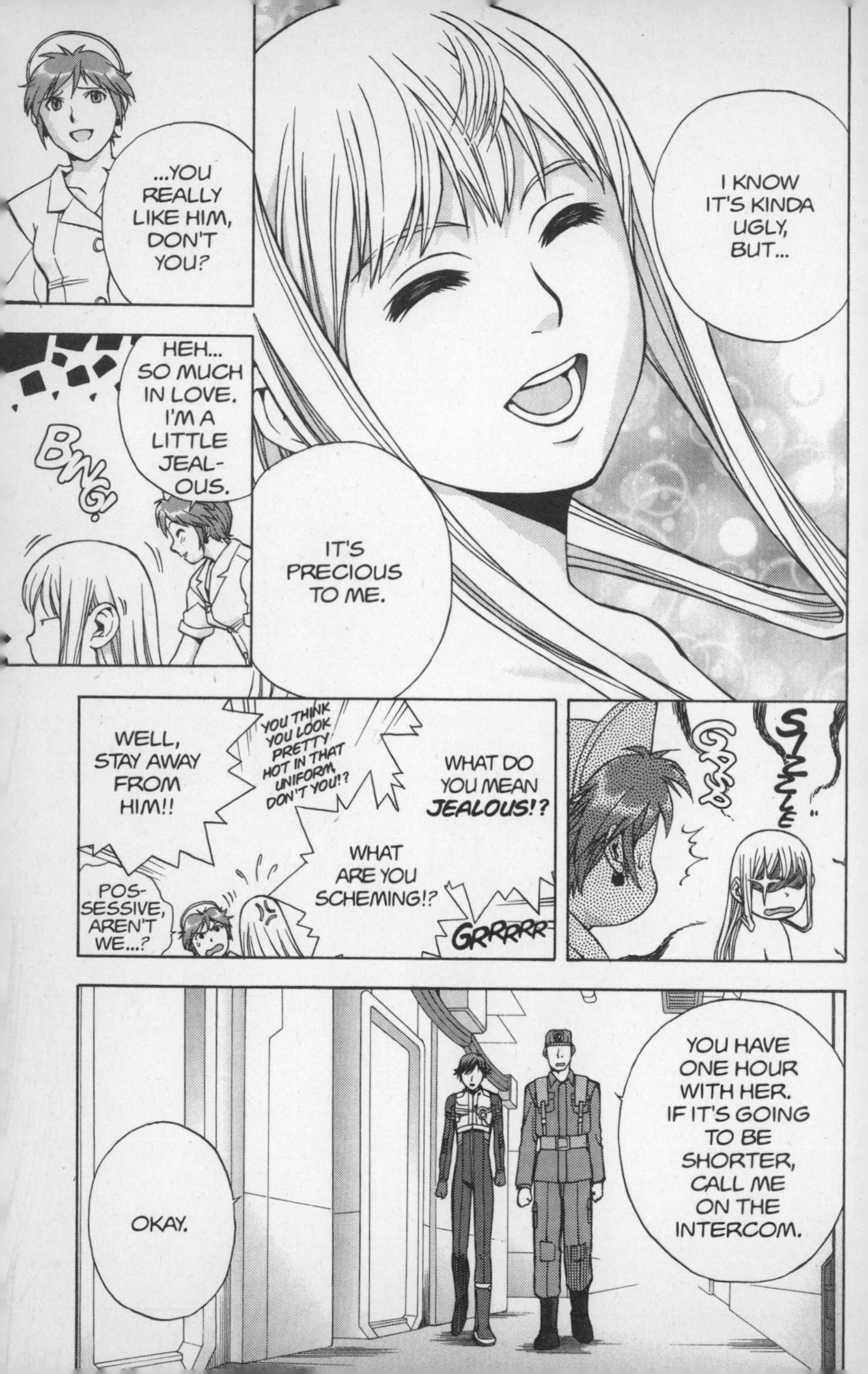
I KNOW IT'S KINDA UGLY, BUT...
IT'S PRECIOUS TO ME.
...YOU REALLY LIKE HIM, DON'T YOU?
HEH... SO MUCH IN LOVE. I'M A LITTLE JEAL-OUS.
BANG
GASP
SIZZLE
WHAT DO YOU MEAN *JEALOUS*!?
YOU THINK YOU LOOK PRETTY HOT IN THAT UNIFORM, DON'T YOU!?
WHAT ARE YOU SCHEMING!?
GRRRRR
WELL, STAY AWAY FROM HIM!!
POS-SESSIVE, AREN'T WE...?
YOU HAVE ONE HOUR WITH HER. IF IT'S GOING TO BE SHORTER, CALL ME ON THE INTERCOM.
OKAY.

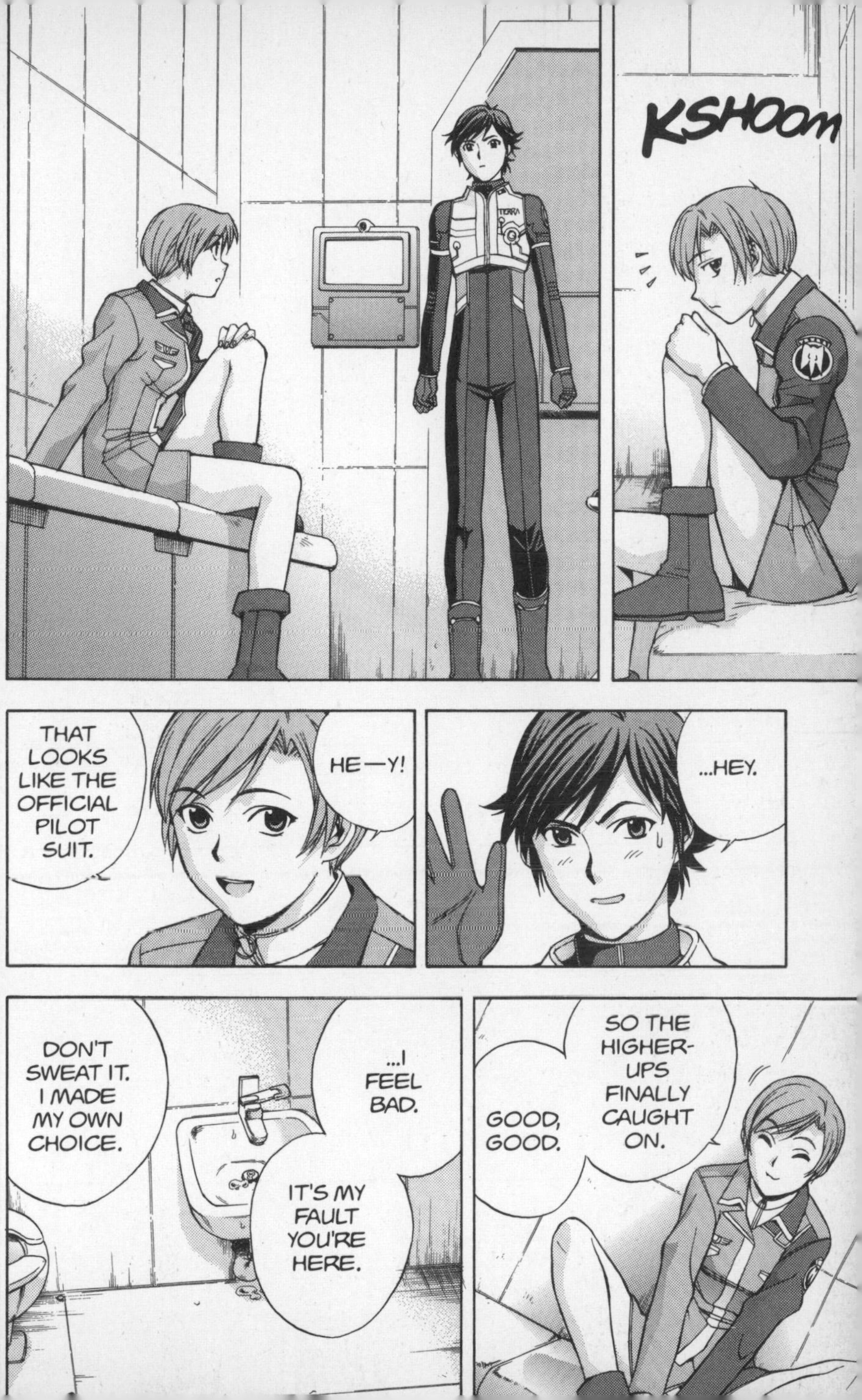
KSHOOM
...HEY.
HE—Y!
THAT LOOKS LIKE THE OFFICIAL PILOT SUIT.
SO THE HIGHER-UPS FINALLY CAUGHT ON.
GOOD, GOOD.
...I FEEL BAD.
IT'S MY FAULT YOU'RE HERE.
DON'T SWEAT IT. I MADE MY OWN CHOICE.

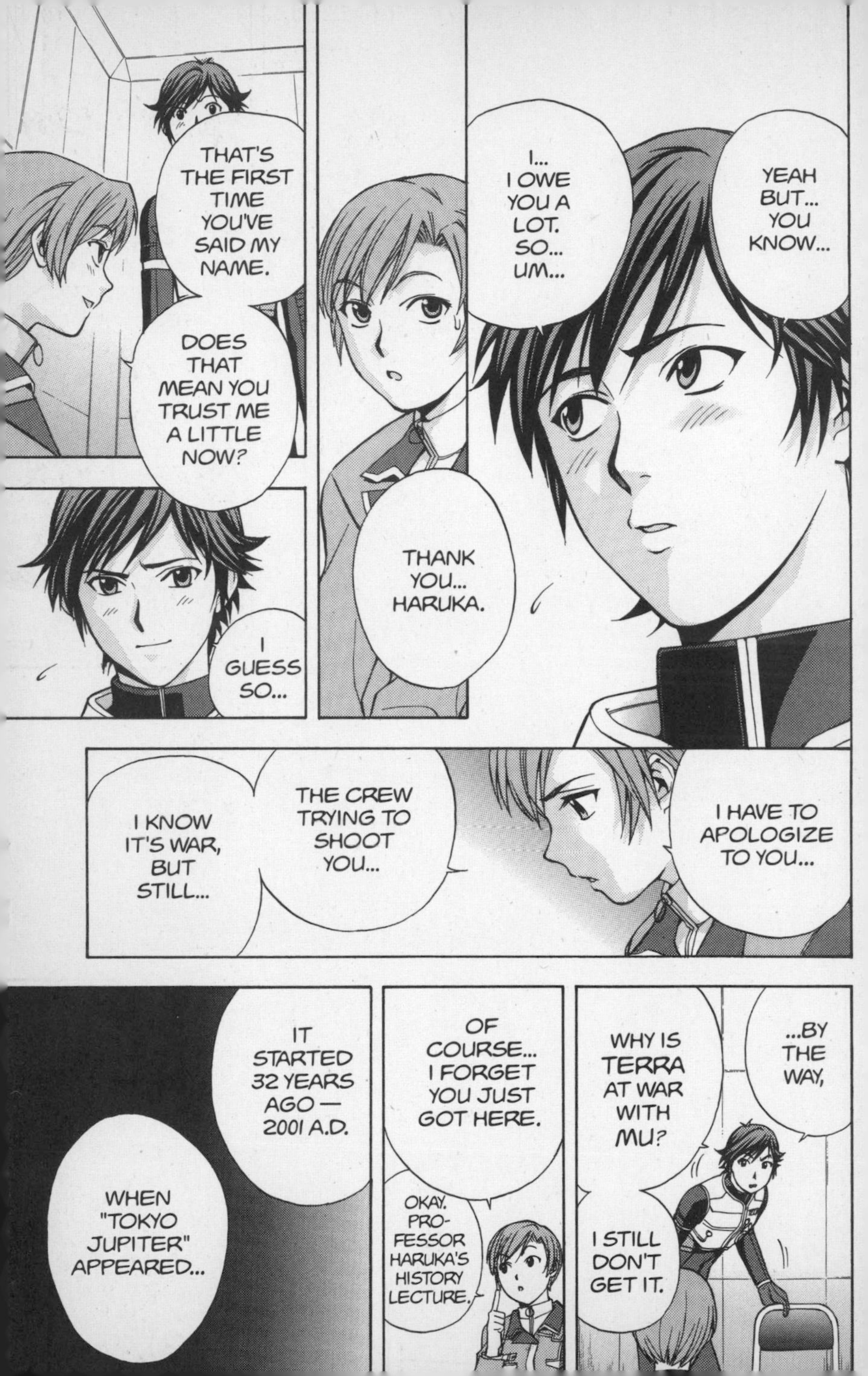
YEAH BUT... YOU KNOW...
I... I OWE YOU A LOT. SO... UM...
THANK YOU... HARUKA.
THAT'S THE FIRST TIME YOU'VE SAID MY NAME.
DOES THAT MEAN YOU TRUST ME A LITTLE NOW?
I GUESS SO...
I HAVE TO APOLOGIZE TO YOU...
THE CREW TRYING TO SHOOT YOU...
I KNOW IT'S WAR, BUT STILL...
...BY THE WAY,
WHY IS TERRA AT WAR WITH MU?
I STILL DON'T GET IT.
OF COURSE... I FORGET YOU JUST GOT HERE.
OKAY. PRO-FESSOR HARUKA'S HISTORY LECTURE.
IT STARTED 32 YEARS AGO — 2001 A.D.
WHEN "TOKYO JUPITER" APPEARED...

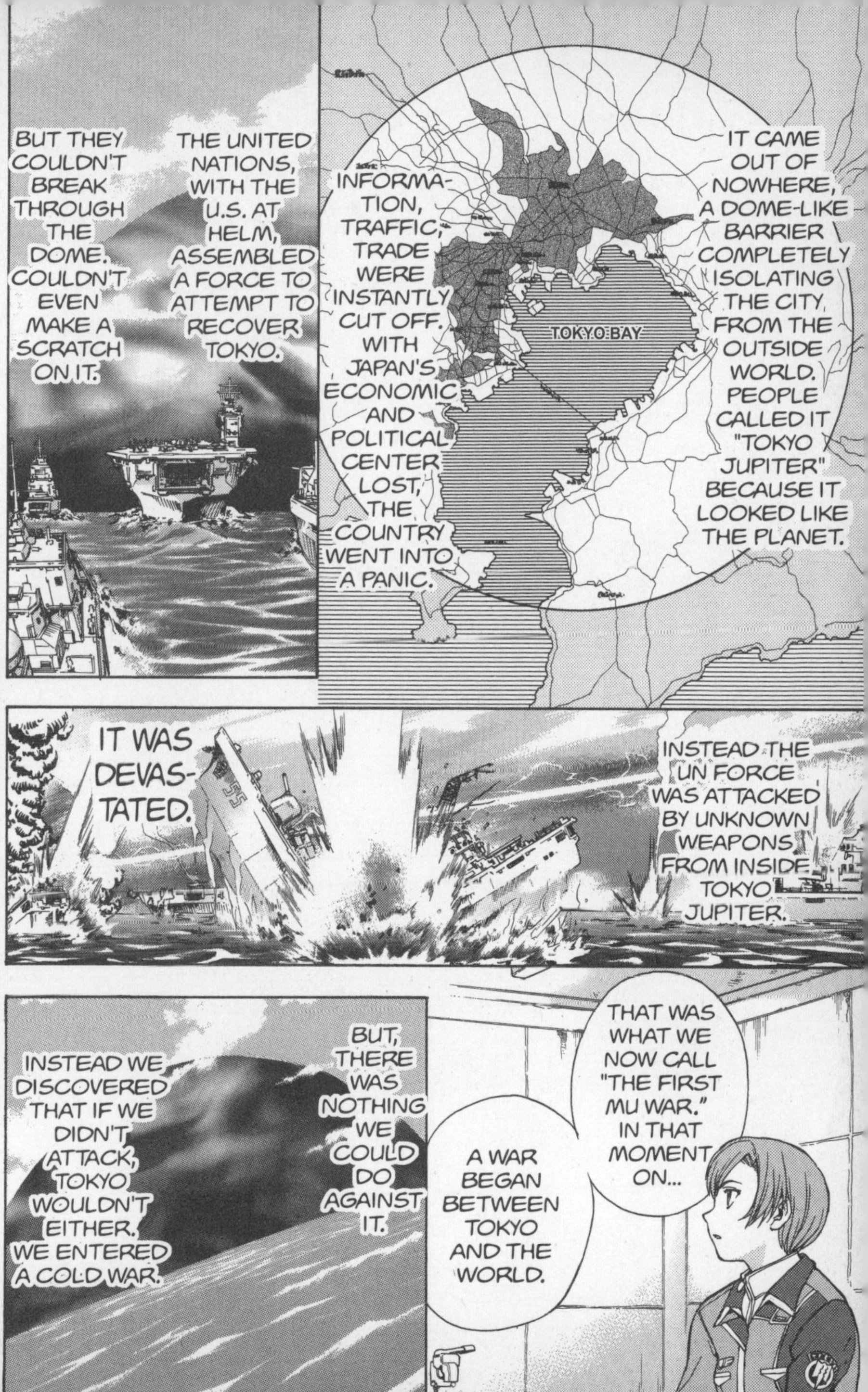
IT CAME OUT OF NOWHERE, A DOME-LIKE BARRIER COMPLETELY ISOLATING THE CITY FROM THE OUTSIDE WORLD. PEOPLE CALLED IT "TOKYO JUPITER" BECAUSE IT LOOKED LIKE THE PLANET.
INFORMATION, TRAFFIC, TRADE WERE INSTANTLY CUT OFF. WITH JAPAN'S ECONOMIC AND POLITICAL CENTER LOST, THE COUNTRY WENT INTO A PANIC.
TOKYO BAY
THE UNITED NATIONS, WITH THE U.S. AT HELM, ASSEMBLED A FORCE TO ATTEMPT TO RECOVER TOKYO.
BUT THEY COULDN'T BREAK THROUGH THE DOME. COULDN'T EVEN MAKE A SCRATCH ON IT.
INSTEAD THE UN FORCE WAS ATTACKED BY UNKNOWN WEAPONS FROM INSIDE TOKYO JUPITER.
IT WAS DEVASTATED.
THAT WAS WHAT WE NOW CALL "THE FIRST MU WAR." IN THAT MOMENT ON...
A WAR BEGAN BETWEEN TOKYO AND THE WORLD.
BUT, THERE WAS NOTHING WE COULD DO AGAINST IT.
INSTEAD WE DISCOVERED THAT IF WE DIDN'T ATTACK, TOKYO WOULDN'T EITHER. WE ENTERED A COLD WAR.

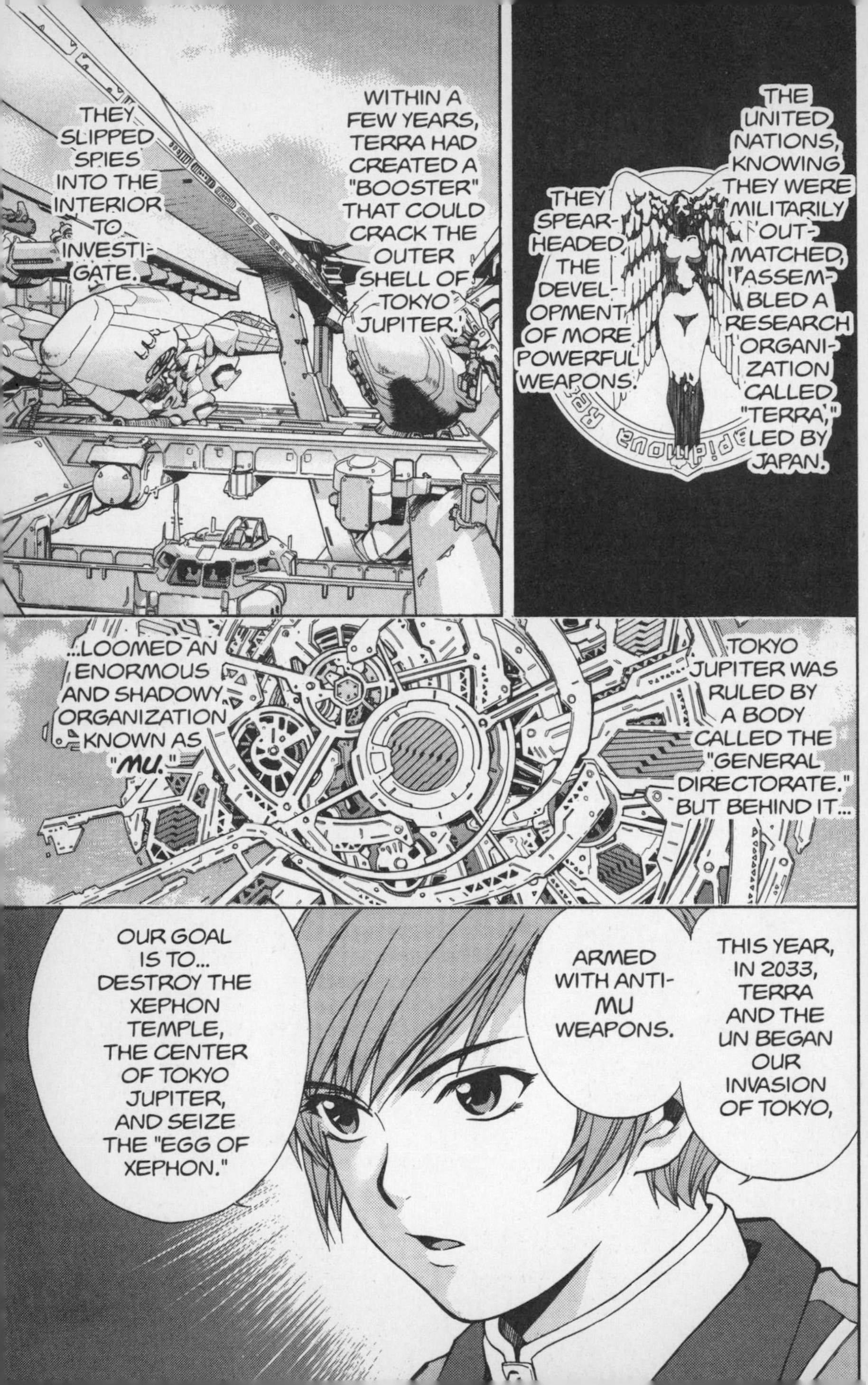
THE UNITED NATIONS, KNOWING THEY WERE MILITARILY OUT-MATCHED, ASSEMBLED A RESEARCH ORGANIZATION CALLED "TERRA," LED BY JAPAN.
THEY SPEAR-HEADED THE DEVEL-OPMENT OF MORE POWERFUL WEAPONS.
WITHIN A FEW YEARS, TERRA HAD CREATED A "BOOSTER" THAT COULD CRACK THE OUTER SHELL OF TOKYO JUPITER.
THEY SLIPPED SPIES INTO THE INTERIOR TO INVESTI-GATE.
TOKYO JUPITER WAS RULED BY A BODY CALLED THE "GENERAL DIRECTORATE." BUT BEHIND IT...
...LOOMED AN ENORMOUS AND SHADOWY ORGANIZATION KNOWN AS "MU."
THIS YEAR, IN 2033, TERRA AND THE UN BEGAN OUR INVASION OF TOKYO,
ARMED WITH ANTI-MU WEAPONS.
OUR GOAL IS TO... DESTROY THE XEPHON TEMPLE, THE CENTER OF TOKYO JUPITER, AND SEIZE THE "EGG OF XEPHON."

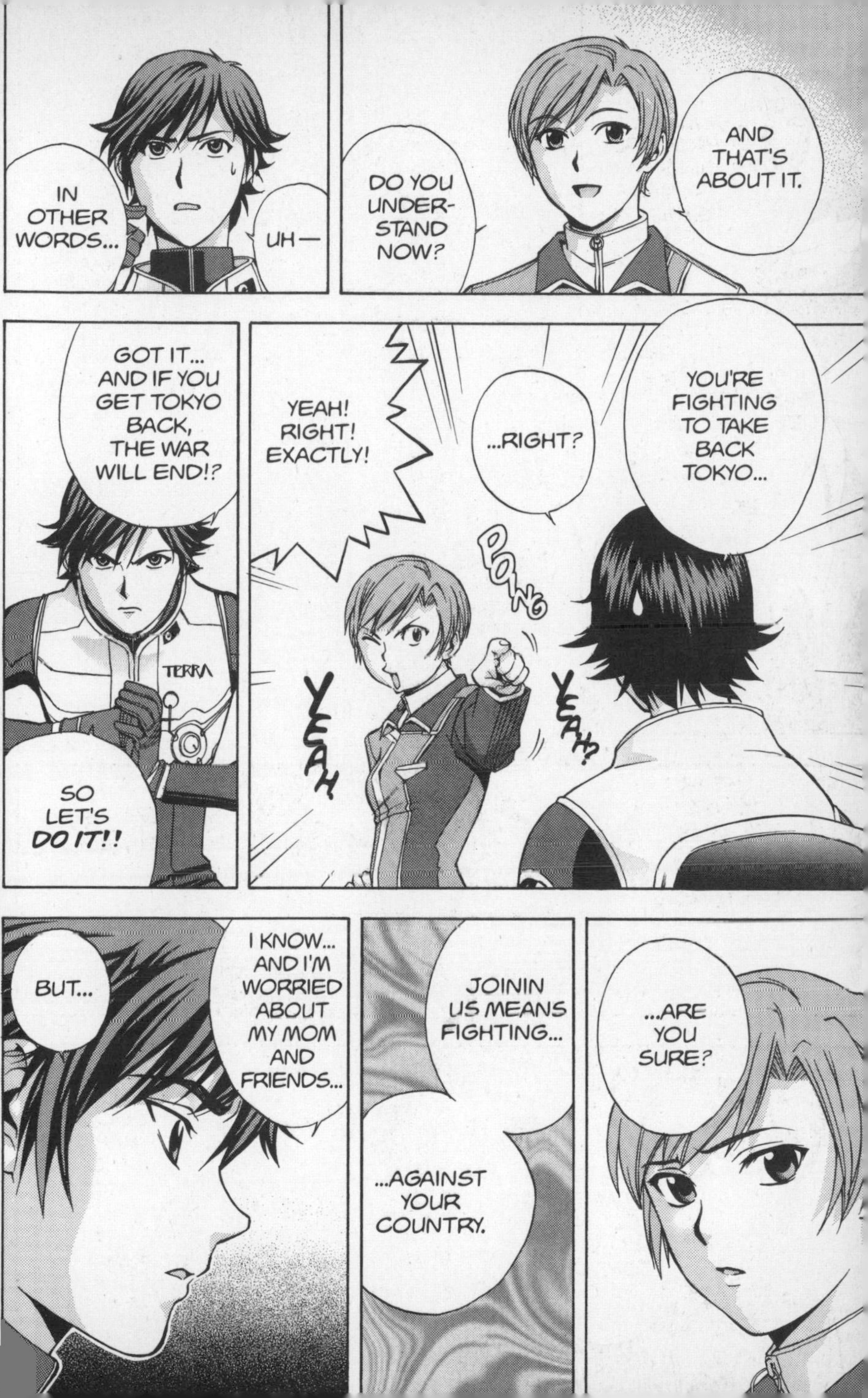
AND THAT'S ABOUT IT.
DO YOU UNDER-STAND NOW?
UH—
IN OTHER WORDS...
YOU'RE FIGHTING TO TAKE BACK TOKYO...
...RIGHT?
YEAH! RIGHT! EXACTLY!
POING
YEAH?
YEAH
GOT IT... AND IF YOU GET TOKYO BACK, THE WAR WILL END!?
TERRA
SO LET'S **DO IT!!**
...ARE YOU SURE?
JOININ US MEANS FIGHTING...
...AGAINST YOUR COUNTRY.
I KNOW... AND I'M WORRIED ABOUT MY MOM AND FRIENDS...
BUT...

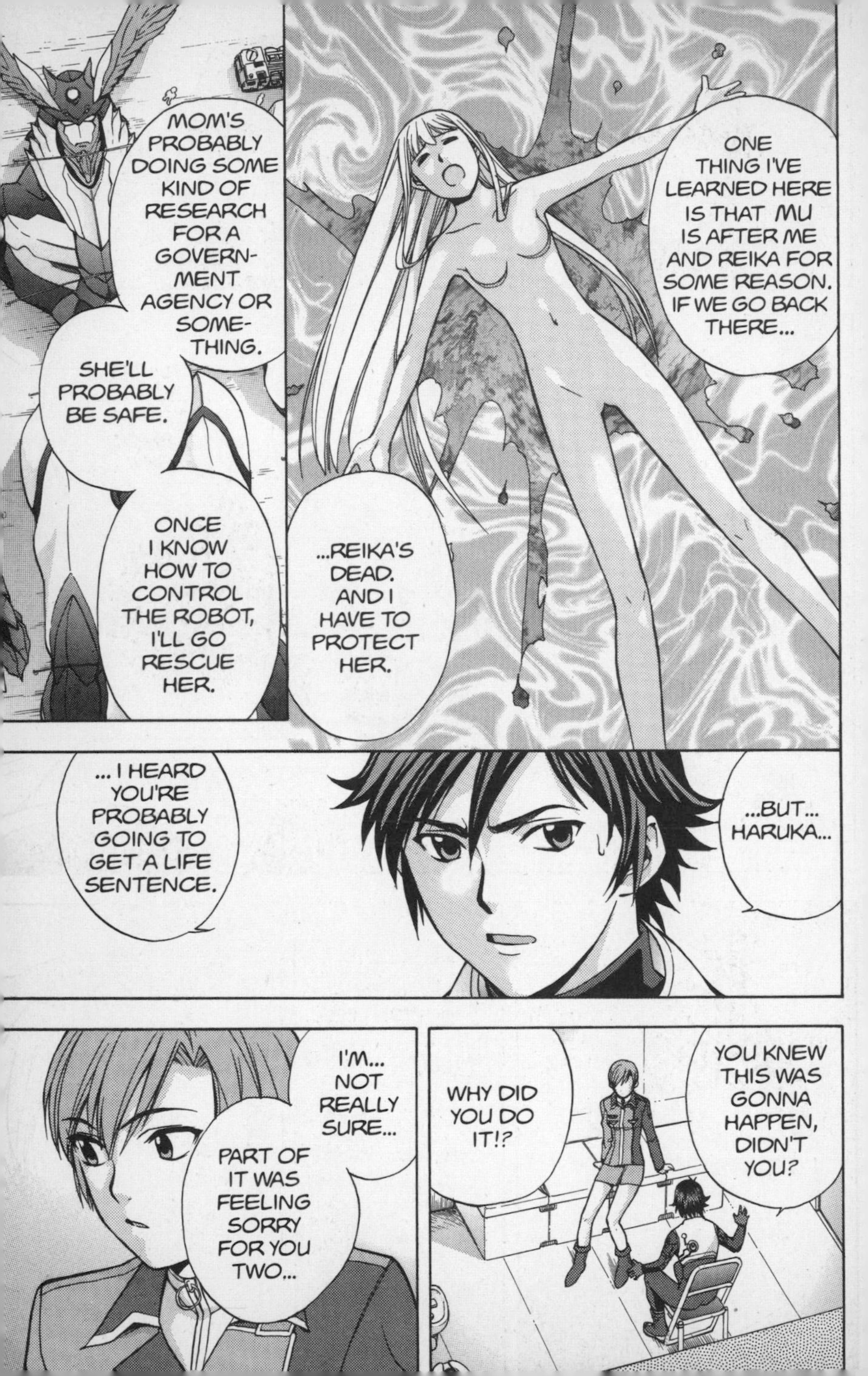
ONE THING I'VE LEARNED HERE IS THAT MU IS AFTER ME AND REIKA FOR SOME REASON. IF WE GO BACK THERE...
...REIKA'S DEAD. AND I HAVE TO PROTECT HER.
MOM'S PROBABLY DOING SOME KIND OF RESEARCH FOR A GOVERNMENT AGENCY OR SOMETHING.
SHE'LL PROBABLY BE SAFE.
ONCE I KNOW HOW TO CONTROL THE ROBOT, I'LL GO RESCUE HER.
...BUT... HARUKA...
... I HEARD YOU'RE PROBABLY GOING TO GET A LIFE SENTENCE.
YOU KNEW THIS WAS GONNA HAPPEN, DIDN'T YOU?
WHY DID YOU DO IT!?
I'M... NOT REALLY SURE...
PART OF IT WAS FEELING SORRY FOR YOU TWO...

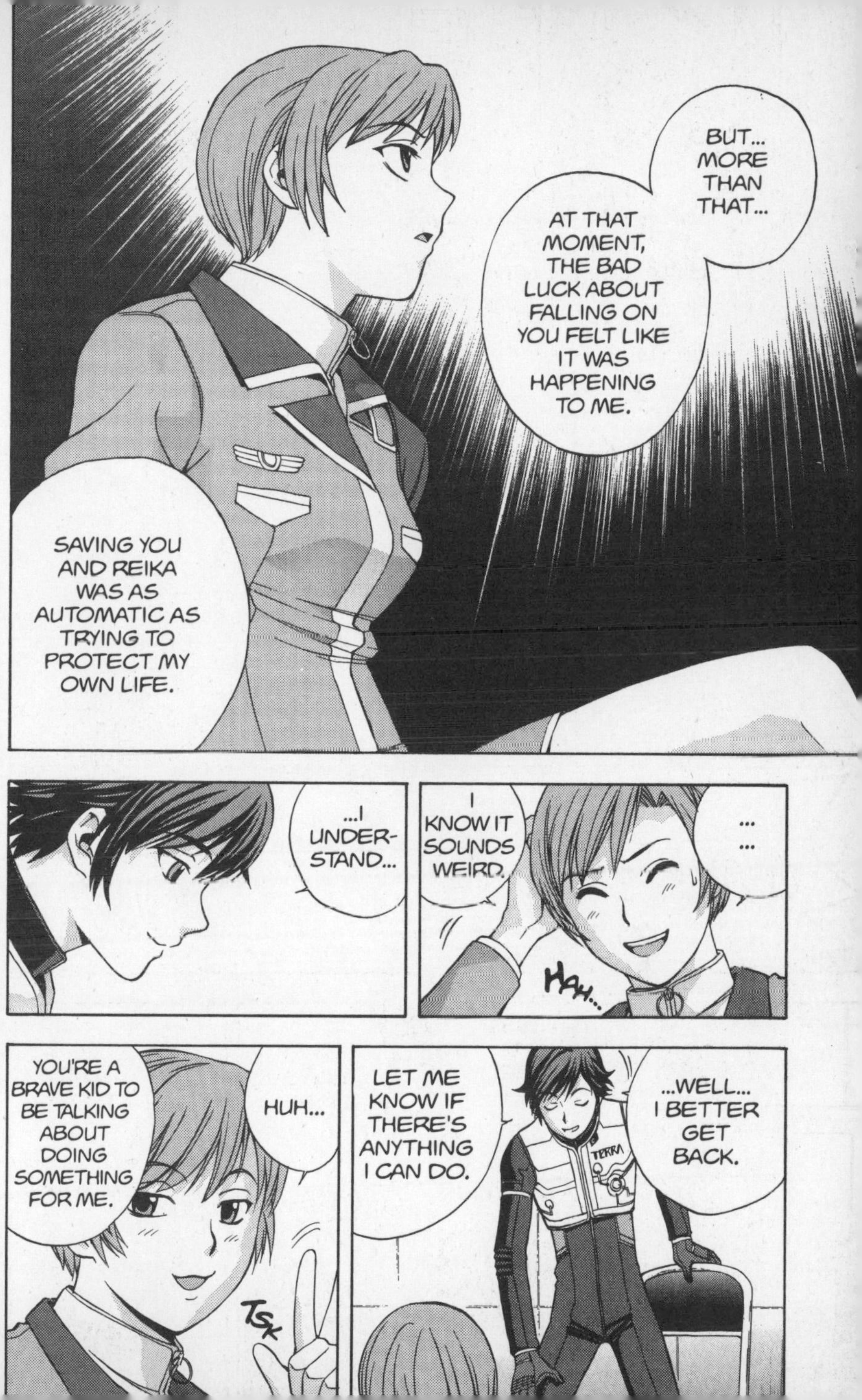
BUT... MORE THAN THAT...
AT THAT MOMENT, THE BAD LUCK ABOUT FALLING ON YOU FELT LIKE IT WAS HAPPENING TO ME.
SAVING YOU AND REIKA WAS AS AUTOMATIC AS TRYING TO PROTECT MY OWN LIFE.
... ...
I KNOW IT SOUNDS WEIRD.
HAH...
...I UNDERSTAND...
...WELL... I BETTER GET BACK.
LET ME KNOW IF THERE'S ANYTHING I CAN DO.
HUH...
YOU'RE A BRAVE KID TO BE TALKING ABOUT DOING SOMETHING FOR ME.
TSK

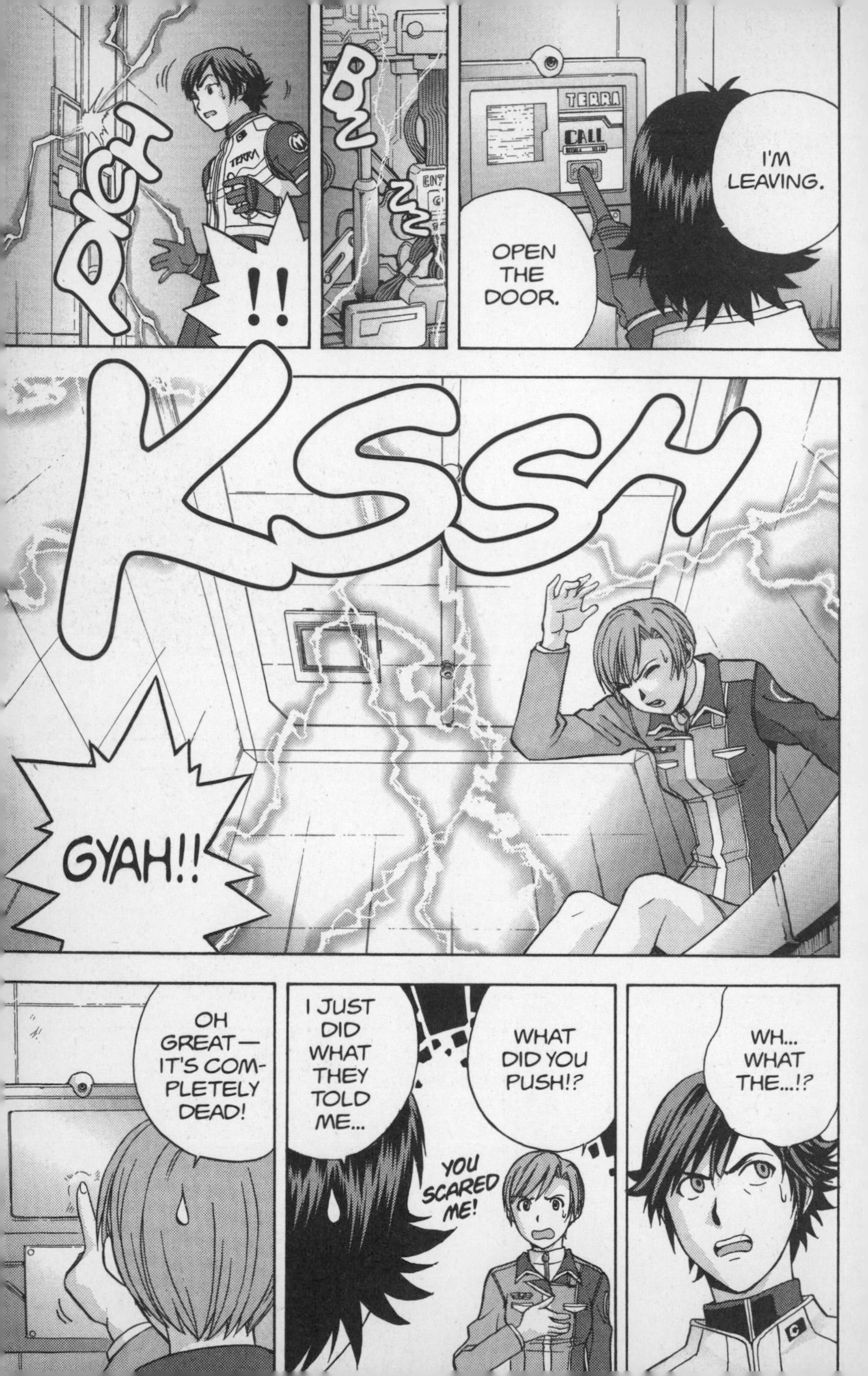
I'M LEAVING.
OPEN THE DOOR.
TERRA
CALL
BZZ
PICH
!!
KSSH
GYAH!!
WH... WHAT THE...!?
WHAT DID YOU PUSH!?
YOU SCARED ME!
I JUST DID WHAT THEY TOLD ME...
OH GREAT— IT'S COM-PLETELY DEAD!

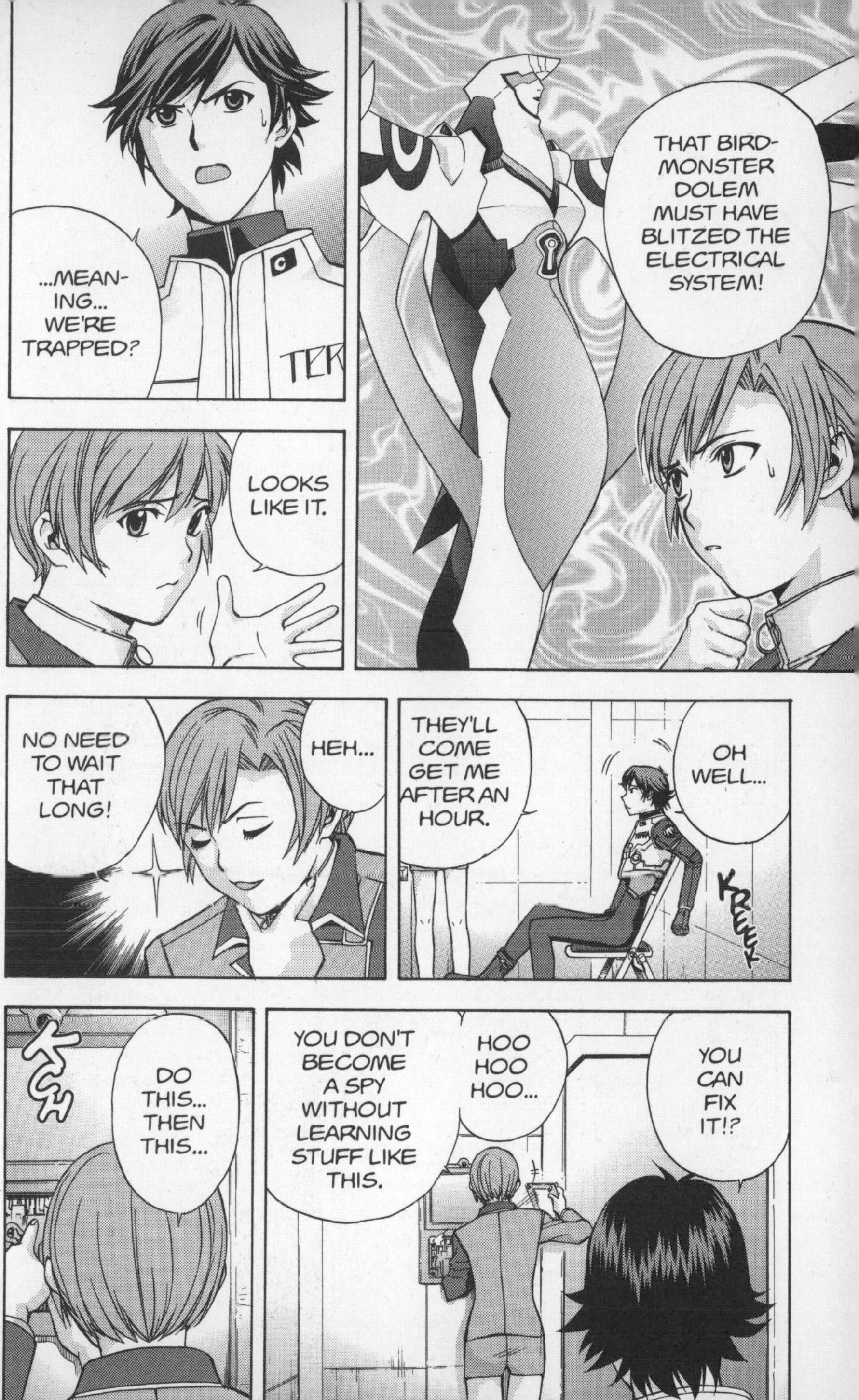
THAT BIRD-MONSTER DOLEM MUST HAVE BLITZED THE ELECTRICAL SYSTEM!
...MEAN-ING... WE'RE TRAPPED?
LOOKS LIKE IT.
OH WELL...
THEY'LL COME GET ME AFTER AN HOUR.
KREEEK
HEH...
NO NEED TO WAIT THAT LONG!
YOU CAN FIX IT!?
HOO HOO HOO...
YOU DON'T BECOME A SPY WITHOUT LEARNING STUFF LIKE THIS.
KCH
DO THIS... THEN THIS...

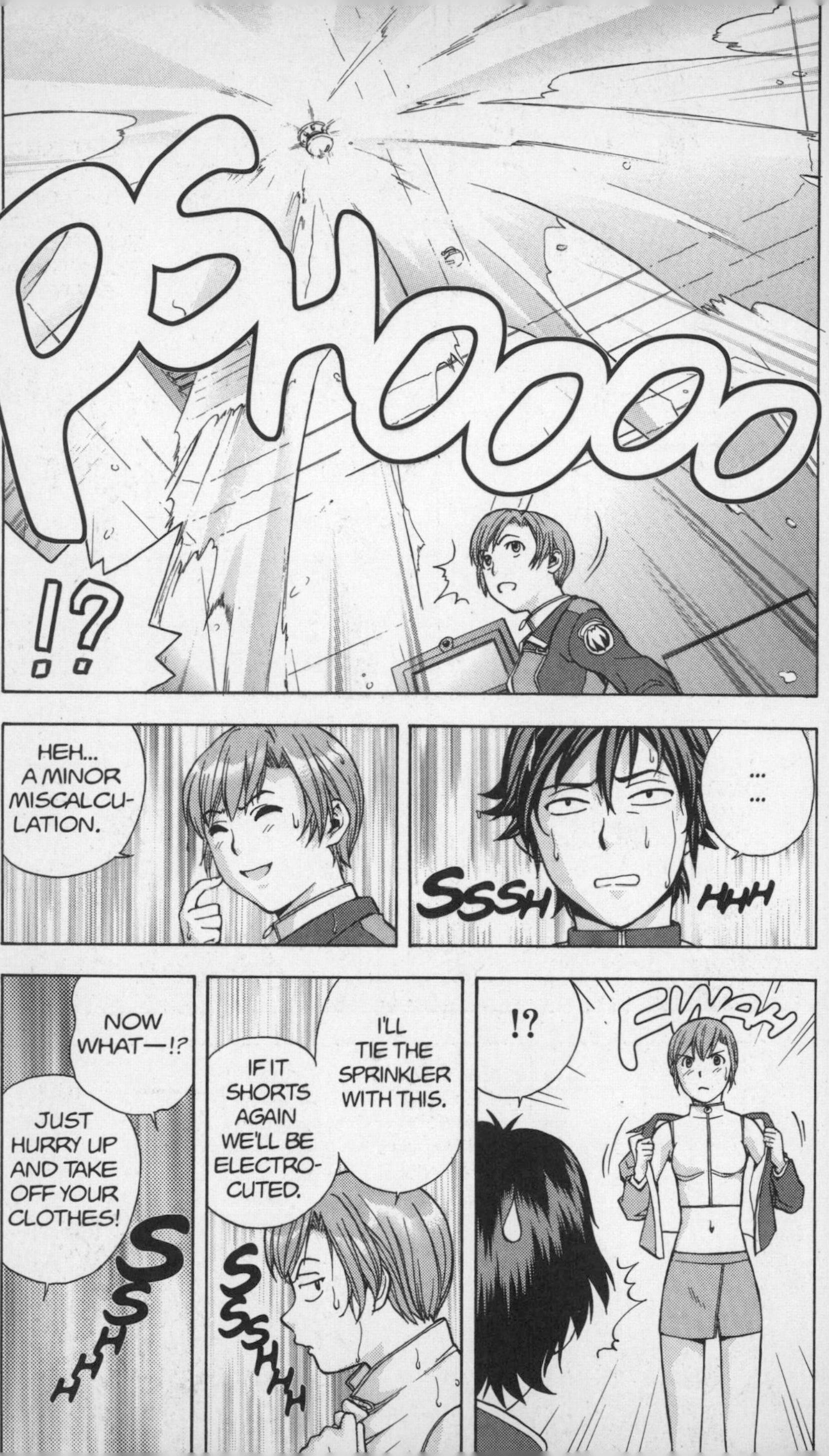
PSHOOOOO
!?
...
...
SSSHHHH
HEH... A MINOR MISCALCULATION.
FWAH
!?
I'LL TIE THE SPRINKLER WITH THIS.
IF IT SHORTS AGAIN WE'LL BE ELECTROCUTED.
SSSHHHH
NOW WHAT—!?
JUST HURRY UP AND TAKE OFF YOUR CLOTHES!
SSHHHH

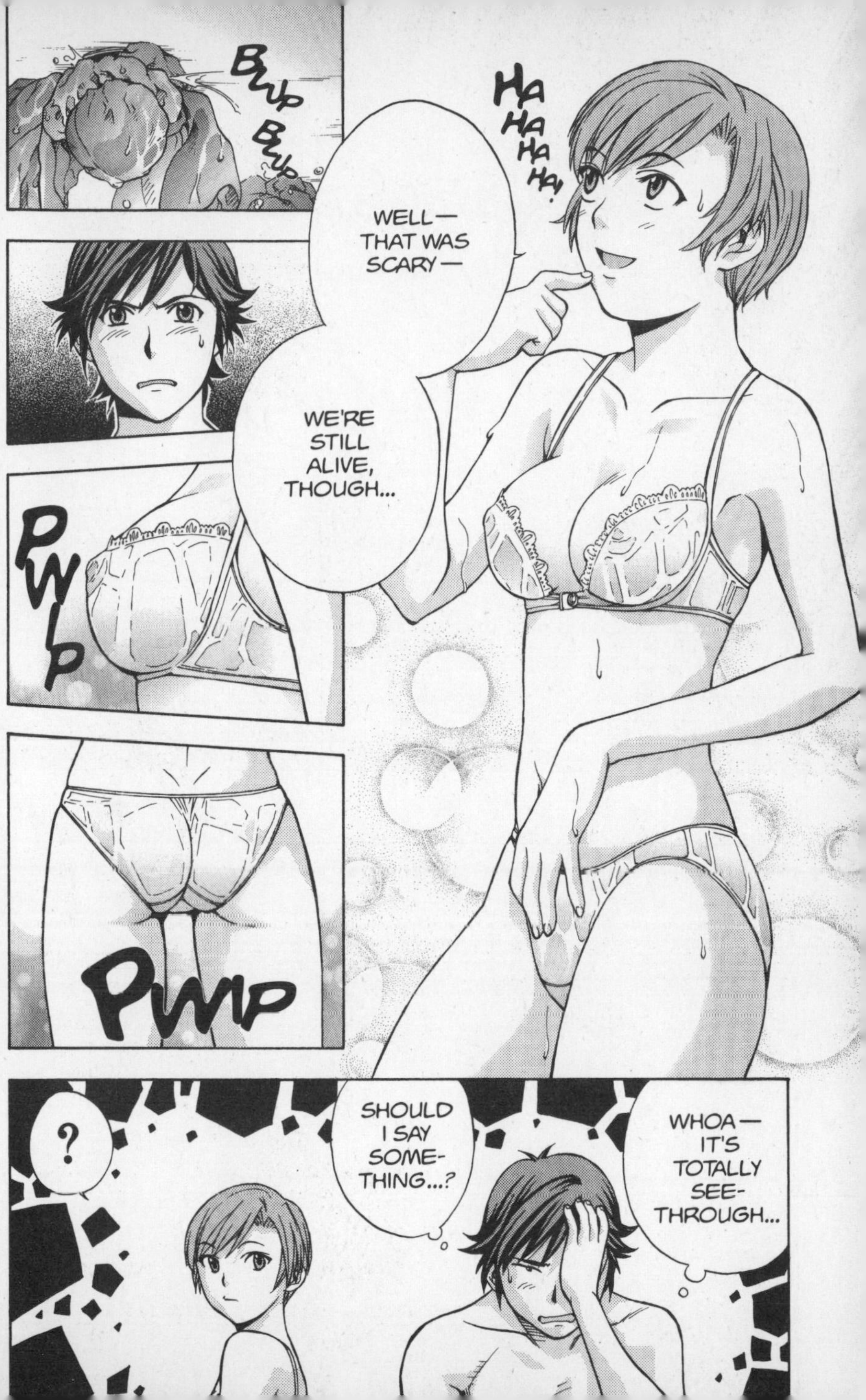
HA HA HA HA HA!
WELL— THAT WAS SCARY—
WE'RE STILL ALIVE, THOUGH...
BLUP BLUP
PWIP
PWIP
WHOA— IT'S TOTALLY SEE-THROUGH...
SHOULD I SAY SOME-THING...?
?

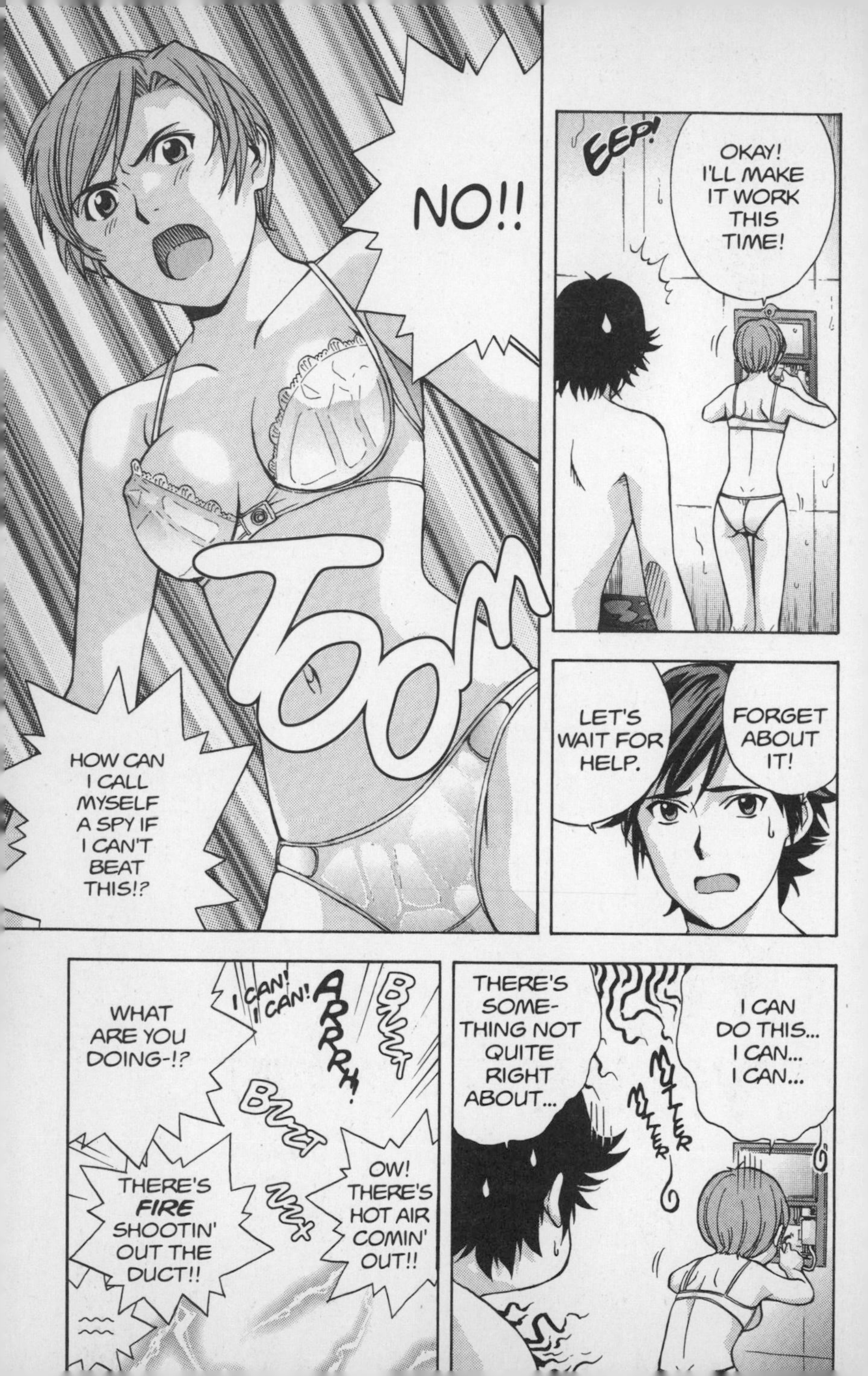
OKAY! I'LL MAKE IT WORK THIS TIME!
EEP!
LET'S WAIT FOR HELP.
FORGET ABOUT IT!
NO!!
TOOM
HOW CAN I CALL MYSELF A SPY IF I CAN'T BEAT THIS!?
I CAN DO THIS... I CAN... I CAN...
MUTTER
MUTTER
THERE'S SOME-THING NOT QUITE RIGHT ABOUT...
BZZT
ARRRH!
I CAN! I CAN!
WHAT ARE YOU DOING-!?
BZZT
OW! THERE'S HOT AIR COMIN' OUT!!
THERE'S **FIRE** SHOOTIN' OUT THE DUCT!!

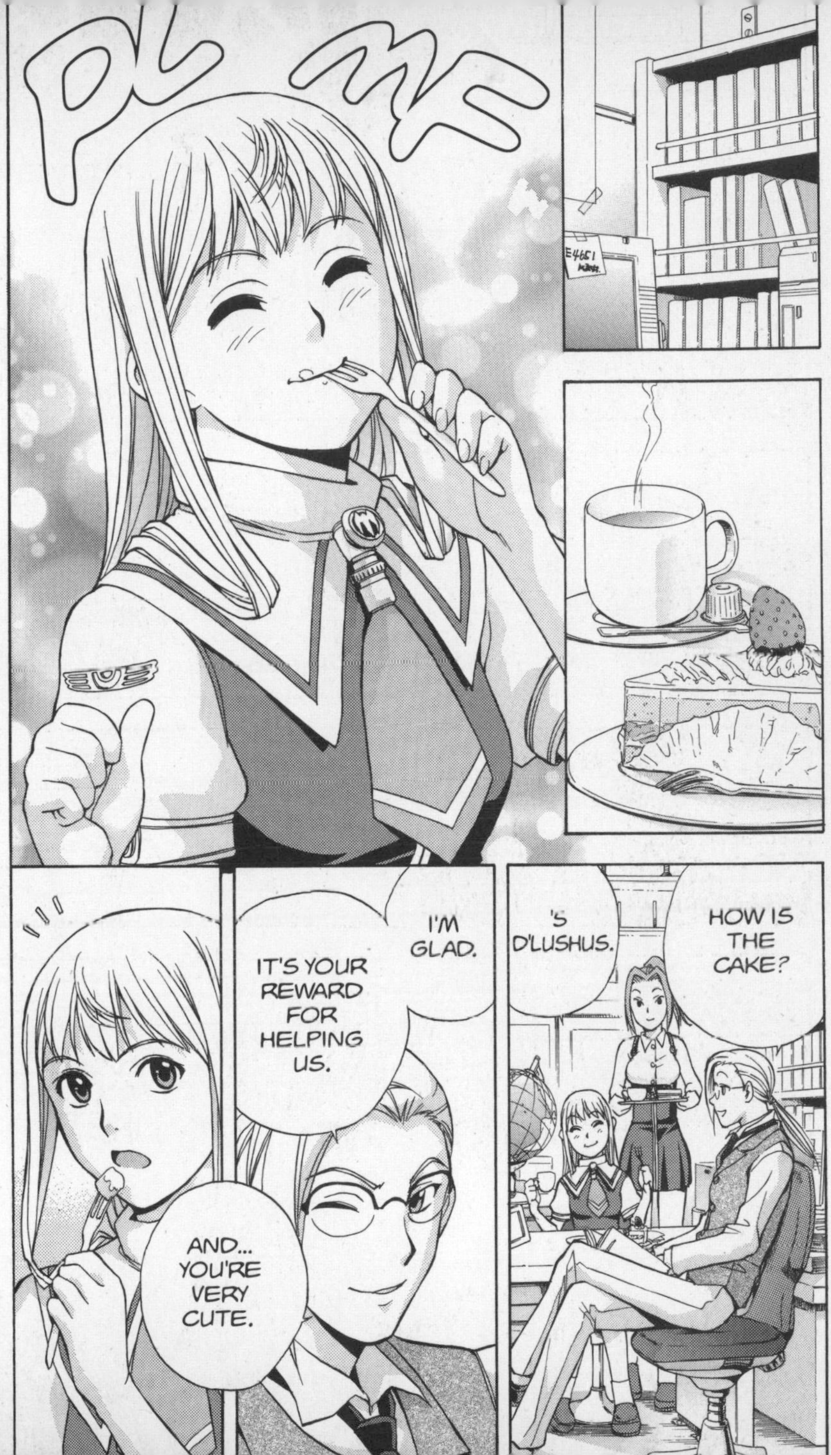
HOW IS THE CAKE?
'S D'LUSHUS.
I'M GLAD.
IT'S YOUR REWARD FOR HELPING US.
AND... YOU'RE VERY CUTE.

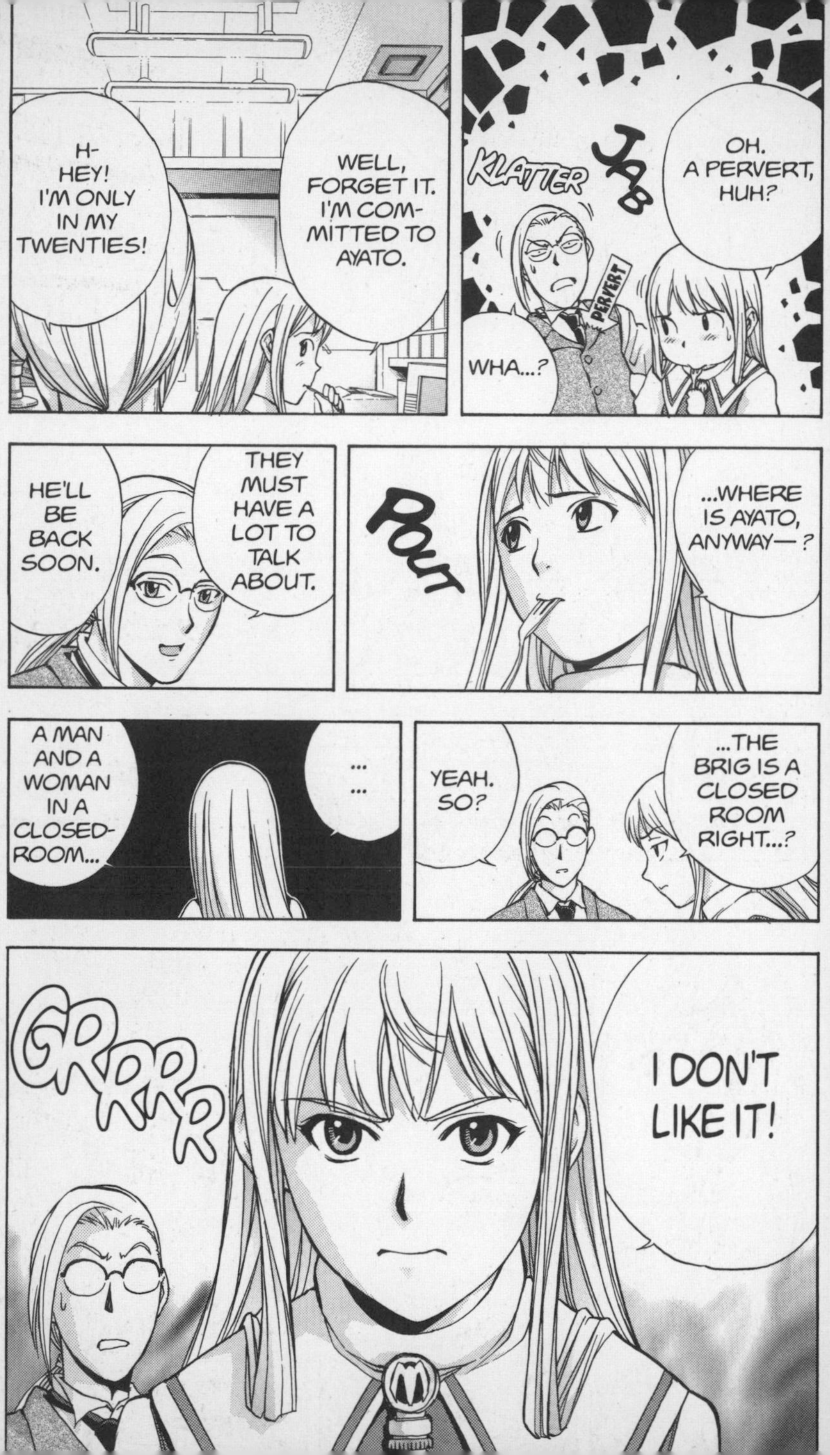
OH. A PERVERT, HUH?
JAB
KLATTER
PERVERT
WHA...?
WELL, FORGET IT. I'M COM-MITTED TO AYATO.
H- HEY! I'M ONLY IN MY TWENTIES!
...WHERE IS AYATO, ANYWAY—?
POUT
THEY MUST HAVE A LOT TO TALK ABOUT.
HE'LL BE BACK SOON.
...THE BRIG IS A CLOSED ROOM RIGHT...?
YEAH. SO?
......
A MAN AND A WOMAN IN A CLOSED-ROOM...
I DON'T LIKE IT!
GRRRR

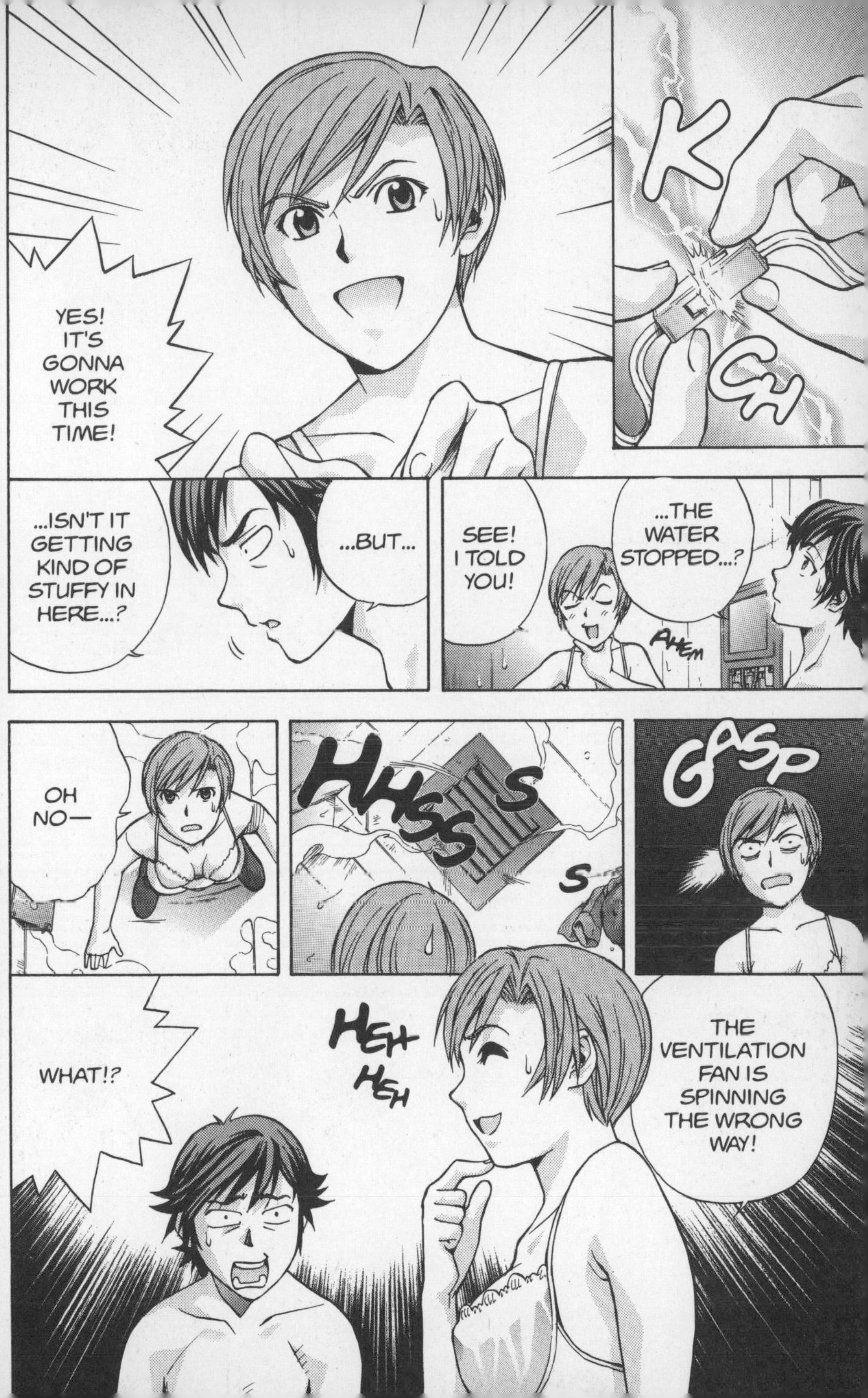
K
CH
YES! IT'S GONNA WORK THIS TIME!
...THE WATER STOPPED...?
SEE! I TOLD YOU!
AHEM
...BUT...
...ISN'T IT GETTING KIND OF STUFFY IN HERE...?
GASP
HHSSS
S
S
OH NO—
THE VENTILATION FAN IS SPINNING THE WRONG WAY!
HEH HEH
WHAT!?

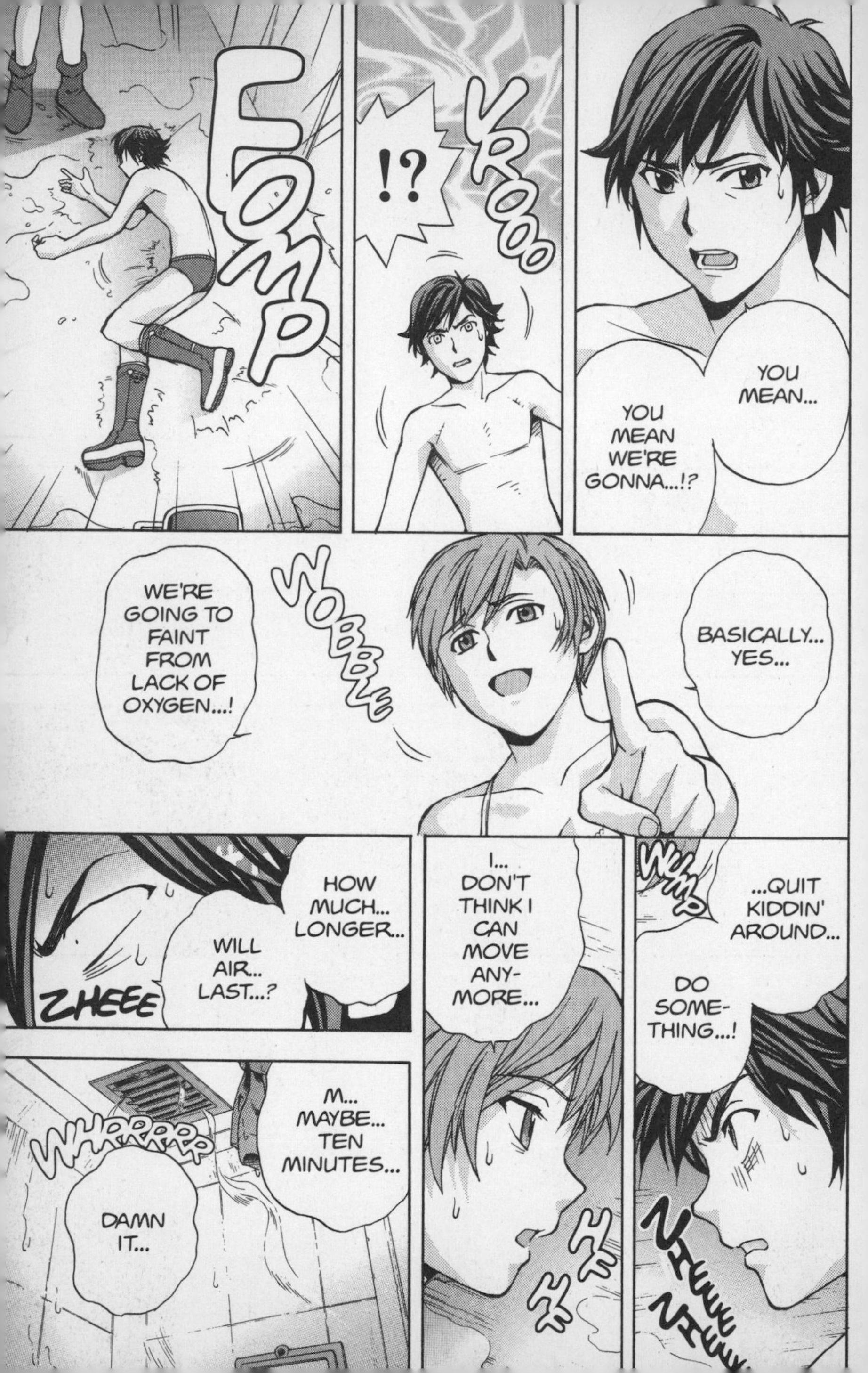
YOU MEAN...
YOU MEAN WE'RE GONNA...!?
VROOO
!?
FLOMP
BASICALLY... YES...
WOBBLE
WE'RE GOING TO FAINT FROM LACK OF OXYGEN...!
...QUIT KIDDIN' AROUND...
DO SOME-THING...!
WUMP
NIUUUU NIUUUU
I... DON'T THINK I CAN MOVE ANY-MORE...
HEH
HOW MUCH... LONGER...
WILL AIR... LAST...?
ZHEEE
M... MAYBE... TEN MINUTES...
WHRRRRR
DAMN IT...

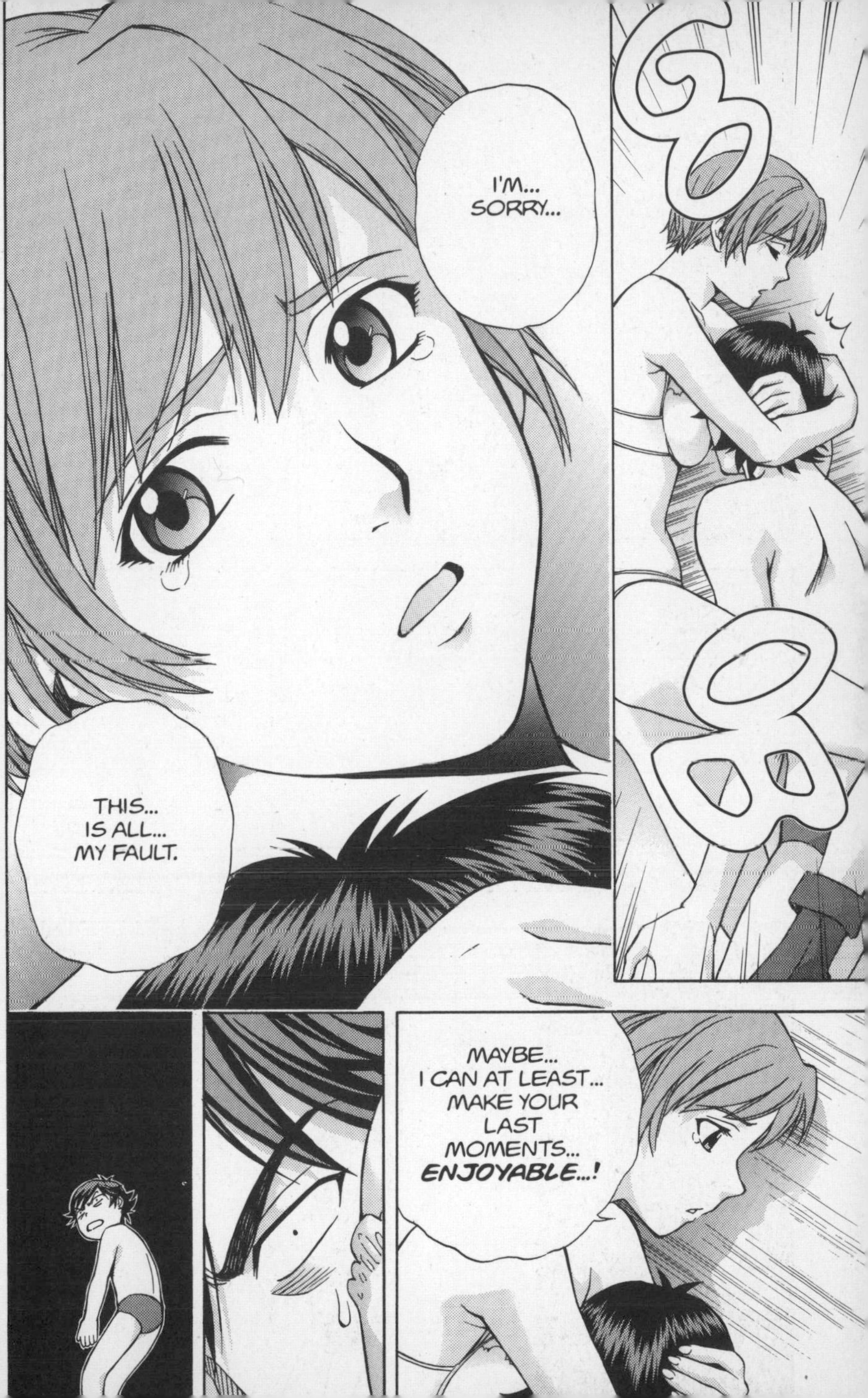
I'M... SORRY...
THIS... IS ALL... MY FAULT.
MAYBE... I CAN AT LEAST... MAKE YOUR LAST MOMENTS... ENJOYABLE...!

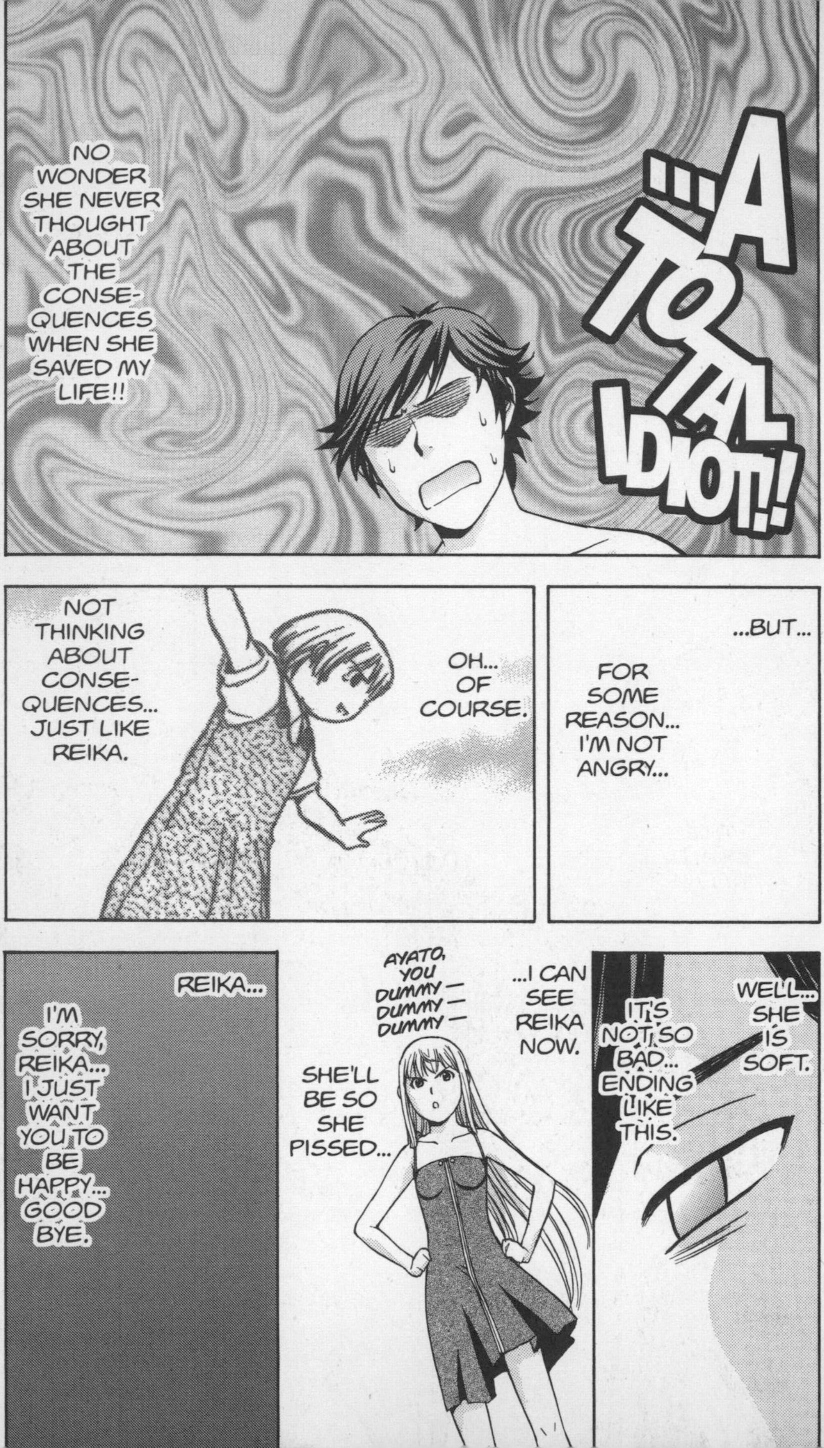
...A TOTAL IDIOT!!
NO WONDER SHE NEVER THOUGHT ABOUT THE CONSE-QUENCES WHEN SHE SAVED MY LIFE!!
...BUT...
FOR SOME REASON... I'M NOT ANGRY...
OH... OF COURSE.
NOT THINKING ABOUT CONSE-QUENCES... JUST LIKE REIKA.
WELL... SHE IS SOFT.
IT'S NOT SO BAD... ENDING LIKE THIS.
...I CAN SEE REIKA NOW.
AYATO, YOU DUMMY— DUMMY— DUMMY—
SHE'LL BE SO SHE PISSED...
REIKA...
I'M SORRY, REIKA... I JUST WANT YOU TO BE HAPPY... GOOD BYE.

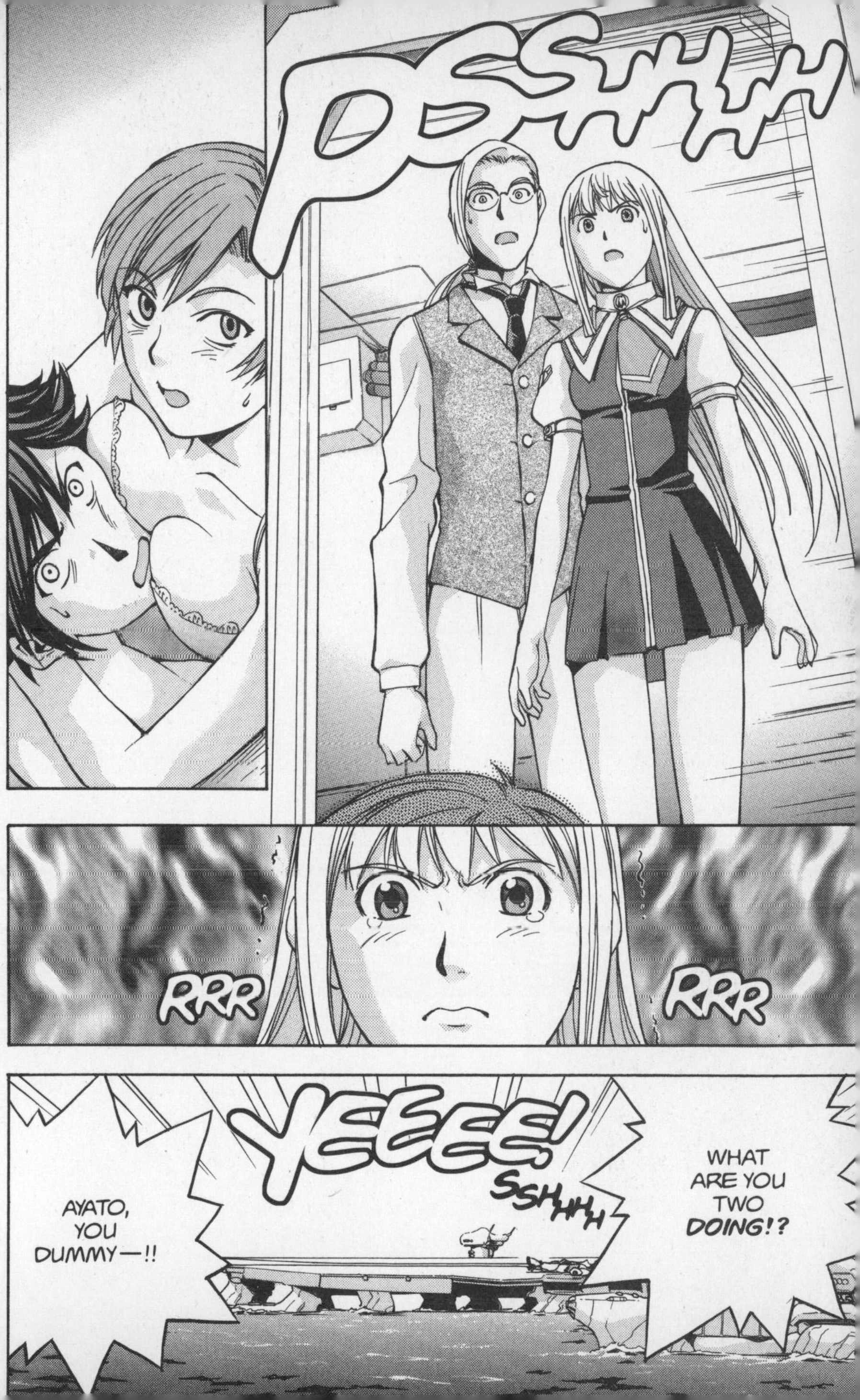
PSSHHH
RRR
RRR
YEEEE!
SSHHHH
WHAT ARE YOU TWO DOING!?
AYATO, YOU DUMMY—!!

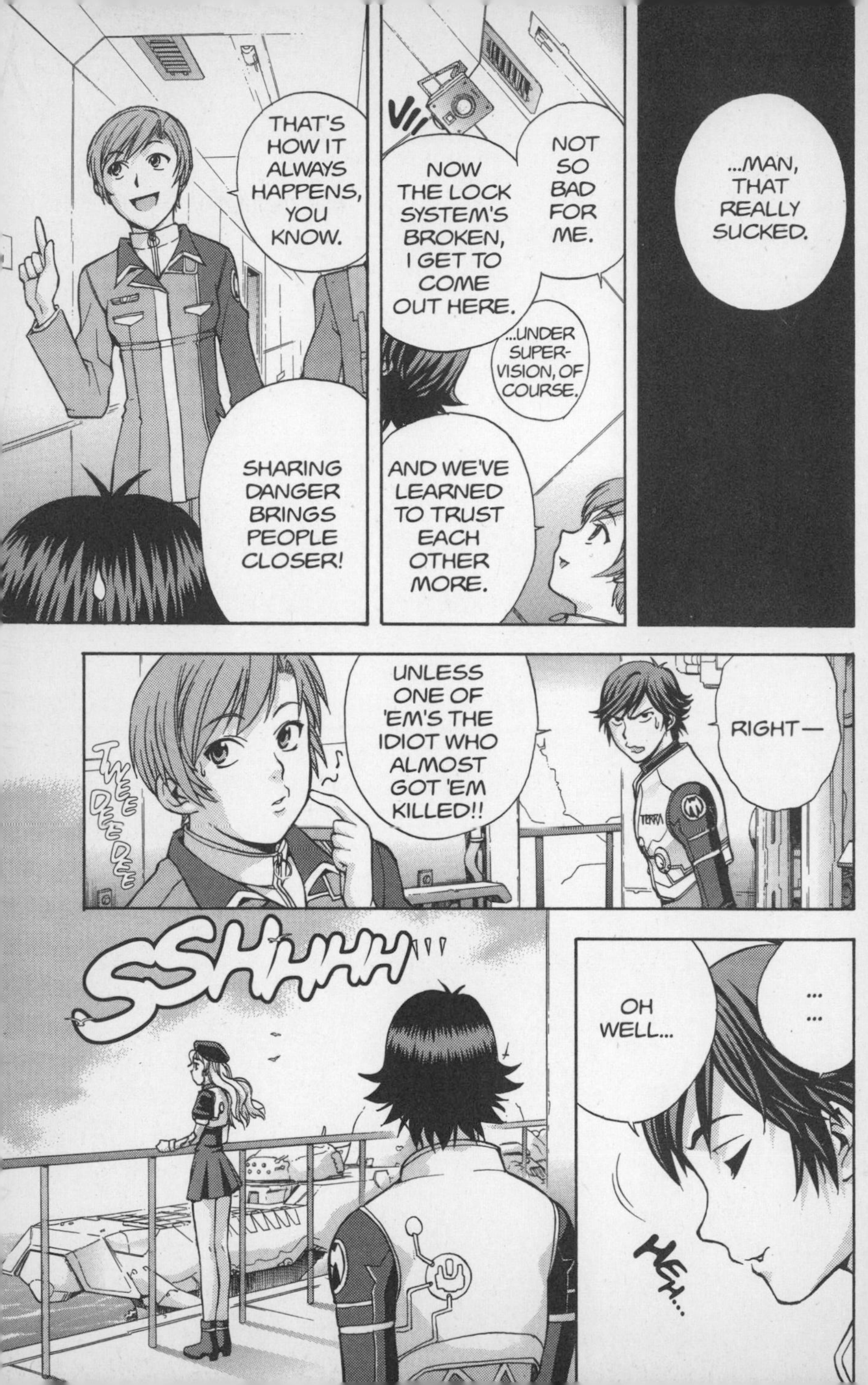
...MAN, THAT REALLY SUCKED.
NOT SO BAD FOR ME.
NOW THE LOCK SYSTEM'S BROKEN, I GET TO COME OUT HERE.
...UNDER SUPER-VISION, OF COURSE.
AND WE'VE LEARNED TO TRUST EACH OTHER MORE.
THAT'S HOW IT ALWAYS HAPPENS, YOU KNOW.
SHARING DANGER BRINGS PEOPLE CLOSER!
RIGHT—
TERRA
UNLESS ONE OF 'EM'S THE IDIOT WHO ALMOST GOT 'EM KILLED!!
TWEE DEE DEE
......
OH WELL...
HEH...
SSHHHH

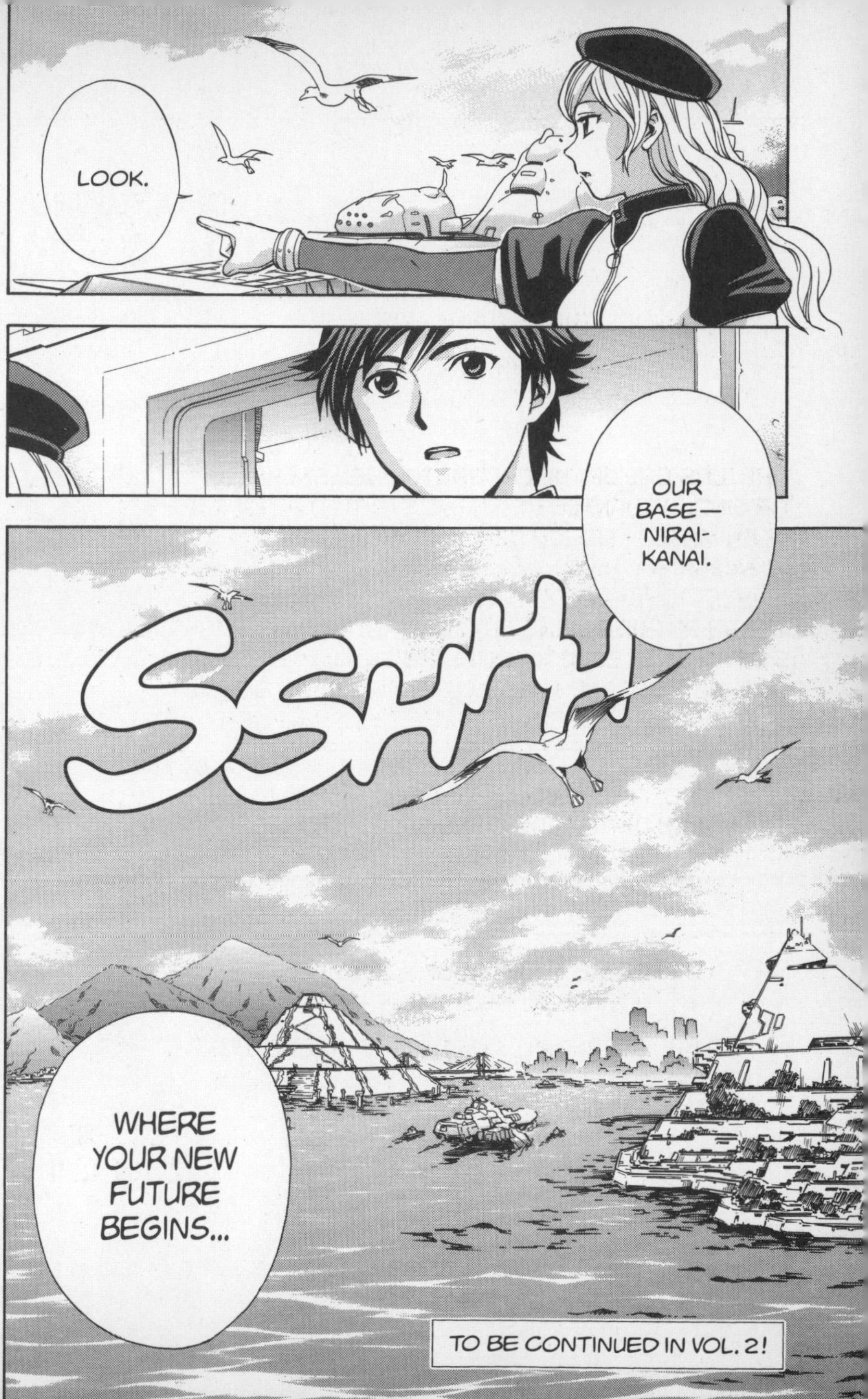
LOOK.
OUR BASE— NIRAI-KANAI.
SSHH
WHERE YOUR NEW FUTURE BEGINS...
TO BE CONTINUED IN VOL. 2!

GOOD TIMING,
THAT'S WHAT IT IS.

GETTING MR. MOMOSE ON
THE "RAHXEPHON" COMIC,
THAT IS.

HE WAS ONE OF THE CHARACTER DESIGNERS WE
ORIGINALLY WANTED WHEN WE STARTED PLANNING
THE ANIMATED VERSION OF "RAHXEPHON." THAT LED TO
HIM WRITING THE COMIC VERSION SO IT'S LIKE FATE,
WE MUST'VE HAD GOOD LUCK. ANIME AND MANGA ARE
SIMILAR BUT DIFFERENT. THE NARRATIVE "GRAMMAR"
IS DIFFERENT. SOMETIMES PEOPLE WANT THE COMIC
TO BE JUST LIKE THE TV SHOW, BUT IT REALLY DOESN'T
WORK THAT WAY, SO YOU HAVE TO BE WILLING TO
ADAPT IT.

...SO, FOR THOSE WHO READ THE MANGA
THEN WATCH THE ANIME, OR THE OTHER
WAY AROUND, THE CHARACTERS MAY
COME OFF A LITTLE DIFFERENT, AND YOU'RE
THINKING, "HEY!"

AS FOR ME, I JUST LOOK FORWARD TO
EVERY NEW ISSUE.

AND UH...I ESPECIALLY LIKE THE EPISODES WITH
BATHING SUITS..., SAYING TO MYSELF "BAD BOY,
BAD BOY" BUT HEY, IT'S OKAY...

**YUTAKA
IZUBUCHI**

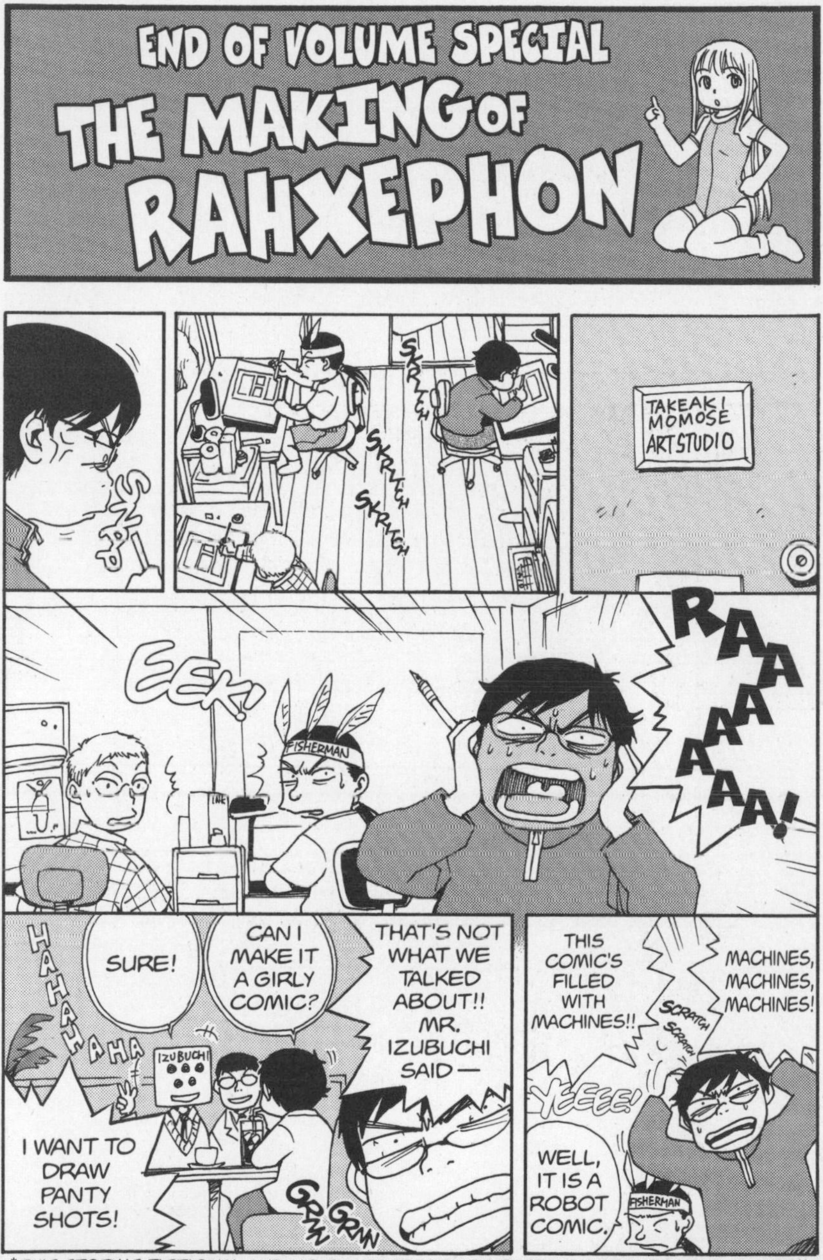
END OF VOLUME SPECIAL
THE MAKING OF RAHXEPHON
TAKEAKI MOMOSE ART STUDIO
SKRITCH
SKRITCH
SKRITCH
SNAP
RAAAAAAAA!
EEK!
FISHERMAN
INK
MACHINES, MACHINES, MACHINES!
THIS COMIC'S FILLED WITH MACHINES!!
SCRATCH SCRATCH
YEEEE!
WELL, IT IS A ROBOT COMIC.
FISHERMAN
THAT'S NOT WHAT WE TALKED ABOUT!! MR. IZUBUCHI SAID—
CAN I MAKE IT A GIRLY COMIC?
SURE!
HAHAHAHAHA
IZUBUCHI
I WANT TO DRAW PANTY SHOTS!
GRNN GRNN

*THIS STORY IS FICTIONAL AND NO CHARACTERS ARE BASED ON REAL PEOPLE...MAYBE!!

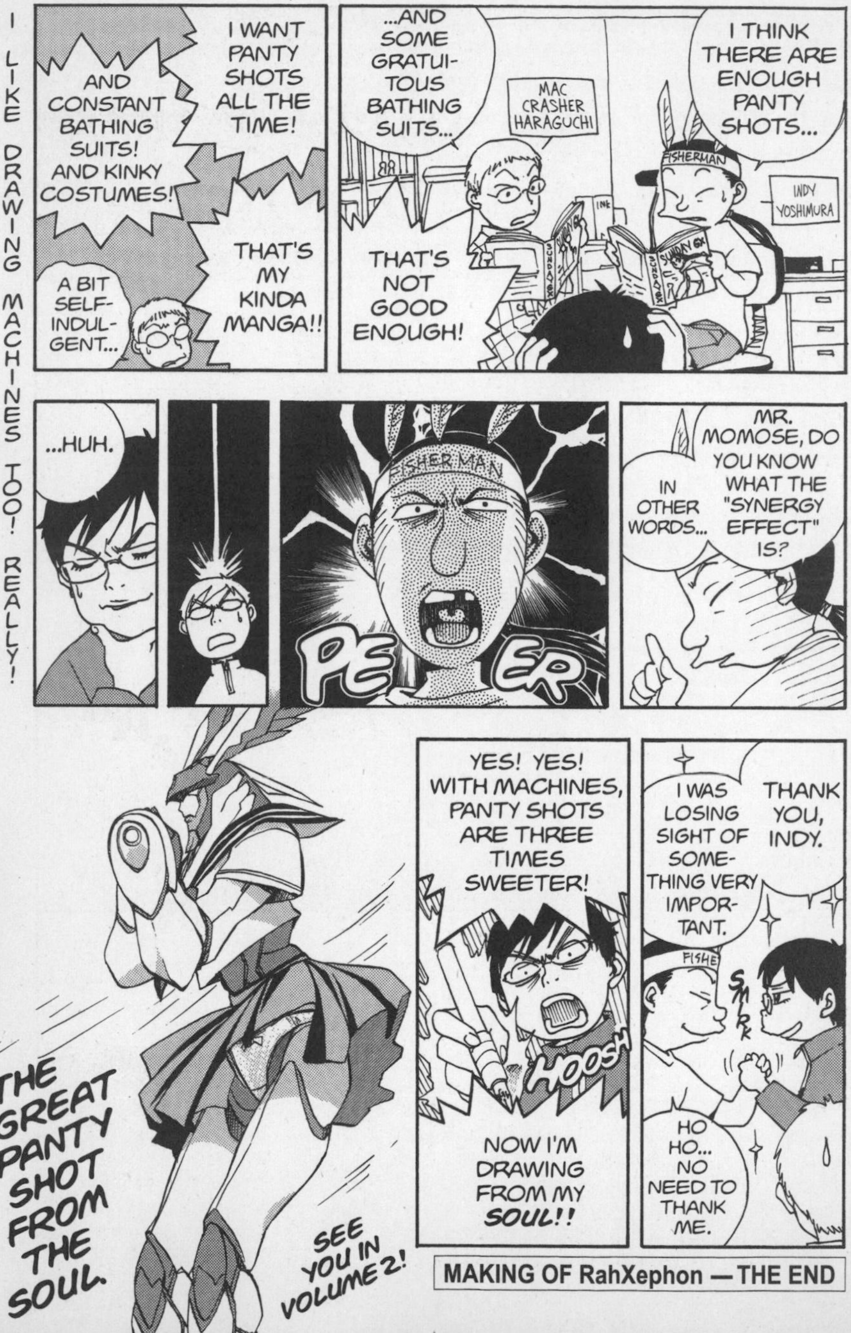

I LIKE DRAWING MACHINES TOO! REALLY!
I WANT PANTY SHOTS ALL THE TIME!
AND CONSTANT BATHING SUITS! AND KINKY COSTUMES!
THAT'S MY KINDA MANGA!!
A BIT SELF-INDULGENT...
I THINK THERE ARE ENOUGH PANTY SHOTS...
...AND SOME GRATUITOUS BATHING SUITS...
MAC CRASHER HARAGUCHI
FISHERMAN
INDY YOSHIMURA
THAT'S NOT GOOD ENOUGH!
...HUH.
FISHERMAN
PEER
MR. MOMOSE, DO YOU KNOW WHAT THE "SYNERGY EFFECT" IS?
IN OTHER WORDS...
THE GREAT PANTY SHOT FROM THE SOUL.
SEE YOU IN VOLUME 2!
YES! YES! WITH MACHINES, PANTY SHOTS ARE THREE TIMES SWEETER!
HOOSH
NOW I'M DRAWING FROM MY SOUL!!
THANK YOU, INDY.
I WAS LOSING SIGHT OF SOMETHING VERY IMPORTANT.
SMIRK
HO HO... NO NEED TO THANK ME.
MAKING OF RahXephon — THE END

Thanks for picking up the first volume of *RAHXEPHON*. I hope you've enjoyed reading it. Some of you familiar with the animated version of *RAHXEPHON* are probably wondering about the various changes in character, setting, and action. It's no simple task condensing an entire television series into three manga volumes, but rest assured that Yutaka Izubuchi, Takeaki Momose, and the rest of the *RAHXEPHON* crew have taken this into consideration. Though the mood is slightly cheekier and the character designs are equally, um...let's just call them cute, fear not the loss of dramatic impact and impending doom. The MU still control Tokyo Jupiter, TERRA is still resolute in its mission to liberate Japan's shining capitol, and Ayato still has a lot to learn about himself and his family. Catch you in Volume 2.

Kit Fox

Editor of *RAHXEPHON*

Did you like *RAHXEPHON*? Here's what VIZ recommends you try next:

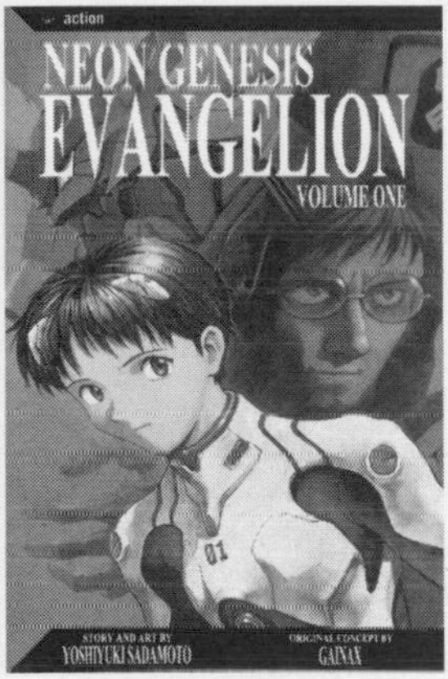
action
NEON GENESIS
EVANGELION
VOLUME ONE
STORY AND ART BY
YOSHIYUKI SADAMOTO
ORIGINAL CONCEPT BY
GAINAX

EVANGELION vol. 1

© GAINAX • Project-Eva • TV Tokyo • NAS 1995

Character designer extraordinaire Yoshiyuki Sadamoto—whose work has appeared in such animated fan favorites as *NADIA–SECRET OF BLUE WATER* and most recently *FLCL*—adapts *NEON GENESIS EVANGELION*, the most controversial and heavily influential anime of the 1990s, into an equally awe-inspiring manga. Shinji Ikari must help Nerv fend off the Angels, adapt to a new life with his estranged father, and come to grips with nothing more than mankind's ultimate fate. All this and more rests on the shoulders of a young man who isn't even old enough to drive.

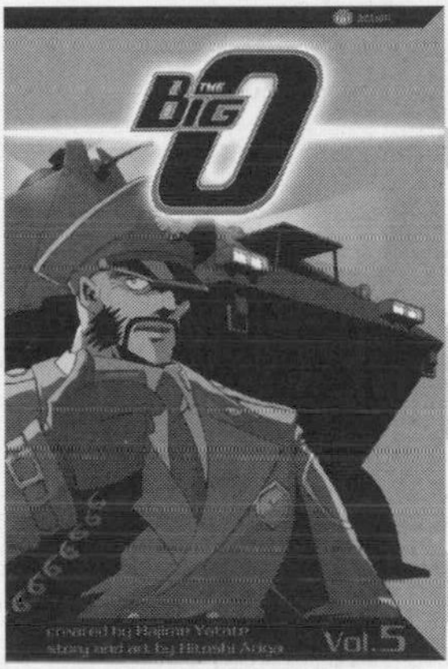
action
THE BIG O
Vol.5

THE BIG O vol. 5

© 2001 Hajime Yatate, Hitoshi Anga • © 2001 Sunrise.

Forty years ago the citizenry of Paradigm City all had their memories erased and were forced to begin their lives anew. Enter Roger Smith, a "negotiator" for anyone and everyone—criminals and citizens alike—who, along with a giant robot dubbed "the Big O," dishes out action-infused justice. From the folks who brought us *GUNDAM WING* comes *THE BIG O*, a manga with giant robot action on a gargantuan scale.

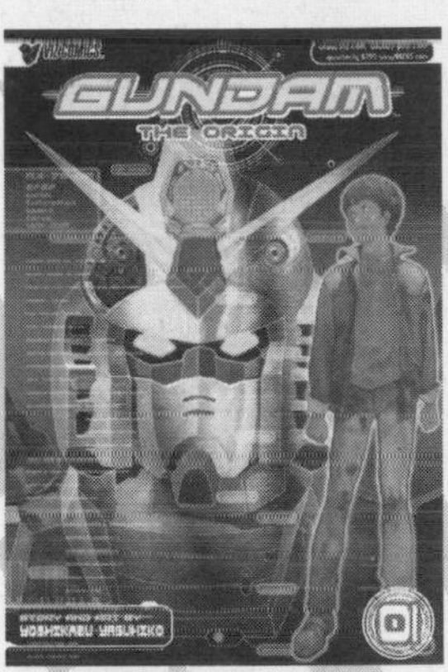
GUNDAM
THE ORIGIN
01

GUNDAM: THE ORIGIN vol. 1

© Yoshikazu YASUHIKO 2001 © SOTSU AGENCY • SUNRISE 2001

Every genre has its forbearers, and where would the world of giant robots be without *MOBILE SUIT GUNDAM*? One of the most popular and prolific anime of all time, *GUNDAM*'s influence can be found in nearly every mecha-infused show of the last thirty years. Yoshikazu Yasuhiko, the original character designer and animation director for that landmark series injects new life into the *GUNDAM* universe with his breathtaking watercolors and adept storytelling.

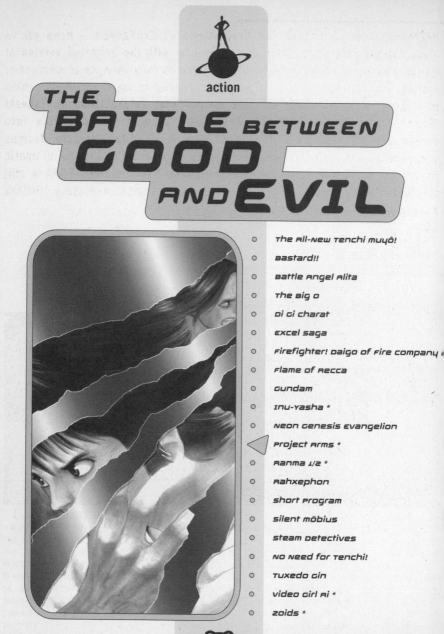

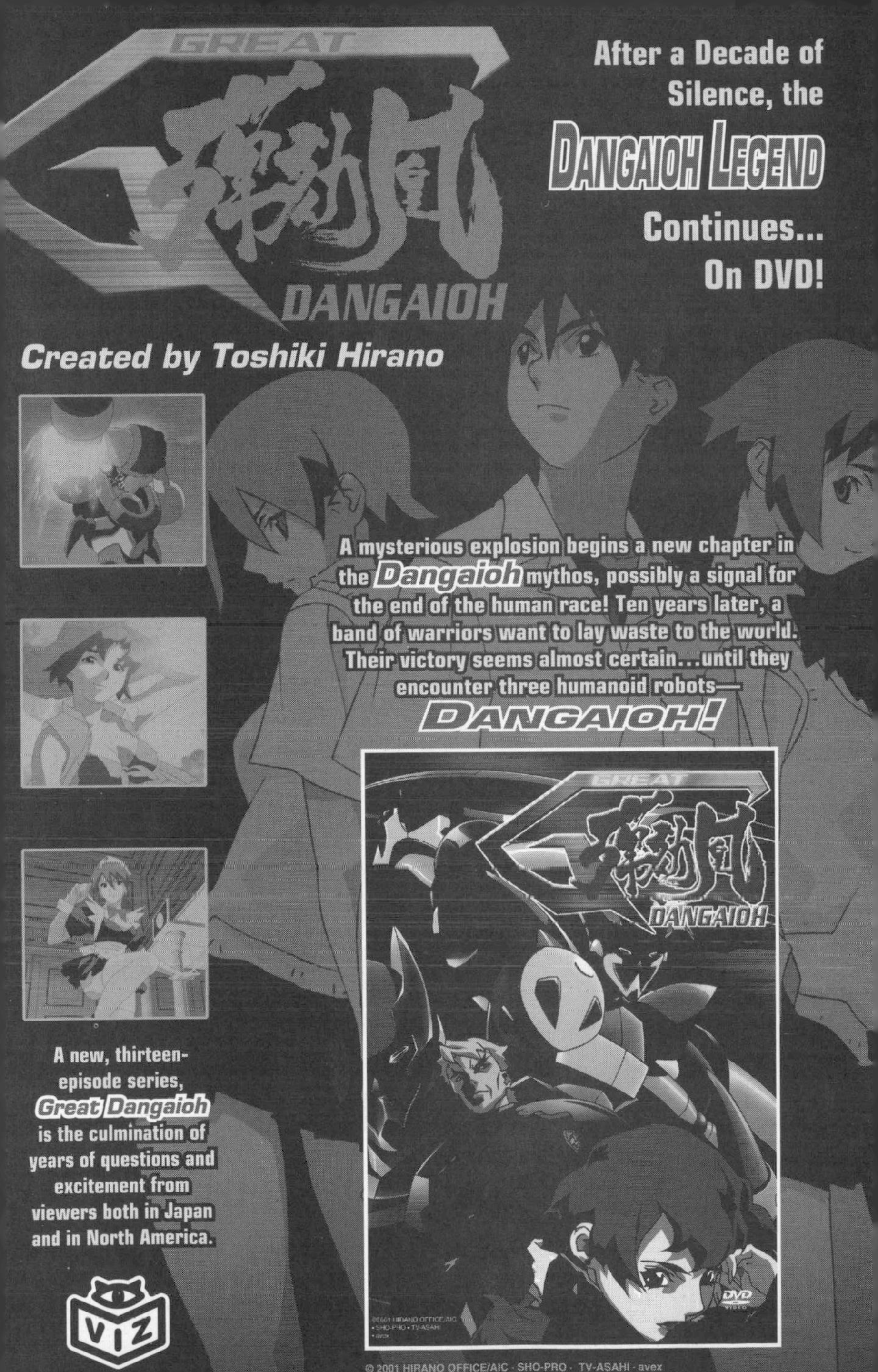
GREAT DANGAIOH
After a Decade of Silence, the
DANGAIOH LEGEND
Continues...
On DVD!
Created by Toshiki Hirano
A mysterious explosion begins a new chapter in the Dangaioh mythos, possibly a signal for the end of the human race! Ten years later, a band of warriors want to lay waste to the world. Their victory seems almost certain...until they encounter three humanoid robots—
DANGAIOH!
GREAT DANGAIOH
A new, thirteen-episode series, Great Dangaioh is the culmination of years of questions and excitement from viewers both in Japan and in North America.
VIZ

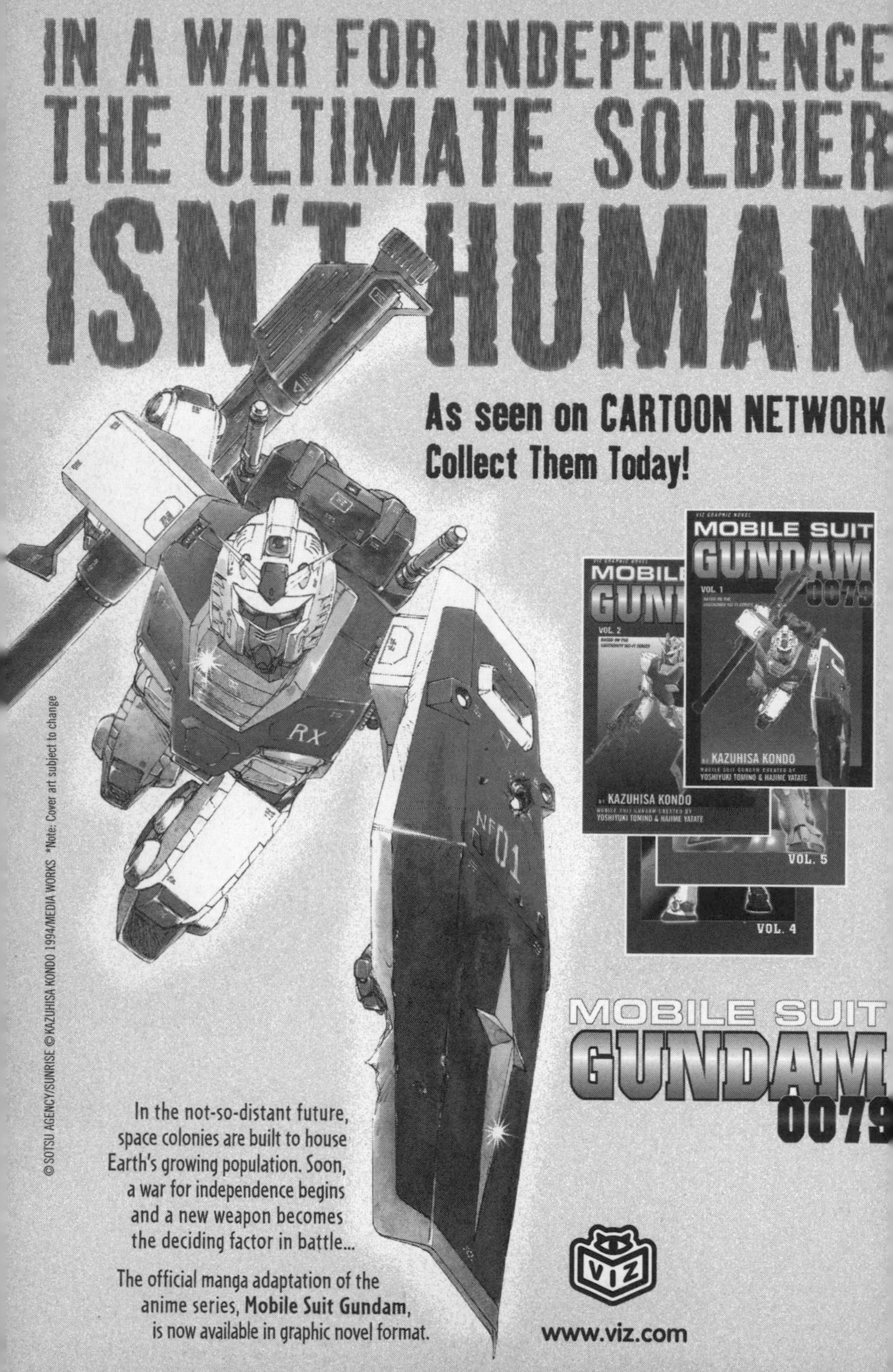
IN A WAR FOR INDEPENDENCE
THE ULTIMATE SOLDIER
ISN'T HUMAN
As seen on CARTOON NETWORK
Collect Them Today!
MOBILE SUIT GUNDAM 0079
VOL. 1
BY KAZUHISA KONDO
YOSHIYUKI TOMINO & HAJIME YATATE
VOL. 2
KAZUHISA KONDO
YOSHIYUKI TOMINO & HAJIME YATATE
VOL. 5
VOL. 4
MOBILE SUIT
GUNDAM
0079
In the not-so-distant future, space colonies are built to house Earth's growing population. Soon, a war for independence begins and a new weapon becomes the deciding factor in battle...
The official manga adaptation of the anime series, Mobile Suit Gundam, is now available in graphic novel format.
VIZ
www.viz.com
© SOTSU AGENCY/SUNRISE © KAZUHISA KONDO 1994/MEDIA WORKS *Note: Cover art subject to change

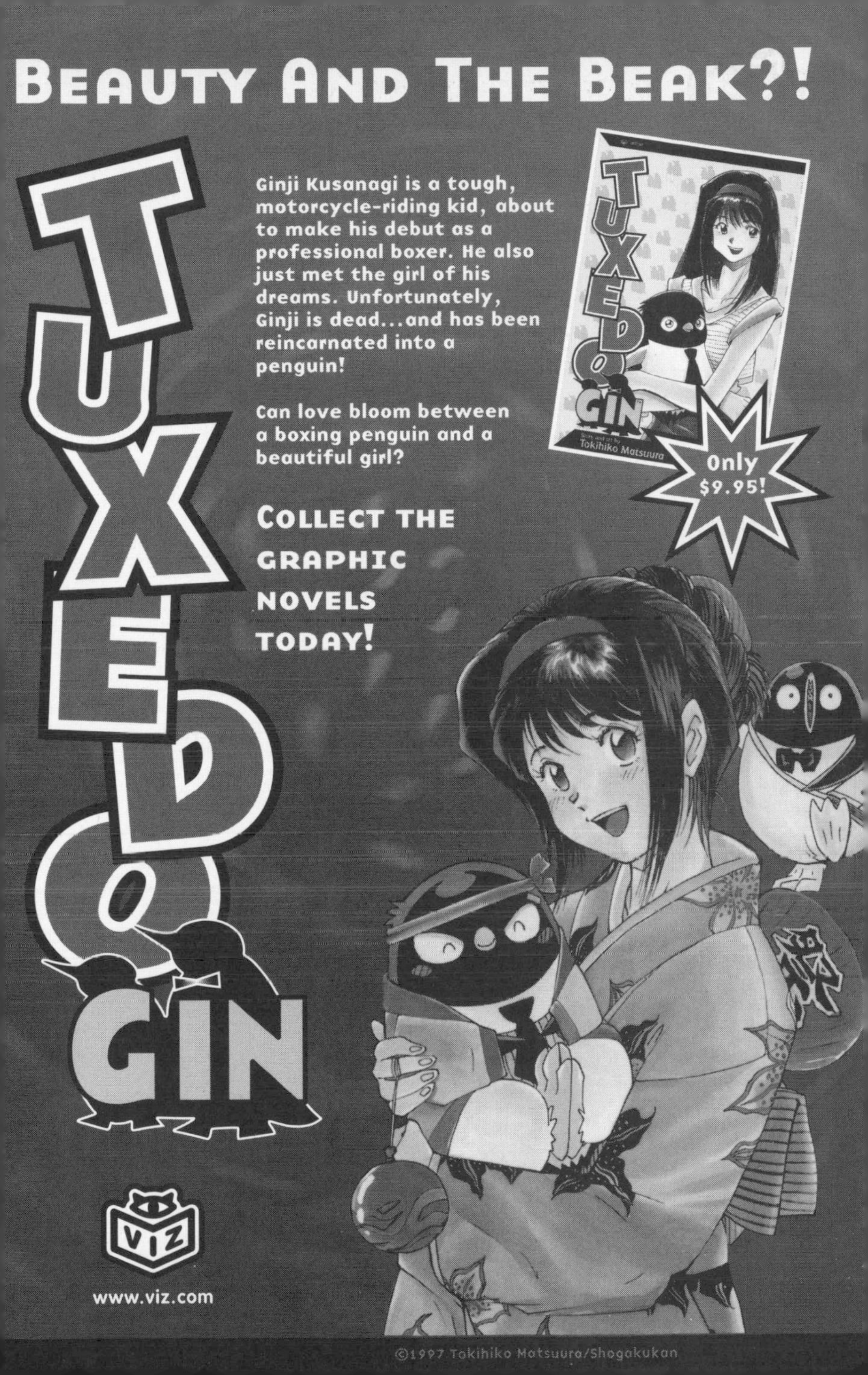
BEAUTY AND THE BEAK?!
TUXEDO GIN
Ginji Kusanagi is a tough, motorcycle-riding kid, about to make his debut as a professional boxer. He also just met the girl of his dreams. Unfortunately, Ginji is dead...and has been reincarnated into a penguin!
Can love bloom between a boxing penguin and a beautiful girl?
COLLECT THE GRAPHIC NOVELS TODAY!
TUXEDO GIN
Story and art by Tokihiko Matsuura
Only $9.95!
VIZ
www.viz.com
©1997 Tokihiko Matsuura/Shogakukan

COMPLETE OUR SURVEY AND LET US KNOW WHAT YOU THINK!

☐ Please check here if you DO NOT wish to receive information or future offers from VIZ

Name: _____

Address: _____

City: _____ **State:** _____ **Zip:** _____

E-mail: _____

☐ **Male** ☐ **Female** **Date of Birth** (mm/dd/yyyy): ___/___/___ (Under 13? Parental consent required)

What race/ethnicity do you consider yourself? (please check one)

☐ Asian/Pacific Islander   ☐ Black/African American   ☐ Hispanic/Latino

☐ Native American/Alaskan Native   ☐ White/Caucasian   ☐ Other: _____

What VIZ product did you purchase? (check all that apply and indicate title purchased)

☐ DVD/VHS _____

☐ Graphic Novel _____

☐ Magazines _____

☐ Merchandise _____

Reason for purchase: (check all that apply)

☐ Special offer   ☐ Favorite title   ☐ Gift

☐ Recommendation   ☐ Other _____

Where did you make your purchase? (please check one)

☐ Comic store   ☐ Bookstore   ☐ Mass/Grocery Store

☐ Newsstand   ☐ Video/Video Game Store   ☐ Other: _____

☐ Online (site: _____)

What other VIZ properties have you purchased/own? _____

_____

How many anime and/or manga titles have you purchased in the last year? How many were VIZ titles? (please check one from each column)

ANIME
- ☐ None
- ☐ 1-4
- ☐ 5-10
- ☐ 11+

MANGA
- ☐ None
- ☐ 1-4
- ☐ 5-10
- ☐ 11+

D0388691

I find the pricing of VIZ products to be: (please check one)
- ☐ Cheap
- ☐ Reasonable
- ☐ Expensive

What genre of manga and anime would you like to see from VIZ? (please check two)
- ☐ Adventure
- ☐ Comic Strip
- ☐ Science Fiction
- ☐ Fighting
- ☐ Horror
- ☐ Romance
- ☐ Fantasy
- ☐ Sports

What do you think of VIZ's new look?
- ☐ Love It
- ☐ It's OK
- ☐ Hate It
- ☐ Didn't Notice
- ☐ No Opinion

Which do you prefer? (please check one)
- ☐ Reading right-to-left
- ☐ Reading left-to-right

Which do you prefer? (please check one)
- ☐ Sound effects in English
- ☐ Sound effects in Japanese with English captions
- ☐ Sound effects in Japanese only with a glossary at the back

THANK YOU! Please send the completed form to:

NJW Research
42 Catharine St.
Poughkeepsie, NY 12601

All information provided will be used for internal purposes only. We promise not to sell or otherwise divulge your information.